# Legislation on Coercive Mental Health Care in Europe

Thomas W. Kallert
Francisco Torres-González
(eds.)

# Legislation on Coercive Mental Health Care in Europe

## Legal Documents and Comparative Assessment of Twelve European Countries

PETER LANG
Frankfurt am Main · Berlin · Bern · Bruxelles · New York · Oxford · Wien

**Bibliographic Information published by Die Deutsche Bibliothek**
Die Deutsche Bibliothek lists this publication in the Deutsche Nationalbibliografie; detailed bibliographic data is available in the internet at <http://dnb.ddb.de>.

ISBN 3-631-55446-X
US-ISBN 0-8204-9938-2



www.peterlang.de

**Foreword**

This book on legislation on coercive mental health care in Europe was written as outcome of scientific work carried out in the research project "European Evaluation of Coercion in Psychiatry and Harmonization of Best Clinical Practice" (acronym: EUNOMIA) funded within the 5th Framework Research Programme of the European Commission. Otherwise, necessary resources for this multinational task would not have been available. Therefore, we would like to express our gratitude to the funding agency for supporting our work.
Furthermore, we gratefully acknowledge the most valuable assistance by Thomas Roche and Gunnar Jaeck in the editing of this book. Janet Schulze deserves special thanks for her excellent work on all details of word processing.

We, the editors and authors of this volume, are clearly aware of the issue that only one half of the countries currently being member states of the European Union are included in our work. Nonetheless, in our view it was more than necessary to start with establishing structured and thus comparable information in a legal field that is highly relevant for the discipline of psychiatry and for human rights in general. We know very well that this work not only needs continuous updates, but should be spread to including all member states of the European Union.

Definitely, diversity of national traditions is among the most precious heritages of the united Europe. However, dealing with the problems of its citizens in a fair, respectful, reliable and equal manner is one of the current and future tasks that might help citizens to increasingly identify themselves with the idea of a united Europe. Mental health is part of the human goods in need of such improvement as concerns public attitudes and politics. One main element in this process would be to establish a clear common legal basis defining how to correctly cope with one of the most sensitive areas of treating people with mental disorders: coercive measures in the field of psychiatry.
It is the hope of the editors and authors of this volume, that their work could humbly provide a small contribution in the long and enduring efforts needed to realize this aim!

Thomas W. Kallert, Dresden, Germany
Francisco Torres-González, Granada, Spain March 2006

## Contents

# CHAPTER 1

# Introduction

Thomas W. KALLERT, Francisco TORRES-GONZÁLEZ

Throughout Europe, the dramatic changes in mental health care practises, which began about 25 to 30 years ago in Western European and about five to ten years ago in Eastern European countries, are still taking place. These changes have focused on: the reduction of hospital beds, the diagnosis-specific differentiation of inpatient treatment, the de-institutionalisation of chronically mentally ill persons, and the establishment of community-based mental health care structures and treatment approaches (Becker 1998, Hinterhuber et al. 2001, Kallert 2000, Leff 1993, Munk-Jorgensen 1999, Priebe et al. 2005, Rössler et al. 1994, Salokangas 1994, Wilkinson et al. 1995).

In general, the guiding principles for this process of change, in conjunction with the issues central to recent mental health service research projects, have been: strengthening the autonomy of the patient, individual needs- or consumer-orientation, flexibility of the treatment approaches in mental health services and the normalisation of the living conditions of those affected (Thornicroft & Tansella 1999). However, recent European mental health services research projects (Baig 2003) have shown that among these states there remains significant variation in approaches to a range of mental health care issues.
Within the context of reforming mental health care, the changes to acutely mentally ill persons' inpatient psychiatric treatment (Szmukler & Holloway 2001), especially those individuals involuntarily admitted to hospital under significantly varied pieces of nation-specific mental health legislation, and the quality of care for these persons who are at risk of having their autonomy, freedom, dignity and human rights infringed upon, have not been reflected upon or scientifically explored on an international European level (Osborn 1999). So far, no cross-nationally accepted guidelines or standards for best practise for treating these patients have been established – for both legal and clinical aspects of treatment.

This fact is most astonishing because nearly all European countries report broadly varying but currently increasing rates of involuntarily admitted psychiatric patients, accounting for up to 30% of all psychiatric hospital admissions (Salize & Dressing 2004, Zinkler & Priebe 2002). Furthermore, several countries have either recently established new mental health acts (e.g. Bulgaria,

Lithuania) or have begun the process of revising existing ones (e.g. United Kingdom, some German Federal States) – reform processes lacking the necessary foundation in empirical data.
All of this coincides with one of the most important general goals of the European Union: equality of health care opportunities and living conditions for citizens in the individual member countries during a special period of psychiatric treatment (closely connected to sensitive ethical and legal considerations (Nilstun & Syse 2000, Olsen 1998, Workman et al. 2000), highly criticised especially from the user's point of view (Committee of the Ministers of the Council of Europe 2000, Hoge et al. 1998, Kaltiala-Heino et al. 1997) and significantly responsible for prejudices and the poor public opinion of psychiatric treatment).

Consequently, the Committee of Ministers of the Council of Europe in 2000 criticised the lack of comparative European studies in the field[1]. Most recently some undertakings have been started to fill this research lacuna.

The first initiative was the "Compulsory Admission and Involuntary Treatment of Mentally Ill Patients – Legislation and Practise in EU-Member States" project, funded by the Health and Consumer Protection Directorate-General of the European Commission from October 2000 to January 2002. This study aimed at gathering, describing and analysing information on the differences or similarities between legal frameworks for involuntary placement or treatment of mentally ill patients throughout the European Union Member States (Salize et al. 2002).
In order to achieve this, a network of experts and collaborators from each member state was set up. These experts filled in a questionnaire for gathering structured information about the current situation and practises relating to legislation on compulsory admissions and the involuntary treatment of mentally ill patients in each member state. They also contributed a chapter describing specific characteristics of their respective member states (e.g. regional differences, historical changes). Numbers and rates of admission per 100 000 of the population from the most recently available year were assessed in all 15 European member states. Complete information relating to the last decade is scarce but for countries where this data was available it was also reviewed. General trends were described and correlations between compulsory admission rates, their change over

[1] Outside Europe, the Mac Arthur Research Networks on Mental Health and the Law and on Mandated Community Treatment (http://macarthur.virginia.edu) in the US have conducted a worldwide unique series of primary research projects on medical-legal and -ethical issues in the field of coercive treatment in mental health care.

time and the respective legislation in member states were analysed and discussed.
Based on the detailed national information the study's co-ordinating centre (Central Institute of Mental Health (CIMH) in Mannheim, Germany) compiled a synopsis of the current situation in the EU. One of the major results of the study was that both the legal regulations and routine procedures for detaining the mentally ill differ considerably throughout the European Union in terms of whether or not these regulations and procedures were regulated by a separate mental health act. National legal traditions, structures or standards of quality with regard to the provision of general health care, as well as national approaches or philosophies regarding mental health care, most strongly determine the legal frameworks or the practise of involuntary placement or treatment of mentally ill patients. Thus, the most significant characteristic of the European Union member states' legal frameworks regarding involuntary placement or treatment of mentally ill is their variety. Although common patterns among member states were identified in comparing crucial legislative or procedural details, these patterns were far from being consistent across all analysed items or approaches. Although compulsory admission is seen as an intervention of last resort across the European Union, only to be applied in an acute crisis or state of emergency, even the most basic legal criteria qualifying a person for involuntary placement in a psychiatric facility differ widely. Globally speaking, these criteria can be categorised into three groups, providing probably the most significant distinction for characterising a member state's legal approach towards involuntary placement or the treatment of mentally ill persons: a serious threat of harm to the person him/herself and/or to others ("dangerousness criterion"), an urgent need for psychiatric treatment ("need-for-treatment criterion"), and a combination of both. The global inconsistency in legal frameworks and practises constitutes a major obstacle to any mutual European actions or policies. However, ongoing activities in the member states to reform or adapt their mental health legislation might offer opportunities for harmonising legal instruments across the European Union. Currently, even within some member states, there might be several legal instruments, each with a different regional scope or pertaining to selected patient groups, in effect simultaneously. The most significant example is Germany, with one nationwide guardianship law and sixteen state commitment laws (corresponding to the sixteen German Federal States) currently in effect that differ remarkably with regard to crucial details. Separate mental health acts are also in effect for large parts of the United Kingdom (Scotland and Northern Ireland), Denmark (Greenland) and in other Member States.

A second valuable initiative was the project "Placement and Treatment of Mentally Ill Offenders – Legislation and Practise in EU Member States", also fi-

nanced by the Health and Consumer Protection Directorate-General of the European Commission. The administrative study has again been coordinated by the CIMH in Mannheim and it has been contributed to by researchers from the fifteen constituting Members Sates of the EU before May 2004. The final report has very recently been handed over to the EC (Salize et al. 2005).
The study aimed at gathering and analysing information about the differences and/or similarities of legislation for the placement and treatment of mentally ill offenders across the referred European Union Member States. The objective of this project deserves some specific comments.
Taking the mentally ill person's rights into consideration whenever dealing with such offenders is controversial. In most EU Member States, and in other countries, the subject receives a great deal of public attention, reinforced from time to time by spectacular cases with intense media coverage. It is indeed a highly disputed issue, particularly because of the double role of the mentally ill offender: on one side patient and on the other a person being processed by the criminal system. Discussions as to whether the patient's needs for treatment should be met and his or her reintegration into society aimed for are contrasted with the public's right to safety.
This study points out the overall shortage of evidence in this much-debated field, despite the high level of public awareness and the mass-media attention to the issue. Partly, this shortage of evidence may be explained by methodological obstacles in analysing the complicated structures and varied systems for regulating forensic cases in the diverse legal and health care systems of the EU Member States. Currently, the judicial, health and criminal reporting systems of the Member States have not sufficiently incorporated forensic indicators into their routine practise. It was demonstrated in the report that standardised European indicators are completely absent.
This aspect of health care seems to suffer from its position at the interface of criminology, jurisprudence and psychiatry. However, these disciplines have not yet developed common methods of assessing and analysing the various aspects of, and problems in the field, in a multidimensional approach and there are no commonly agreed criteria for evaluating the judicial procedures and for placement or health care of mentally ill offenders.
It is agreed, nevertheless, that a meticulous and evidence-based forensic psychiatric assessment is crucial for placing and treating mentally disordered offenders and that both the mental health system and the criminal justice system have to be considered in this assessment. Such practise should make the process for obtaining mentally disordered offenders' release less problematic and may also be relevant for to the judge's verdict. "Therefore it is a crucial question whether legal regulations require a psychiatric assessment as mandatory for trials where the suspect is thought to be mentally ill. Such regulations may reflect the aware-

ness of the problem and may even indicate the interdependencies between the mental health system and the criminal justice system", reports the study.
One particular issue is of outstanding importance. Increasingly, the potential dangerousness of mentally disordered offenders who have been convicted of a crime and the public's right to safety are discussed in polemic terms by the media. This growing contradiction – the public's right to safety versus the right to freedom of an individual about whom only dubious clinical predictions of dangerousness have been made – is also relevant for the verdict of the courts. The judge must make concrete decisions about placement and treatment and as a consequence, he or she expects evidence in the expert's assessment on which his or her own decisions can reasonably rely. Nonetheless, the implicit weakness in clinical predictions of possible further dangerous behaviour has been well known for a long time, and much more research is needed in this field.

As already emphasized, one major factor hindering harmonising the national laws, acts or procedures, is the shortage of clinical evidence that could guide best practise.

The first important recent international clinical initiative in Europe is the Nordic study on the use of coercion in the Nordic mental health care system. This study has been carried out in all five Nordic countries (Denmark, Finland, Iceland, Norway and Sweden). One aim of the study was to identify the justifications for the use of coercion in the mental health acts of these countries. A major finding was that in spite of varying degrees of coercive powers of the different mental health acts, there was an agreement among the interviewed professionals as to when civil commitment was justifiable (Syse & Nilstun 1997). It was also found that a narrow concept of coercion (hospitalization is coercive if the patient has no option, and the patient refuses or lacks the competency to express an opinion) was in use in some countries, while a wide concept (hospitalization is coercive if the patient has no option, regardless if the patient refuses, or is incompetent, or not) was in use in other countries (Nilstun & Syse 2000).
Another main aim of the Nordic study was to explore the concept of coercion by looking at the kind of events and circumstances determining the patient's perception of coercion. More than 900 patients at twelve centres in the five countries were interviewed within five days from admission, using the Nordic Admission Interview, including the Coercion Ladder and the MacArthur Perceived Coercion Scale. A main finding was that perceived coercion tends to be a dichotomised phenomenon, rather than graded and normally distributed (Høyer et al. 2002). Committed patients' reports of perceived coercion at admission differed substantially between countries, with lower levels of perceived coercion in countries with a wide legal concept of coercion (Kjellin et al, manuscript in pro-

gress). In Sweden, differences in perceived coercion at admission among committed patients were found between centres with different local care traditions (Kjellin et al. 2004).

As the second important initiative, the "European Evaluation of Coercion in Psychiatry and Harmonization of Best Clinical Practise" (acronym: EUNOMIA) project, funded for 45 months (October 2002 to June 2006) by the Research Directorate-General of the European Commission in its Quality of Life and Management of Living Resources programme, aims to fill part of this specific clinical research gap (Kallert et al. 2005).
The main goal of this project is to analyse existing cross-national variation in coercive psychiatric treatment (i.e. forced admission to a psychiatric hospital, involuntary detention after voluntary admission, seclusion/isolation in a room that the patient is not allowed to leave, restraint/fixation by holding and/or mechanical devices, forced medication), its influencing factors and outcomes.
In designing the project, regions of comparable size from all areas of Europe were included in order to cover as much of the existing variation as possible. The regions included are: Dresden, Germany; Sofia, Bulgaria; Prague, Czech Republic; Thessaloniki, Greece; Tel-Aviv, Israel; Naples, Italy; Vilnius, Lithuania; Wrocław, Poland; Michalovce, Slovakia; Granada and Malaga, Spain; East-London, United Kingdom; and Örebro, Sweden.
Within a 28 month period of data collection (i.e. the main part of the project) two groups of patients will be assessed at three time-points (at the end of the first week after admission to a psychiatric hospital, four weeks after admission, and three months after admission) using a battery of survey instruments covering psychopathology, social functioning, satisfaction with treatment, subjective quality of life, auto- and hetero-aggressive behaviour, and perceived coercion. Furthermore, each individual incident involving the administration of coercive treatment measures within the initial four weeks of hospital treatment is to be recorded in detail. Relatives' attitudes to hospital admission are assessed separately. The *first group* to be assessed – and the aim is to cover all such hospital admissions in each catchment area within the period of data collection - has experienced legally legitimate coercive measures (as defined by nation-specific legislation) motivated by either the patient's dangerousness to others (for the prevention of harm to the society), dangerousness to self (for the prevention of harm to the patient) or by the need for treatment (for the good of the mentally ill person). These coercive measures can either refer to the admission procedure which does not take place directly at a care institution (pre-authorization of involuntary hospital admission) OR to direct admission which takes place at the hospital itself (e.g. patient is being brought to the hospital with the use of physical or mechanical force). Because of the project's interest in patients' rights and

the inclusion of a wide range of European countries with different service traditions and cultures the *second group* to be assessed comprises of patients who (according to a screening procedure) experience a significant amount of perceived coercion (Cascardi & Poythress 1997, Lidz et al. 1995, Monahan et al. 1995) during the admission process although they have been voluntarily admitted from the legal point of view.

One further objective of the EUNOMIA project is to provide information on the legal basis for coercive measures in the participating countries and on their current practise. A special legal counselling group, involving one prominent legal expert from each country is responsible for this task. In order to compile all national regulations concerning coercive measures in psychiatry – and in this significantly extending the methodological approach of the project "Compulsory Admission and Involuntary Treatment of Mentally Ill Patients – Legislation and Practise in EU-Member States" – each local EUNOMIA team produced a "legal report". These reports from twelve countries (Bulgaria, Czech Republic, England, Germany, Greece, Israel, Italy, Lithuania, Poland, Slovak Republic, Spain, and Sweden) constitute the individual chapters of this book.
In order to facilitate a homogeneous structure, these national reports have been written according to a guideline established by Professor Francisco Torres-Gonzalez, Granada, Spain, and Professor Thomas Kallert, Dresden, Germany (co-ordinator of the EUNOMIA project), who are the editors of this volume. Each chapter starts with preliminary remarks on issues like the nation-specific situation covering historical developments of laws and general norms, upcoming changes to the legislation, and the specificity of the political system, or with a definition of principal legal terms. This is followed by a section on applicable laws and general norms which is subdivided into constitutional norms, general laws, international conventions and agreements incorporated into national laws, and the second level of legal norms. Comments on the particular laws are provided, focusing on: the improvement intended by the law, the consequences for clinical practise, criticism of this law, and planned revisions. The section on jurisprudence covers major sentences set down by judicial bodies, either national or international. Furthermore, each report has tried to identify and describe the contents of those protocols and internal norms related to coercive measures or compulsory treatment. Another section gives the details of reports of national organizations, international organizations, and of non-governmental organizations evaluating the application of the coercive measures in the respective countries. Monitoring and checking systems are identified in a special section of the reports differentiating checking procedures relevant for the individual person or case from abstract monitoring procedures. Finally, information on other legal data which might be pertinent for the use of coercive measures in

mental health care is provided, and each report concludes with a graphic representation of the most frequently used or the typical legal procedure administered in the field of coercive measures in mental health care.
Two chapters of the book aim at comparatively assessing and commenting on the extensive information provided for each national situation. From a clinical and legal point of view these chapters try to extract similarities between the country-specific situations as well as important future perspectives (e.g. outpatient commitment (Bonnie & Monahan, in press)), and indicate a standard that should be achieved in order to harmonize both the clinical and the legal situation across Europe.
Thus, this book significantly contributes to the main result of the EUNOMIA project. This should be – not only from a legal point of view – the identification of best clinical practise of coercive treatment in psychiatry based on the observed variation, followed by the development of a European guideline ("patient charter") for the best practise of coercive measures in psychiatry.

**References**

Baig SS (2003) Consolidated report on projects funded under research and technological development activities of a generic nature and support for research infrastructures. Office for Official Publications of the European Communities, Luxembourg

Becker T (1998) Gemeindepsychiatrie. Entwicklungsstand in England und Implikationen für Deutschland. Thieme, Stuttgart New York

Bonnie RJ, Monahan J. From Coercion to Contract: Reframing the Debate on Mandated Community Treatment for People with Mental Disorders. Law and Human Behavior, in press

Cascardi M, Poythress NG (1997) Correlates of perceived coercion during psychiatric hospital admission. International Journal of Law and Psychiatry 20: 445-458

Committee of Ministers of the Council of Europe (2000) "White Paper" on the protection of the human rights and dignity of people suffering from mental disorder, especially those placed as involuntary patients in a psychiatric establishment.

Hinterhuber H, Liensberger D, Trasser A, Schwitzer J, Rizzuti E, Meise U (2001) Stand der Entwicklung der psychiatrischen Versorgung in Italien. 22 Jahre nach Franco Basaglias Reformgesetz Nr. 180. Nervenarzt 72: 501-510

Hoge SK, Lidz CW, Eisenberg M, Monahan J, Bennett N, Gardner W, Mulvey EP, Roth L (1998) Family, clinician, and patient perceptions of coercion in mental hospital admission. International Journal of Law and Psychiatry 21: 131-146

Høyer G, Kjellin L, Engberg M, Kaltiala-Heino R, Nilstun T, Sigurjónsdóttir M, Syse A (2002) Paternalism and autonomy: A presentation of a Nordic study on the use of coercion in the mental health care system. International Journal of Law and Psychiatry 25: 93-108

Kallert TW (2000) Versorgungsbedarf und subjektive Sichtweisen schizophrener Patienten in gemeindepsychiatrischer Betreuung. – Evaluationsstudie im Jahr nach Klinikentlassung in der Versorgungsregion Dresden -. (Monographien aus dem Gesamtgebiete der Psychiatrie, Band 101) Steinkopff, Darmstadt

Kallert TW, Glöckner M, Onchev G, Raboch J, Karastergiou A, Solomon Z, Magliano L, Dembinskas A, Kiejna A, Nawka P, Torres-González F, Priebe S, Kjellin L (2005) The

EUNOMIA project on coercion in psychiatry: study design and preliminary data. World Psychiatry 4: 168-172

Kaltiala-Heino R, Laippala P, Salokangas RKR (1997) Impact of coercion on treatment outcome. International Journal of Law and Psychiatry 20: 311-322

Kjellin L, Andersson K, Bartholdsson E, Candefjord IL, Holmström H, Jacobsson L, Sandlund M, Wallsten T, Östman M (2004) Coercion in psychiatric care – patients' and relatives' experiences from four Swedish psychiatric services. Nordic Journal of Psychiatry 58: 153-159

Leff J (1993) The TAPS project: evaluating community placement of long-stay psychiatric patients. British Journal of Psychiatry 162 Suppl 19

Lidz CW, Hoge SK, Gardner WP, Bennett NS, Monahan J, Mulvey EP, Roth LH (1995) Perceived coercion in mental hospital admission: pressures and process. Archives of General Psychiatry 52: 1034-1039

Monahan J, Hoge SK, Lidz CW, Roth LH, Bennett NS, Gardner WP, Mulvey EP (1995) Coercion and commitment: understanding involuntary mental hospital admission. International Journal of Law and Psychiatry 18: 249-263

Munk-Jorgensen P (1999) Has deinstitutionalization gone too far? European Archives of Psychiatry and Clinical Neuroscience 249: 136-143

Nilstun T, Syse A (2000) The right to accept and the right to refuse. Acta Psychiatrica Scandinavica 101: 31-34

Olsen DP (1998) Toward an ethical standard for coerced mental health treatment: least restrictive or most therapeutic? Journal of Clinical Ethics 9: 235-246

Osborn DPJ (1999) Research and ethics: leaving exclusion behind. Current Opinion in Psychiatry 12: 601-604

Priebe S, Badesconyi A, Fioritti A, Hansson L, Kilian R, Torres-Gonzales F, Turner T, Wiersma D (2005) Reinstitutionalisation in mental health care: comparison of data on service provision from six European countries. British Medical Journal 330: 123-126

Rössler W, Salize HJ, Biechele U, Riecher-Rössler A (1994) Stand und Entwicklung der psychiatrischen Versorgung. Ein europäischer Vergleich. Nervenarzt 65: 427-437

Salize HJ, Dressing H (2004) Epidemiology of involuntary placement of mentally ill people across the European Union. British Journal of Psychiatry 184: 163-168

Salize HJ, Dressing H (2005) Placement and treatment of mentally ill offenders – legislation and practise in EU-member states. Final report of the research project. Mannheim

Salize HJ, Dressing H, Peitz M (2002) Compulsory admission and involuntary treatment of mentally ill patients – legislation and practise in EU-member states. Final report of the research project. Mannheim

Salokangas RKR (1994) Community care and need for treatment of schizophrenic patients in Finland. British Journal of Psychiatry 164 Suppl 23: 115-120

Syse A, Nilstun T (1997) Ulike regler – lik lovforståelse? Om tvangsregulering og verdikonflikter i nordisk psykiatri. Tidskrift for Rettsvitenskap 5: 837-918

Szmukler G, Holloway F (2001) In-patient treatment. In: Thornicroft G, Szmukler G (eds) Textbook of community psychiatry. Oxford University Press, Oxford, p 321-338

Thornicroft G, Tansella M (1999) The mental health matrix. A manual to improve services. Cambridge University Press, Cambridge

Wilkinson G, Piccinelli M, Falloon I, Krekorian H, McLees S (1995) An evaluation of community-based psychiatric care for people with treated long-term mental illness. British Journal of Psychiatry 167: 26-37

Workman RH, McCullough LB, Molinari V, Kunik ME, Orengo C, Khalsa DK, Rezabek P (2000) Clinical and ethical implications of impaired executive control functions for patient autonomy. Psychiatric Services 51: 359-363

Zinkler M, Priebe S (2002) Detention of the mentally ill in Europe – a review. Acta Psychiatrica Scandinavica 106: 3-8

**CHAPTER 2**

# Legal Report – Bulgaria

Yonko GROZEV, Georgi ONCHEV

## 2.1 Preliminary Remarks

This report has the purpose of describing Bulgarian law on the use of coercion in psychiatric treatment. It reviews issues of involuntary placement in psychiatric hospitals or other institutions for the mentally ill, involuntary treatment and the use of restraint at such institutions.

Bulgaria is a unitary state, with a system of government defined in its Constitution adopted in 1991. The Constitution established a parliamentary system of government, with executive powers vested predominantly in the Council of Ministers headed by the Prime Minister, elected and accountable to Parliament. The head of state is the President, who is elected at popular elections, and who has some limited executive powers, none of which, however, relate to health care. Bulgaria has a strong tradition of rather centralized government. Although the Constitution of 1991 did set a trend towards transferring powers to the local level, as local governments have no tax raising powers, government in all its aspects, including medical care, remains centralized.

The system of providing medical care underwent wide reforms at the end of the 90s, when a transition was made from a system of hospitals and clinics administered by the central or local authorities, to a system of health insurance, with minimum mandatory health insurance. In 1998 the Bulgarian Parliament adopted the Health Insurance Act, which introduced both compulsory and voluntary health insurance. The Health Insurance Act established the National Health Insurance Fund (NHIF), which is a government body responsible for the management of the compulsory health insurance scheme in Bulgaria, a system guaranteeing a package of health-related services on the basis of contracts between the NHIF and medical care providers.

Psychiatric health care reform was not a priority in the 90s, with the government making practically no effort in this area. The Bulgarian Psychiatric Association, a professional organization of psychiatrists that was created in 1992, was the organization that made efforts to introduce a human rights perspective by translating and disseminating international standards. Despite the efforts of professionals, users and NGOs to engage the government administration in reforming mental health care, a sustained interest on behalf of the latter in carrying out reform was not demonstrated until the year 2000. In 2000, as part of the overall health care reform, facilities providing psychiatric health care went through a process of accreditation. In 2001, the Ministry of Health adopted a reform plan for psychiatric health care in Bulgaria ("National Mental Health Program for the Citizens of the Republic of Bulgaria, 2001 to 2005"), envisaging a process of moving away from hospitalization of patients. With respect to legal regulation of coercion and improving clinical practise in psychiatric health care there had been no substantial changes until the adoption of the new Health Act, which came into force on January 1, 2005.

The Ministry of Health developed a draft law that addressed these issues and introduced important standards and guarantees for the proper use of coercion in psychiatry. This draft legislation, part (Chapter V) of the new general Health Act[1], placed increased emphasis on the rights of patients, and was subject to discussion among professionals, users and the general public as well before final adoption. The new Health Act was adopted by the Parliament on July 29, 2004, published in the *State's Gazette*, and came into force on January 1, 2005. With this new Act, for the first time under national law, detailed regulations on consent for treatment and use of restraints are provided, and procedural safeguards introduced. It also improves legislative safeguards concerning the rights of patients with respect to institutional placement and compulsory treatment.

### 2.2 Applicable Laws and General Norms

The Constitution of the Republic of Bulgaria does not contain any specific referral to psychiatric treatment. It does guarantee, however, the basic rights relevant to psychiatric treatment: the right to life[2], the prohibition of torture and inhuman and degrading treatment[3] and the right to liberty[4]. More specifically, the Constitution refers to "medical, scientific and other experiments", which can only be performed given an individual's "voluntary informed consent"[5]. Although its wording is limited to medical experiments, it could be argued that the Constitution requires informed consent for any form of medical treatment. The Constitution also sets a standard with respect to the detention of individuals. Where detention is not ordered by an agent of the judicial power (under Bulgarian law this

---

1 Health Act, *State's Gazette*, issue 70/10.08.2004, in Bulgarian.

2 Article 28 of the Constitution reads: "Everyone has the right to life. An encroachment on human life shall be punished as a heaviest crime".

3 Article 29 of the Constitution, which prohibits "cruel, inhuman or degrading treatment".

4 Article 30 of the Constitution guarantees the right to individual liberty, providing that no one can be detained, except where the power to detain is explicitly provided for by law.

5 Article 29 paragraph 2 of the Constitution of the Republic of Bulgaria.

includes both prosecutors and judges) an agent of the judicial power should be informed of the detention and rule on its legality within 24 hours[6].

The Bulgarian Constitution, however, has had little practical impact as a guarantee of basic rights in general and no impact at all with respect to rights of patients and rights of the mentally ill. The main reason for this is that the Constitutional Court, which is the judicial body empowered to enforce the Constitution, has no powers to review complaints of individuals about violations of their basic rights. Instead, it may only consider complaints, filed by a very limited number of institutions: Parliament, the President, the Council of Ministers and the Prosecutor General, in compliance with the Constitution of Parliamentary Legislation's abstract. Those institutions have never challenged legislation regulating or affecting the rights of medical patients and/or the rights of the mentally ill. As a result, none of the provisions of the Constitution cited above have been interpreted by the Constitutional Court with respect to the rights of the mentally ill, and the Court has never ruled on the compliance of domestic legislation with those constitutional norms in regard to mentally ill persons.

### 2.2.1 Placement in Psychiatric Establishments

Under Bulgarian law a person may be placed, by the courts, against her/his will in a psychiatric establishment for treatment following two different proceedings, one administrative, the other criminal. A person may also be placed in a psychiatric establishment for treatment by her/his guardian if that person has been deprived of legal capacity and been placed under guardianship.

The two procedures differ in terms of how they are initiated, the steps taken in the process, the substantive grounds on which placement and treatment can be ordered by the court and the type of treatment ordered. Probably the major difference is that the criminal law procedure is applied to individuals suspected of having committed a crime but who have been found unfit to stand trial because of their psychiatric condition. In accordance with this procedure courts can order only inpatient treatment. The other procedure, which is regulated by administrative law, regulates involuntary treatment of individuals that might be a danger to the public or themselves. The courts may order either inpatient or outpatient psychiatric treatment in accordance with this procedure. Initially, only placement for the purpose of psychiatric assessment is possible, which can be ordered by the prosecutor for up to 30 days. Both procedures are described in more detail below.

6 Article 30 paragraph 3 of the Constitution of the Republic of Bulgaria.

### 2.2.1.1 Administrative Procedure

This procedure is referred to by national legislation as "compulsory treatment", as the final decision is made by a court, which orders treatment, possibly including placement in a psychiatric establishment on an inpatient basis. The second option the courts have under this procedure is to order psychiatric treatment without placement, that is, in a day-centre on an outpatient basis. The grounds on which an individual can be placed in a psychiatric establishment are described in Article 36, paragraph 3 of the People's Health Act (1974), which reads:

> *"Persons suffering from schizophrenia, paranoia, manic-depressive psychosis, epilepsy, senility, pre-senility, traumatic, vascular and organic mental disorders, infectious, somatogenic, psychogenic and intoxication psychoses, oligophrenia and severe psychopathy who, due to their illness, are likely to perpetrate crimes constituting a serious danger to society or are dangerous to their relatives or others, or seriously threaten their own health shall be admitted for compulsory treatment in a state or municipal treatment facility under a judicial decree."*

The procedure for ordering "compulsory treatment" is described in art. 59, 61-63 of the PHA. The decision to commit someone to psychiatric treatment against his will is made by the lowest level courts, the *Raionen Sad* ("District Court"). It is only the prosecutor with the respective District Court, *Raionen Prokuror* ("District Prosecutor"), who may submit a request for the "compulsory treatment" of an individual, with the *Raionen Sad* having territorial jurisdiction, in accordance with the individual's place of residence.

The procedure, however, may be initiated by any individual who files a complaint with the respective District Prosecutor. The District Prosecutor, following such a complaint, should conduct an investigation[7]. The prosecutor would rarely question witnesses him- or herself, but rather instruct a police officer to question relatives and neighbours of the person against whom a complaint was made. The prosecutor should also order a forensic psychiatric examination, which is done by directing a letter to a psychiatrist, including evidence collected. The psychiatrist would invite the individual for a voluntary examination. If the person refuses to submit himself/herself to an examination voluntarily, the psychiatrist should report this to the prosecutor, who can order placement in a psychiatric institution for up to 30 days for psychiatric assessment. This time period can be extended in certain cases up to three months[8]. Secondary legislation treats both time limits as the maximum period of time, and stipulates that the length of placement should

---

7 Article 61 of the People's Health Act.

8 Article 61, paragraph 2 of the People's Health Act. This provision was introduced in response to complaints to the European Court of Human Rights (see the *Varbanov vs. Bulgaria* case below). Detailed regulations are set forth in Articles 69-73 of the Regulation on the People's Health Act of the Council of Ministers and Articles 4-7 of Instruction no. 1 of the Minister of Public Health.

be determined on the basis of individual case needs and should not exceed the time necessary for the examination. On the basis of the evidence collected and the psychiatric examination the prosecutor then should decide whether to request from the court an order for the placement in compulsory treatment.

One issue that is not resolved clearly by the law is whether medicinal treatment can be administered during the preliminary placement in a psychiatric establishment for examination. On the face of it, the law refers only to placement for the purposes of psychiatric assessment, and involuntary treatment should not be allowed. Treatment in emergency cases, however, is allowed upon psychiatric discretion.

On the basis of the police investigation and the forensic examination, the District Prosecutor makes a decision as to whether to file a request for compulsory treatment with the District Court. The court must schedule a hearing within two weeks of receiving the proposal and give the individual whose compulsory treatment was sought one week prior notice in order to organize his defence[9]. The person may be arrested by the police and brought in attendance in front of the court for the court hearing, if he/she failed to appear voluntarily. The court is required to hear that individual in person. The court may do this in the courtroom or hold a hearing in the treatment facility if his/she/her condition does not allow him/her to appear in court. The individual has the right to legal representation. Courts do appoint lawyers to patients for these proceedings, although free legal aid is not fully guaranteed according to an interpretative decision of the Supreme Court of 1984 that the participation of a defence lawyer in legal proceedings under art. 59 of the People's Health Act is not obligatory[10]. Amendments to the People's Health Act of 1997 provided courts with the power to order compulsory treatment both in a hospital and on an outpatient basis. Were the court to find that compulsory treatment is necessary, it should also specify the type of treatment and the psychiatric facility required. The judgment of the *Raionen Sad* may be appealed by both parties through the *Okrajen Sad*, ("Regional Court"). The decision of the *Okrajen Sad* is final and there is no further appeal from it.

Every six months, the court should rule on the extension of the compulsory treatment, whether to terminate or extend the course of treatment on the basis of a psychiatric report presented by the health institution where the individual is treated. The law also requires psychiatrists to report to the prosecutor for release

9 In practice it takes much longer to have the court hearing and a final judgment.

10 There is no statistical data or other research suggesting in what percentage of these proceedings free legal aid is granted or denied. Observations suggest that court practices vary, depending among other things on financial resources.

of patients who in their view no longer need treatment, and the prosecutor in his/she/her turn should address the court.

Monitoring has established that although placement for assessment should not exceed the time necessary for the examination, prosecutors tend to order the full time period allowed by law. Even the enforcement of the maximum time period is sometimes problematic, as courts schedule hearings at great intervals, and patients placed for assessment might stay well beyond the statutory time limits in the psychiatric institution where they are placed.

The new Health Act (2004) has substantially rewritten the whole procedure, introducing better guarantees for the rights of the patients. Individuals with mental disorders that according to this law could be subject to obligatory treatment are defined as:

> *"1. mentally ill with evidence of a serious disturbance in psychic functions (psychosis or severe personality disorder) or with salient permanent disability due to mental illness; 2. individuals with moderate or severe mental retardation or dementia" (Article 146 (1)).*

Obligatory detention and treatment according to the new Act is applied to subjects with a mental disorder (as defined above) who

> *"...due to their illness may perpetuate crimes of significant community danger or constitute a danger for their relatives or others or seriously jeopardize their own health" (Article 155 (1)).*

The delineation between detention and treatment was not made in the People's Health Act from 1974.

As in the law of 1974, a request to the District Court is filed by the District Prosecutor (Article 157). The law establishes, however, 2 court hearings in open trials: one before psychiatric forensic assessment (Article 158 (2)), and another after it is done (Article 162 (1)). The first court hearing is held within two weeks of the District Prosecutor's application with participation of the subject concerned (Article 158 (2)), a prosecutor, psychiatrist, and defence lawyer (Article 158 (4)). The court's decision could be either non-suit (Article 159 (4)), or order for forensic psychiatric assessment, including the setting: in- or outpatient (Article 159 (1)), the health service and the expert(s), the period for inpatient assessment – up to 14 days, and timing the next court hearing – not later than 48 hours after the expert assessment is done (Article 159 (2)). One-time prolongation of the assessment period up to ten days is possible (Article 159 (3)). One of the main advantages of the new law in comparison with the law from 1974 is establishing a stricter (and shorter) time frame for the assessment (initial 14 days with a possibility of ten days extension), but also the explicit linking the timing of the assessment report with the timing of the second court hearing – within two days after the deadline of the psychiatric assessment. As one of the major deficiencies of the system at present is the major delays between the assessment and court hearings, this procedural safeguard is of considerable importance.

Other major developments in the new Health Act (2004), as compared with the People's Health Act (1974), are:

a) Differentiation between detention and treatment;
b) Detention for assessment is possible only with court decision, not prosecutor's;
c) During the inpatient assessment no treatment is provided unless informed consent is given or in emergency cases (Article 160 (2)).
d) Requirement for assessment of the capacity to give informed consent for treatment along with the assessment concerning need for obligatory treatment (Article 160 (3)), and consequently, the court's decision on obligatory detention/treatment, decision about this capacity should be also reached (Article 162 (2)), and, in cases where it is judged as being absent, about the person who can express it for the patient (Article 162 (3)). The latter could be either a close relative or, in cases of conflict of interests or lack of relatives, a representative appointed by the regional municipal health department or the local mayor.
e) The Health Act (2004) limits the time for re-examination of the need for placement and treatment, which should take place every three months, instead of the six months according to the People's Health Act (1974) (Article 164 (2)). Detention and treatment can be terminated by court even before term's expiry if the pre-conditions for obligatory treatment are not present, after application by the subject concerned, the prosecutor or the head of the health service (Article 164 (3)).

Options for appeal are scheduled at every stage of the process: after the District Prosecutor's request, copies of which the court is obliged to send to the person concerned – within seven days (Article 158 (1)), after the first court hearing and the order for forensic assessment – within three days (Article 161 (1)), and after the court decision for obligatory detention and treatment – within seven days (Article 163 (1)).

### 2.2.2 Placement in Emergency Cases

The People's Health Act (1974) provides emergency powers to the psychiatrist, who might take a patient for compulsory treatment in a psychiatric establishment, if the condition of the patient requires emergency measures. The head physician at the psychiatric establishment, who has those powers by law, must report the case immediately to the prosecutor who in turn should request the court to order compulsory treatment following the standard procedure[11].

The main failure of domestic law with respect to emergency placement is the lack of clearly established procedure after an emergency placement by the head of psychiatric facility. The law requires the head of psychiatric facility to inform the prosecutor and the prosecutor would then order placement. However, prosecutors have powers only to order placement for the purposes of psychiatric assessment, not treatment, leaving a gap in the regulation of the process.

The new Health Act (2004) provides a separate procedure for emergency psychiatric care that can be applied to

> *"...subjects with conspicuous signs of mental disorder when their behaviour or state constitute a direct and imminent danger for their own health or for the health or lives of others" (Article 153 (1)).*

Placement on an emergency basis could be decided upon by the head of a psychiatric service in 24 hours (Article 154 (1)), with one-time prolongation for up to 48 hours permitted by judge (from the Raionen Sad, or the District Court) (Article 154 (2)), or 72 hours in total. If further treatment is deemed necessary, the head of the psychiatric service should immediately submit application for obligatory treatment with their grounds, along with the psychiatrist's statement, to the Raionen Sad (Article 154 (3)), which should, in turn, immediately hold a hearing (Article 158 (3)). After that, the procedural pathway for legal obligatory detention and treatment is the same as the described above under Administrative procedure.

In summary, the major developments in the Health Act (2004) as compared with the People's Health Act, concerning emergency treatment, are:

a) Differentiation between emergency detention and detention sought by prosecutor
b) Requirement of "direct and imminent danger" for emergency care
c) Feasible hospitalization up to 24 hours by doctor's decision only; and up to 72 hours with permission by a judge only (expert report not required in this case)
d) Requirement for immediate submission of request for obligatory treatment to the District Court, and for immediate examination of the case by the court, in turn, when obligatory treatment is deemed needed in emergency cases.

---

[11] See Article 36 paragraph 5 of the People's Health Act.

Despite the advantages in the new Health Act (2004), as compared with the People's Health Act (1974), there is evidence since the beginning of 2005 (when the new Act came into force) of shortcomings in the law's implementation – due mainly to lack of capacity in the legal system in the country of adhering to the procedural requirements, e.g. court hearings are postponed for a period longer than the deadlines prescribed by the law.

### 2.2.3 Placement with the Consent of a Guardian

Bulgarian law treats placement for treatment in a psychiatric establishment upon the request or with the consent of a guardian as a form of voluntary treatment and there are no separate procedural safeguards set by law, besides the safeguards with respect to guardianship. The law distinguishes between full guardianship and limited guardianship. In the first case all legal decisions including consent for treatment are made by the guardian, while in the second, they are made by the individual, with the consent of the guardian.

Bulgarian law does not have detailed regulation on matters of legal capacity of individuals with a mental illness. Instead, the law uses the same categories as those developed for children. Children up to the age of 14 have no legal capacity at all and their parents make all decisions on their behalf, while children between the age of 14 and 18 years of age can make legal decisions, but only with the consent of the parent. The law refers to those two categories as full and limited guardianship.

The legal standard for placing someone under guardianship occurs when the person cannot take care of his/she/her own interests[12]. The procedure for placing someone under guardianship is described in Articles 275 to 277 of the Civil Procedure Code. A person can be placed under guardianship by a court. The procedure can be initiated by a close relative, or anyone with an interest in the matter. The court is under a duty to hear the individual, this hearing can also take place in a psychiatric institution. The court decisions should be based on all relevant evidence, including a psychiatric report.

### 2.2.4 Criminal Procedure

This procedure is referred to by national legislation as "involuntary treatment" and is applied to individuals who are either charged with committing a crime or were convicted of committing a crime. It is described in Articles 89 to 91 of the Penal Code. A person can be placed in a psychiatric hospital under this procedure only if he or she has committed the crime for which he or she was charged in a state of legal insanity, or who has fallen into such a state before the pronouncement of the sentence or in the course of serving the sentence. The court

12 Article 5 of the Persons and Family Act.

may order three alternative measures, to surrender the person to the guardianship of his(she/her next-of-kin, order involuntary treatment at an ordinary psycho-neurological facility, or order treatment at a special psychiatric hospital, or a special ward in an ordinary psycho-neurological establishment. A proposal for such treatment may be made by the regional or district prosecutor. The proposal should be supported with a psychiatric forensic report and evidence as to the fact that the person presents a danger to society. Under this procedure the participation of a defence lawyer in the court proceedings is mandatory and the courts are under a duty to appoint a lawyer free of charge if the person does not hire one. Every six months following the beginning of the treatment, the court should rule *ex officio* on the need of continued treatment.

### 2.2.5 Treatment, Seclusion and Restraint

#### 2.2.5.1 Consent for Treatment of Patients

Once a person is placed in a psychiatric establishment, whether voluntarily or by a court order, the law leaves specific treatment almost entirely to the discretion of the health professionals. Voluntary consent given by the patient or their guardian is formulated in very general terms, where agreement on treatment at a specific institution is given without any further specifications. The law does not require any further specifications, and the physician decides on the specific nature of the treatment. The court decisions committing a person to psychiatric treatment do, however, need to specify the institution and whether treatment will be done on an in- or outpatient basis, but need not specify the treatment.

The general rule on consent to medical treatment is set forth in Article 25 paragraph 3 of the People's Health Act (1974), which says that

> *"examinations, vaccinations and treatment should be carried out with the consent of the patient, with the exception of cases in which the law envisages compulsory examinations, vaccinations and treatment".*

The provisions of the PHA (1974) regarding informed consent, though applicable to all inpatient psychiatric care facilities, lack specific instructions as to what the form of informed consent for treatment should be. As there are no requirements for explicit consent for specific forms of treatment under Bulgarian law, the general consent for treatment or order for compulsory treatment leave the specific course entirely to the discretion of health professionals.

Article 31 of the People's Health Act (1974) repeats this rule with a more detailed description of treatment particularly related to psychiatric patients. It states that

> *"disease prevention, diagnostic, and treatment methods which have not been generally accepted may be used only in the interest of the patient's health in accordance with the procedure established by the Ministry of Health ... diagnostic and treatment methods leading to a temporary change in human consciousness, such as hypnosis and narcosis, may be applied only in duly equipped health care facilities by specially trained professionals."*

In both cases described in the previous sentence, the law requires that

> *"diagnostic and treatment methods covered under paragraphs 3 and 4 shall be applied only with the patient's advance consent or, if the patient is legally incapacitated, with the consent of his/she/her lawful representative or guardian".*

Again, there is no requirement for a detailed description of particular therapy or explicit consent or approval of a certain therapy besides the general agreement for treatment or decision committing a patient to treatment.

Electro-convulsive therapy and other types of shock therapy fall into the second category of methods, those of diagnosis and treatment, which lead to a temporary change in consciousness. According to Instruction No. 5 of 1975 on the implementation of methods for diagnosis and treatment which lead to a temporary change in consciousness the following are defined as such:

> *"biological shock methods with the use of electric shock, insulin, cardiasol and other medicines; hypnoses, narcoses".*

Besides the non-existence of detailed regulation of consent for a specific course of treatment, observers have raised concerns with respect to two other issues. One is the unmodified electro-convulsive therapy, which is electro-convulsive therapy without anaesthetic or muscle relaxants[13]. Bulgarian law has no explicit prohibition of unmodified ECT and for lack of financial resources and staff some psychiatric establishments administer electro-convulsive therapy without anaesthetics and muscle relaxants. The second issue is treatment and particularly drug treatment during the commitment to a psychiatric institution by a prosecutor for a psychiatric examination. According to Bulgarian law, such commitment is for the sole purpose of examining the patient, and the examination should assist the court in reaching a well-informed decision regarding compulsory treatment. For practical purposes, however, as judicial proceedings tend to take substantially longer than the two weeks provided by law, treatment starts shortly if not immediately after a person is committed to a psychiatric institution for an examination. Some legal ground for such treatment might be found under the emergency pow-

---

[13] Concerns with respect to unmodified ECT were first raised by the Committee on the Prevention of Torture (CPT) in its report on its first visit in Bulgaria in 1995. According to monitoring done by the Bulgarian Helsinki Committee unmodified ECT is still practiced in Bulgaria.

ers of heads of psychiatric hospitals, but the legislation certainly needs more clarity.

One of the major developments of the new Health Act (2004), already discussed above, is the differentiation between placement and treatment, which can no longer be considered the same thing by law. The District Court rules separately on placement, and separately on whether the person has the capacity to give consent to treatment. Where the court finds that the individual does not have the capacity to give consent for treatment, the District Court appoints a relative or other person, to give consent to treatment on behalf of the patient[14].

The Health Act (2004) stipulates that all medical activities shall be done only after informed consent of the patients is voluntarily expressed (Article 87 (1)). In cases where the capacity to give informed consent is disturbed by mental illness, the court appoints a relative or others to express informed consent for the patient, as described in Article 162 (3)). All interventions requiring general anesthesia or other invasive methods should be done only after obtaining the informed written consent of the patient (Article 89 (1)). These interventions can be applied without informed written consent only in cases of imminent life-threatening conditions when receiving such consent is not possible because of the physical or mental state of the patient, or the legal guardian, in cases of legal incompetence, cannot be reached (Article 89 (2)). In psychiatric patients judged unable by court to give informed consent (see Article 162) such interventions can be applied only with the permission of the ethical committee of the health service, or by the head of the service where such committees are nonexistent (Article 89 (3)).

On the level of "internal norms", all hospitalizations in the country (including the voluntary psychiatric hospitalizations) should be done with the informed written consent of the patients.

**2.2.5.2 Seclusion and Restraint**

Bulgarian legislation does not contain any standards on the use of restraint and seclusion of psychiatric patients during their stay in a psychiatric establishment. After the year 2000 all psychiatric establishments had to be accredited and for this accreditation process they had to adopt protocols for the application of coercive measures. Although such establishments do run registers of incidents describing measures of restraint, there seem to be variations in the way different institutions do that, if they do it at all. Organizations that have carried out monitoring of psychiatric establishments have failed on different occasions to estab-

---

[14] See Article 162 paragraph 1 through 3 of the Health Act (2004).

lish the existence of internal rules adopted by the institutions themselves, which reveals a need for better enforcement of such internal rules[15]. Seclusion and restraint of patients are routinely practiced in Bulgarian psychiatric establishments[16]. A diverse arsenal of restraints is used, like leather and canvas belts, with which the patient's wrists are strapped to the bed frames or springs, which seems to be the most widely used restraint, and in some cases a longer belt is also used to immobilize the waist. Chains ending in either self-locking or clasp-locked irons are also used in some institutions. In its first report on Bulgaria, the CPT recommended that the two sets of handcuffs found in the psychiatric section of the Lovech Prison Hospital be removed from the premises. Incidents of restraint are recorded in patients' case histories and/or in the doctors' and nurses' report sheets.

Seclusion of patients in separate rooms for isolation is also a relatively common practice in Bulgarian psychiatric establishments[17]. As in the case of restraint, there is no clearly formulated policy, much less a set of written rules, for the guidance and training of the staff on the use of isolation.

The new Health Act (2004) for the first time regulates this matter on legal level. According to Article 150 measures for temporary physical restraint can be applied to patients with confirmed mental disorders that have deteriorated to states constituting a direct and imminent danger for their own health or life or for the health or lives of others (1), clarifying that: restraining measures only create conditions for treatment and do not replace the treatment itself (2), are ordered by medical doctor, who assigns the type of measure and its duration – up to six hours (3), the measures are applied by trained staff (4), are documented in a special journal of the service and in the patient's hospital file (5), and do require constant monitoring: by a doctor or a nurse (6).

**2.3 Jurisprudence**

There is little jurisprudence on the use of coercion in psychiatric treatment in Bulgaria. As far as domestic courts go, the decision of a court under Article 36 of the People's Health Act (1974) to place a person in a psychiatric establishment is not subject to appeal before the Supreme Court, which is the only court that can establish precedents. As the Constitutional Court can be addressed only by a very limited number of government agencies, the President, the Council of Ministers,

---

15 These include the Council of Europe Committee on the Prevention of Torture, Amnesty International and the Bulgarian Helsinki Committee.

16 Reports of Amnesty International and the Bulgarian Helsinki Committee (see below).

17 Seclusion in separate rooms is reported in most of the psychiatric establishments, one exception being the 1995 report of the CPT on the Radnevo State Psychiatric Hospital.

the General Prosecutor and a number of Members of Parliament, it has never ruled on the rights of psychiatric patients.

The one exception to that rule of lack of jurisprudence on the issue is a judgment by the European Court of Human Rights in the case of Varbanov vs. Bulgaria, judgment of 5 October 2000. There, the European Court of Human Rights established a violation of two provisions of the European Convention of Human Rights, Article 5.1, concerning the lawfulness of the detention in psychiatric facilities and Article 5.4, concerning the right to judicial review of the legality of detention. These two violations occurred in the procedure of mandatory placement in a psychiatric establishment for the purpose of psychiatric examination. The Court ruled that in that particular case the prosecutor ordered the placement of the patient who had no prior medical history in a hospital for 30 days, without a preliminary medical opinion from a medical expert. This, according to well established case law of the Court was in violation of Article 5.1e of the European Convention of Human Rights. The Court said in this judgment

> *"that a prior appraisal by a psychiatrist, at least on the basis of the available documentary evidence, was possible and indispensable... In these circumstances, the Court cannot accept that, in the absence of an assessment by a psychiatrist, the views of a prosecutor and a police officer on the applicant's mental health ... sufficed to justify an order for his arrest..."*

The People's Health Act in force at the time of the plaintiff's commitment, and as of June 2003, did not oblige prosecutors to seek such an appraisal. They could and still can base their decision to commit a person for an involuntary examination in a psychiatric establishment on the basis of a refusal of the person to undergo voluntary examination[18].

In the Varbanov judgment the Court found also a violation of the Convention because the prosecutor who ordered the commitment did not have clear powers to do so under domestic law, a deficiency, which was overcome in 1997, while the case was still pending, with amendments to the People's Health Act. The Court ruled, that

> *"the expressions 'in accordance with the law' and 'in accordance with a procedure prescribed by law' require that the impugned measure should have a basis in domestic law and also should refer to the quality of the law in question, requiring that it should be accessible to the person concerned and foreseeable as to its effects".*

And finally, the Court established a third problem with Bulgarian law, which was the lack of a clearly established procedure to challenge the decision of the prosecutor before the courts. For this reason the Court ruled a violation of Article 5

---

[18] Government is working on legislative amendments that will provide the proper guarantees in light of the Varbanov judgment.

paragraph 4 of the European Convention of Human Rights. The Court ruled that both in general and in the concrete case, the possibility of appeal can only be provided in two forms. When a court orders the initial detention, the detainee must be given access to a hearing either in person or through some form of representation. When a non-judicial body orders the initial detention, the detainee must be given the opportunity to appeal the decision before a court[19].

### 2.4 Protocols and Internal Norms Related to Coercive Measures or Compulsory Medical Treatment

Coercive measures and compulsory treatment are regulated by a parliamentary and secondary legislation. As cited above, the major legislation is the People's Health Act (1974), or, since January 1, 2005, the Health ACT (2004), and the Penal Code and the Criminal Procedure Code regulating placement of the criminally irresponsible. Secondary legislation of particular importance is the Regulation on the Enforcement of the People's Health Act, adopted by the Council of Ministers and Instruction no. 1 of the Minister of Public Health.

A process of accreditation *de novo* of all health services in Bulgaria took place after the year 2000. This process required extensive documentation of all treatment procedures and the adoption of protocols for the application of coercive measures. As a result all psychiatric establishments had to adopt such protocols, with each establishment adopting its own protocols. The protocols on use of coercive measures of the different psychiatric hospitals and psychiatric departments however, are to a large extent similar, with only minor differences. Those protocols concern immobilization, seclusion, forced medication, and detention. There are no separate protocols or guidelines on involuntary placement, as placement is regulated by the law. Individual files of patients would only note that the patient is placed on an involuntary basis. The protocols, however, have guidelines as to how the staff should treat patients' "aggressive and auto-aggressive behaviour". Protocols on coercive measures are usually short and to a certain extent operational. They commonly list:

---

[19] While the European Court of Human Rights was hearing the Varbanov case, the Bulgarian government introduced amendments to the People's Health Act in February 1997. The amendments gave clear powers to prosecutors to detain persons for inpatient psychiatric examination. These powers were given with the new Article 61 paragraph 2 of the People's Health Act: *"If the person refuses to undergo psychiatric expertise voluntarily without good reason, the prosecutor shall order that this would be conducted by compulsion – on an outpatient or inpatient basis."* The other two problems, however, remained unsolved – prosecutors were not obliged to seek any medical opinion prior to a patient's placement in an inpatient facility for expertise, and there is still no clear procedure for the appeal of detention by a prosecutor before a court.

- Indications for the measure in behavioural or diagnostic terms, e.g. imminent threat to self or to others, destructive and disorganized behaviour, catatonic excitement, impossibility for application of alternative measures;
- Who orders the measure, e.g. a doctor, or a nurse in case of emergency when a doctor is not present;
- Description of the procedure itself, e.g. a staff member for each limb, method of physical restraint and parts of the body (usually wrists and/or ankles), place of muscular injection, etc.;
- Monitoring of the measure, e.g. examination of the immobilized body parts, assessment of vital signs, behaviour and state of arousal, etc.;
- Written record of the measure in patient's documentation and in the "on duty" doctor's and nurse's book, as well as in a separate "journal of incidents". Time when measure was started and time when measure was discontinued should clearly be noted.

The monitoring of the implementation of these protocols, however, is still to a large extent an unresolved issue.

To better understand the development of such norms, the background in the development of those "internal norms", the protocols, should be taken into consideration. They have been the result of almost a decade of discussion within the psychiatric community in Bulgaria. Shortly after the political changes in 1989 a heated debate broke out in the community as to the ethics of the profession. Coercion in psychiatry was discussed in the framework of searching for a new professional identity, ethically centred on the concept of patients' autonomy. Alleged abusive practices and a need to change practices to better guarantee human rights have been part of the ongoing discussion within the Bulgarian Psychiatric Association (BPA). The Association had carried out a significant amount of work during the 90s in publication, training and dissemination of internationally recognized instruments on bioethics, psychiatric ethics and on coercion in psychiatry. The 90s were, thus, a time of the psychiatric community in Bulgaria getting familiar with and integrating international ethical standards.
It was only in the last few years, that efforts were directed towards the creation and adoption of national standards. In this effort a number of organizations cooperated, among them the BPA, the Medical Universities, the Ministry of Health, the National Health Insurance Fund, and patient's organizations. Guidelines for the management of aggression and dangerous behaviour, concerning application of coercive measures have been developed, and integrated into the National Standard in Psychiatry, adopted by the Ministry of Health (2004).

**2.5 Reports**
There have been several reports by independent organizations on psychiatric institutions in Bulgaria. These include two reports by the Council of Europe Committee on the Prevention of Torture, drafted after their visits in 1995 and 1999, a report by the Bulgarian Helsinki Committee on psychiatric hospitals and a report by Amnesty International on Social Care Homes[20].

The Committee on the Prevention of Torture visited the Radnevo Psychiatric Hospital, the Lovech Neuropsychiatric Hospital, the Lovech Prison Hospital and the Social Care Home in Terter. In its reports the Committee on the Prevention of Torture raised concerns dealing with the lack of proper living conditions, nutrition, heating, clothes, policy and recording of the use of restraints and isolation rooms, proper training for the use of restraints, use of unmodified ECT, insufficient alternatives to pharmacotherapy, insufficient staff as well as the lack of proper complaint and regular reports proceedings.

The Amnesty International report is based on visits during October 2001 and January 2002 by representatives of Amnesty International, the Bulgarian Helsinki Committee and Mental Disability Rights International of three state psychiatric hospitals in Karlukovo, Patalenitsa and Kardzali, and five social care homes for children with mental disabilities in Borislav, Dzhurkovo, Strazha, Mogilino and Vidrare, and eight social care homes for adults in Sanadinovo, Radovets, Razdol, Pastra, Podgumer, Dragash Voyvoda, Samuil and Cherni Vrah. The report covers a broad number of concerns ranging from legal provisions and practices regarding compulsory treatment, to lack of rehabilitation for mentally disabled children, to living conditions and treatment available in social homes for adults. The latter, according to the report were "in a shocking state and conditions and treatment of residents in seven of the eight social homes visited, in the delegation's view, were considered to amount to cruel, inhuman and degrading treatment".

The report of the Bulgarian Helsinki Committee was drafted on the basis of joint visits with representatives of the Bulgarian Psychiatric Association to eight State Psychiatric Hospitals, SPH-Lovech, SPH-Tserova Koria, SPH-Radnevo, SPH-Kurdjali, SPH-Tsarev Brod, SPH-Sevlievo, SPH-Karvouna, SPH-Karloukovo, SPH-Patalenitsa, SPH-Novi Iskur, SPH-Byala in 2001 trial observations, and interviews with health professionals. The report covers a range of issues like or-

---

20 All reports are available on the internet on the web pages of the respective organizations, www.cpt.coe.int, for the CPT, www.amnesty.org for Amnesty International and www.bghelsinki.org for the Bulgarian Helsinki Committee.

ganization of psychiatric establishments, legal regulation of compulsory placement and treatment and its implementation, living conditions, nutrition, staff and inspections of psychiatric hospitals.

**2.6 Safeguards**

There are a number of government institutions that have the powers to inspect psychiatric establishments, respectively concerning different requirements. These include the Hygiene and Epidemiology Inspectorate, the Ministry of Health, the Ministry of Social Affairs, the regional health care centres, the Labor Inspectorate, the State Financial Monitoring authorities and the Prosecutor's Office. The Prosecutor's Office is obliged to inspect psychiatric establishments under Article 127 paragraph 2 of the Constitution and Article 118 paragraph 2 of the Judiciary Act, requiring the Prosecutor's Office to exercise supervision over the enforcement of all measures of compulsion.

In practice, however, inspections of psychiatric institutions do not seem to be rigorous and thorough, failing to address many issues. During its first visit in 1995, the Committee for the Prevention of Torture summarized in its evaluation that the complaints and inspection procedures effective then in the psychiatric establishments "were not satisfactory", and that external supervision of these psychiatric establishments "is at best sporadic". There is no practice of visits on a regular basis by an independent outside body, carrying a thorough research, including confidential interviews with patients and publishing the findings. Observers have noticed that most inspections are on hygiene, fire safety, and of financial issues. Prosecutor's Offices, which are specifically obliged to monitor the use of compulsory measures in psychiatric establishments, seem to be particularly inactive[21].

In its report on its visit of 1999 the CPT recommended, concerning the Social Home in Terter, that "specific arrangements be made enabling residents to lodge formal complaints with a clearly designated body" and also that "an independent outside body responsible for the inspection of patients' care, visiting on a regular basis" be created[22]. Similar recommendations were made with respect to the psychiatric hospitals visited by the CPT in 1995.

---

21 The Bulgarian Helsinki Committee noted in its report that monitoring of "The Bulgarian Helsinki Committee and the Bulgarian Psychiatric Association did not find any evidence that prosecuting authorities visited the facilities."

22 See CPT Report on Bulgaria of 1999, paragraph 186. The recommendations with respect to psychiatric hospitals can be found in the CPT Report on Bulgaria of 1995, paragraph 222.

## Diagram 2.1: Flowchart of Legal Procedures for Involuntary Treatment in Bulgaria (People's Health Act 1974)

**Article 36. (3) People's Health Act** Signs of mental disorder (specified by the law, e.g. schizophrenia, paranoia, manic-depressive psychosis, etc.)

+

"...who, due to their illness, are likely to perpetrate crimes constituting a serious danger to society or are dangerous to their relatives or others, or seriously threaten their own health..."

↓ **OR** ↓

Application from virtually anyone (e.g. relatives, physicians) to the District Prosecutor | Admission to psychiatric inpatient facility on emergency basis

↓ ↓

Order by the Prosecutor for ambulatory assessment | Evaluation on admission that the criteria of Art. 36 above are fulfilled

↓ ↓ ↓

Ambulatory assessment (by 1 or 2 psychiatrists) | Refusal to be assessed ambulatory | Director of the facility immediately (in 24 hours) informs the Prosecutor - Art. 36. (5)

↓ ↓ ↓

Submission of written expertise report to Prosecutor | Order by the Prosecutor for inpatient assessment in 30 days *Note: Allowance for treatment in the assessment period not specified; in practice: frequently delivered based on medical judgment*

↓ ↓

Submission of written expertise report (signed by three psychiatrists, in most cases) to the Prosecutor. After the 30-day period patient should be released.

↓ ↓

→ Prosecutor's motion to court (submitting expertise along with other evidence)

↓

Open trial with obligatory presence of the patient with a defendant, and with experts in vivo as witnesses

↓

Court decision: Prosecutor's motion denied or involuntary treatment ordered, specifying the setting: outpatient, semi-inpatient or inpatient, and the facility where it is to be administered

↓

Involuntary treatment subject to termination, change or continuation based on experts' written report in six months. In cases of significant improvement written report offer for termination of the involuntary treatment could be submitted before expiry of the six-month period.

## Diagram 2.2: Community Health Act (2004), Chapter Five

**Art. 150 (1)** Individuals with a **mental disorder** that according to this law could be subject to "special measures": 1. mentally ill with evidence of a serious disturbance in psychic functions (psychosis or severe personality disorder) or with salient permanent disability due to mental illness; 2. individuals with moderate or severe mental retardation or dementia.

**Art. 154** (1) Measures for temporary physical restraint could be applied to patients with *confirmed mental disorders* that have deteriorated to states constituting *a direct and imminent danger* for their own health or life or for the health or lives of others. The measures:
(2) only create conditions for treatment and **do not replace the treatment itself**;
(3) are ordered **by medical doctor**, who assigns the type of measure and its duration – up to **six hours**;
(4) are applied by **trained** staff;
(5) are **documented** in a special journal of the service and in patient's hospital file;
(6) require constant **monitoring**: by a doctor or a nurse.

**Art. 159 (1) Obligatory detention and treatment:** subjects with a mental disorder (as defined in **Art. 150 (1), it. 1 & 2**), who *due to their illness may* commit a *crime* of significant community danger or constitute a danger for their relatives or for others *or seriously jeopardize their own health.*

↓

**Art. 161.** Application by a prosecutor.

↓

**Art. 162 (1)** The district court sends copies of the application to the subject concerned. Within *seven days* appeal is possible.

↓

↓

**Art. 162 (2)** Open trial with the participation of the subject concerned in *two weeks period.*

**Art. 157 (1) Emergency psychiatric care:** could be applied to subjects *with conspicuous signs* of mental disorder, when their behaviour or state constitute *a direct and imminent danger* for their own health or life or for the health or lives of others.

↓

Mental disorder present (**Art. 150 (1), it. 1 & 2**) and need for continuation of treatment after emergency management.

↓

**Art. 158 (1)** Decision from the head of the health service for temporary detention for treatment – for *up to 24 hours*; informing the relatives.

↓

**Art. 158 (2)** One-time prolongation for *up to 48 hours* with permission by a judge.

↓

Obligatory treatment needed (**Art. 159**)

↓

**Art. 158 (3)** *Immediate* application by the head of the service to the district court with motivation, along with a statement by a psychiatrist.

↓

**Art. 162 (3)** *Immediate* examination of the case by court. Copies are submitted in the trial. The head of the service ensures appearance of the subject.

↓

**Art. 162 (4)** The participation of *psychiatrist, defence, and prosecutor* is obligatory.

↓

**Art. 162 (5)** The subject concerned is interrogated in person. When needed he/she is brought compulsorily. When subject's health does not allow appearance in trial, the court should acquire a *first hand impression* of his/she/her condition.

↓

**Art. 163 (4)** Non-suit when circumstances according the Art. 159 are absent or when mental disorder as judged by the psychiatrist is not present.

**OR**

**Art. 163 (1)** Order for psychiatric expertise assessment, its form – outpatient or inpatient, **(2)** the health service and the expert(s), the period – *up to 14 days*, timing the next trial – not later than 48 hours after the expert assessment is done.
↓
**Art. 163 (3)** One-time prolongation of the assessment period for up to *ten days*.

**Art. 164 (2)** During the expert assessment no treatment is provided *unless informed consent is given or in emergency cases.*

**Art. 164 (3)** Along with the expert assessment, the expert judges the *capacity for giving informed consent for treatment.*

↓
**Art. 165 (1)** The decision for non-suit or for expert assessment is subject to appeal or protest *within three days.* The appeal cancels the expert assessment unless otherwise decided by the court.
↓
**Art. 165 (2)** The appeal court decides in open trial. Non-appearance of the subject without a reasonable excuse is not obstacle for case consideration.
↓
**Art. 166 (1)** Court decision, **(2)** about the need for *obligatory detention*, the *health service* that should provide it, the *capacity for giving informed consent*, the *period*, and the *form* of the treatment – outpatient or inpatient; **(3)** when capacity for informed consent is absent, the court orders *obligatory treatment* and *appoints a person* among the subject's relatives who should express informed consent on his/she/her behalf. In cases of a conflict of interests or a lack of relatives the court appoints a representative of the regional municipal health department or a representative appointed by the local mayor who should express informed consent for treatment of the subject concerned.
↓
**Art. 167 (1)** The court decision is subject to appeal within *seven days.* **(2)** The appeal cancels its execution unless otherwise decided by the district or the appeal court.
↓
**Art. 168 (1)** The obligatory treatment terminates with expiration of the term or by court's decision. **(2)** On the basis of expertise psychiatric report the court decides every *three months* in favour of termination or prolongation of the obligatory detention and treatment. **(3)** When the pre-conditions for obligatory treatment are not present any more, the obligatory detention and treatment may be terminated by a court before the term's expiry after *application by the subject concerned, the prosecutor or the head of the health service.*

**Art. 160 (1)** Obligatory treatment is ordered by court.

Note: "Obligatory" is the term accepted in this law and in all norms in this country, synonymous to "compulsory" in other legislations. The very term "compulsory" in our legislation is used in the Penalty Law for treatment of those that have already committed crime and, due to insanity, are not subject to penalty but to "compulsory" treatment (Art. 89).

**Art. 160 (2)** Obligatory treatment could be provided in practically all health services.

**Art. 169 (2)** The order for obligatory detention and treatment and the order for expert assessment are to be executed by the health services, with the cooperation of the police when needed.

**Diagram 2.3: Main Changes in the CHA (2004) as Compared to PHA (1974)**

- Differentiation between emergency detention and obligatory detention applied for by a prosecutor
- Requirement for "direct and imminent danger" for emergency care and for measures for physical restraint
- Feasible hospitalization up to 72 hours with only permission by judge; expertise not required
- Detention for hospital expert assessment possible only with court decision, not prosecutor's
- Two court trials: one for review of applications (by the prosecutor or by the head of the health service in cases of emergency) and for order of expert assessment, and a second one for review of expert report and decision for obligatory detention/treatment
- Differentiation between obligatory detention and obligatory treatment
- Requirement for expert assessment not only for the need for obligatory treatment according to Art. 159 but for the capacity to also give informed consent for treatment
- Court decision not only about obligatory detention / treatment but also about the capacity to give informed consent, and in cases where this capacity is absent, about the person who can express it for the patient
- Shortening of all procedural deadlines (up to "immediately" in emergency)
- Requirement for "first hand impression" about the patient when his appearance in court is impossible
- Definition of the conditions for treatment when detained for expert assessment
- Definition of the conditions for application of measures for temporary physical restraint
- Feasibility for obligatory treatment to be provided not in "special" health services but practically in all health services, including wards in general hospitals, dispensaries, etc.

# CHAPTER 3

# Legal Report – Czech Republic

Štěpán PEICHL

## 3.1 Preliminary Remarks

Both the Czech constitutional law and legal system are based on the principles of the universality of human rights, the rights of citizens, and the sovereign character of law. Each person is free and under no obligation to undertake courses of action other than those stipulated by specific legal acts. Therefore, each person may freely decide on questions regarding their health and it is solely at their discretion whether they undergo medical care. The inviolability of personal integrity is a constitutional principle. However, this principle is neither absolute nor unlimited and can be restricted through general laws stipulating certain conditions whereby an individual must undergo a specific course of medical care – even if this is against their will. The above legal concept prevailed following the democratic changes of 1989.

## 3.2 Applicable Laws and General Norms

### 3.2.1 Constitutional Norms

Act No. 1/1993 Coll., the Constitution of the Czech Republic of December 16, 1992, as amended (the "Constitution"):

> *"Article 1(1). The Czech Republic is a sovereign, unitary and democratic, law-abiding State, based on respect for the rights and freedoms of the individual and the citizen."*

> *"Article 2(4). Everybody may do that which is not prohibited by law and nobody may be forced to do that which the law does not instruct them to do."*

> *"Article 3. An integral component of the constitutional system of the Czech Republic is the Charter of Fundamental Rights and Freedoms."*

> *"Article 4. The fundamental rights and freedoms shall be protected by the judiciary power."*

The Charter of Fundamental Rights and Freedoms adopted by the Act No. 2/1993 Coll. (the "Charter"):

> *"Article 2(3). Everybody may do that which is not prohibited by law and nobody may be forced to do that which the law does not command."*

> *"Article 7(1). Inviolability of the individual and of privacy is guaranteed. This may be limited only in cases specified by law.*
> *(2) Nobody may be subjected to torture or to inhuman or degrading treatment or punishment."*

*"Article 8(1). Personal freedom is guaranteed.*
*(2). Nobody may be prosecuted or deprived of his or her freedom except on certain grounds and in a manner specified by law.*
*(6) The law shall determine cases where a person may be admitted to or kept in a medical institution without his or her consent. This shall then be reported within twenty-four hours to a court that shall then decide on the permissibility of such placement within seven days."*

*"Article 31. Everybody has the right to the protection of his or her health. Citizens are entitled under public insurance to free medical care and to medical aid under conditions set by law."*

*"Article 36(1). Everybody may assert, in a set procedure, his or her right in independent and unbiased legal proceedings and in specified cases to another legal body.*
*(2) Anybody who claims that his or her rights have been violated by a decision of a public administration body may turn to a court for a review of the legality of such a decision, unless the law stipulates otherwise. However, a review of the decisions affecting the fundamental rights and freedoms listed in the Charter may not be excluded from the jurisdiction of courts."*

**Remarks**

The Charter of Fundamental Rights and Freedoms adopted in the Act No. 2/1993 Coll. (hereinafter the Charter) is a major part of the constitutional system of the Czech Republic. The Charter was adopted, by the Czech Republic, from the constitutional system of former Czechoslovakia.

### 3.2.2 General Laws

#### 3.2.2.1 Administrative Legislation

Act No. 20/1966 Coll., Act on People's Health Care, as amended (hereinafter "The Healthcare Act"):

*"Section 23(2). Diagnostic and therapeutic measures may be carried out only with the concerned person's consent or if their consent can be anticipated.*
*(3). A parent or a representative of an underage person, or the guardian of a person who has been deprived by a court of the capacity to provide consent, may give such consent. The doctor in charge has the capacity to make decisions regarding emergency diagnostic or therapeutic measures necessary for saving the life or health of a child or a person who has been deprived by a court of the capacity to provide consent, if the parent or the guardian refuses to give his or her consent.*
*(4) Diagnostic and emergency measures without the patient's consent may be carried out, or a patient may be admitted to a medical establishment if the following conditions are met:*
*(a) there is an illness which is specified in a particular law for which compulsory treatment may be ordered,*

*(b) a person with signs of a mental disorder or intoxication poses a threat to himself or herself or to members of his or her community*[1]*, or*
*(c) measures are necessary in order to save the life or health of an individual due to the present health conditions of the person whose consent cannot be required."*

**Remarks**
Essentially, the diagnostic and therapeutic measures may be carried out only with the concerned person's consent or if their consent can be expected (Section 23(2) of the Healthcare Act). Parents, a representative of an underage person, or the guardian of a person who has been deprived by a court of their legal capacity to provide consent, may also give such consent. In accordance with Section 23(3) of the Healthcare Act, the doctor in charge has the power to make decisions relating to the implementation of emergency diagnostic or therapeutic measures necessary for saving the life or health of a child, or an individual who has been deprived by a court of the capacity to provide consent, if the parents or the guardian refuse to give their consent. Diagnostic and any necessary course of medical action may be carried out or a patient may be admitted to a medical establishment without the patient's consent, if the conditions stipulated in the Section 23(4) of the Healthcare Act are met.

There is neither a specific act on mental health in Czech law nor a comprehensive act regulating involuntary treatment, involuntary admission or the use of preventive safety measures with respect to mentally ill persons. Involuntary admission and involuntary treatment are differentiated by particular circumstances only. The use of preventive security measures and order are not regulated by general law. However, an amendment no. 260/2001 Coll. to the Healthcare Act stipulates in Section 67a ff. that a medical establishment must keep records containing information on the treatment of each patient and significant events relating to the patient's state of health as well as procedures in connection with the health care provided. The above-mentioned measures undoubtedly constitute "significant events" or "procedures in connection with health care" which must be kept in the records.

However, the Ministry of Health is preparing an entirely new act on healthcare, which is expected to contain provisions regulating treatment/admission without the person's consent and a definition of informed and qualified consent in a similar manner to the Healthcare Act, but with provisions that are expected to be

1 The wording of the provision is not clear and certain doubts exist as to whether the provision shall apply when such a person poses a threat to property. The interpretation used herein shall comply with the constitutional principle of minimal restriction of individual freedoms.

more precise. The act is also expected to contain provisions allowing a person to appoint a representative in the event that they are not able to express their opinion or consent. Additionally, new provisions will regulate the management of aggressive patients as well as police involvement in such cases.

### 3.2.2.2 Civil Legislation

Act no. 99/1963 Coll., the Civil Procedure Code:

*"Section 191a. (1) An institution providing medical care (hereinafter the 'institution') in which persons are placed for reasons referred to in a special regulation must, within 24 hours, inform the court in whose district the institution is located of institutionalising an individual, who has been placed therein without their written consent (hereinafter the 'ill person').*
*(2) If the person who was placed in medical care with his or her written consent has had their free movement or contact with the outside world restricted in the course of medical care, the institution must inform the court according to paragraph 1 within 24 hours after such restriction has occurred.*
*Section 191b. (1) The court in whose district the institution is located shall commence proceedings on the permissibility of admitting the ill person on whose behalf the institution must inform the court according to Section 191a; however, these proceedings shall not be commenced if admission and keeping the ill person in the institution were ordered by a court in another proceeding.*
*(2) If the person who has been admitted to the institution has no other representative, the court shall appoint a guardian for these proceedings.*
*(3) The court shall collect evidence necessary for considering whether the ill person was admitted (Section 191a paragraph 1 and 2) for lawful reasons; the court shall also hear the ill person and the attending doctor. A meeting usually need not be ordered.*
*(4) Within seven days after the restriction according to Section 191a occurred, the court shall decide whether the admission procedure was legally sound and grounded (Section 191a paragraph 1).*
*Section 191c. (1) The ruling according to Section 191b paragraph 4 shall be delivered to the person who has been admitted unless he or she is unable to understand the contents of such a decision in the opinion of the attending doctor; the ruling shall be also delivered to his or her representative (guardian) and to the institution.*
*(2) An appeal against this ruling shall have no deferring effect. An appeal may also be filed by the institution if the court has decided that the admission procedure was not legally sound.*
*(3) The institution may release the placed person even if the court has declared that the admission procedure was legally sound and grounded.*
*Section 191d (1) If the court has stated that the admission was in accordance with legal practice and if the placed person's contact with the outside world is restricted or excluded, the court shall then continue proceedings on the permissibility of prolonged institutionalisation.*
*(2) In order to examine the placed person's health condition, the court shall appoint an expert. The task of this expert is to state whether holding the placed person in the institution and restricting or excluding his or her contact with the outside world is necessary. A*

*doctor who works in the institution where the placed person is kept cannot be appointed as expert.*
*(3) The court shall order a meeting to which the court shall summon the placed person (if, according to a statement of the attending doctor or a written expert's report, he or she is able to understand the course and content of the meeting) and his or her representative (guardian). In the meeting, the court shall examine the expert and, depending on the circumstances, the attending doctor and the placed person; depending on the specifics of the case, the court shall also collect other pertinent evidence.*
*(4) In a judgment that must be issued within three months after the verdict on the permissibility of admission to the institution, the court shall decide whether the prolonged institutionalisation is permissible and if so, the period of time necessary. The provisions of Section 191c paragraphs 2 and 3 shall apply analogously.*
*Section 191e. (1) The effects of the judgment according to Section 191d paragraph 4 shall expire after the lapse of one year after its passing unless a shorter period was determined therein. If institutional care for the patient is to be prolonged beyond this period, it shall be necessary to carry out a new examination of the patient and the court must decide again on permissibility of prolonged care. The provisions of Section 191c paragraphs 2 and 3 shall apply analogously.*
*(2) The judgment according to paragraph 1 shall prevent neither the institution from releasing the person kept in the institution before the lapse of the period referred to in paragraph 1 nor the custodian court from taking other measures.*
*Section 191f. The person being kept in the institution who is capable of taking action, their representative (guardian) and persons close to them may, even before the set time period for care has lapsed, request a new examination and subsequent decision about release if there is a justified belief that keeping the person in the institution for any further period of time is not necessary. If the court then dismisses a petition for release, it may also decide that further examinations shall not be carried out before the lapse of the originally stipulated time period.*
*Section 191g. The costs of proceedings shall be paid by the state. However, the state shall not pay costs of legal representation except for cases referred to in Section 30 paragraph 2 of this Act."*

**Remarks**

Juridical control over involuntary admission/detention was fundamentally changed in 1991 in accordance with the principles of rule of law after democratic changes in Czechoslovakia. A major amendment to the Civil Procedure Code added seven new Sections 191a ff. governing specific proceedings that should ensure that involuntary admission/detainment in a medical establishment is not abused and that the rights of the person concerned are protected. Such proceedings are usually commenced following the proposal of the medical establishment to which the person is admitted/detained. However, a court shall commence such proceedings in every case where it is aware of a person being admitted/detained in a medical establishment without their written consent, or if such consent has been withdrawn. The proceedings shall not commence if the court ordered the admission in other proceedings (e.g. compulsory treatment).

### 3.2.2.3 Criminal Legislation

The Act No. 140/1961 Coll., Criminal Code, as amended (hereinafter the Criminal Code"):

> *"Section 12. A person has no criminal liability if due to a mental disorder the person was not able to determine the jeopardy society was placed in or if the person was not able to control his or her behaviour when committing the criminal offence."*

> *"Section 25. The court may waive the punishment if the offender committed the crime in a state of impaired mental functioning and the court is of the opinion that compulsory treatment (Section 72), ordered at the same time, would be more effective than punishment. This provision shall not apply if the offender caused the reduced sanity himself through the abuse of addictive substances."*

> *"Section 32(2). If the court is of the opinion that due to the offender's state of health, the aims of punishment may be achieved through ordering compulsory treatment (Section 72), then the court shall order compulsory treatment whilst simultaneously imposing an imprisonment punishment with a lower than minimal penal charge, notwithstanding Section 40(3)."*

> *"Section 72. (1) The court shall order compulsory treatment in cases stipulated in Sections 25 and 32(2) or if the offender has no criminal liability and if their free movement is dangerous.*
> *(2) The court is entitled to order compulsory treatment also if a) the offender committed a crime in a state of impaired mental functioning due to a mental disorder and their freedom is dangerous or b) the offender abusing addictive substances committed the crime in connection with substance abuse; compulsory treatment shall not be imposed if it is clear that the purpose of such treatment cannot be achieved due to the personality of the offender.*
> *(3) The court may order compulsory treatment simultaneously with punishment or it may waive punishment.*
> *(4) If the court imposes the punishment of imprisonment, compulsory treatment shall usually start in a penitentiary after the offender's arrival. In other cases, compulsory treatment shall be usually carried out in a medical establishment. The court may also order ambulatory compulsory treatment if the nature of the disorder and treatment options allow that the aims of treatment to be so achieved. The court may also change the manner of treatment. If the length of the imprisonment is not sufficient for the purposes of treatment, the court may decide that the treatment shall continue in a medical establishment or as ambulatory treatment following imprisonment.*
> *(5) The compulsory treatment shall last as long as necessary in order to fulfil its purpose. Compulsory treatment under paragraph 2 b) may be terminated if its purpose cannot be achieved. The court shall decide on the discharge from compulsory treatment."*

**Remarks**

The Criminal Code stipulates cases, where the court must order compulsory treatment and cases, where the court may order compulsory treatment.
Compulsory treatment is usually carried out in a medical establishment, but the court may order ambulatory treatment according to the nature of the concerned person's disorder. Compulsory treatment shall last until its aims have been

achieved and the court does not specify the length of its duration. The medical establishment, where the compulsory treatment is carried out, shall inform the court when the treatment has achieved its aims. It also submits to the court medical records and reports on the course and results of treatment. The court shall review documents and shall decide on the termination of compulsory treatment and release the person if satisfied that its aims have been achieved.

### 3.2.2.4 Compulsory Treatment of Alcohol and Drug Addicted Persons

Act No. 37/1989 Coll., on Protection against Alcoholism and other Drug Abuse, as amended (hereinafter "The Act on Alcohol"):

> *"Section 8. (1) A person who raises scandal in public, or is a threat to him or herself, his or her family or to public order or property due to the abuse of alcohol, must accept admission and medical treatment at a special medical unit until acute intoxication is over.*
> *(2) Admission may be ordered by the doctor in charge upon the request of police and other state authorities."*

> *"Section 9. A court, on the recommendation of a family member or the medical establishment where the person was treated, may order compulsory outpatient treatment."*

**Remarks**

The state has focused on the prevention and reduction of the abuse of alcohol and other drugs for many years. The Act on Alcohol has imposed strict measures on persons abusing alcohol and other drugs and also on addicted persons. The Act on Alcohol adopted in 1989 was an administrative-type act authorizing local authorities *inter alia*, to order compulsory treatment. Certain parts of those provisions were not in compliance with the new Czech Constitution adopted in 1993 and the Constitutional Court abolished them. Other provisions were amended by Parliament in the same manner. Moreover, the Act on Alcohol is expected to be replaced by a new act in the near future. The new act regulating protection against alcohol and other drugs is expected to allow emergency involuntary admission of a person who is a threat to himself or his community (see Health Care Act in part A.2) due to intoxication, and as such a person could be kept in a special medical unit until acute intoxication is over. The new acts' proposal contains no other provisions regarding compulsory admission or treatment.

### 3.2.2.5 Compulsory Observation of a Person in a Medical Establishment Ordered by a Court in the Course of Certain Proceedings

*Proceedings on deprivation of legal capacity*

Civil Procedure Code:

> *"Section 187(3). (3) Regarding the examined person's health condition, the court shall always hear from an expert. If it is necessary to examine the person's health condition, the*

> *court may order upon an expert's petition so that the examined person can be observed in a health care institution for up to a maximum of three months."*

**Remarks**

During the proceedings on deprivation of legal capacity, the court may decide, on the recommendation of an expert, that the person shall be observed in a medical establishment in order to examine their state of health. The observation may last up to three months. Such a decision is a significant hindrance to personal freedom and therefore, prior to such a decision, the court shall investigate all facts and circumstances relevant to the case and it may order the observation only if an expert is not able to assess the mental state of that person within a brief limited period of time.

*Criminal proceedings*

Act No. 141/1963 Coll., Criminal Procedure Code, as amended (hereinafter "The Criminal Procedure Code"):

> *"Section 116. (2) The court or, during the proceedings' preparatory phase a judge at the public prosecutor's proposal, may decide that the accused person shall be observed in a health care institution to examine their mental state."*

**Remarks**

During the criminal proceedings, the court or, during the proceedings' preparatory phase a judge on the public prosecutor's proposal, may decide that the accused person shall be observed in a medical establishment or special prison unit, in order to examine their mental state. Such a procedure is a serious obstruction of constitutional rights and therefore it should be ordered only if the court has tried all other possible methods to examine the person's mental state, particularly if an expert appointed by the court is not able to provide a credible and qualified opinion without observation in a medical establishment (R 25/1967, R 24/1990, R 18/1997). The observation should last up to two months and it can be extended for one additional month. The person must be represented by an advocate in accordance with Section 36 (1) of The Criminal Procedure Code. The expenses of this representation may be borne by the state if the accused person attests that he or she does not have sufficient means to pay the representative.

### 3.2.2.5 Act No. 283/1991 Coll., on Police, as Amended (Hereinafter "Act on Police")

Although this act mainly regulates the rights and obligations of police forces, it is, from time to time, applied to manage persons with a mental disorder. The Police may arrest a person who poses an imminent threat to their own or another person's life, health or property in accordance with Section 14(1) of the Act on

Police. If alcohol, drugs or other addictive substances influence the person concerned or if such a person claims to suffer from a serious illness, or if there is a reasonable suspicion of serious illness, a doctor shall examine the person. The doctor decides whether the person shall be admitted to a medical establishment or a special medical unit if there are grounds for admission.

Such an examination shall be also carried out if the above-mentioned conditions are met during arrest in accordance with Section 28 and Section 32 of the Act on Police. If, in practice, there is a suspicion of a mental disorder, the person is to be transported by police to the psychiatric unit for the above-mentioned examination. If the person suffers from a mental disorder in the opinion of the examining doctor and arrest would be inappropriate, the doctor shall follow the general rules regarding treatment and admission of ill people (see section 3.2.2 of this report).

### 3.2.3 International Conventions and Agreements

- The Universal Declaration of Human Rights of December 10, 1948.
- International Covenant on Civil and Political Rights of December 19, 1966.
- International Covenant on Economic, Social and Cultural Rights of December 19, 1966.
- Convention for the Protection of Human Rights and Fundamental Freedoms of November 4, 1950.
- European Convention for the Prevention of Torture and Inhuman or Degrading Treatment or Punishment of November 26, 1987.
- Convention for the Protection of Human Rights and Dignity of the Human Being with regard to the application of Biology and Medicine (Oviedo Convention) of April 4, 1997.

**Remarks**

Pursuant to Article 10 of the Constitution, promulgated international agreements, the ratification of which has been approved by the Czech Parliament and which are binding on the Czech Republic, shall all constitute a part of the legal order; should an international agreement make provision contrary to a national law, the international agreement shall be applied.

### 3.2.4 Second Level of Juridical Norms

#### 3.2.4.1 Methodical Provision of the Ministry of Health no. 31829/2004/OZP of January 6, 2005 on the Use of Restriction Measures of Patients in Psychiatric Hospitals in the Czech Republic

*"Restriction measures may be used only if no other options exist and if it is necessary for the protection of: the patient, other patients, hospital staff or other persons."*

*"1. Restriction shall mean placement of a patient in a closed ward, placement of a patient in a protective (net) bed, placement of a patient in therapeutic isolation in a special room, restriction of patient's free movement (restricting straps, straitjacket), parenteral administration of drugs."*

*"3. With respect to voluntarily admitted patients, the use of a restriction measure is a reason to commence proceedings in accordance with Sections 23 and 24 of the Healthcare Act, i.e. notification to the relevant court within 24 hours, unless the patient's consent to restriction is obtained subsequently. With respect to the persons deprived of the legal capacity to give consent, consent must be obtained from their guardian within the stated time limit. With respect to patients under 18, the attending physician shall subsequently inform their parents or other legal representatives about the use of restriction measures and shall request their consent."*

*"4. A physician shall prescribe the use of restriction measures. Only health service personnel may use restriction measures. Such personnel should be trained regularly including model training."*

*"5. The restricted patient shall be checked regularly, the time of such checks must be specified." ... "Restriction measures shall be used for the shortest period necessary and it should be reviewed during the checks whether the restriction measure is still necessary and whether a less restricting measure would be sufficient."*

*"6. A physician shall prescribe the use of a restriction measure and shall make a written record including: the prescribing person's name, the kind of restricting measure used, the reason for restriction, time of commencement, time of termination, frequency of checks by health service personnel and physicians, description of physical and mental status of the patient, function which must be observed. Health service personnel shall inform the attending physician on any changes of the patient's status. A head physician shall sign the record subsequently during the ward round."*

*"7. The restricted patient shall be placed out of direct contact with patients who are not being restricted."*

*"10. In accordance with the above principles, it is recommended that each psychiatric hospital elaborates its internal rules regulating the use of restrictive measures."*

#### 3.2.4.2 Methodical Regulation of the Ministry of Health no. LP-270-22.5.72 of June 27, 1972 on the Transport of Agitated and Aggressive Mentally Ill Patients to Psychiatric Establishments (hereinafter "The Regulation on Transport")

The Regulation on Transport unifies procedures on the transport of mentally ill patients who are agitated and aggressive. Such a patient shall be transported by a medical transport service after they have been quietened down by a doctor in accordance with the principles of first aid provided to mentally ill patients. In exceptional cases restricting measures (e.g. straitjacket, restricting straps) may be used. The regulation does not specify who may order such measures and subsequent steps after their application. Generally, the doctor on duty will cooperate with the paramedics carrying out the transport of such a patient. The Regulation on Transport also stipulates that paramedics carrying out such transport and the doctors on duty shall be regularly trained in ordering the use of restricting measures properly.

#### 3.2.4.3 Methodical Provision no. ZD16/98 Published in the Official Journal 7/1998 of the Ministry of Health on June 1, 1998, which Governs the Evaluation of Medical Establishments

It stipulates certain standards, which should be met by medical establishments in order to receive accreditation. With respect to the rights of patients, the standards include, *inter alia*, the right of patients to be fully informed, and the limited use of restricting measures only in duly justified and documented cases, in order to protect patients' safety in compliance with Czech law.

However, the above-mentioned standards are not currently obligatory and only a certain number of medical establishments participate in the quality of care evaluation program in which compliance with these standards is monitored.

## 3.3 Jurisprudence

### 3.3.1 Ústavní Soud (Constitutional Court)

The Decision of the Constitutional Court No. IV. ÚS 23/97. The facts of the case: The local authority ordered the plaintiff to undergo compulsory treatment in accordance with The Act on Alcohol. The plaintiff appealed against the order. The general court deciding on the appeal interrupted the proceedings and filed the preliminary question to the Constitutional Court. The Constitutional Court decided that only an act stipulates in which cases a person may be admitted to or kept in a medical establishment without their written consent. The relevant court must be notified of such measures within 24 hours. Only a court is entitled to decide on permissibility following obligatory notification by the medical establishment. No other authorities may decide on permissibility and an act may not override its decision.

The Decision of the Constitutional Court No. IV. ÚS 639/2000. The facts of the case: The plaintiff was required by their general physician to undergo an examination at a psychiatric hospital. The plaintiff refused both transportation to the psychiatric hospital and examination. The physician asked the police to assist in transporting the plaintiff due to the physician's suspicion that the plaintiff was suffering from a mental illness. Despite not agreeing to transport or examination, the plaintiff obeyed the police, was transported to the psychiatric hospital and examined by a psychiatrist. The psychiatrist did not find any psychiatric disorder and the plaintiff was released. The Constitutional Court decided that all individuals are free and only an act may impose an obligation on a person. It is at the sole discretion of the individual to decide whether to undergo medical treatment and only a legal act may impose an obligation to do so. The Health-care Act stipulates that a person must undergo medical treatment if such a person poses a threat to himself or herself or to members of his or her community due to a mental disorder, and such treatment is necessary to save that person's life or health. These conditions were not met in this case; there were no grounds for police action. It is neither acceptable nor permissible that police's actions are based purely on a physician's personal opinion, because, as the Constitutional Court stressed, a diagnosis of mental illness shall not limit the rights of the ill person. Therefore, the application of any provision of law allowing the restriction of personal freedom must be carried out with respect to constitutional principles and must avoid the abuse of such provisions for other "non-care based" purposes. Provisions can be applied only with extreme caution.

### 3.3.2 Krajský Soud (Regional Courts)

The Decision of the Regional court in Hradec Králové on case no. 8 Co 272/93. The court decided that the hearing of the person concerned and his or her doctor may be sufficient evidence for the decision of the court in proceedings on the permissibility of admission without the person's consent, in accordance with paragraph 191b of The Civil Procedure Code (see section 3.6 of this report). It is not necessary to determine how long a person may be kept in a medical establishment without his or her consent.
Note: The decision may not be applied to a further decision of a court in accordance with paragraph 191d (see section 3.6 of this report).

The Decision of the Regional Court in České Budějovice on case no. 5 Co 441/92. The court decided that the written consent to admission of a person admitted to a medical establishment ceases to be relevant at the moment when such a person is restricted in their free movement or in their contact with the outside world. In such a case, the medical establishment must notify the relevant court within 24 hours and the court must commence proceedings on the permissibility of admission in accordance with paragraph 191a (1) of Civil Procedure Code (see section 3.6 of this report).

The Decision of the Municipal Court in Prague on case no. 20 Co 490/96. The court decided that the medical establishment must notify the court within 24 hours and the proceedings on permissibility of admission in accordance with paragraph 191a ff. of the Civil Procedure Code must be commenced if a person admitted with their written consent withdraws this consent. The court shall decide in the same manner as if the person had been admitted without their consent. The medical establishment need not notify the court if a person admitted without written consent gives such written consent within 24 hours of admission. In the event that proceedings were commenced for such a case, the court shall cease them.

**Remarks**

The hierarchical system of general courts is composed of the *Nejvyšší soud* (Supreme Court), *Vrchní soudy* (High Courts), *Krajské soudy* (Regional Courts)[2] and *Okresní soudy* (District Courts)[3]. Moreover, the Supreme Administrative Court was established on January 1, 2003 and it may play an important role in the future with respect to coercive measures.

The District Courts decide on actions regarding permissibility of placement/detainment in medical establishments and additionally are normally responsible for decisions regarding compulsory treatment. The Regional Courts decide on appeals against the decisions of the District Courts. The High Courts and the Supreme Court play only a minor role in decisions regarding involuntary treatment and/or admission, but such decisions would have a strong if not definitive bearing on the case.

As mentioned several times herein, the Czech legal system has gone through fundamental changes since 1989, when a democratic system and rule of law was established. In fact, only according to the changes thereby enacted may coercive measures generally be reviewed and revised by courts.

In matters concerning the protection of human rights, including the restriction of free movement of persons, the primary authority is the *Ústavní soud České republiky* (the Constitutional Court of the Czech Republic), which was established in 1993 in connection with the foundation of the Czech Republic as a successor to the Czech and Slovak Federal Republic. The Constitutional Court is not a part of the general court system; it is a specific court and the highest interior competent authority deciding, *inter alia*, on cases where human rights and fundamental freedoms are affected. The Constitutional Court has issued several key decisions regarding involuntary admission and treatment with respect to mental disorders. Some of these cases concerning the use of coercive measures in the Czech Republic attracted interest from the general public.

---

2 *Městský soud v Praze* (Municipal Court in Prague) is of the same hierarchic level.

3 *Obvodní soudy* (District Courts) in Prague *Městský soud v Brně* (Municipal Court in Brno) are of the same hierarchic level.

### 3.4 Internal Norms

#### 3.4.1 Internal Ordinance Regarding the Physical Restriction of a Patient Issued by the Psychiatry Hospital Bohnice, Prague as of April 17, 2002

The ordinance defines "restriction" as the therapeutic restraining of a patient's movement in bed through straps designed for such measures or the placement of the patient in therapeutic isolation in a purpose built room. A doctor, based on findings from an examination only, may for therapeutic reasons, and only for a limited period of time, order restriction. The doctor and paramedics shall make every effort to ensure that the use of restriction is as minimal as possible. The grounds for therapeutic restriction include primarily:

- serious symptoms of restlessness and hetero-aggressiveness;
- event of limited or non co-operation of the patient;
- symptoms of auto-aggressiveness with an imminent risk of self harm or suicide;
- necessity to separate a patient from other patients, and;
- cases which have a high probability of leading to the above-mentioned symptoms.

Decisions regarding restriction shall be duly justified in the patient's records along with the exact time of restriction, the patient's heart rate and blood pressure, and the signature of the doctor on duty. The relevant court must be notified immediately by fax of each case of restriction unless the patient is being treated involuntarily.

During restriction in bed, a paramedic must check the patient at least once every hour. Such a check shall review the patient's state of health, including particularly their state consciousness and the restricting straps' tightness and circulation of blood in their extremities. The results of the check shall be kept in the patient's records and shall contain the decision either to terminate or continue restriction. At least every third hour, heart rate and blood pressure shall be monitored. Similar measures shall be carried out with respect to a patient who is restricted in a suitable room.

A doctor shall examine the patient's state after every three hours of restriction in bed or every twelve hours of restriction in a room used for such purposes, as the case may be, and they shall decide either to terminate or continue restriction if therapeutic reasons exist. Each decision shall be documented in the patient's records with the time, justification for the restriction, the patient's state of health and a signature from the doctor in charge.

### 3.4.2 Internal Standards: Restriction of a Patient; Psychiatric Hospital Havlíčkův Brod, Issued on August 1, 2003

The norm stipulates that the main principles to be applied when considering restriction of a patient due to restlessness and/or aggressiveness (the norm shall not be applied if restriction is ordered to prevent falls, self-mutilation or dangerously excessive water drinking). A doctor may, in writing, order restriction only if no other measures are effective. Such an order shall be duly documented in the patient's record and revised daily, and a senior psychiatrist shall review records. The patient shall be informed about the reasons for restriction, and be duly examined. The restricted patient shall be checked periodically and the findings shall be documented in their records no less than every five hours (or one hour where restricting straps are used). Should the duration of restriction be longer than fifteen hours (or three hours where restricting straps are used), a new evaluation and a new order for restriction must take place. Moreover, the hospital director shall be notified in each case of restriction by a form specifying: the names of the patient and the ordering doctor, the reasons for restriction, the exact time restriction commenced and other relevant information. If restriction is ordered for a voluntarily admitted patient, the procedure used for involuntarily admitted patients shall be used.

### 3.4.3 The Internal Norm for the Management of Restless and Aggressive Patients; Psychiatric Hospital Kosmonosy, Un-Dated

The norm allows the use of restriction if other measures are not sufficient to calm a patient. Restriction may be ordered only in writing by a doctor. Paramedic staff shall inform the patient of the reasons for restriction, and record the times when restriction commences and terminates, additionally a description of the patient's state and all other relevant information shall be made in the patient's record. They shall also measure and record the patient's blood pressure and heart rate in accordance with the doctor's instructions. If restriction is ordered for a voluntarily admitted patient, the procedure used for involuntarily admitted patients shall be used.

### 3.4.4 Internal Directive of the Director of the Psychiatric Hospital Bílá Voda Issued on September 1, 2003

This directive allows the use of restriction only if no other measure is available. Restriction is to be performed by a paramedic on the basis of a doctor's order (such an order may also be given in advance, but no more than one day before). The paramedic shall inform the patient of the reasons for their restriction, measure the patient's blood pressure and heart rate, as well as record the times when restriction commenced and was terminated. During restriction the patient shall be checked each hour by a paramedic, particularly his/she/her state of con-

sciousness should be monitored, as well as their movement and the restriction's tightness. If the restriction needed is longer than three hours in bed or twelve hours in the case of therapeutic isolation, a new evaluation and a new order for restriction must be given by a doctor.
If restriction is ordered for a voluntarily admitted patient, the procedure used for involuntarily admitted patients shall be used.

### 3.4.5 Internal Standards: Use of Restriction; Psychiatric Hospital Dobřany, Issued on January 1, 2003

This norm stipulates that restriction may be used for a limited period of time in order to insure the safety of the patient and other persons. The patient may be placed in isolation in specified departments solely on the basis of the doctor's written order. The patient shall be continuously watched through the video monitoring system. Other means of restriction include placement in a netted- or a caged-bed with continuous monitoring or the use of restricting straps with a thorough health check of the patient every twenty minutes. For every case where restriction is used, the paramedic staff shall enter in the patient's record: the times when restriction commenced and was terminated, reasons for restriction and course of the restriction.

### 3.4.6 Internal Directive of the Director of the Psychiatric Hospital Opava, Issued on December 3, 2001 and Amended on March 18, 2003

This directive stipulates that restriction shall be used in connection with other methods of treatment such as psychotherapy. The directive specifies, apart from the use of a net-bed and restricting straps, the use of pharmaceutical treatment as a form of physical restriction. Any restriction measure may be applied only on the basis of the doctor's written order, duly justified in records (specifying also the conditions, form and extent of the restriction) and upon the approval of a senior psychiatrist. Each case of restriction shall also be recorded, including the time of restriction, in a special book of restrictions kept in each department.

**Remarks**

The Ministry of Health issued in January 2005 guidelines regulating the use of preventive security measures in medical establishments. Prior to the January 2005, there were almost no legal regulations governing the use of coercive measures in medical establishments and it was at the discretion of each establishment how to regulate the use of such measures. Therefore, there have been major differences among establishments, varying from no written rules in some to detailed internal directives in others. However, most of the establishments have recently issued internal norms, and development in this field is rapid.

## 3.5 Reports

### 3.5.1 National Institutions

*The Annual Report on the State of Human Rights in the Czech Republic* issued by the Government Council for Human Rights[4] first mentioned the situation of mentally ill persons placed in medical establishments in 2001. The report says *inter alia*:

> *"In practice, the mentally ill frequently do not receive equal treatment even at court proceedings which are to decide on their placement in an institution. This is mostly due to the existing paternalism, which is often based on a* bona fide *humanistic conviction. However, such situations also exist due to the fact that the legislation regulating the rights of such persons has not undergone any changes since 1989[5], which is in strict contrast with the development of the human rights of other handicapped groups (the convicted, the disabled, etc.).*
>
> *The existing information on various cases indicates that there are often enormous differences between various facilities, or even between various departments of the same facility, in the following areas: the standards of patient treatment; of the respect for human dignity; providing information to patients about their care; the level of control over restrictions of their personal freedom or interventions in their personal integrity; and complaint resolution mechanisms. While the best establishments try to develop humanistic element in their psychiatric care, according to existing models in developed EU members, the situation in other facilities has undergone only minimum changes since 1989."*

The non-governmental organization *Centre for Mental Health Care Development,* in co-operation with the Government Council for Human Rights and the Ministry of Health, have carried out the project APEL (Audit of rights and ethics during treatment in psychiatric establishments) on the basis of which the nationwide standard of evaluation of psychiatric establishment should be established. This should be the first step towards setting up nationwide standards evaluating human rights protection in psychiatric establishments. A further step would include proposals for legal provisions, which would provide a higher standard of human rights protection in these facilities. The project team has found several cases of unsatisfactory practice in some establishments:

- Due to technical reasons (e.g. the fax machine not being accessible at weekends) the court is not notified of involuntary admission within the legal limit of 24 hours.

---

4 The Government Council for Human Rights is an advisory body of the Czech government with respect to the protection of human rights and fundamental freedoms in the jurisdiction of the Czech Republic. The Council was established in 1998 by the government resolution no. 809 dated December 9, 1998. It monitors the observance of the Czech Constitution, the Charter of Fundamental Rights and Freedoms and international treaties regarding the protection of human rights.

5 The fall of the communist regime and the establishment of democracy.

- The patients sign the general written consent to treatment on admission, but later they are not asked to agree with particular treatment measures (electro-convulsive therapy is an exception).
- It is not properly documented whether the patient was duly informed on possible methods of treatment, its risks and adverse effects.
- The consent to treatment is not distinguished from the consent to admission.
- There are no formalized rules in establishments regulating how to deal with complaints. Patients usually have no idea how and to whom they could complain.
- There were significant differences among the establishments with respect to the use of restricting measures and frequency of their use. In some establishments there were no written rules regarding the use of restricting measures. The issuing of such rules is within the competence of the establishments and there are significant differences in the methods and number of details in such rules. However in most cases there are no internal mechanisms to check compliance with such rules.
- In most establishments there is no central statistic on the use of restricting measures. Such use is documented in medical records regarding a particular patient.
- There is no definition of open or closed departments of these establishments.
- There are in fact no organizations or institutions which carry out the protection of mentally ill or hospitalized patients.
- There is no systematic supervision by state authorities and institutions with respect to the rights of mentally ill patients.

In many cases the decision of the courts on the permissibility of involuntary admittance tends to be carried out informally.

### 3.5.2 International Organizations

*The 2002 Regular Report on the Czech Republic's Progress towards Accession* issued by the Commission of the European Communities declared that significant improvements had been achieved in the field of mental health care and the rights of the mentally ill, with a request for further steps to be taken. However the Report is not specific.

*The European Committee for the Prevention of Torture and Inhuman or Degrading Treatment or Punishment (CPT) Report to the Czech Government* based on the visit of the CPT in Opava Psychiatric Hospital[6], carried out in April 2002. The Report states *inter alia* that the CPT heard no allegation of mistreatment – and gathered no other evidence of such treatment – of patients at the establishment visited, and therefore the CPT appreciated the professionalism and commitment demonstrated by the medical and nursing staff towards their patients. With respect to the involuntary placement procedure, the CPT reported that the procedures were generally carried out in compliance with their requirements. Upon admission, every patient was first examined by a psychiatrist in the admission unit, and, once transferred to the specialized unit, by a second psychiatrist and a senior psychiatrist. A judge visited the establishment on a regular basis (at least one day per week). However, the CPT noted that the three-month deadline for the court to pronounce itself on permissibility of continued detention was not always respected. In some cases, this deadline was missed by several months. The CPT also noted that the person concerned was frequently not notified of court decisions, by making use of legal exception (see section 3.6 of this report). The CPT stressed that all patients should be given a copy of court decisions concerning their involuntary placement, apart from in exceptional circumstances. Further, the delegation observed that in the context of involuntary admission procedures, whenever a patient did not have a legal representative, the secretary of the court was appointed as a guardian. Given the large number of such cases, the secretary was supposed to act as guardian without being able to effectively deal with cases of involuntary placement. The CPT also pointed out that persons who have been deprived of the legal capacity to consent could be admitted to hospital solely with the written consent of their guardian. However, they were considered voluntary patients, and, thus, the court was not notified of their admission. In the CPT's view, detaining incapacitated persons in a psychiatric hospital, without benefiting from the procedural safeguards otherwise provided by law (including the judicial review of their cases) is a highly questionable practice.

With respect to the restraint of an agitated and/or violent patient, the CPT reported the use of a variety of instruments of physical restraint, such as soft fixation to the bed with straps, the use of a straight-jacket and placement in a net-bed, but not a seclusion room. The report says that such instruments of physical restraint were used in accordance with the internal guidelines issued by the director in the case of patients displaying disturbed or aggressive behaviour, and only if initial non-physical attempts to restrain and manually care for the patient

---

6 Opava Psychiatric Hospital is one of the largest in-patient psychiatric establishments in the Czech Republic accommodating almost 1000 in-patients, of whom approximately 11% were placed there involuntarily.

had failed. The decision to apply instruments of physical restraint was made by a doctor. In the case of an emergency, a doctor was informed immediately after instruments of restraint had been used. Every instance of patient restraint was recorded in the patient's medical file. However, there was no specific register for this purpose, which is not in compliance with general CPT requirements.

**Remarks**

Only in the last few years, the rights of persons placed in medical establishments due to mental illness have become the focus of public attention. Official annual reports did not mention this field until 2001. Non-governmental organizations focusing on the protection of the rights of the mentally ill, which operate in the Czech Republic, are not highly developed. There is, in fact, no organization focusing specifically on the monitoring of conditions in psychiatric establishments or on the provision of legal aid to such persons.

### 3.6 Safeguards

#### 3.6.1 Juridical Supervision

See section 3.2.2.2 of this report entitled "Civil Legislation".

#### 3.6.2 Supervision of State Authorities Other Than a Court

##### 3.6.2.1 Office of a State Prosecutor

Act No. 283/1993 Coll. on State Prosecutors, as amended, (hereinafter only the "The Act on State Prosecutors"):

> *"Section 4. (1) State Prosecutors shall, in extension and under conditions and in a manner stipulated by an act:*
> *a) act as a public prosecutor in criminal proceedings and perform other duties stipulated by the Criminal Procedure Code,*
> *b) supervise compliance with legal regulations in institutions where custody is carried out, imprisonment, compulsory treatment, protective or institutional education and in other places in which personal freedom is limited in accordance with the law,*
> *c) ..."*

**Remarks**

The role of the state prosecutor office was substantially extended in 1999 by introducing their supervision of the implementation of applicable laws in detention facilities, prisons, protective treatment facilities, protective or education institutions and in all other places where the freedom of persons is restricted by law. Such supervision is carried out within the scope of and under the terms set out in a special law. Such a special law, however, does not exist with respect to medical establishments and therefore the capacity of the state prosecutor to supervise is significantly limited, and in practice is not carried out in the medical establishments.

### 3.6.2.2 Ombudsman

Act No. 349/1999 Coll. on the Public Protector of Rights as amended (hereinafter "The Act on the Ombudsman"):

> *"Section 1. (1) The Public Protector of Rights (hereinafter "The Ombudsman") shall act in order to protect persons both against acts by the authorities and institutions specified herein if such acts are: contrary to law, are not in compliance with the principles of the democratic state of law and good practice; and in instances where the authorities and institutions have failed to act. Therefore the ombudsman shall contribute to the protection of fundamental rights and freedoms.*
> *(2) The ombudsman is entitled to review, in accordance with paragraph 1, ministries and other authorities, the Czech National Bank, the Council for Radio and Television Broadcasting, Czech Republic's Police Force, Czech Republic's Army, the Castle Guard, Czech Republic's Prison Authorities, all establishments in which persons are detained in custody, as well as: imprisonment, protective or institutional education, compulsory treatment and public health insurance companies."*

**Remarks**

It was in 1999 that the office of public protector of rights (ombudsman) was first introduced into Czech law. The ombudsman shall act *ad hoc* in order to protect people from illegal actions, including the decisions not to act on behalf of the authorities and they shall help to protect all citizens' fundamental rights and liberties. A medical establishment, in which compulsory treatment ordered by a court in criminal proceedings is carried out, is considered as being among such authorities. Moreover, the ombudsman may review any act of a state authority (e.g. The Ministry of Health's response, or even its decision not to respond to a person's complaint regarding treatment/admission). The ombudsman shall start proceedings either upon the request of the concerned person or without such a request. They are entitled to check relevant documents and hear in private both the establishment's employees and the placed person, and the establishment shall co-operate accordingly. On the basis of this investigation the ombudsman may *inter alia* request reparation of the conditions not complying with the law. However, no case regarding compulsory treatment/admission has been reported to this date. The Ministry of Justice and Government Council for Human Rights is currently proposing an amendment to the Act on Ombudsman, which would extend the ombudsman's direct supervision of all medical establishments where people are kept involuntarily.

## Diagram 3.1: Regular Judicial Procedure Concerning Involuntary Admission and Detention in the Czech Republic

Pre-condition (paragraph 23(4) of the Healthcare Act):

1a) signs of a mental disorder or intoxication
AND
2a) the patient poses a threat to himself or herself or to members of his or her community
OR
1b) emergency medical measures are required in order to save the patient's life or health
AND
2b) the patient's written consent cannot be required due to their health conditions

*up to 7 days*

a medical establishment where the patient is kept notifies the relevant court within 24 hours of the patient's admission[7]

↓

the court proceedings on permissibility of admission (paragraph 191a ff of the Civil Procedure Code)

- participation of the patient's representative or guardian
- hearing of the patient and the doctor in charge and an examination of evidence
- decision[8]

↓

*up to 3 months*

court proceedings on the permissibility of detention

- hearing of an expert concerning the patient's health state and detention's necessity[9]
- participation of the patient[10], his representative or guardian and examination of evidence
- decision[11]

↓

detention may be extended only by new proceedings on the admissibility of detention[12]

---

7 notification is not required if the patient provides consent to admission and treatment within the above said period.

8 appeal against this decision is allowed without deferring effect

9 an expert is a psychiatrist certified as an expert, this expert must not work in the medical establishment where the patient is held

10 provided that the patient is capable of comprehending the proceedings

11 appeal against the decision is allowed without deferring effect; detention may be allowed for up to one year

12 a medical establishment may release the person at any time without any approval of the court

**CHAPTER 4**

# Legal Report – England

Christina KATSAKOU, Guy DAVIS, Martin ZINKLER

## 4.1 Preliminary Remarks

The law most relevant for psychiatry in England and Wales is the Mental Health Act from 1983. The act regulates

> *"the circumstances in which the liberty of persons who are mentally disordered may be restricted and where there is conflict, to balance their interests against those of public policy"*

(R. v. Secretary of State for the Home Department, ex p.K (1990) 3 All E.R. 562, 570 per McGowan L.J.). It also covers provisions for mentally disordered offenders. Scotland and Northern Ireland have separate laws with similar although not identical provisions.

Mental Health legislation in England can be traced back to 1339 when the Statute de Prerogativa Regis

> *"limited the King's jurisdiction over the estates of idiots or natural fools, whose profits he was to take, but for whom he was to find necessaries. For anyone 'that before time hath had his wit and memory' and should 'happen to fail of his wit' ... the King was to keep his estate safe and maintain him and his household competently out of his profits, but the King was to take nothing for his own use"* (Keely 1944).

The *Criminal Lunatics Act* from 1800 for the first time regulated the safe custody of insane persons charged with offences. The *County Asylums Act* from 1808 provided the legal basis to build asylums. The basis of modern mental health law is the *Mental Health Act 1959*. It

> *"incorporated the principles that no one should be admitted to hospital if care in the community would be more appropriate, and that where admission to hospital was required compulsion, which was to be a medical instead of a judicial matter, should if possible be avoided"* (Jones 2001).

There is no written constitution for the UK. Instead, the relationship between the State and the people relies on statute law, common law and conventions. Some principles of common law relevant to psychiatric treatment are outlined in the next paragraph under "Constitutional norms".

In 1998 the UK incorporated the European Convention of Human Rights into UK law: *The Human Rights Act 1998*. It gives people in the UK the right to take court proceedings if they believe their Convention rights are breached.
Also in 1998 the Government commissioned an Expert Committee to advise on

> *"how mental health legislation should be shaped to reflect contemporary patterns of care within a framework which balances the need to protect individual patients and the need to ensure public safety"*

(Department of Health 1999). A Draft Mental Health Bill for England and Wales is now subject to pre-legislative scrutiny. It is unclear at the time of writing this report when the new law will be presented to parliament. Key proposals for change are the introduction of non-resident compulsory orders, which have become known as community treatment orders (CTOs), for non-offenders similar to the current conditional discharge arrangements for mentally disordered offenders, a wider definition of mental disorder, and special provisions to detain people perceived as particularly dangerous. A broad coalition of user organizations, voluntary organizations including MIND, trade unions and professional bodies including the Royal College of Psychiatrists regard the proposed changes as too complicated, unworkable, discriminating and infringing on users' rights (Mental Health Alliance 2004).

In 2003 Scotland introduced a new Mental Health Act with broad consensus, which will come into effect in 2005. It includes CTOs, but only after treatment in hospital, one of the criteria for compulsory treatment is the patient's impaired ability to decide on treatment, substance abuse is not regarded as a reason for compulsory treatment, and there are no special provisions for particularly dangerous people.

## 4.2 Applicable Laws and General Norms

### 4.2.1 Constitutional Norms

> *"In most countries whole areas of law are contained in a single code rather than, as in England, being divided between the common law, which is derived from decisions of judges over the centuries, and statute law enacted by Parliament."* (The Law Commission 2004)

General principles relating to medical treatment under common law can be found in relevant judgements:

> *"1. It is a criminal and tortuous assault to perform physically invasive medical treatment, however minimal the invasion might be, without the patient's consent if the patient has the capacity to decide.*
> *2. Prima facie every adult has the right and capacity to decide whether or not he will accept medical treatment, even if a refusal may risk permanent injury to his health or even lead to premature death. (...)*

*4. A person lacks capacity if some impairment or disturbance of mental functioning renders the person unable to make a decision whether or not to consent to or refuse treatment.*
*(...)*
*5. If an adult patient did not have the capacity to decide at the time of the purported refusal and still does not have that capacity, it is the duty of the doctors to treat him in whatever way they consider, in the exercise of their clinical judgement, to be in his best interest."* (Jones 2001)

### 4.2.2 General Laws: The Mental Health Act 1983

Legal regulations covering involuntary hospital admission and treatment of the mentally ill are described in the Mental Health Act (MHA) from 1983. The MHA covers a number of different issues, such as the definition of mental disorder, compulsory admission to hospital, guardianship, criminal commitment, and consent to treatment. The various paragraphs in the MHA 1983 are called sections. The most important sections referring to coercive measures will be described here.

Section 1: Definition of Mental Disorder
The first section of the MHA 1983 refers to the definition of mental disorder. In effect, it describes four categories of mental disorder: mental illness, mental impairment, severe mental impairment and psychopathic disorder.

*Mental illness* is not defined in the Act or in the Code of Practice however the Department of Health has issued guidance defining mental illness by the presence of one or more of the following characteristics:
(i) more than temporary impairment of intellectual functions shown by a failure of memory, orientation, comprehension or learning capacity;
(ii) more than temporary alteration of mood of such degree as to give rise to the patient having a delusional appraisal of his situation, his past or his future, or that of others or to the lack of any appraisal;
(iii) delusional beliefs, persecutory, jealous or grandiose;
(iv) abnormal perceptions associated with delusional misinterpretation of events;
(v) thinking so disordered as to prevent the patient making a reasonable appraisal of his situation or having reasonable communication with others.

Severe mental impairment, mental impairment and psychopathic disorder are defined in the Act:
*Severe mental impairment means* a state of arrested or incomplete development of mind which includes severe impairment of intelligence and social functioning and is associated with abnormally aggressive or seriously irresponsible conduct on the part of the person concerned.

*Mental impairment* means a state of arrested or incomplete development of mind (not amounting to severe mental impairment) which includes significant impairment of intelligence and social functioning and is associated with abnormally aggressive or seriously irresponsible conduct on the part of the person concerned.
*Psychopathic disorder* means a persistent disorder or disability of mind (whether or not including significant impairment of intelligence) which results in abnormally aggressive or seriously irresponsible conduct on the part of the person concerned.

Civil Sections (2, 3) and Emergency section (4):
Sections 2, 3 and 4 describe the procedure that needs to be followed for involuntary admission of mentally disordered patients for assessment or treatment.

Section 2 allows the involuntary admission of a patient for assessment for up to 28 days. It is usually appropriate for patients who are not known to the mental health system and for whom there is no previous information on diagnosis, prognosis or care planning.
*Criteria for detention* under section 2 are the presence of a mental disorder and the need to be detained in the interest of the person's own health or safety or for the protection of other persons. Section 2 cannot be renewed, as the 28 days are considered sufficient for the assessment of the patient's clinical status. If it is deemed necessary for the patient to remain in hospital after this period, he should either stay as a voluntary patient or be detained under section 3 of the MHA.

Section 3 allows for the involuntary admission and treatment of a patient for up to six months. However, a patient can get discharged from section 3 earlier within this period, before the section expires. If it is considered necessary for the patient to stay in the hospital for longer, section 3 can be renewed for another six months in the first place and for one-year periods afterwards.
*Criteria for detention* under section 3 are:
(i) the patient is suffering from mental illness, severe mental impairment, psychopathic disorder or mental impairment and his mental disorder is of a nature or degree which makes it appropriate for him to receive medical treatment in a hospital; and
(ii) in the case of psychopathic disorder or mental impairment, such treatment is likely to alleviate or prevent a deterioration of his condition; and
(iii) it is necessary for the health or safety of the patient or for the protection of other persons that he should receive such treatment and it cannot be provided unless he is detained under this section.

Section 4 allows detention in the hospital for up to 72 hours. It is used for emergency detention when a patient needs to get admitted immediately, with the intention that once he/she is in the hospital, an application for a section 2 will be submitted.

Application for detention under a section of the MHA:
The application for detention under sections 2 or 3 can be submitted by the patient's nearest relative or an approved social worker (ASW). Two medical recommendations (one for section 4) or one joint medical recommendation by two doctors demonstrating the criteria for detention are required. One of the doctors involved in the application should be approved to detain patients under the MHA. Furthermore, one of the doctors should, if possible, have previous acquaintance with the patient and his/ her condition. Only one of the doctors can be employed in the hospital where the patient will be admitted. For an application for section 4 to be submitted, the application by the nearest relative or social worker is needed (as for sections 2 and 3) together with only one medical recommendation, as this is a section used for emergency situations.

Treatment for patients detained under the MHA:
A patient who is detained under section 2 or 3 can be given medical treatment without his consent for the first three months beginning with the date treatment for mental disorder was first administered according to section 63 of the MHA under the direction of a trained psychiatrist (Responsible Medical Officer, RMO). Health professionals should always seek the patient's consent for the administration of medication. However, if this is not possible, treatment can still be given. The treatment must be for the mental disorder from which the patient is suffering and must not be an intervention described in sections 57 or 58 (in the case of ECT) of the Act. After three months, if the patient does not consent and/or lacks the capacity to consent to the particular treatment, a second opinion must be obtained to continue with medical treatment.

Under section 4 (emergency detention for up to 72 hours), consent should be asked for the administration of any kind of treatment. However, when it is deemed necessary and the patient does not comply, treatment can be given under Common Law.

Discharge from detention under the MHA:
There are various ways to get discharged from sections 2, 3 and 4. If the responsible Medical Officer (RMO) believes that the patient should not be detained anymore, he/ she can discharge him/ her before the section expires.

If a patient believes that he/she shouldn't be detained under section 2 or 3, he/she can apply to the Hospital Managers or to a Mental Health Review Tribunal (MHRT) for discharge. If the nearest relative wishes to discharge the patient he/ she must notify the Hospital Managers at least 72 hours before the discharge. In this case, the RMO is informed and can bar the discharge if he/she believes that the patient is likely to act in a manner dangerous to himself or others. If such an action is taken, the Hospital Managers are then obliged to consider holding a review of the patient's detention. When a patient is detained under section 3, the nearest relative has the right to apply to a MHRT if the treating doctor has barred the order for discharge.

As far as section 4 is concerned, the nearest relative cannot appeal against this section, but the patient can. The RMO can discharge the patient, even before the section expires, if he/ she believes that the patient should not be detained any longer.

Police Powers (sections 135, 136):
Sections 135 and 136 allow the police to remove a person that appears to be suffering from mental disorder to a place of safety. With section 135(1), an Approved Social Worker obtains a warrant for a policeman to enter premises (the home of a patient), whereas with section 136 a police officer can remove a mentally ill person from a public place.

Forensic sections (37, 45a, 47 and 48):
Section 37 allows the courts to direct that a person, who suffers from a mental disorder and has committed a crime, stays in a psychiatric hospital at sentencing. A restriction order (Section 41) can be included which has the effect of restricting the patient's discharge, transfer or leave of absence from hospital without the consent of the Home Secretary. Under section 42, the Home Secretary can exercise powers directing that the patient comply with certain conditions after discharge from hospital, e.g. to reside at a specific place, to comply with medication, to see mental health professionals, and to attend specific places of treatment (day centres, psychological treatment).

Section 45a allows the Crown Court to require that a mentally disordered offender (suffering from psychopathic disorder) stays in hospital at sentencing. Moreover, they can later be transferred back to prison.
Sections 47 and 48 allow the transfer of a mentally disordered prisoner to a psychiatric hospital for treatment.

Guardianship (sections 7 and 8):
Section 7 allows for a patient suffering from a mental disorder to be allocated a guardian. The nearest relative or an approved social worker can submit the application for guardianship. Two medical recommendations from two doctors are also required. The order is for six months and it can be renewed when expired. The R.M.O., the nearest relative or the authority can discharge the patient. He/she also has the right to appeal against the guardianship to a Tribunal.
Section 8 refers to the powers of a guardian. More specifically, the guardian can oblige the patient to stay in a specified place and attend specified meetings for medical care, education or employment. Furthermore, he can give permission to mental health professionals to have access to the patient's residence whenever this is deemed necessary.

*The Mental Health (patients in the Community) Act 1995 (Section 25A-J, after-care under supervision):*
This Act came into power in April 1996 and supplements the MHA 1983 on issues related to supervised discharge from hospital. More specifically, it extends the period that a patient can be on leave while subject to return to hospital, as well as the period within which a patient who has absconded can be taken back to the hospital. A patient can be put on a supervision order after discharge, which directs the patient to attend specific places for treatment and to reside at a specified place, but cannot include an order to comply with medication.

Guardianship and after-care under supervision have rarely been used in practice and are not included in the proposals for a new mental health act.

### 4.2.3 International Conventions and Agreements Incorporated into National Law: The Human Rights Act 1998

The European Convention for the Protection of Human Rights is the only international document against which the MHA can be judicially tested. The Convention was written after the Second World War. The UK signed up to the Convention in 1953. The countries that have signed up to this instrument constitute the Council of Europe.

The Convention is divided into 'Articles'. Articles 2 to 14 describe the rights that are protected by the Convention. Article 3 (protection against torture or inhuman or degrading treatment), Article 5 (protection against arbitrary detention), Article 6 (right of access to a fair hearing in civil and criminal proceedings), Article 8 (the right to respect for privacy, family life and freedom of correspondence) and Article 10 (the right to receive information) are all related to compulsory psychiatric treatment. Over the years the Convention has been supplemented by a number of protocols that have been agreed by the Council of Europe.

The Human Rights Act 1998 (HRA) was later introduced in order to promote the rights and safeguards secured under the European Convention on Human Rights. The HRA achieves this goal in several ways. First, it states that the courts in the UK should interpret the law in a way that the rights guaranteed under the Convention are taken into account. Second, it requires that public authorities act in a manner that is compatible with the regulations introduced by the Convention. The HRA also allows anyone who believes that their Convention rights have been breached to take court proceedings.

The Human Rights Unit in the Department of Constitutional Affairs of the UK government has also been founded to monitor the successful implementation of the Human Rights Act 1998 in the UK.

#### 4.2.4 Second Level of Legal Norms: The Code of Practice

The Code of Practice (Department of Health and Welsh Office 1999), published by the Secretary of State, is a valuable tool in offering guidance for good practice regarding hospital admission and treatment. However, it does not have the legal force of a statute. Its legal status is that of an official guidance. This is because there is a need for the Code to be updated and amended regularly to cover any current aspects of good practice. In its recent judgement in R. (on the application of Munjaz) v Ashworth Hospital Authority (2002) EWHC Admin 1521, the Court of Appeal confirmed that the Mental Health Act 1983 Code of Practice should be observed by all to whom it is addressed unless they have good reason for departing from it in relation to an individual patient. The Court has also made clear that good reasons for particular departures may be identified in relation to an individual or to groups of patients who share particular well-defined characteristics, so that if a patient falls within that category there will be good reason for departing from the Code in his or her case. The Department of Health considers it best practice for the reasons for any departure from the Code to be recorded. Further, it should be noted that the Mental Health Act Commission's policy is to treat unsubstantiated departures from the Code to be prima facie evidence of poor practice.

The government-established *Mental Health Act Review Expert Group* is keen on enhancing the role of the Code of Practice. The Committee has considered a number of different ways to achieve this goal. They are currently reflecting on recommending that the consultation requirements imposed on the Secretary of State in the Act be made more specific. Furthermore, the Code could be included within the expectations of clinical governance or within individual employment contracts.

Furthermore, the *Mental Health Act Commission* was founded in 1983, together with the publication of the MHA. Lawyers, laypersons, doctors, nurses, social workers, psychologists and other professionals constitute the Commission. Its main role is to monitor the implementation of the MHA and Code of Practice and to collect and investigate detained patients' complaints regarding their treatment. In addition, the Commission is responsible for appointing health professionals to provide second opinions in the cases where this is required by the MHA.

## 4.3 Jurisprudence

### 4.3.1 European Court of Human Rights

Article 3 of the Convention states that

> *"no one shall be subjected to torture or to inhuman or degrading treatment or punishment"* (Jones 2001).

The European Court of Human Rights (ECHR) has considered several cases relating to this article. In Keenan v. United Kingdom (Keenan v. United Kingdom App. No. 27229/95, April 3, 2001; *The Times,* April 18, 2001, quoted from Jones 2001) it said that the

> *"treatment of a mentally ill person may be incompatible with the standards imposed by article 3 in the protection of fundamental human dignity, even though that person may not be able, or capable of, pointing to any specific ill-effects."*

However until now there has been no successful case on Article 3 relating to psychiatric treatment at the ECHR. In Bolam v. Friern Barnet Hospital (Bolam v. Friern Hospital Management Committee (1957) 1 W.L.R. 582) the court held

> *"that treatment which would be considered by a responsible body of psychiatrists as being therapeutically necessary could not be regarded as inhuman or degrading" (Jones 2001). Also, "removal from association, such as seclusion of a mentally disordered patient, does not normally amount to inhuman or degrading treatment"*

(A v. United Kingdom (1998), app. no. 6840/74, *The Times,* October 1, 1998; quoted from Jones 2001).

In October 2004 the ECHR ruled in H.L. v. The United Kingdom on the detention of an incapacitated patient who was kept as a "voluntary" patient in a psychiatric hospital under common law. He had not refused admission and had not made any attempts to leave the hospital. The court found H.L. was deprived of his liberty, when he was admitted to hospital. Hospital staff effectively controlled his care and his movements. It held there was a violation of Article 5, paragraph 1 as regards the lack of protection against arbitrary detention and a violation of Article 5 paragraph 4 (Application no. 45508/99). This case is one of the most important involving the care of people with mental disorder and the government issued interim advice in December 2004 on its implications; essentially that all healthcare organizations provide appropriate care to those people who lack capacity to decide for themselves, which does not amount to deprivation of liberty without the legal safeguards provided under such primary legislation as the Mental Health Act. The government also stated its intention to provide additional procedural safeguards to incapacitated patients who are not formally detained, but at the time of writing it is not clear whether this will be a part of the proposed Mental Health or Capacity legislation, if there will be a separate piece of legislation introduced, or if the current Mental Health Act will be amended.

### 4.3.2 UK Jurisprudence

There is very little recent case law in the UK on the use of coercive measures like mechanical restraint, forced medication and the use of locked wards. As indicated above there is extensive guidance by the Government on how coercive measures are to be used in psychiatric institutions. The Code of Practice (Department of Health and Welsh Office 1999) does not

> *"impose a legal duty to comply with the Code but as it is a statutory document, failure to follow it could be referred to in evidence in legal proceedings"* (Jones 2001).

In the Munjaz case, the court held that seclusion is medical treatment for the purposes of the Mental Health Act and that the seclusion policy at Ashworth (a special forensic hospital) was unlawful because it did not comply with the Code of Practice. In contrast to the Code of Practice the seclusion policy at the hospital did not include a review by a doctor every four hours.

Treatment for a mental illness can be given without consent for a patient who is detained in hospital. In a number of cases the courts considered what kind of treatment this includes. In St George's Healthcare NHS Trust v. S (1998, 3 All E.R. 673, CA) it said that

> *"a person detained under the Act cannot be forced into medical procedures unconnected with her mental condition unless she is deprived of her capacity to decide for herself, in which case the treatment would be authorized under common law"* (Jones 2001).

In a similar case a patient suffering from schizophrenia had refused amputation of his gangrenous leg and was found capable to make this decision (Re C, (Adult: Refusal of Medical Treatment), (1994) 1 All E.R 819).

The Court of Appeal decided that the feeding by naso-gastric tube of a patient suffering from borderline personality disorder was treatment according to the

Act, because anorexia was a way of self-harm e.g. a symptom of mental disorder. (B v Croydon Health Authority 1995 1 All E.R. 683).

The English Mental Health Act does not impose incapacity to decide on treatment as a condition for treatment without consent, however several court decisions have clarified that

> *"if a patient has the mental capacity to exercise a choice he 'must consent if medical treatment of him is to be lawful. ... Treating him without his consent or despite a refusal of consent will constitute the civil wrong of trespass to the person and may constitute a crime'"*

(Re T (Adult Refusal of Medical Treatment) (1992) 4 All E.R. 649; quoted from Jones 2001).

Common law rules apply for advance decisions to refuse treatment (advance directives). This was clarified in Re C (Adult Refusal of Medical Treatment (1994) 1 WLR 290; 1 All ER 819): a person with mental capacity to do so can make a valid advance refusal of consent. Such statements (which need not be in writing) must be treated as capable refusal of treatment even where the patient subsequently loses mental capacity. Under particular circumstances, when it is determined that the patient did not appreciate the implications of treatment at the time they did so, such statements may be ineffective. The Mental Capacity Bill seeks to codify the common law rules in respect of advance directives.

### 4.4 Protocols and Internal Norms

#### 4.4.1 The Code of Practice

The Secretary of State (Department of Health and Welsh Office 1999) has published the Code of Practice to provide guidelines for professionals on the implementation of the MHA and on inpatient treatment.

According to the Code, during involuntary treatment in the hospital, a number of coercive measures can be applied to patients as a last resort, under emergency situations, even against their will. There are a number of different measures mentioned in the Code of Practice, which can be used when a patient is considered to be a risk to himself or others. Staff members are receiving training in restraining a patient's bodily parts, when this is deemed necessary. No mechanical restraints can be used and the restraining procedure is based on written guidelines. Forced medication can also be administered when a patient is overagitated or aggressive. However, before such an action is taken the doctor in charge should take into consideration the medication's long-term effects and the patient's clinical benefits from treatment. Seclusion in a locked room under the constant supervision of a staff member can also be used to contain behaviour that could be harmful for others. Patients who are at risk of self-harming or at-

tempting suicide can be put under staff observation. In such cases there should be a balance between assuring a patient's safety and allowing them to have the personal space that they need. Furthermore, when there is a risk for a patient to abscond, the doors of the ward can be locked. The patient should be informed of the reasons and the rationale for such an action. Last, when a patient's behaviour is too disruptive or dangerous for him/her to be treated in an open ward, a transfer to locked or secure wards can be considered, until the patient is ready to return for treatment in an open ward.
Furthermore, some of the sections in the MHA describe specific interventions that cannot be administered without the patient's consent and/or a second opinion. Section 57 refers to treatments, such as psychosurgery and the surgical implementation of hormones for the reduction of male sexual drive. Such interventions require both the patient's consent and a second opinion given by a doctor. Section 58 refers to ECT (in every case) and the administration of medication for a patient's mental disorder (after three months). Such treatments can only be administered either with the patient's consent or with a second opinion provided by a Second Opinion Approved Doctor, appointed by the Mental Health Act Commission.

### 4.5 Reports

#### 4.5.1 National Reports

The government appoints the Mental Health Act Commission. It visits and meets detained patients in private and visits all hospitals and registered nursing homes with detained patients. It publishes a biennial report that is laid before parliament. More information on this commission will be provided in section 4.6.

The latest biennial report from 2001/03 (Mental Health Act Commission 2003) makes 70 recommendations, most of which are directed to Government and Parliament. It draws attention to the need for legal reform following the Human Rights Act 1998, the need to provide equal and non-discriminatory services, and recommends statutory regulation of specific areas of compulsion including seclusion to ensure uniform good practice. Main concerns are the vulnerability of children and adolescents admitted to adult facilities, and of women patients admitted to largely male environments, the problems to access therapeutic and recreational facilities on many inpatient wards and the over-representation from Black and minority ethnic groups. It specifically addresses racial harassment of patients. It also comments on the draft for a new mental health law and criticises government plans to extend compulsory treatment to prison. The government later stepped back and compulsory treatment in prison was not included in the mental health bill.

The commission also comments on restraint: physical restraint, which is being held by nurses trained in this procedure, and mechanical restraint, which is being tied to a device like a bed or a chair, or being handcuffed. While the Code of Practice prohibits mechanical restraint there seems to be a grey area of patients, usually elderly, being tied to chairs to prevent them from falling. These patients are usually not detained under mental health law, and would not come under the remit of the Mental Health Act Commission. The commission proposes the use of mechanical restraint in all mental health services as a possible area of study under future monitoring arrangements.
In the chapter on racial harassment the report draws its recommendation from the investigations into the death of David Bennett, a patient who died having been restrained for 25 minutes after an incident which was sparked by racial abuse directed against him. The commission recommends establishing policies to protect patients from racial harassment. The death of this patient was also subject of an independent inquiry by the regional health authority, which produced a report at the request of the government. It made 20 recommendations, among them mandatory training on cultural awareness, competency and sensitivity, acknowledgement of institutional racism in mental health services, a maximum of three minutes restraint in a prone position and collection of data on all deaths in psychiatric inpatients including ethnicity (Norfolk, Suffolk and Cambridgeshire Strategic Health Authority 2003).

In 1999 the government published the report on reform of mental health legislation (Department of Health 1999). A committee chaired by Professor Genevra Richardson made detailed recommendations for a new mental health act. Based on general principles of non-discrimination, patient autonomy, provision of the least restrictive alternative, respect for the role of carers and reciprocity (detention and compulsion entitle to treatment, care and aftercare) all parts of the current mental health act are reviewed. This includes diagnostic criteria for detention, compulsory powers in hospital and the community, regulations for mentally ill offenders, safeguards, transfers from prison and controlled treatments (neuro-surgery, ECT and others). Main recommendations were to introduce the concept of capacity (capable patients could only be treated against their will if public safety is concerned), to introduce community treatment orders, to replace the nearest relative with a person nominated by the patient, to improve safeguards for voluntary patients, to introduce advance agreements on care and to provide advocacy.
The National Institute for Mental Health in England (NIMHE) in 2003 published a report on mental health services for black and minority ethnic communities (NIMHE 2003). Rates of compulsory admission are markedly higher for

black and minority ethnic groups in comparison to whites. It acknowledges that institutional racism exists within mental health care. It recommends

> *"co-ordinated action to reduce and eliminate ethnic inequalities in mental health service experience and outcome"*

and investment in

> *"community development of minority ethnic groups aimed at achieving greater community participation and ownership around mental health".*

In 1999 the Department of Health published a report prepared by researchers from King's College and St. George's Medical School on research relating to the Mental Health Act from 1983 (Department of Health 1999(2)). It found a "dramatic increase" of more than 80% in the absolute number and in the proportion of compulsory admissions between 1984 and 1996. Being young, male and black increases the risk of being detained. Many voluntary patients see their admission as coercive. Many mentally disordered people are being assessed, treated, or simply ignored in prison. People brought to psychiatric hospitals by the police are more likely to be young, male, black, violent and suffering from schizophrenia.

### 4.5.2 International Reports

The Council of Europe's Committee for the Prevention of Torture and Inhuman or Degrading Treatment or Punishment (CPT) has visited the UK on several occasions since 1990. The reports form the visits in 2003 and 2004 have not been published yet. Only on one visit in 1994 the CPT visited a psychiatric institution: Rampton Special Hospital, a high-security forensic psychiatric hospital for mentally disordered offenders with over 500 beds. The CPT delegation heard no allegations and gathered no evidence of torture of patients, and hardly any allegations of other forms of ill-treatment (Council of Europe 1996). CPT heard about a patient who had died in 1992 following the use of control and restraint techniques and requested to see the results of judicial and health authority enquiries. It felt the psychiatrist/patient ratio was too low to be considered adequate. Further concerns expressed were: night cover, nurses' working shifts, limited access to fresh air, limited privacy, and the practice of seclusion.

### 4.5.3 Reports by NGOs

In 2002 The Sainsbury Centre for Mental Health published "Breaking the circles of Fear" a review of the relationship between mental health services and African and Caribbean communities (Sainsbury Centre for Mental Health 2002). Black people in the UK are more likely to be subject to compulsory admission, readmission, over-diagnosis of schizophrenia, involvement of police in hospital admission, over-use of medication, and less likely to receive psychotherapy. The report makes 15 recommendations, among them to fund a national programme of mental health promotion owned by the Black community, free advocacy services for users and carers, provision of counselling and psychotherapy services, to review inpatient care for Black people, to organize training programmes for Black staff in primary care, housing agencies, probation, social services and the police, and to set relevant performance targets.

WNUSP, the World Network of Users and Survivors of Psychiatry recently published a report on human rights problems faced by people with psychiatric disabilities (WNUSP 2005). The report notes "increased coercive psychiatry in UK, US, Japan and Netherlands". The draft Mental Health Act for England and Wales

> *"would legalise compulsory treatment in the community, broaden the criteria for compulsory detention and remove the 'treatability' criterion for psychiatric detention".*

## 4.6 Safeguards

### 4.6.1 Procedures: How to Make a Complaint

Every patient who is treated in a hospital of the National Health Service (NHS) in the UK can complain about any aspect of care to the hospital managers. All hospitals have a complaint policy and a complaint procedure. National guidance on how to complain is provided by the Department of Health (Department of Health 2005). Complaints can be made verbally or in writing. Every nurse in a hospital in the UK will have a complaint form for a patient on request. The hospital management will respond to the complaint in writing within 20 days and advise on how the complaint can be taken further if the complainant is unhappy with the response. The relatives of a patient can lodge a complaint in the same way. Complaints are common, and hospitals produce a yearly report on complaints that have been made and the outcomes.

Patients in psychiatric hospitals have the same rights as other patients and complaints will be dealt with in the same way. Patients who are detained in hospital under the Mental Health Act can appeal against their detention and treatment order to a mental health tribunal. Mental health tribunals have a judicial function, they are independent from the hospital and typically consist of three persons: a legal professional, an independent psychiatrist, and a lay member of the public. Appeals against treatment orders will be heard within 21 days by the tribunal (within seven days for assessment orders), who has the power to discharge the patient. The patient is entitled to free legal representation and can choose a solicitor. Before hearing the appeal the tribunal will request reports from the treating psychiatrist, from the nurses, and from a social worker. The reports need to provide a care plan for hospital treatment and also for aftercare, in case the tribunal discharges the patient. It is not uncommon that a tribunal decides on a deferred discharge, for example it orders the hospital to discharge the patient within seven days to allow the hospital to put a care plan in place. The patient and the hospital can ask for a judicial review of a tribunal decision by a high court. From there the case can be taken further up to the Court of Appeal, and finally to the House of Lords and the European Human Rights Court.

Another way to complain about specific aspects of care is to direct a complaint to the Mental Health Act Commission, or to the Ombudsman for Health in Parliament. Most psychiatric hospitals now offer an advocacy service, which will assist in formulating such complaints. Complaints involving racial discrimination can be taken to the Commission for Racial Equality, complaints about individual professionals can be directed to the relevant professional bodies (General Medical Council, Royal College of Nursing etc.).

The proposals for a new mental health act include tribunal hearings for all detained patients whether they apply against their order or not, and all psychiatric hospitals will be obliged to provide free advocacy.

**4.6.2 Authorities for Control: the Mental Health Act Commission**

The Mental health Act Commission (MHAC) was established by parliament with the Mental Health Act in 1983 to ensure the lawfulness of patient detention. It's main functions are: to review the exercise of powers and duties within the Mental Health Act, to visit and interview detained patients, to investigate complaints, to appoint doctors for second opinions on specific treatments (ECT and others) and to submit proposals for the content and revision of the Code of Practice. The MHAC visits all institutions (hospitals and nursing homes) where patients are detained under the MHA at least three times during a two-year period. Its members meet with detained patients in private, observe the conditions of detention and compulsion, scrutinise legal documents relating to detention, identify good and bad practice and provide service managers with detailed reports and recommendations for improvement. It also monitors adherence to the Code of Practice and produces a biennial report for parliament.

The MHAC has also commented on aspects of care, which were not exactly within its remit e.g. the protection of voluntary patients, or deaths of patients during psychiatric inpatient treatment. The government plans to transfer MHAC functions to a new Commission for Healthcare Audit and Inspection (CHAI) with the introduction of a new mental health act. CHAI would safeguard the rights of both detained and voluntary patients.

### 4.6.3 Internal Procedures: MHAct Offices in Every Hospital, Policies on Seclusion and Restraint

Every hospital where patients are detained under the MHA operates a so-called MHA Office with staff trained in the administration of the Mental Health Act. The MHA office scrutinises legal documents of detention, arranges for second opinion doctors, arranges for tribunal hearings, and reminds clinicians of their duties under the act. It also arranges training events for all staff involved in procedures of the MHA and associated legislation, and produces yearly statistical records of admissions and detentions under the MHA.

All Mental Health Care providers have to produce policies on seclusion and restraint if seclusion and restraint are practised in their hospitals. A typical example is available on www.elcmht.nhs.uk/uk/pdf/aboutus/seclusion.pdf (accessed on 16.01.2005). A qualified nurse within sight and sound must monitor patients under seclusion. The need for seclusion must be reviewed by two nurses every two hours and by a doctor every four hours. A typical restraint policy can be accessed on www.elcmht.nhs.uk/pdf/aboutus/restraint_policy_final.pdf (accessed on 16.01.2005).

### 4.7 Other Information

This report was produced with the referenced sources of information, but also with the authors' clinical, managerial, administrative and research experience in the area, for the EUNOMIA research project. Any other use or publication is prohibited without permission by the authors.

### 4.8 Practical Exercise

The following examples are given, to illustrate typical pathways through the procedures of the MHA. There are of course many more outcomes of assessments, treatments, appeals and court decisions, than those given here. Appeals against decisions can be made at least once during each stage; complaints can be made at any time.

### 4.8.1 Involuntary Admission (Civil Patient)

Mental disorder, assessment requested by family member (or housing agency, family doctor, neighbour)

↓

Assessment by Approved Social Worker and two doctors (family doctor & Psychiatrist), nearest relative is contacted

↓

Involuntary admission under section 2 MHA (for assessment and treatment, up to 28 days)

↓
Further diagnostic assessment and treatment in hospital
↓
Patient appeals against detention, reports prepared by clinicians, tribunal arranged within seven days
↓
Mental Health Review Tribunal hears the case and does not discharge
↓
Clinicians decide on further treatment and apply for section 3 MHA (for treatment up to six months
↓
Assessment by Approved Social Worker and two doctors (family doctor and psychiatrist)
↓
Further treatment, significant clinical improvement, care plan in place, patient willing to continue with voluntary treatment
↓
Psychiatrist (RMO) decides to discharge the patient from S. 3 MHA, patient continues with voluntary treatment (in hospital or in the community)

**4.8.2 Involuntary Admission (Forensic Patient)**
Mentally disordered offender, assessment requested by criminal court
↓
Assessment by two psychiatrists who recommend a hospital (and restriction) order
↓
Criminal court decides on a hospital and restriction order (section 37/41 MHA)
↓
Admission, further diagnostic assessment and treatment in a forensic psychiatric hospital
↓
Patient appeals against section, tribunal hearing, tribunal does not discharge
↓
Further treatment, considerable improvement
↓
Risk assessment allows treatment in the community, clinicians recommend conditional discharge, conditional discharge granted by the Home Office (Ministry of Interior Affairs)
↓

Conditions of discharge under section 42 can include that the patient continues to take and receive medication as prescribed by local psychiatric services. A patient who fails to take the prescribed medication runs the risk of being recalled to hospital.

↓

Further treatment with long-term stability and low risk of re-offending, clinicians recommend absolute discharge, absolute discharge granted by the Home Office

↓

Further treatment as a voluntary patient in the community

## References


Council of Europe (1996) Report to the United Kingdom Government on the visit to the United Kingdom carried out by the European committee for the Prevention of Torture and Inhuman or Degrading Treatment or Punishment (CPT) from 15 to 31 May 1994. Strasbourg CPT/Inf (96) 11

Department of Health (1999) Report of the Expert Committee. Review of the Mental Health Act 1983. London: The Stationary Office

Department of Health (1999(2)) A systematic review of research relating to the Mental Health Act (1983). London: The Stationary Office

Department of Health and Welsh Office (1999) Government Guidance. Code of Practice Mental Health Act 1983. London: The Stationary Office

Department of Health (2005) How to make a complaint about the NHS www.dh.gov.uk/ PolicyAndGuidance/OrganizationPolicy/ComplaintsPolicy/NHSComplaintsProcedureArticle/fs/en?CONTENT_ID=4080900&chk=nxiG%2B5 (accessed 16.01.2005)

Institute of Mental Health Act Practitioners (2005) www.imhap.co.uk (accessed 23.01.2005)

Keely TS (1944) One Hundred Years of Lunacy Administration. The Cambridge Law Journal 8: 195-200

Jones R (2001) Mental Health Act Manual (7th ed.) London: Sweet & Maxwell

Mental Health Act Commission (2003) Tenth Biennial Report 2001-2003. Placed amongst strangers. Twenty years of the Mental Health Act 1983 and future prospects for psychiatric compulsion. London: The Stationary Office

Mental Health Alliance (2004). What is the Draft Mental Health Bill? www.mentalhealth.org.uk/page.cfm?pagecode=PRCMMH. (accessed 28.12.2004)

NIMHE (2003) Inside Outside. Improving Mental Health services for Black and Minority Ethnic Communities in England. London: The Stationary Office

Norfolk, Suffolk and Cambridgeshire Strategic Health Authority (2003) Independent Inquiry into the death of David Bennett. pdf download at image.guardian.co.uk/sys-files/Society/documents/2004/02/12/Bennett.pdf (downloaded on 08.01.2005)

Sainsbury Centre for Mental Health (2002) Breaking the Circles of Fear. A review of the relationship between mental health services and African and Caribbean Communities. London: The Sainsbury Centre for Mental Health

The Law Commission (2004) About the Law Commission. www.lawcom.gov.uk/77htm (accessed 27.12.2004)

WNUSP (2005) Report for the quadrennial review of the implementation of the world programme of action on disability. www.wnusp.org (accessed 08.01.2005)

## CHAPTER 5

# Legal Report – Germany

Gerhard HEGENDÖRFER, Matthias GLÖCKNER, Thomas W. KALLERT

### 5.1 Preliminary Remarks

The Reunification of Germany happened in 1990. One of the consequences was the harmonization of two separate judicial systems that were previously clearly divided in the case of mental health laws. In fact, the common structures of the legal system of mental health care valid in the *Länder*[1] of the former West Germany[2] had to be transferred to the "re-founded" *Länder* of the former East Germany (Brandenburg, Mecklenburg-Western Pomerania, Saxony, Saxony-Anhalt, Thuringia), including East-Berlin, and regulations established in the German Democratic Republic were completely abandoned.[3]

### 5.1.1 Survey of the Legal Framework

The German legislation on mental health comprises three different areas of law: civil, public administrative and criminal law. The civil law mainly regulates the relationship between a person with a mental disorder and a psychiatric health care facility by defining the legal conditions for contracts[4] requiring the concerned person's consent. In particular, it provides the criteria for the role and the rules of a guardianship, which, especially in the context of an involuntary placement or involuntary treatment, may be necessary to protect a person with a mental disorder from significant danger of serious harm to his or her life or

---

1 The 16 *Länder* or States of the Federal Republic of Germany constitute their proper government, parliament and jurisdiction and have the power of legislation.

2 Another historical and specifically German dimension still relevant for different (clinical and legal) aspects of involuntary (treatment) measures in psychiatry is the national-socialistic period (1933 to 1945) with its tremendous amount of crimes against mentally disordered persons. – The authors of this report strongly recommend that the readers inform themselves about the details of German psychiatry in this period by studying at least one of the available books on this subject.: e.g. Schmidt 1983, Mitscherlich and Mielke 1989, Schilter 1999.

3 Notably the Mental Health Act of the German Democratic Republic (GDR) about the placement of mentally ill persons into psychiatric establishments of June 11, 1964 (Einweisungsgesetz - EinwG), came into force on July 1, 1968 (Law Gazette of the GDR, I 1968 N°13, p. 273).

4 These conditions concern (e. g.) the obligations and duties of mental health care personnel (care, treatment etc.) and the holder of a mental health facility (accommodation, meals etc.) to the patient and the patients' rights.

health (self-destructive behaviour). The public administrative law, on the other hand, deals with the specific measures and procedure either to protect a mentally disordered person from self-destructive behaviour or to ensure the legal protection of important interests of other people or the public that have been endangered by the behaviour of a person with a mental disorder. The criminal law is aimed at sanctioning mentally disordered offenders, who have committed a crime or a severe criminal offence but are not guilty because of their mental status, with detention in a psychiatric hospital if they are considered to be dangerous delinquents. Both administrative and criminal law pursue the prevention of danger of harm to other persons or to public safety and order resulting from a person's mental disorder.

#### 5.1.1.1 The Civil Law in Mental Health Matters

The legal acts dealing with the conditions and procedure for involuntary measures in mental health under civil law are exclusively reserved to federal legislation. Volume 4 of the German Civil Code, with the title "Family Law," contains the definitive provisions for the prerequisites (of involuntary measures).[5] The judicial proceedings and in particular the role of the Guardianship Court, which represents a specific division of the County (Local) Court, are codified in the German Code on Matters of Non-contentious Jurisdiction.[6]

#### 5.1.1.2 Public Administrative Law

In contrast to civil law, the legislative competence for the legal conditions and procedure concerning involuntary measures in mental health care under public administrative law is allocated to the sixteen *Länder*. Thus, there are sixteen independent Mental Health Acts in Germany with quite varying provisions. In order to keep the presentation of this area of the German legal system concise, the Saxon Mental Health Act of June 16, 1994 for the Aid and Placement of Persons with Mental Disorders[7] is given by way of an example. The Federal legislation is limited to providing the rules for proceedings before a court or a tribunal, especially in relation to an appeal from the decisions taken by administrative authorities.

---

5 Bürgerliches Gesetzbuch of August 18, 1896, came into force on January 1, 1900, Viertes Buch, Familienrecht.

6 Gesetz über die Angelegenheiten der freiwilligen Gerichtsbarkeit of May 20, 1898 (Freiwillige-Gerichtsbarkeit-Gesetz - FGG) entered into force on January 1, 1900 (Law Gazette RGBl. 1898, p. 369, 771).

7 Sächsisches Gesetz über die Hilfen und die Unterbringung bei psychischen Krankheiten (SächsPsychKG) from June 16, 1994 (Saxon Law Gazette SächsGVBl. 1994, p. 1097).

#### 5.1.1.3 Criminal Law

In addition to civil and public administrative law, the criminal justice system is also involved in providing specific sanctions and measures against certain persons with mental disorders. They are called "Preventive Measures for the Reform and Security of Mentally Disordered Criminal Offenders".[8] The legislation in this legal area is in Federal competence as far as it concerns decisions on sanctioning, sentences and the procedural rules. The legal conditions are stated in sections 61 and following of the German Penal Code. The procedural rules for the criminal courts or tribunals are fixed in the German Penal Procedure Code. As concerns the implementation and enforcement of criminal sanctions or measures, the competence of legislation belongs to the 16 *Länder*. Most of them apply the provisions of the mental health acts as far as they are suitable for mentally disordered criminal offenders;[9] others have codified specific legal acts about the implementation and enforcement of preventive measures for reform and security based on criminal law.

### 5.1.2 Definition and Structure of Involuntary Measures in Psychiatric Health Care

The legal conditions and requirements for ordering and enforcing involuntary measures against patients with mental disorders mainly concern the involuntary placement, involuntary treatment and the so-called preventive measures for protection against imminent danger of serious harm during the implementation and/or enforcement of an involuntary placement. Therefore, in this context, involuntary measures generically comprise all legalised powers for acting against a person with a mental disorder without or against his or her relevant consent, either on the occasion of placement in a psychiatric establishment or otherwise. The following distinctions and legal definitions are intended to emphasize the differing characters and uses of these measures in the context of clinical practise.

### 5.1.3 The Different Levels of Legal Acts Authorizing Involuntary Measures

The legal procedure and the application and implementation of particular acts authorizing involuntary measures in psychiatric care are systematically divided into two different procedural steps ("levels") that have to be strictly observed: Whereas level 1 consists of the basic (= primary) legal act of power which orders the appropriate measure, level 2 concerns the implementation and, if necessary, the enforcement of the order or decision (= secondary act of power).

---

8 "Maßregeln der Besserung und Sicherung".

9 E.g. the Saxon Mental Health Act of June 16, 1994 for the Aid and the Placement of Persons with Mental Disorders, see section 38 subsection 1.

### 5.1.3.1 The Basic (= Primary) Legal Act of Power: LEVEL 1

The primary legal act of power is the order or the decision to encroach upon the patient's rights to personal freedom, self-determination and physical integrity and constitutes the legal basis for measures against the patient without or against his or her relevant consent. There are three different laws, according to the three legal framework areas shown before (civil, public administrative and criminal law), on which orders or decisions to restrain the rights to personal freedom and personal integrity of mentally disordered or ill persons are based. Concerning these orders or decisions, a strict distinction must first be made between (a) *involuntary placement*, (b) *involuntary treatment*,[10] and (c) *preventive measures of protection against imminent danger of serious harm.*

a) Involuntary placement

The term *"involuntary placement"* describes an involuntary *admission*[11] or *committal*[12] to a psychiatric hospital or facility. It comprises the legal procedure for restraining the personal freedom of a mentally disordered person either in order to protect him or her from a present and considerable danger to his or her own life or health (self-destructive behaviour) or in order to prevent a present and considerable danger to legally protected important interests of the public or of other individuals (dangerous behaviour) due to mental illness.

b) Involuntary treatment

In a legal context, involuntary treatment deals with the medical-therapeutic or other therapeutic treatments of the patient's mental or behavioural disorder(s) regardless of placement in a psychiatric establishment. The types of involuntary treatment can be defined as *compulsory treatment* and *emergency treatment.* Whereas a compulsory treatment is supposed to represent a broad, general term for legalizing any treatment of a mental illness or disorder against the (relevant) consent of the person, an emergency treatment only authorizes a treatment in case of significant danger of serious harm to the patient's life or health in a particular situation where the patient is not able to consent due to his or her mental disorder.

---

10 See: *Council of Europe*, Steering Committee on Bioethics (CDBI), "White Paper" on the protection of the human rights and dignity of people suffering from mental disorders, especially those placed as involuntary patients, from February, 10 2000, p. 2 and the draft Recommendation of the Committee of Ministers to member States to ensure the protection of the human rights and dignity of people with mental disorders, especially those placed as involuntary patients in a psychiatric establishment; *European Commission*, Research Project on Compulsory Admission and Involuntary Treatment of Mentally Ill Patients – Legislation and Practise in EU-Member States, Final Report, May 15, 2002, p. 85.

11 Term used for a decision based on civil or public administrative law.

12 Term used for a decision based on criminal law (court or tribunal sentence).

c) Preventive measures of protection against imminent danger of serious harm
Besides involuntary placement and involuntary treatment, a third form of involuntary measures exists for particular situations of imminent danger resulting from the patient's behaviour during his or her detention in a psychiatric facility. These are special measures or treatments in order to prevent acts of violence against the patient him/herself, other people (patients or staff members of the institution) or other legally protected important interests, or to safeguard law and essential order within a psychiatric establishment (e. g.: in case of threats or attacks by the patient against persons or objects). They comprise measures like the seizure or retention of (dangerous) objects, overnight observation, separation from other patients, restraint of outdoor stays, physical restraint by use of mechanical devices or isolation/seclusion in a particular safeguarding cell without dangerous objects and with no other patients.

#### 5.1.3.2 The Enforcement = (Secondary) Legal Act of Power: LEVEL 2

The secondary legal act of power represents the enforcement of the basic legal acts shown under level 1. A proper legal basis is required to carry out these measures by applying physical force. These so-called *coercive measures* are a particular means for exercising legalized compulsory powers like involuntary placement, involuntary treatment or preventive measures of protection against imminent danger of serious harm by "breaking" the involuntary patient's will and behaviour with the use of *direct (physical) force* or its *auxiliary means* (e. g. fetters, hand cuffs etc.).

## 5.2 Applicable Laws and General Norms

### 5.2.1 Constitutional Norms

Basic Law of the Federal Republic of Germany (May 23, 1949)
There are no specific provisions for mental heath concerning involuntary placement or involuntary treatment.

#### 5.2.1.1 General Fundamental Rights

Article 1.1 of the German Basic Law – protection of human dignity:

> *"The dignity of man is inviolable. To respect and protect it shall be the duty of all public authority."*

Article 2 of the German Basic Law – rights of liberty, protection against personal injuries:

> *„(1) Everybody shall have the right to the free development of his personality in so far as he or she does not violate the rights of others or offend against the constitutional order or the moral code.*

*(2) Everybody shall have the right to life and to inviolability of the person. The freedom of the individual is inviolable. These rights may only be encroached upon pursuant to a law."*

#### 5.2.1.2 Rule-of-Law Principles

Article 20.3 of the German Basic Law – the principle of Rule-of-Law:

*"The legislature shall be bound by the constitutional order, the executive and the judiciary by law and justice."*

#### 5.2.1.3 Fundamental Rights in Case of Judicial Proceedings

Article 104 of the German Basic Law – legal guarantees in the event of deprivation of liberty:

*"(1) The liberty of the individual may be restricted only pursuant to a formal law and only with due regard to the forms prescribed therein. Detained persons may not be subject to mental or physical ill-treatment.*
*(2) Only a judge may decide on the admissibility or continuation of any deprivation of liberty. Where such deprivation is not based on the order of a judge, a judicial decision must be obtained without delay. The police may not hold anybody on their own authority in their own custody longer than the end of the day after the day of apprehension. Details shall be regulated by legislation.*
*(3) Any person provisionally detained on suspicion of having committed a criminal offence must be brought before a judge not later than the day following apprehension; the judge shall inform him or her of the reasons for the detention, examine him or her and give him or her an opportunity to raise objections. The judge must, without delay, either issue a warrant of arrest setting forth the reasons therefore or order his or her release from detention.*
*(4) A relative or a person enjoying the confidence of the person detained must be notified without delay of any judicial decision ordering or continuing the deprivation of liberty."*

### 5.2.2 Primary Law (Acts of Parliament)

The different legal acts at the federal or state level provide conditions and rules for the procedures of placement and treatment.

#### 5.2.2.1 Acts Governing Involuntary Placement in a Psychiatric Establishment, Hospital or Similar Facility

a) Civil law (Federal Law)

Section 1906.1 to 1906.3 and 1906.5 of the German Civil Code – requirements for placement:

*"(1) Placement of a person under legal guardianship based on a decision of his or her guardian that involves a loss of personal freedom is only permitted, as long as it is required for the well-being of the person under guardianship, if*
*1. by reason of a mental illness or a mental or psychical handicap of the person under guardianship, there is a danger that he or she may commit suicide or cause substantial injury to his or her own health, or*

*2. an examination of his or her state of health, a therapeutic treatment or a medical intervention is necessary that cannot be carried out without placement of the person under guardianship and owning to a mental illness or a mental or psychic handicap the person is not able to recognise the need for his or her admission or to act according to such recognition.*
*(2) A placement can only be put into effect by leave of the Guardianship Court. Exceptionally, a placement without leave of the court is permitted if any delay may involve danger; the leave shall be subsequently obtained afterwards without delay.*
*(3) The guardian shall terminate the placement if the prerequisites therefore no longer apply. He or she has to inform the Guardianship Court of the termination of placement.*
*(4) ...*
*(5) A placement based on a decision of an authorized representative and the consent of an authorized representative to measures mentioned in subsection 4 require that the authorization be granted in written from and include explicitly the measures mentioned in subsections 1 and 4. Besides, subsections 1 and 4 are also applicable."*

**Remarks**
The civil law provides for the possibility of involuntary placement in case of self-destructive behaviour by a person with a mental disorder. If the person is under guardianship, the decision of his or her guardian has to be approved in advance by the guardianship court. If an authorized representative of the person has taken the decision, a placement requires the informed written consent of the person concerned and the leave of the guardianship court. In case of imminent danger, the placement can be put into effect without in advance of the leave of the guardianship court, but must thereafter be approved as soon as possible by the court.

Section 1631b of the German Civil Code – requirements for placement of a child:

*"The placement of a child that involves a loss of personal freedom is permitted only by the leave of the Family Court. A placement without leave of the court is only permitted if any delay may entail a risk; the leave shall be subsequently obtained afterwards without delay. The court shall withdraw the leave if the well being of the child requires no further placement."*

b) Administrative law (State Law)
Sections 10.1 and 10.2 of the Saxon Act of June 16, 1994 for the Aid and Placement of Persons with Mental Disorders (Saxon Mental Health Act)- requirements for confinement:

*"(1) A confinement requiring that a person with a mental disorder be admitted to a hospital or committed to remain there for further time against or without his or her consent must be based on a court decision, preliminary admission order or an order of admission to care or detention pursuant to the provisions of this act.*

*(2) A person with mental disorder may be subject to a confinement only if he or she represents a significant and obvious danger to his or her life or health or to legally protected important interests of other persons due to his or her mental disorder and if the danger cannot be prevented otherwise."*

**Remarks**

This provision states the legal prerequisites for involuntary placement of a person with a mental disorder in case of self-destructive behaviour and/or if such a person represents a significant danger to others (= confinement).

Section 17 of Saxon Act of June 16, 1994 for the Aid and the Placement of Persons with Mental Disorders (Saxon Mental Health Act) – preliminary confinement:

*"(1) Before a preliminary measure of confinement is taken, the court gives the local public health authority of the district where the patient usually resides the opportunity for an official comment except in case of imminent danger; in case of imminent danger, the opportunity for an official comment must be given to the local public health authority as soon as the preliminary measure of confinement is taken.*
*(2) At the end of the term of a preliminary confinement fixed by the court, the patient shall be released if the court does not prolong the confinement by rendering a further preliminary decision or a decision on final confinement. Regardless of this provision, a decision pursuant to section 18 should also be rendered.*
*(3) If the further placement of a patient subject to a preliminary confinement is medically no longer necessary he or she should be released. The court and the administrative authority shall be informed. With regard to minors or patients under guardianship relating to the right to determine his or her place of residence or health care, the legal representative shall be informed immediately."*

Sections 18.1 and 18.2 of the Saxon Act of June 16, 1994 for the Aid and Placement of Persons with Mental Disorders (Saxon Mental Health Act) – immediate preliminary confinement:

*„(1) If existing reasons strongly suggest that the prerequisites for a confinement apply and if a court decision cannot be brought about in time to prevent an impending danger, the administrative authority should impose immediate preliminary confinement and enforce it pursuant to section 14. The administrative authority shall inform immediately the competent court about the placement, at the latest by 10:00 of the day following the day when the detention began.*
*(2) In accordance with subsection 1, the patient shall be examined immediately by a medical doctor. If the results of the medical examination confirm that the prerequisites for a confinement do not apply, the patient shall be released. Exceptionally, he or she may remain in the hospital under a legally relevant consent. The competent court and the administrative authority shall be informed immediately about the release."*

Section 18.3 of the Saxon Act of June 16, 1994 for the Aid and Placement of Persons with Mental Disorders (Saxon Mental Health Act) – immediate preliminary confinement in case of imminent danger:

> *"(3) In case of imminent danger and under the criteria of subsection 1, the police are authorized to bring a patient to a competent hospital pursuant to section 15 without decision of an administrative authority. So far as possible, a medical doctor shall first be consulted. The patient shall be examined immediately. If the results of the medical examination confirm that the prerequisites for a confinement do apply, the patient should be subject to admission or placement in care against or without his or her consent. Sentence 1 is also applicable if the patient refuses the care of the hospital contrary to the decision of the court."*

Section 18.4 of the Saxon Act of June 16, 1994 or the Aid and Placement of Persons with Mental Disorders (Saxon Mental Health Act) – immediate preliminary restraint:

> *"(4) A patient admitted to a hospital without being detained pursuant to the provisions of this Act should be restrained in the hospital against or without his or her consent if the criteria of subsection 1 apply but the administrative authority is not able to take a decision on time."*

Sections 18.5 to 18.7 of the Saxon Act of June 16, 1994 for the Aid and Placement of Persons with Mental Disorders (Saxon Mental Health Act) – administrative procedures:

> *„(5) Under the criteria of subsections 1, 3 and 4, the hospital shall inform immediately the court and the administrative authority, at the latest by 10:00 of the day following the day when the confinement of the patient began, by producing an expert's report containing explicitly the answers to the questions of section 13, subsection 1, sentence 1.*
> *(6) Under the criteria of subsections 1 to 4, the patient shall have the opportunity, granted by the administrative authority, the police and the hospital, to inform his or her relatives or a person in whom he or she has personal confidence. The persons mentioned in sentence 1 shall be heard by the court according to the patient's demand if this does not interfere with the purpose of placement, and if this does not lead to a disproportionate disturbance of the proceedings.*
> *(7) If a court decision has not been rendered by the end of the day following the day when the patient was detained or the confinement of the patient began, the patient shall be released. The court, the administrative authority and, with regard to minors and to persons under guardianship relating to the right to determine their place of residence or health care, the legal representative shall be informed immediately."*

c) Criminal law (Federal Law)
Section 63 of the German Penal Code – commitment to a psychiatric hospital

> *"If someone has committed an unlawful act and at the time lacked capacity to be adjudged guilty (section 20) or was in a state of diminished capacity (section 21), the court shall sentence the person to committal to psychiatric hospital if a comprehensive evaluation of the perpetrator and his or her act reveals that, as a result of his or her condition, serious*

*unlawful acts can be expected of him or her and he or she therefore represents a danger to the general public."*

Section 19 of the German Penal Code – criminal incapacity of the child to be adjudged guilty
Whoever upon commission of a criminal act is not yet fourteen years of age lacks the capacity to be adjudged guilty.

Section 20 of the German Penal Code – lack of capacity to be adjudged guilty due to mental disorder

*"Whoever upon commission of a criminal act is incapable of appreciating the wrongfulness of the act or acts in accordance with such appreciation due to a pathological mental disorder, profound consciousness disorder, mental defect or any other serious mental abnormality, acts without guilt."*

Section 21 of the German Penal Code – diminished capacity to be adjudged guilty

*"If the capacity of the perpetrator to appreciate the wrongfulness of the act or to act in accordance with such appreciation is substantially diminished upon commission of the act due to one of the reasons indicated in section 20, then the punishment may be mitigated pursuant to section 49 subsection (1)."*

Section 64 of the German Penal Code – commitment to an institution for withdrawal treatment[13]

*"(1) If someone has a proclivity to consume alcoholic beverages or other intoxicants to excess and is convicted of an illegal act he or she committed while intoxicated or as a result of his or her proclivity, or is not convicted solely because his or her lack of capacity to be adjudged guilty has been proven or may not be dismissed, then the court shall sentence the person to committal to an institution for withdrawal treatment if there is a danger that he or she will commit serious illegal acts as a consequence of his or her proclivity.*
*(2) A sentence to committal shall not be issued if withdrawal treatment appears to be without prospects from the onset."*

### 5.2.2.2 Legal Provisions Permitting an Involuntary Treatment of Mentally Disordered or Ill Persons

a) Civil law (Federal Law)
Section 1904 of the German Civil Code – application of medical measures:

---

13 Pursuant to the decision of the Federal Constitutional Court of March 16, 1994 (Federal Law Gazette, BGBl. I S. 3012), the following shall apply: Section 64 is incompatible with Article 2 subsection (1) and subsection (2), sentence 2 of the Basic Law and is void because it also provides for an order of placement under the provisions of its first subsection when there is no sufficiently concrete prospect for successful treatment.

*"(1) The consent of the guardian to an examination of the state of health, a therapeutic treatment or a medical intervention requires the leave of the Guardianship Court if there is a substantial apprehension that the person under guardianship may die as a consequence of those measures or suffer severe and long term health injury. Those measures may only be carried out without leave of the court if a delay involves jeopardy.*
*(2) Subsection 1 applies analogously to the consent of an authorized representative. The consent is only legally relevant if the authorization is given in written form and includes explicitly the measures mentioned in subsection 1, sentence 2."*

b) Administrative law (State Law)
Section 16 of the Saxon Act of June 16, 1994 for the Aid and Placement of Persons with Mental Disorders (Saxon Mental Health Act) – treatments under judicial decision:

*„If a patient, having attained his or her majority, is not under guardianship relating to the right to determine his or her place of residence or health care at the moment when the court renders a decision on confinement, the court rules also on the lawfulness of treatments and those applicable without the patient's consent."*

Section 21 of the Saxon Act of June 16, 1994 for the Aid and Placement of Persons with Mental Disorders (Saxon Mental Health Act) – treatment:

*„(1) The patient is entitled to necessary treatment. This includes the necessary examinations as well as measures of social therapy, psychotherapy, pedagogical, occupational and work therapy. The treatment takes place according to a treatment plan. It also encompasses measures that are necessary to enable the patient, after his or her release, to lead an independent life in society.*
*(2) The treatment plan must be discussed with the patient. The patient shall be informed comprehensively and entirely about the necessary diagnostic procedures and treatment as well as the attendant risks."*

Section 22 of the Saxon Act of June 16, 1994 for the Aid and Placement of Persons with Mental Disorders (Saxon Mental Health Act) – treatment without the patient's consent:

*„(1) For all therapeutic treatment measures required according to valid and reliable standards of medical practice, the explicit and informed consent of the patient or his or her legal representative must, in principle, be obtained. If approval according to section 16 or consent of a guardian charged with the health care of the patient or, in the case of minors, the person with custody, has not been submitted, a treatment and all examinations necessary for a treatment may only be carried out without the patient's consent if any delay significantly endangers the life or the health of the patient.*
*(2) Medical interventions and methods of treatments pursuant to subsection 1 that are combined with a surgical intervention or a significant danger of serious harm to the life or the health of a patient are permitted only upon the patient's informed and legally relevant consent or, if he or she is not able to assess the significance and implications of such an intervention and of the consent thereof, the legally effective consent of his or her legal representative.*

*(3) Feeding against the patient's will is permitted only when it is necessary to prevent an imminent and significant danger of serious harm to the life or the health of the patient.*
*(4) All measures may not injure the patient's dignity and may only be carried out by the order of and under direct supervision and responsibility of a physician. "*

**Remarks**
The Saxon Law permits an involuntary treatment of a patient only in cases of patients under guardianship with the consent of his or her guardian or in an emergency situation. The law does not allow any general compulsory treatment.

### 5.2.2.3 Legal Provisions for Preventive Measures of Protection Against Imminent Danger of Serious Harm Regarding Mentally Disordered or Ill Persons

a) Civil law (Federal Law)
Sections 1906.4 and 1906.5 of the German Civil Code ) – measures to restrain personal freedom:

*"(4) Subsections 1 to 3 are also applicable if it is intended to restrain the freedom of a person under guardianship living in an institution, a home or another, similar facility without his or her being detained, for a longer period or regularly by mechanical devices, medication or in some other manner.*
*(5) A placement based on a decision of an authorized representative and the consent of an authorized representative to measures mentioned in subsection 4 require that the authorization be granted in written form and include explicitly the measures mentioned in subsections 1 and 4. Besides, subsections 1 and 4 are also applicable."*

**Remarks**
The civil law permits the application of mechanical devices, medication or other similar measures only in the case of a person under guardianship with the guardian's written consent *and* by the official approval of the Guardianship Court. In case of imminent danger, the measures can be applied without leave of the court but have to be approved later without undue delay.

a) Administrative law (State Law)
Section 31 of the Saxon Act of June 16, 1994 for the Aid and Placement of Persons with Mental Disorders (Saxon Mental Health Act) – measures of security:

*"(1) A patient shall only be subject to such measures of security as are indispensable for the purpose of a placement or to avoid or eradicate a serious disturbance of security and order in the hospital. The following measures of security are applicable*
*1. the seizure or retention of objects,*
*2. overnight observation,*
*3. separation from other patients,*
*4. the restraint or limitation of outdoor stays,*
*5. seclusion in a special safeguarding cell without dangerous objects and*

*6. physical restraint by use of mechanical devices.*
*(2) Measures of security according to subsection 1 are still applicable if the behaviour of a patient or his or her mental state increasingly implies the danger of escape attempts, acts of violence against persons or objects or of suicide or self-injuries.*
*(3) A physical restraint by using mechanical devices in order to lead patients out, to bring them before the judge or to transport them is also applicable in case of increased danger of an escape attempt.*
*(4) The restrictions mentioned in subsection 1 shall only be maintained as far as their purpose requires."*

**Remarks**
This provision includes the seizure or retention of (dangerous) objects, overnight observation, separation from other patients, restraint of outdoor stays, physical restraint by using and/or applying mechanical devices, and seclusion in particular safeguarding cells without dangerous objects and with no other patients. The law does not however allow any sedation with drugs.

### 5.2.2.4 Legal Provisions for the Enforcement of Legal Basic Acts by Applying Coercive Measures

Section 23 of the Saxon Act of June 16, 1994 for the Aid and Placement of Persons with Mental Disorders (Saxon Mental Health Act) – application of direct force:

*„If therapeutic measures and other interventions that a patient is committed to endure pursuant to this law or orders provided by this law cannot otherwise be enforced, the personnel of the hospital is authorized to apply direct physical force against a patient after it has been announced. An announcement is not necessary if the particular circumstances of an individual case are not convenient."*

**Remarks**
The Saxon law permits the use of direct (physical) force. However, the law does not allow the use of any auxiliary means (e.g. fetters, hand cuffs etc.).

### 5.2.2.5 Legal Provisions Governing the Proceedings Before a Court or a Tribunal

a) Federal laws

Section 70 to section 70 n of the German Code on Matters of Non-Contentious Jurisdiction:
Section 70.1 – competent court:

*„(1) The following provisions apply to proceedings concerning measures of detention. Measures of detention are*
*1. the leave of the court for a placement representing a loss of personal freedom*
*a) of a child (sections 1631b, 1800, 1915 of the German Civil Code) and*

*b) of a person under guardianship (section 1906.1 to section 1906.3 of the German Civil Code) or a person who has authorized a third person to make decisions regarding his or her placement representing a loss of personal freedom (section 1906.5 of the German Civil Code);*
*2. the leave of the court for a measure pursuant to section 1906.4 of the German Civil Code and*
*3. the decision on a placement representing a loss of personal freedom pursuant to the legal acts of the States (*Länder*) regarding the placement of persons with mental disorder.*
*The Guardianship Courts are the competent jurisdictional bodies for measures of detention except of those pursuant to section 1631b of the German Civil Code."*

## Section 70 a – competence of a person to conduct proceedings in his or her own name:

*„The person concerned has the competence to participate in proceedings in his or her own name, regardless of his or her legal competence, on reaching the age of fourteen."*

## Section 70 b – curatorship during proceedings:

*„(1) As far as it is necessary for the pursuit of the interests of the person concerned, the court assigns a curator for the proceedings to assist the person concerned. In particular, an assignment is necessary if it is intended not to hear the person concerned in person pursuant to section 68.2. Section 67.3 is applicable accordingly.*
*(2) If the court does not assign a curator for the proceedings to assist the person concerned, the reasons shall be adduced in the decision ordering a measure of detention.*
*(3) A curator for the proceedings to assist the person concerned should not be assigned or a decision for an assignment should be revoked if the person concerned is represented by a lawyer or by another appropriate representative for the proceedings.*
*(4) The assignment of a curator is terminated provided that the decision on it has not already been revoked when*
*1. the decision concluding the proceedings becomes final or*
*2. the proceedings are otherwise concluded."*

## Section 70 c – hearing of the person concerned:

*„The court shall hear the person concerned in person and gain a direct impression of him or her before rendering a decision on a measure of detention. As far as it is necessary, the court gains the direct impression in the ordinary surroundings of the person concerned. The court informs the person about the possible course of proceedings. Proceedings according to sentence 1 should not be executed by a requested judge. Furthermore, section 68 subsection 1 sentence 5 and section 68 subsections 2 to 5 apply analogously."*

## Section 70 d – hearing in accordance with the law/opportunity for comments:

*"(1) Before rendering a decision on a measure of detention, the court gives the opportunity for an explanation to*
*1. the spouse of the person concerned if the spouses are not permanently separated,*
*1a. the common law spouse of the person concerned if the common law spouses are not permanently separated,*

*2. each of the parents and all children with whom the person concerned was living during proceedings,*
*3. the guardian or tutor of the person concerned,*
*4. a reliable person nominated by the person concerned,*
*5. the head or director of the institution where the person concerned lives, and to*
*6. the competent authority.*
*In addition, State Law (the Law of the* Länder*) may provide the opportunity for an explanation to other persons or authorities.*
*(2) If the person concerned is a minor, his or her parents, if vested with the care for the person of the child, his or her legal representative for personal affairs and his or her foster parents shall be heard in person."*

## Section 70 e.1 – expert report of a medical doctor:

*"(1) Before rendering a decision on a measure of detention pursuant to section 70 subsection 1 sentence 2 Nos. 1 and 3, the court shall ask for the opinion of an expert, who is bound to examine and interrogate the person concerned in person. The expert should ordinarily be a doctor in psychiatry; in any case, he or she must be a medical doctor experienced in psychiatry. For decisions on a measure of detention based on section 70 subsection 1 sentence 2 No. 2, a doctor's certificate is sufficient."*

## Section 70 f – content of decision:

*"(1) A decision on a measure of detention shall comprise*
*1. the personal details of the person concerned,*
*2. the specific description of the measure of detention,*
*3. the date by which the measure of detention must be terminated if no extension has been ordered; the indicated date must not exceed one year following the pronouncement of the decision or two years in case of an evident need for a long detention,*
*4. the instructions about a person's right to appeal.*
*(2) A decision shall also state the reasons in case of rejection."*

## Section 70 g – announcement of decision:

*„(1) In any case, the decisions must be announced in person to the person concerned. Exceptionally, an announcement of the reasons for a decision to the person concerned is not necessary if a medical certificate states consequently significant detriments to his or her health.*
*(2) A decision on a measure of detention shall also be announced to the persons and authorities mentioned in section 70 d and to the head or director of the institution where the person concerned is intended to be detained. In any case, the decisions must be announced to the competent authority if the court has given the opportunity for an explanation to that authority pending the proceedings.*
*(3) The decision on ordering or rejecting a measure of detention will take effect at the moment when it becomes final. The court, however, may declare immediate effect for a decision. In this case, the decision will become final upon being announced, together with the decree for immediate effect, to the person concerned, to the curator for the proceedings or to the guardian or tutor of the person concerned , upon submittal of the decision together*

*with the decree for immediate effect to the registry of the court for announcement, or upon informing a third person, charged with carrying out the decision, about the decision and the decree for the immediate effect; the date must be noted on the decision.*
*(4) The decision of the court to bring the person before a judge must be carried out by the competent authority.*
*(5) On request, the competent authority shall assist the tutor, the parents, the guardian or the curator of the person concerned in transferring him or her to a placement pursuant to section 70 subsection 1 sentence 2 No. 1. The use of force by the competent authority requires a specific decision of a court. The competent authority has the power to request the assistance of the police if required."*

Section 70 h – preliminary decision:

*„(1) A provisional measure of detention may be taken by a preliminary decision. Section 69f subsection 1 and section 70 g are applicable accordingly. Section 70 d applies accordingly except in case of imminent danger.*
*(2) A provisional measure of detention must not exceed a term of six weeks. If such a term is not sufficient, the period of a detention may be prolonged by a further preliminary decision for a total term of three months after an expert has been heard. The period of detention for preparing an expert opinion (section 70 e subsection 2) shall be included in that total term.*
*(3) Subsections 1 and 2 apply analogously if it is intended to take a measure of detention pursuant to section 1846 of the Civil Code."*

Section 70 i – termination or prolongation of detention:

*„(1) A measure of detention shall be terminated if the prerequisites no longer apply. Before terminating a measure of detention pursuant to section 70 subsection 1 sentence 2 No. 3, the court gives the opportunity of an official comment to the competent authority except in a situation where the progress of the proceedings would be delayed in a more than insignificant manner. The termination of that measure of detention shall always be announced to the competent authority.*
*(2) The provisions for taking a decision on a measure of detention for the first time apply analogously to the prolongation of a measure of detention. If the total period of a detention exceeds a term of four years the court, should ordinarily not appoint an expert who was hitherto involved in the treatment of the person concerned or charged with rendering an opinion or who is employed at the institution where the person concerned is detained."*

Section 70 k – stay of execution:

*„(1) The court may stay the execution of a detention pursuant to section 70 subsection 1 sentence 2 No. 3. The stay can be subject to certain obligations. The stay should not exceed regularly a term of six months; a prolongation to one year is possible.*
*(2) The court may revoke the stay of execution if the person concerned does not discharge his or her obligations or if it is necessary because of the state of the person concerned.*
*(3) Section 70 d applies accordingly to the proceedings concerning the stay of execution and its revocation."*

Section 70 l – motion for a court decision to review the measures regulating the conditions and the implementation of a detention:

„*(1) The person concerned has the right of motion for a court decision to review the measures regulating the special conditions and the implementation of a detention pursuant to section 70 subsection 1 sentence 2 No. 3. The person concerned may also move for the court to compel the competent public authority to perform a rejected or omitted measure during a detention.*
*(2) The admissibility of the motion requires that the person concerned assert a violation of his or her rights caused by the performance, rejection or omission of a measure during a detention.*
*(3) The motion itself does not imply a suspensory effect. The court may decree the suspensory effect of a motion.*
*(4) The court decision is non-appealable.*"

Section 70 m.1 and 70 m.2 – appeal subject to a time-limit:

„*(1) An immediate appeal is admissible against decisions taking effect from the date the decision becomes final.*
*(2) Without affecting section 20, the persons or authorities mentioned in section 70 d are entitled to appeal against measures of detention, preliminary measures of detention or against the rejection of the termination of those measures.*"

Section 70 n sentence 2 – information about a decision on detention:

„*The head or director of the institution where the person concerned lives shall be informed about the termination of a measure of detention pursuant to section 70 i subsection 1 sentence 1 and about the stay of execution of a detention pursuant to section 70 k subsection 1 sentence 1.*"

b) State law

Section 18.8 of the Saxon Act of June 16, 1994 for the Aid and Placement of Persons with Mental Disorders (Saxon Mental Health Act) – motion for a court decision to review measures regulating the conditions and the implementation of a detention before a court decision on a placement has been rendered:

„*(8) The patient has the right of motion for a court decision to review a measure regulating the special conditions and the implementation of a detention pursuant to the provisions of this act even before a court decision on a placement or detention has been rendered.*"

### 5.2.3 International Conventions and Agreements

The principle international conventions or agreements concerning the legal conditions of persons with mental disorders in psychiatric establishments which have been ratified by Germany and implemented into national law (legally binding acts) are:

1. on the UN-level:
   - The International Covenant on Civil and Political Rights (CCPR) of December 19, 1966, ratified by Germany on November 15, 1973 and entered into force on March 23, 1976[14]
   - The International Covenant on Economic, Social and Cultural Rights (CESCR) of 19 December 1966, ratified by Germany on ... and entered into force on January 3, 1976[15]
   - The UN Convention Against Torture and Other Cruel, Inhuman or Degrading Punishment (CAT) of December 10, 1984 ratified by Germany on ... and entered into force on June 26, 1987[16]

2. on the Council of Europe-level:
   - The European Convention for the Protection of Human Rights and Fundamental Freedoms of November 4, 1950, ratified by Germany on December 5, 1952 and entered into force on November 3, 1953[17]
   - The European Convention for the Prevention of Torture and Inhuman or Degrading Treatment or Punishment of November 26, 1987, ratified by Germany on February 21, 1990 and entered into force on June 1, 1990[18]

**Remark**
The European Convention for the protection of Human Rights and dignity of the human being with regard to the application of biology and medicine (so-called "Oviedo Convention") of April 4, 1997, has not been signed yet by Germany.

### 5.2.4 Secondary Law (Administrative Decrees, Regulations, Ordinances or Instructions of Public Authorities)

As the States (*Länder*) are exclusively competent and responsible for the implementation and the enforcement of measures of involuntary placement and involuntary treatment even if those measures are based on Federal Legislation (principle of Article 83 of the German Constitution) no Federal provisions on secondary law exist. Therefore, the States and the respective local public authorities have the power to issue the specific rules. They are empowered by special enabling provisions of primary law to pass legal norms at the secondary level, such as administrative decrees, regulations, ordinances or instructions of public authorities. For example, section 42 of the Saxon Act of June 16, 1994 for the Aid

---

14 See *Federal Law Gazette* (Bundesgesetzblatt=BGBl.) II 1973, p. 1533 (1534, 1570).
15 See *Federal Law Gazette* (Bundesgesetzblatt=BGBl.) II 1976, p. 428.
16 See *Federal Law Gazette* (Bundesgesetzblatt=BGBl.) II 1990, p. 247.
17 See *Federal Law Gazette* (Bundesgesetzblatt=BGBl.) II 1952, p. 685 (953).
18 See *Federal Law Gazette* (Bundesgesetzblatt=BGBl.) II 1989, p. 946.

and Placement of Persons with Mental Disorders (Saxon Mental Health Act) states:

Section 42 – provisions for implementation

*"(1) The State Ministry for Social Affairs is enabled to regulate the composition and the duties of the monitoring commissions, the appointment and the duties of the patients' advocates, the procedures for visits, holidays, measures of security, measures easing restrictions of detention, for placement and for guardianship, the obligatory information necessary for ensuring the intent of a detention and the grant of remuneration for the purposes of section 19 subsection 4 sentence 2, as well as the fixing of catchment areas for the purposes of section 2 subsection 2 by issuing administrative decrees in agreement with the State Ministry of Home Affairs and the State Ministry of Justice.*

*(2) The institution is enabled to regulate the details on the furnishing of rooms with objects of the patients, the procedure and the surveillance of visits and exchange of letters and mail, as well as the use of direct force by issuing ordinances or house regulations in compliance with the provisions of legal acts.*

*(3) In other respects, the State Ministry for Social Affairs in agreement with the State Ministry of Justice issues the necessary regulations for implementing the provisions for the enforcement of preventive measures of rehabilitation and security against criminal offenders with mental disorders according to the eighth passage."*

Apart from some ordinances and house regulations of psychiatric institutions in Saxony, no general administrative decrees or regulations have been issued by the ministry at the moment.

## 5.3 Jurisprudence

### 5.3.1 National Jurisdictional Bodies

Bavarian Constitutional Court of December 19, 1957, ref.-no. Vf.92-VII-55: (limits of compulsory treatment for persons with mental illnesses)

*„Despite the absence of explicit provisions in the Bavarian Constitution (BC) compared to article 2 subsection 2 sentence 1 of the German Federal Basic Law, physical integrity is also protected by the Bavarian constitutional law in so far as infringements would represent a violation of fundamental rights expressed in article 100 (protection of human dignity), article 101 (general freedom of action) or article 102 (personal freedom) of the BC. The fundamental rights of human dignity, freedom of action and freedom of movement are general human rights and therefore also belong to persons with mental disorders. An involuntary or compulsory treatment ordered and carried out in accordance with the provisions of the Mental Health Act does not infringe upon the substance of those basic rights."*

Moenchengladbach Regional Court, division of civil law, 5th chamber of April 19, 2002, ref.-no. 5 T 99/02, concerning section 1906 subsection 1 of the German Civil Code, sections 10, 11 and 18 subsection 4 of the Mental Health Act of North Rhine-Westphalia:

(distinction between involuntary admission based on civil law and involuntary placement or detention based on public administrative law)

*„In principle, involuntary placement or confinement based on public administrative law is subsidiary to the involuntary admission based on civil law. However, involuntary placement or confinement based on public administrative law is considered to be exceptionally permitted simultaneously with an already existing involuntary admission based on civil law if a medical intervention of involuntary treatment is necessary even against or without the consent of the guardian or tutor in order to prevent a significant danger of serious harm to the public safety. In particular, this can be the case if the guardian or tutor refuses to consent to a necessary involuntary and compulsory treatment pursuant to section 18 subsection 4 of the Mental Health Act of North Rhine-Westphalia."*

Higher Regional Court of Thuringia of February 5, 2002, ref.-no. 6 W 44/02, concerning section 1906 of the German Civil Code and section 70 g of the German Code on Matters of non-contentious Jurisdiction:

*„The use of physical force in order to carry out and enforce a medical intervention is not regulated explicitly by the law on guardian- and tutorship. A recourse in particular to section 1906 subsections 1 and 4 of the German Civil Code is precluded. No more than the law on guardian- and tutorship provides a legal basis for compulsory measures on the part of the court against a person under guardianship beyond section 1906 of the German Civil Code and section 70 g of the German Code on Matters of non-contentious Jurisdiction. If the use of physical force against a person under guardianship who is competent to understand is not permitted in order to carry out a medical intervention, its use is only required against a person under guardianship who, for reason of a mental illness or a mental handicap, is not able to understand the necessity of a treatment and if such an intervention is indispensable for protecting his or her life."*

Federal Supreme Court of October 11, 2000, ref.-no. XII ZB 69/00, concerning section 1906 subsection 1 no. 2, subsection 2 and subsection 4 of the German Civil Code:

*„A permanent medical intervention consisting of a regular application of neuroleptica every two weeks and the use of coercive measures for a short time against an unwilling person under guardianship in order to carry out each application of that treatment do not represent a placement depriving personal freedom (=detention) or a similar measure. Therefore, those measures cannot be subject to a leave of the court pursuant to section 1906 subsection 2 of the German Civil Code in liaison with subsection 1 no. 2 or section 1906 subsection 4 of the German Civil Code."*

Higher Regional Court of Schleswig-Holstein of May 7, 2003, ref.-no. 2 W 73/03, concerning section 1906 subsection 1 of the German Civil Code:
(involuntary placement of a person under guardianship: justification of a committal of a person suffering from chronic schizophrenia for medical examination and involuntary treatment)

*„A detention of a mentally disordered person under guardianship in a psychiatric hospital may not be justified if that person refuses to take the necessary drugs for his or her treatment and therefore causes a relapse of his or her condition if such a relapse does not induce the risk of chronification and thereby require a permanent in-patient treatment.*

*Rather, it is necessary to ascertain, based on concrete facts resulting from a disease, that a certain probability exists for suicide, risk of substantial injury to the health of the person concerned or for the detriment of others. When the paranoid schizophrenia of the person concerned has already taken a chronic progress, a detention may be justified if further psychotic outbreaks implicate the risk of serious aggravation of the disease. The detention of the person concerned for reason of an examination with medical devices through CCT that is deemed necessary for his or her well being may not be justified if the measures are not permitted to be carried out without consent and the person concerned does not consent to such examinations due to an existing ability to understand the consequences of those measures. The detention of the person concerned for a definite period for reason of attempting a lengthy treatment by coercive medication may represent a justified and appropriate measure to induce the subsidence of the symptoms and the stabilization of the ability to understand and control one's own actions. In case of a treatment by coercive medication, the interference with fundamental rights resulting from the deprivation of liberty and the use of force involved in a coercive medication and its consequences for the person concerned must be considered in proportion to the expected development without those measures. "Liberty of illness" must be conceded to the person concerned in such a way that he or she may have the choice between life with psychotic crisis and the – from his or her point of view – insufferable consequences of a detention or compulsory treatment (ensuing Federal Constitutional Court of March 23, 1998, ref.-no. 2 BvR 2270/96, published in New Weekly Journal of Law (NJW) 1998, p. 1774)."*

Karlsruhe Higher Regional Court of February 11, 2002, division for matters of family law, ref.-no. 20 WF 112/01, concerning section 70 h subsection 2 sentence 2 of the German Code on Matters of non-contentious Jurisdiction and sections 1643, 1904 of the German Civil Code:
(preliminary detention: prolongation of a preliminary decision on a provisional measure of detention for more than six weeks; no leave of the court for the therapeutic treatment of minors)

*„The prolongation for more than six weeks up to a total period of three months (section 70 h subsection 2 sentence 2) of a detention of a minor based on a preliminary decision shall be reserved to those exceptional cases in which the decision on the final detention cannot be rendered earlier due to particular reasons. The therapeutic treatment of a minor is not amenable to the leave of the Guardianship Court. The provision for guardianship stipulated in section 1904 of the German Civil Code is not applicable in connection with the law for minors; an extension of the number of legal transactions of minors subject to the leave of the court is excluded by analogy."*

Bremen Hanseatic Higher Regional Court of June 12, 1996, ref.-no. 1 W 3/96, concerning section 1906 subsection 4 of the German Civil Code:

*„The coercive medication of a person under tutorship/guardianship living in a psychiatric hospital without being detained involuntarily does not require the leave of the Guardianship Court if the person concerned has to be restrained only for a short period in order to administer the medicine. The same principle shall apply when the coercive medication takes place regularly."*

Kassel Regional Court, division of civil law, 3rd chamber of January 5, 1996, ref.-no. 3 T 859/95 and 3 T 860/95, concerning section 1901 subsection 1, 2 and 3 and section 1906 subsection 1 no. 2 of the German Civil Code, section 69a subsection 1 of the German Code on Matters of non-contentious Jurisdiction and article 104 subsection 1 and 2 of the German Basic Law:
(law of guardianship/tutorship: individual rights of a person under guardianship/tutorship who is competent to understand and control his or her actions in case of medication)

> *„In the field of therapeutic treatments (here: coercive medication), the will of a person concerned who is able to understand and control his or her individual actions takes absolute precedence. The individual rights resulting from the detention of a person under tutorship/guardianship shall also not apply by analogy to the therapeutic treatment of persons under tutorship/guardian-ship."*

Hamm Higher Regional Court of September 7, 1981, ref.-no. 7 VAs 30/81, concerning section 136 of the Correction of Criminal Offenders Act and sections 23 and following of the Introductory Act to the Judicature Act:
(judicial control of medical measures of treatment)

> *„Medical treatment measures for a detained person may represent measures in terms of section 23 of the Introductory Act to the Judicature Act that are appealable by declaratory proceeding. Section 136 of the Correction of Criminal Offenders Act cannot be interpreted to the effect that a judge should be charged with the final binding decision on medical inquiries and the instruction of doctors for medical treatment principles working in psychiatric establishments for mentally disordered criminal offenders. Exceptionally, a treatment representing a medical practise that obviously does not comply with valid and reliable medical standards may require the intervention of a judge."*

Koblenz Regional Court of January 6, 1977, ref.-no. 4 T 697/76, concerning section 1 of the Mental Health Act Rhineland-Palatinate:
(Admission to a psychiatric hospital in case of danger of self-destructive behaviour)

> *„The jeopardy of the public safety and order and the danger of self-destructive behaviour represent two independent reasons for admission. Therefore, an involuntary placement may be justified in case of suspected considerable detriment to the health of the person concerned even though the public safety and order shall not be affected."*

Stuttgart Higher Regional Court of April 29, 2003, Civil Division, ref.-no. 8 W 135/03, concerning section 1906 of the German Civil Code:
(guardianship/mentorship: prerequisites for the leave of the Guardianship Court in order to place a person under guardianship and with a mental disorder and alcohol addiction in a psychiatric hospital)

> *„A placement initiated by a guardian according to section 1906 of the German Civil Code in order to prevent self-injury due to mental illness requires that the person under guardi-*

*anship lack free exercise of will due to that illness, meaning the person is unable to make decisions conditional upon reasonable considerations. In principle ,alcohol addiction justifies a placement only if there is a causal connection with mental afflictions, particularly a mental disorder, or if the condition of the person concerned due to alcohol abuse has assumed the extent of mental afflictions."*

Bavarian Higher Court Munich of July 28, 1999, Civil Division, ref.-no 3Z BR 212/99, concerning Article 1 section 1 1st sentence of the Bavarian Act for the Placement of Persons with Mental Disorders:
(Placement of persons with mental disorders; the principle of proportionality; definition of mental illness)

*„The principle of proportionality represents the main criterion for interpreting the prerequisites of a placement based on public administrative law. It determines the standards for the clarification of the circumstances and requires the total consideration and appreciation of the circumstances of the individual case. The use of the term mental disease must indicate a seriousness of personality disorder sufficient for justifying a deprivation of liberty. In the same way, it is indispensable that the risk of harm for individuals and legally protected important interests of others coming from a person with mental disorder corresponds with the seriousness of an encroachment on personal freedom."*

Frankfurt Regional Court of November 12, 1992, division of civil law, 9th chamber, ref.-no. 2/9 T 428/92, concerning section 1896, 1906 1st subsection no. 2 of the German Civil Code:
(leave of the court for involuntary placement or guardianship without consent to therapeutic treatment)

*„In case risk of serious harm to the health of the person concerned is lacking, the necessity of a placement for therapeutic treatment pursuant to section 1906 of the German Civil Code must be denied if the intended therapeutic treatment does not offer a reasonable prospect of success because of the vehement refusal of treatment by the person concerned. A placement for diagnostic purposes and treatment by compulsion are impermissible even if treatment is necessary from a medical point of view. If the person concerned refuses any kind of therapeutic treatment and if the involuntary placement is impermissible, the order of guardianship concerning the area of responsibility "consent to and make decisions regarding therapeutic treatment" does not seem sensible."*

Koblenz Regional Court of January 6, 1977, ref.-no. 4 T 697/76, concerning section 1 of the Rhineland-Palatinate Act for the Placement of Persons with Mental Disorder:
(Admission to a psychiatric hospital in case of self-destructive behaviour)

*„The jeopardy to public safety and order and the risk of self-destructive behaviour are each a separate criterion for a detention in psychiatric hospital. Consequently, an involuntary placement is even justified provided that significant detriment to the health of the person concerned can be expected, even if public safety and order are not affected."*

Kassel Regional Court of January 5, 1996, ref.-no. 3 T 859/95, concerning sections 1901 and 1906 of the German Civil Code and Article 104 of the German Basic Law:

*„In connection with therapeutic treatments, the true intention of a person concerned who is competent to understand takes absolute precedence. The rights resulting from an involuntary placement of a person under guardianship are also not applicable by analogy to a therapeutic treatment of a person under guardianship."*

Zweibrücken Higher Regional Court of November 16, 1999, ref.-no. 3 W 223/99, concerning sections 1904 and 1906 of the German Civil Code and section 70 g of the German Code on Matters of non-contentious Jurisdiction:

*„Neither section 1906 subsection 1 no. 2 of the German Civil Code nor section 1906 subsection 4 of the German Civil Code do apply to the leave of the Guardianship Court for a outpatient medication of the person concerned consisting of a regular application of depot neuroleptica even if it seems necessary in a medical point of view to avoid a placement. However, the leave of the court is necessary if the prerequisites of section 1904 subsection 1 of the German Civil Code do apply. Regardless of whether a guardian or tutor charged with the health care of the person concerned requires the permission for a measure of therapeutic treatment in such a situation a permanent outpatient therapy consisting of the injection of depot neuroleptica must not be enforced against the free determination of the person's concerned will. In this respect a legal basis lacks to implement coercive measures."*

Hamm Higher Regional Court of April 6, 2000, ref.-no. 15 W 76/00, concerning sections 1906 and 1904 of the German Civil Code and section 28 of the German Code on Matters of non-contentious Jurisdiction:

*„Section 1906 subsection 1 no. 2 of the German Civil Code provides the legal basis for the leave of the court to enforce a repeated and brief admission of the person concerned to a psychiatric hospital provided that the admission merely represents a restraint of personal freedom in order to apply depot neuroleptica, and if, in accordance with the principle of proportionality, such a measure represents an encroachment on the rights of the person concerned that is less intrusive than would an otherwise necessary, fairly long-term commitment representing a deprivation of liberty. In such a case, the leave of the court must not be granted without considering simultaneously the requirements of a leave for therapeutic treatment pursuant to section 1904 subsection 1 sentence 1 of the German Civil Code."*

Bavarian Higher Court Munich of March 15, 1990, ref.-no. BReg 3 Z 23/90, concerning sections 1846, 1915 and 1910 of the German Civil Code:

*„A preliminary confinement ordered by the Guardianship Court pursuant to section 1846 of the German Civil Code does not justify a therapeutic treatment against the will of the person concerned. Such a treatment is only permitted before assigning a curator if the person concerned is legally incapable in this field and if the Guardianship Court explicitly allows a specified therapeutic measure."*

Bremen Hanseatic Higher Regional Court of March 12, 1996, ref.-no. 1 W 319/96, concerning section 1906 of the German Civil Code:

*„In principle, a guardian or tutor charged with the health care of a person placed in a psychiatric institution is authorized to consent to a necessary, coercive medicinal treatment of the person concerned against his or her will (here: medicinal treatment by applying 2 ml of ciatyl-z depot every 10 days for a period of one year). In this respect, the leave of the Guardianship Court is not necessary. Measures depriving personal freedom only require the leave of the Guardianship Court when they are applied regularly. A regular deprivation of personal freedom implies, among other things, recurrent occasions. Unintended repetitions may involve the duty to obtain the leave of the Guardianship Court pursuant to section 1906 subsection 1 of the German Civil Code if the recurrence of an occasion is estimated. Physically restraining the person under guardianship for only a few moments (here: in order to give an injection) does not involve the duty to obtain the leave of the Guardianship Court pursuant to section 1906 subsection 4 of the German Civil Code. This provision must be given a narrow interpretation and the application field is confined to measures similar to detention. The application of simple physical restraint by force for only a very short period does not qualify as such a measure."*

### 5.3.2 International Jurisdictional Bodies

European Commission of Human Rights/European Court of Human Rights

European Commission of Human Rights of October 16, 1986, application no. 11249/84, concerning Articles 3, 4, 5 paragraph 1 (a), 8, 13, 14 and 17 (art. 4, art. 5-1-a, art. 8, art. 13, art. 14, art. 17) of the European Convention on Human Rights:

The applicant had initially complained that he did not receive a special rehabilitation in prison and that the courts maintained the order of 1979 according to which the sentence to imprisonment was to be executed prior to the detention in a neuropathic hospital. The Commission notes that by letter of September 25, 1986 the applicant expressed his wish to withdraw these complaints on the ground that he had nearly served the time of his prison sentence. It considers that there are no reasons of a general character affecting the observance of the Convention which necessitate a further examination of these complaints. It concludes that it is no longer seized of the applicant's initial complaints. The applicant now complains that, though his character changed, the order of 1979 that he be detained in a neuropathic hospital is still in force. The applicant has complained that his detention in a mental hospital is neither justified by subpara. (a) or (e) of Article 5 paragraph 1 (art. 5-1-a, 5-1-e) of the Convention, because he could not be considered as a person of unsound mind. As the applicant is no longer serving sentence but is detained in a mental hospital and as subparas. (a) and (e) are not mutually exclusive, it has, in the first place, to be examined whether the requirements for detention under Article 5 paragraph 1 (e) (art. 5-1-e) of the Convention are fulfilled.

*"However, the Commission is not required to decide whether or not this new complaint discloses any appearance of a violation of the Convention as, under Article 26 (art. 26) of the Convention, it may only deal with a matter after all domestic remedies have been exhausted according to the generally recognised rules of international law. In the present case, no court proceedings have yet taken place under S. 67 c of the German Penal Code which provide for a review of the initial court order that the applicant be detained in a neuropathic hospital after he had served a sentence to imprisonment. The applicant has not applied for a discontinuance of the order of 1979 on the grounds of an alleged change of circumstances. He has, therefore, not exhausted the remedies available to him under German law. Moreover, an examination of the case does not disclose the existence of any special circumstances which might have absolved the applicant, according to the generally recognised rules of international law, from exhausting the domestic remedies at his disposal."*

European Commission of Human Rights of May 4, 1987, application no. 11457/85, concerning Article 5 paragraphs 1, 4 and 5 of the European Convention on Human Rights:
The applicant first complains that his detention in various mental hospitals between 1980 and 1984 was unjustified because the relevant committal orders were based on wrongful psychiatric evidence stating that he suffered from schizophrenia. New psychiatric reports of 1984 in fact confirmed that the applicant had never suffered from schizophrenia and these reports were relied upon in several subsequent court decisions, including in particular a decision by the Munich Court of Appeal of October 24, 1986 by which the original committal order of 1 October 1980 was declared to be without object in view of the new psychiatric reports.

*"The Commission considers that despite this latter decision the applicant can still claim to be a victim, within the meaning of Article 25 (art. 25) of the Convention, of a violation of his Convention rights in connection with his above detention. The effect of this decision, which operated ex nunc, was limited to terminating the probationary supervision which still was applicable to the applicant as a consequence of the committal order. The original committal order was not revoked or annulled and the applicant did not obtain any compensation or other redress regarding his claim that the detention had been unjustified from the onset. He therefore can still complain of that order. However, the Commission is not required to decide whether or not the facts alleged by the applicant disclose any appearance of a violation of Article 5 (art. 5) as, under Article 26 (art. 26) of the Convention, it may only deal with a matter after all domestic remedies have been exhausted according to the generally recognised rules of international law."*

European Commission of Human Rights of October 6, 1987, application no. 12485/86, concerning Article 5 subsection 1a and 1e of the European Convention on Human Rights:
The applicant has complained that his detention in a mental hospital is justified neither by subpara. (a) nor (e) of Article 5 paragraph 1 (art. 5-1-a, 5-1-e) of the

Convention, because he could not be considered as a person of unsound mind. As the applicant is no longer serving sentence but is detained in a mental hospital and as subparas. (a) and (e) are not mutually exclusive it has, in the first place, to be examined whether the requirements for detention under Article 5, paragraph 1 (e) (art. 5-1-e) of the Convention are fulfilled.

*"The term 'unsound mind' as employed in Article 5 paragraph 1 (e) (art. 5-1-e) does not only refer to mental illness in the strict sense of psychiatric science, but also to any kind of mental disorder, the kind or degree of which must be such as to warrant compulsory confinement (judgment of the Eur. Court HR of April 5, 1981, case of X v. United Kingdom, Series A, Vol. 46, p. 18, paragraph 40). In the present case the German courts have, on the basis of several consecutive and concordant medical expert opinions and taking into account his numerous previous convictions relating to violent offences and his aggressive and violent behaviour in detention, concluded that there is concrete danger that the applicant, who, up to now, has refused treatment and also refuses to accept any kind of treatment or examination after his eventual release, might again commit serious offences."*

European Commission of Human Rights of November 8, 1989, application no. 13957/88, concerning Article 8, paragraphs 1, 10, paragraphs 1 and 6 of the European Convention on Human Rights:
The applicant complains about the dismissal by the Federal Court of his action tending to obtain access to the medical file concerning his treatment in the psychiatric clinic of the Free University of Berlin. This complaint is not that the State has acted but that it failed to act. It therefore has to be examined whether the handling by the Federal Court of the applicant's request for access to his clinical record was, as claimed, in breach of a positive obligation forthcoming from Article 8 (art. 8) (respect for private life) or Article 10 (art. 10) (freedom of information) of the Convention.

*"The Commission first notes that according to the Federal Court's jurisprudence a patient has in principle a right to inspect his/she/her clinical records insofar as they relate to objectively justified findings and reports on measures of treatment. It also notes the view of the Federal Court that in the field of psychiatric and psychotherapeutic treatment therapeutical reasons may exist to deny a former patient access to the clinical record even if his/she/her conditions have improved. It agrees that account has to be taken of the fact that the attending practitioner was personally involved and that subjective elements of evaluation could play an important role in the treatment, justifying leaving to them to decide in the individual case whether to and to what extent the patient should be granted access to the clinical records."*

European Commission of Human Rights of February 13, 1990, application no. 13770/88, concerning Article 2 to 14, 17 and 18 of the Convention, Article 1 and 2 of Protocol No. 1 and Article 2 of Protocol No. 4 of the European Convention on Human Rights:

The applicant complains about the proceedings in 1986 before the Aachen Regional Court and the Cologne Court of Appeal concerning his further detention in a mental hospital. He submits, inter alia, that in these proceedings he was not assisted by a counsel. The applicant's complaint falls within the scope of Article 5 paragraph 4 (art. 5-4) of the Convention which provides:

*"Everyone who is deprived of his liberty by arrest or detention shall be entitled to take proceedings by which the lawfulness of his detention shall be decided speedily by a court and his release ordered if the detention is not lawful."*

The respondent Government consider the applicant's complaint as inadmissible under Article 26 (art. 26) of the Convention for non-exhaustion of domestic remedies. They submit that the applicant failed to request assistance by an official defence counsel in the proceedings concerned and that the proceedings in 1986 were in accordance with Article 5 paragraph 4 (art. 5-4) of the Convention. They contend that this provision does not in general guarantee the right to have free legal assistance. In the present case, an official counsel was not required by the interests of justice or of the applicant, who represented himself and had not requested legal assistance. In particular, the applicant was not obviously unfit to plead his case due to his mental illness.

*"It is true that under Article 26 (art. 26) of the Convention the Commission may only deal with a matter after all domestic remedies have been exhausted according to the generally recognised rules of international law. The Commission notes that on March, 12 1986, the Aachen Regional Court, upon a petition by the applicant, informed him that there was no legal basis for detainees to be assisted by official counsel in proceedings of the kind in question. Furthermore, the Federal Constitutional Court, in its decision of February 10, 1987 refusing to accept his constitutional appeal, dealt with the merits of the applicant's complaint. In these circumstances the Commission finds that the applicant has properly exhausted the remedies available to him under German law. The Commission considers that, in the particular circumstances of the present case, the applicant's complaint about the proceedings before the Aachen Regional Court and the Cologne Court of Appeal in 1986 raises questions of fact and of law which are of such a complex nature that their determination requires an examination of the merits. The application cannot, therefore, be declared manifestly ill-founded within the meaning of Article 27 paragraph 2 (art. 27-2) of the Convention. No other ground for declaring it inadmissible has been established."*

European Commission of Human Rights of May 18, 1992, application no. 14219/88, concerning Article 5 subsections 1 and 5 and Article 3 of Protocol No. 7 of the European Convention on Human Rights:

The applicant first complains under Article 5 paragraph 1 (art. 5-1) of the Convention that his detention in the years 1980 to 1984 was unlawful because he never suffered from a mental disease justifying this detention. The applicant further complains under Article 5 paragraph 5 (art. 5-5) of the Convention that he was unjustifiably refused compensation for unlawful detention. He claims compensation under Article 5 paragraph 5 (art. 5-1) of the Convention because his detention allegedly was not lawful under Article 5 paragraph 1 (art. 5-1).

> *"The Commission notes that the finding in question only appeared in the reasons, but not in the operative part of the decision of the Court of Appeal of October 24, 1986. It thus could not be considered in the German legal system as an authoritative statement on the lawfulness or otherwise of the applicant's detention. The Commission notes that in the retrial proceedings the German courts considered very carefully the evidence underlying the original detention order as well as new expert evidence. Ultimately it was found that the doubts, which might exist concerning the correctness of the diagnosis which had led to the detention order of 1980, were unjustified. While the assumption of a chronic schizophrenia could not be upheld, it could not be excluded that the applicant had in fact suffered in 1980 from an acute schizophrenic psychosis excluding his criminal responsibility and thus justifying his detention as a person of unsound mind. Without expressly referring to art. 5, paragraph 1 (e) (art. 5-1-e) of the Convention, the German courts thus in substance confirmed that the applicant's detention had been covered by this provision. The Commission finds no indication that their decisions were unreasonable or arbitrary."*

European Commission of Human Rights of October 13, 1993, application no. 19791/92, concerning Article 5, paragraphs 3, 3 and 6 of the European Convention on Human Rights:
The applicant complains under Article 5 paragraph 3 (art. 5-3) of the Convention about the length of his detention on remand. Article 5 paragraph 3 (art. 5-3), so far as relevant, provides as follows:

> *"Everyone arrested or detained in accordance with the provisions of paragraph 1 (c) of this Article ... shall be entitled to trial within a reasonable time or to release pending trial."*

The respondent Government consider that the applicant can no longer claim to be the victim of a violation of his right under Article 5 paragraph 3 (art. 5-3), as any possible breach was remedied by the Freiburg Regional Court's judgment of 20 December 1990. The Government further submit that the overall length of the applicant's detention on remand of less than 32 months and eighteen days was not unreasonable in the circumstances. They refer in particular to the complexity of the facts and of the investigations, which necessitated the taking of expert evidence. They contend that there were no undue delays on the part of the German authorities. The applicant considers that the proceedings until the applicant's conviction could have been terminated after 18 months as a maximum. He submits that the case was not complex, and that the relevant results of the investigations were already available in September and October 1988. The experts could have been appointed simultaneously. According to the applicant, his refusal to make any statements on the charges against him did not render the investigations more difficult. The applicant points at several delays in the course of the proceedings, in particular the delay in preparing the first report on the result of the investigations and transmitting it to the Public Prosecutor's Office.

The forensic expert opinion on the circumstances of the offence should have been ordered from the very beginning of the investigations. Following a first contact with the forensic expert, it took a month until he was appointed as expert in January 1989. The applicant further submits that the appointments of the psychiatric and the psychological experts were belated. The Public Prosecutor's Office could have also started to prepare the indictment earlier and thus have it preferred one month earlier.

> *"The Commission recalls that, as regards complaints about a breach of Article 6, paragraph 1 (Art. 6-1), mitigation of sentence and discontinuance of prosecution on account of the excessive length of proceedings do not in principle deprive the individual concerned of his status as a victim within the meaning of Article 25 (Art. 25), unless the national authorities have acknowledged either expressly or in substance, and then afforded redress for, the breach of the Convention (Eur. Court H.R., Eckle judgment of 15 July 1982, Series A no. 51, p. 30, paragraph 66). The Commission finds that the Freiburg Regional Court, though referring to an extraordinary length of the applicant's detention on remand, did not thereby make any finding of a violation of Article 5 paragraph 3 (Art. 5-3). Moreover, this length and its impact on the applicant were only indeterminate elements in fixing his sentence. Consequently, the applicant may still claim to be victim of a violation of his right under Article 5, paragraph 3 (Art. 5-3) of the Convention. The Commission recalls that it is in the first place for the national authorities to ensure that, in a given case, pre-trial detention of an accused person does not exceed a reasonable time. To this end, they must examine all the facts arguing for or against the existence of a genuine requirement of public interest justifying, with due regard to the principle of the presumption of innocence, a departure from the rule of respect for individual liberty and set them out in their decisions on the question of release. It is essentially on the basis of the reasons given in these decisions and of the true facts mentioned by the applicant in his appeals, that the Convention organs are called upon to review the reasonableness of the length of detention (cf. Eur. Court H.R., Letellier judgment of June 26, 1991, Series A no. 207, p. 18, paragraph 35; W. v. Switzerland judgment of January 26, 1993, paragraph 30, to be published in Series A no. 254). The Commission considers that especially the period of almost two years for completing the preliminary investigations may at first sight appear excessive."*

European Court of Human Rights of June 12, 2003, final judgement, application no. 44672/98, concerning Article 50 paragraphs 1 and 4, 6, paragraphs 1 and 13 of the European Convention on Human Rights:
The applicant has been detained in three different psychiatric institutions. He complains that his second placement in a psychiatric hospital was unlawful because a mental disease justifying this detention had never been revealed. In his point of view the condition of "urgent reasons" required for a preliminary detention never existed because of the lack of a written medical report and individual hearing on his state of health and because the telephone diagnosis which was carried out instead could not have been sufficient. The public authorities did not require a current medical examination although the medical report they took as basis for their decision dated from 1995. Furthermore the applicant complains

that he has not had any possibility to lodge an appeal before a tribunal in order to review the legitimacy of his detention. Furthermore he claims a compensation for damage consisting of loss of earnings during his commitment.

> *"The Court reminds that article 5 paragraph 1 of the Convention is principally addressed to national legislation and must be respected in implementing substantive and procedural provisions. Thus any deprivation of liberty strictly requires conformity to the intention of that article namely to protect the individual against state arbitrariness (Winterwerp a. The Netherlands, decision of October 24, 1979, n. 33, p. 17, paragraph 39 and Hutchison Reid a. UK, n. 50272/99, decision of February 20, 2003, paragraph 46). In the Court's view an emergency situation can justify a preliminary detention based on moral evidence like telephone diagnosis or other means of substantial evidence without further medical examination or immediate hearing of the person concerned. No violation of article 5 paragraph 1 of the Convention can be found. Concerning the applicant's complaint of no right to judicial relief after his temporary detention a finding of violation of article 5 paragraph 4 of the Convention is to be made. Even when a detention has terminated the subsequent review of all the facts justifying a deprivation of individual liberty by a judicial body is necessary to guarantee full judicial review. Otherwise the intention of article 5, paragraph 4 of the Convention would fail. The Court does not adjudge a compensation for damage because a causality between the violation of Article 5 paragraph 4 of the Convention and the loss of earnings cannot be found. Nevertheless the applicant is entitled to receive a compensation for pain and suffering of 3500 Euro caused by partial violation."*

European Court of Human Rights of October 26, 2004, decision on admissibility, application no. 61603/00, concerning articles 3, 5, 6 and 8 of the European Convention on Human Rights:
The applicant complained that her placement in different psychiatric hospitals against her will constituted a deprivation of her liberty and amounted to a breach of Article 5 of the Convention. She submitted that, in particular due to the interpretation of the relevant provisions of national law by the courts and the assessment of the expert evidence by them, she did not have a fair trial within the meaning of Article 6 of the Convention.

> *"In the Court's view, the applicant, who complained not only that she had been deprived of her liberty in the different psychiatric institutions, but also about the medical treatment she received there against her will, can be taken to have claimed, in substance, that there had also been an interference with her private life as guaranteed by Article 8 of the Convention. The Court considers, in the light of the parties' submissions, that the complaint raises serious issues of fact and law under Article 5, paragraph 1 of the Convention, the determination of which requires an examination of the merits. The Court concludes therefore that this complaint is not manifestly ill-founded within the meaning of Article 35, paragraph 3 of the Convention. No other ground for declaring it inadmissible has been established."*

### 5.4 Protocols and Internal Norms

#### 5.4.1 International Declarations and Recommendations

As distinguished from the legally binding international conventions or agreements, international declarations or recommendations do not oblige a State to implement them into national law and therefore a disregard or infringement cannot be sanctioned by judicial authorities or international bodies. Nevertheless, such international legal instruments shall be considered as guidelines or principles for national legislation.

1. on the UN-level:
   - The Universal Declaration of Human Rights of December 10, 1948, signed by Germany on November 4, 1950
   - The Principles for the Protection of Persons with Mental Illness and for the Improvement of Mental Health Care of December 17, 1991

2. on the WHO-level:
   - Ten Basic Principles on Mental Health Care Law of 1996, based on the UN Principles for the Protection of Persons with Mental Illness and for the Improvement of Mental Health Care of December 17, 1991 (*www.who.int/mental_health/media/en/75.pdf*)

3. on the Council of Europe-level:
   - Recommendation No R 1983(2) of the Committee of Ministers to Member States concerning the legal protection of persons suffering from mental disorders placed as involuntary patients of February 22, 1983[19]
   - Recommendation No R (1994)1235 of the Parliamentary Assembly of the Council of Europe on psychiatry and human rights of April 12, 1994
   - Recommendation No. R (2004)10 of the Committee of Ministers to Member States concerning the protection of the human rights and dignity of persons with mental disorders of September 22, 2004.

#### 5.4.2 Identification and Description of the Contents of Those Protocols That Are More Widely Used by National Health Institutions

German Medical Association (Bundesärztekammer/Landesärztekammern)

The German Medical Association (Bundesärztekammer) publishes official statements/recommendations and guidelines on various medical issues. However, using the German terms "Zwangsmaßnahmen or Unterbringung AND Psychiatry" no specific document on coercive measures in psychiatry could be found. The only publication mentioning this problem was a guidelinc for physi-

---

[19] The Representatives of Germany reserved the right of their government to comply or not to comply with the provisions in Articles 3.a and 6.b of the rules appended hereto.

cians on dealing with patients' advanced directives. In these directives, details of placement and treatment can be defined; these have to be respected by the physicians, but the physicians must review if the patient was in a state to give informed consent when the directive was written. In any cases of doubt, a court's decision on these issues should be established.

Federal and State Ministries of Health and Justice (Bundes- und Landesministerien für Gesundheit und Justiz)

Using the same search terms as mentioned above, no official publications on the specific issues covered in this report could be found on the websites of the German Federal Ministries of Health and of Justice. This statement refers also to the official publications of the Saxon Ministries of Social Affairs and Justice.

German Hospital Association (Deutsche Krankenhausgesellschaft)

On the website of the German Hospital Association, which acts as representative of the hospitals to governmental/parliamentary bodies and financial carriers of the health insurances in the establishment of any legal or financial regulations concerning hospitals (and also collects all these materials), no documents could be found with a special focus on coercive measures during inpatient hospital treatment. Published documents include the general legal frameworks for establishing external and internal quality assurance in hospitals (see 5.4.3).

Federal Organization of the Health Insurance Companies (Bundesverband der Krankenversicherungen)

Again, no documents could be found with a special focus on coercive measures during inpatient hospital treatment.

German Society for Psychiatry, Psychotherapy and Nervous Diseases (Deutsche Gesellschaft für Psychiatrie, Psychotherapie und Nervenheilkunde (DGPPN))

This national association of psychiatrists started to publish guidelines for best clinical practice in 1998. They focus on (mainly psychopharmacological) treatment approaches for specific mental disorders, and try to define algorithms for adequate treatment options during different stages of the disorders. Up to now – and this statement is also valid for the most recent guideline on "psychosocial treatment approaches" (DGPPN, in press) – none of these publications has defined any norms related to coercive measures or compulsory medical treatment. Obviously, the guideline authors appointed by DGPPN overlooked the publication by Steinert et al. (1998) presenting guidelines for quality assurance of coercive measures (isolation, fixation, medication) during hospitalization; these specific guidelines were established from the clinical perspective in a large psychiatric hospital. In 2000, DGPPN organized the first national scientific meeting on this issue. The presentations focused on current practical experiences and empirical data regarding the mental health laws in all 16 states of the Federal Republic of Germany.

Journal "Deutsches Ärzteblatt"
From 1996 onwards, no articles or official statements by federal medical bodies concerning involuntary admissions to psychiatric hospitals and/or coercive treatment measures in psychiatry were published in the weekly journal addressing all German physicians of all medical disciplines – i.e. the group of those working in hospitals and the group not working in hospitals.

Journal "Der Nervenarzt"
Within the period of the last seven years, the official journal of the German Society for Psychiatry, Psychotherapy and Nervous Diseases "Der Nervenarzt" published no official statement of the society on this issue. The journal published two scientific articles on this subject: 1. Structure of care in psychiatric hospital units 22 years after the "Psychiatrie-Enquete": This national survey (59% response rate of 319 clinical units) identified – among other differences like size of the wards, number of open wards etc. – differences in the frequencies of coercive measures used between the federal states (Gebhardt and Steinert 1998). 2. Involuntary treatment in psychiatry from the patient's point of view: This is a small study in one hospital assessing the patients' perceptions/attitudes towards coercive treatment measures experienced during hospital treatment (Smolka et al. 1997).

German Society for Public Health Services [Öffentlicher Gesundheitsdienst/(Journal „Das Gesundheitswesen")]
Within the period of the last seven years, the official journal of the association of physicians specialized in public health services published only one article specifically dealing with coercive treatment. Ten years after the introduction of the new legislation, it reviews the development of legislation for the care of the mentally ill ("Betreuungsrecht") as seen by the psychiatrist (v. Oefele 2002).

### 5.4.3 Identification and Description of the Contents of Any Internal Normative Regarding National Hospitals

Guideline on quality assessment in inpatient psychiatric services
In the mid-1990s, a guideline on quality assessment in inpatient psychiatric services was developed by a project group funded by the Federal Ministry of Health (Bundesministerium für Gesundheit 1996). It proposed a matrix of 28 dimensions or components of the care process and service management on the one hand (1-28), and 23 evaluation criteria on the other hand (A – W; see table 5.1).

**Table 5.1: Guideline for Quality Assessment in Inpatient Psychiatric Services: Care Process/Service Management (Evaluation Domains 1-28), and Quality Criteria (Criteria A-W) (Bundesministerium für Gesundheit 1996)**

| Evaluation domains | Quality criteria |
|---|---|
| admission procedure (1); diagnostic procedures (2); drug and other somatic treatment (3); generic and specific psychotherapy (4); work and physiotherapy (5); residential care / helping with self-support (6); help concerning work, employment, school (7); support with social contacts, leisure time (8); liaison with family (9); benefits (10); discharge planning and discharge (11); handling of coercive measures (12); general medical and somatic liaison care (13); key worker / therapeutic relationship (14); treatment and (nursing) care planning (15); time management (16); therapeutic milieu (17); ward concepts (18); treatment team (19); information and communication system (20); documentation system (21); ward organization and administration (22); staff management (23); service organization and management structure (24); management-clinician cooperation (25); public relations work (26); patient advocacy (27); service accessibility (28) | reduction of psychopathological symptoms (A); enhancing responsibility, illness understanding, compliance, empowerment (B); supporting social integration (C); protection of patient dignity / human rights (D); user satisfaction (E); prevention of damage, social and data protection (F); legal safety (G); positive outside effects (H); person-centred care planning (I); relationship-oriented care (J); transparency of treatment and care planning (K); multidimensional disease concept (L); methodological-scientific orientation (M); integration of treatment components, multiprofessional care (N); outside orientation, social network-oriented care and help with non-psychiatric support systems (O); preference for non-residential care (P); adequate documentation (Q); reflection (R); cost-effectiveness (S); care based on maintenance and development of personal resources (T); task-oriented input from professional groups (U); clear professional responsibility (V); adequate service resources (W) |

Handling of coercive measures (12) was one of the evaluation domains, and protection of patient dignity/human rights (D), legal safety (G) were examples of quality criteria specifically referring to coercive measures. The general idea of this guideline was for the evaluation to look at each cell, i.e. to evaluate the degree to which the quality criteria were met, in a particular inpatient service, when considering the various aspects of the care process and service management one by one. The guideline has been used by some inpatient services, but has not been accepted generally in the field.

In 1997, the Aktion Psychisch Kranke e.V., a federal clearing body (based in Bonn) at the junction of professional practice, psychiatric reform and federal health policy, organized a national symposium entitled „Violence and coercion in psychiatric hospitals“, and published the presentations in a book (Kebbel, Pörksen & Aktion Psychisch Kranke, 1998). Especially concerning the legal practice of involuntary admissions (see contributions of Dodegge & Marschner) important suggestions for improving this area were formulated. Their starting point was the clinical reality that the structure of regional mental health services and the local organizational aspects of the procedure of involuntary admissions are more relevant than written law when it comes to the involuntary admission of an individual mentally ill person. Furthermore, there are big regional differences concerning the rates of involuntary admissions under public and civil law, and it was foreseen that advance directives would influence clinical practice in the future significantly. Therefore, the legal experts established the following suggestions (quoted in brief): 1. The State Mental Health Laws should define the mandatory establishment of community services including those for emergency and crisis situations which could decrease the number of involuntary hospital admissions; 2. The preconditions for involuntary admissions should be changed to reflect a sense of crisis intervention in acute mental disorders (which increases the role of civil law for this measure), narrowing the definition of these preconditions which have been previously referred more or less to the respective categories of police law; 3. the use of physical force for bringing a patient to the hospital should only be allowed after several other measures haven't been effective (example for the definition of these states: Thuringen State Mental Health Law); 4. because the frequency of pre-authorized detentions is low (as is the rule according to law), the court itself cannot influence the procedure or any decisions in advance of the hospital admission: therefore, a thorough psychiatric examination should be done as early as possible in every case, and police should bring patients to the hospital in the presence of two persons experienced with the mentally disordered; any changes of State Mental Health Laws should take into consideration that emergency detentions (not pre-authorized) are the rule for the practice of the law; 5. forced medication should be clearly restricted to measures relating to the disorder relevant for the current detention; the measure has to be explained to the patient in order to obtain his informed consent; 6. situations for allowing the use of mechanical restraint as well as the clinical standard (e.g. personal supervision) for practicing this measure or similar measures have to be clearly defined in the mental health laws; 7. detention in open wards should be the rule; 8. patients have to be informed in detail (along with written information material) about their rights in the detention procedure; because knowledge about judicial options does not mean that the patient actually has the capability to use these options, a lawyer (Verfahrenspfleger) acting for the patient has to be appointed; establishment of external safeguards is of high importance (see 5.6.2); 9. any development of the mental health laws should be oriented towards clinical practice/practical problems; particularly, this applies to regulations for special procedures within the detention procedures; one should not avoid to clearly defining these procedures in the law in order to establish standards from the judicial point of view which can be overseen and guaranteed in a reliable way.

Federal directive on staffing in in- (and day-) patient psychiatric services

Staffing levels are at the heart of most attempts to address quality issues in psychiatric services. The Psychiatrie-Personalverordnung (Psych-PV; psychiatry staffing act) is a directive for staffing levels in psychiatric services which is valid at the federal level, i.e. for the whole country, and includes inpatient and partial hospitalization. Since 1990, this has given new impetus to improving quality of care in in-patient services (Kunze & Kaltenbach 1996). The directive applies to general adult, substance misuse and child and adolescent psychiatric in-patient services. It provides a matrix of care classes or groups and allocates minutes of staff time per professional group (e.g. psychologist, nursing staff, etc.) per week on the basis of these categories.

The effects of the implementation of the Psych-PV have been described in a comprehensive survey of in-patient mental health services covering the period 1990 to 1995 comprising 216 in-patient services which provide in-patient care for 75% to 80% of the German population (Aktion Psychisch Kranke e.V. et al. 1998). The overall staff increase was 24%. This increase in staffing also provided scope for considerable improvement in service quality. During the 1990s there has been a shift towards shorter hospital stays, along with changes in the distribution of Psych-PV care groups, namely an increase in the share of acute care categories (all acute and intensive care categories: 51% in 1990 to 64% in 1995) and a decrease of the share of long-term care and rehabilitation case groups (from 39% to 25%).

Quality assurance in psychiatric hospitals

Quality assurance (QA) in hospitals has a legal basis in the German system of social security (paragraph 112 and paragraph 137 Social Code Book V). In the last few years, several important initiatives at the state level have been undertaken. For example, in North Rhine-Westfalia, inpatient treatment for people suffering from schizophrenia (Janssen et al. 2000), and in Baden-Württemberg, inpatient depression treatment (Wolfersdorf et al. 1997). These studies have developed a clear conceptual framework for conducting QA in psychiatric inpatient care. This includes attempts to assess treatment quality in defined target areas (e.g. standardization and documentation of treatment procedures, treatment of "new" chronically mentally ill, minimization of coercive measures, satisfaction of patients, relatives and staff, and the economic and administrative quality) (Schneider et al. 2001). However, instruments for implementing this concept, and the empirical data, are currently lacking.

Three hospitals located in three federal states have started an attempt to realize this concept with regard to coercive measures and developed a collaborative model for quality management of coercive treatment measures (Ketelsen et al. 2000). This consists of a so-called 'event-related' standardized documentation system (Fähndrich 2000). The data (e.g. considerable differences in the number of ordered restraint measures) are discussed on a regular basis, not only in each hospital individually, but also in a joint working group.

Quality assurance professional workgroups
In recent years, there has been some interest in peer review groups (German: Qualitätszirkel, quality circles) mostly – but not on a national, systematic basis – established for critical analysis of professional practice in outpatient care (Härter & Berger 1997). The groups discuss issues of clinical care using a variety of approaches such as case reports and case discussion, clinical guidelines and management of problem situations using best evidence.
As concerns coercive treatment measures in psychiatric hospitals there is only one initiative at state level. In Baden-Württemberg, several hospitals participate in a project of standardized documentation of these measures. Results are discussed in quality circles established for this group of hospitals (Steinert et al. 2001, Kuster et al. 2002). New research initiatives plan to implement documentation and quality assurance measures concerning coercive measures in all hospitals in two Federal States (Kallert & Steinert 2003).

Statements of the national conference of the senior consultants of psychiatric hospitals (Verlautbarungen der Bundesdirektorenkonferenz psychiatrischer Krankenhäuser)
In 2000, the national workgroup of the senior consultants of the psychiatric departments integrated in somatic hospitals published a paper outlining the perspectives of inpatient psychiatric treatment (Bauer 2000). One of their arguments for integrating psychiatry within the other medical disciplines was the specific treatment of psychiatric crisis or emergency situations. Because of the increasing number of intoxications, delirious states, acute psychoses due to somatic illnesses, and suicide attempts which require in many cases coercive treatment measures also from the somatic point of view, provision of these care approaches should happen in psychiatric departments integrated in somatic hospitals. This would also be in line with general recommendations to provide community-oriented services and decrease stigma.

## 5.5 Reports

### 5.5.1 Reports Elaborated by National Organs on the Topic

The Rodewisch Theses
An international symposium on psychiatric rehabilitation in 1963 can be viewed as the first initiative to formulate principles and quality standards of humane mental health care in the former GDR (Renker 1965). The assembly of psychia-

trists established ten theses and addressed the health ministries of the socialist countries with these. Thesis 8 covers coercive treatment and requires the states

> *"to restrict administrative and legally defined coercive measures administered towards mentally ill persons to the absolute minimum needed.... Existing laws and decrees should be adapted to this guideline, and revisions of respective laws and decrees have to take this into consideration."*

Reviewing the realization of the Rodewisch Theses Waldmann (1998) states that in 1968 a progressive law for compulsory admissions was established in GDR. For the first six weeks, the decisions related to a hospital stay were in the range of physicians'/psychiatrists' responsibilities, though they had to inform the prosecutor about this. A court's decision had to be established only for a longer period of compulsory stays. The rates of patients treated under the regulations of this law were relatively low.

Enquete-committee appointed by the Federal Government (Enquetekommission)

In 1975, the Enquete-committee, an expert group appointed by the Federal Government, published its comprehensive final report on the current situation of psychiatry in the Federal Republic of Germany (Deutscher Bundestag, Drucksache 7/4200). This report covered in detail all fields of mental health care, and established recommendations for each sector of mental health care. Concerning the State Mental Health Laws the committee required a reform that should take into consideration: a) emphasis of the care aspects of involuntary admissions/hospital stays, e.g. by including preventive and after-care measures; b) simplification and flexible performance of the legal procedures, e.g. by concentrating competencies; c) reliable regulations to guarantee cooperation of all authorities/bodies involved in the process of involuntary admissions; d) sufficient and continuous information of all professional groups participating in this process by specific training and education measures/courses; e) simplification and harmonization of the respective terminology; f) adequate regulation of costs. In general, the committee stated that the primary and most relevant purpose of involuntary admission/hospital stay should be the protection and provision of help in the interest of the mentally ill person. Because this should apply for a high percentage of the mentally ill, the committee suggested to include the legal regulations of involuntary admission/hospital stay in the reform of the guardianship law, thus establishing a judicial act of civil law. The public law of the Federal States would consequently regulate only the detention of those rather few mentally ill persons for whom the primary reason of detention is to prevent acts of violence against others.

Expert committee appointed by the Federal Government (Expertenkommission der Bundesregierung)

In 1988, an expert committee appointed by the Federal Government reviewed again the state of mental health care in Germany, and gave detailed recommendations for future developments focusing especially on community mental health care. Concerning care in psychiatric hospitals the central recommendation was that inpatient treatment should be provided using a community-oriented approach and integrated in the care provided by other medical disciplines. Each hospital should take the full responsibility for offering all forms of psychiatric care to a geographically and population-based defined sector of ca. 150,000 inhabitants. This responsibility includes admitting all patients from this sector whose involuntary hospital stay is necessary and legally defined according to the state mental health laws (Empfehlungen der Expertenkommission der Bundesregierung zur Reform der Versorgung im psychiatrischen und psychotherapeutisch/psychosomatischen Bereich, 1998, p 281/282, p 293).
In an official statement on the report of this expert committee, the Federal Government (Stellungnahme der Bundesregierung zu dem Bericht "Empfehlungen der Expertenkommission der Bundesregierung zur Reform der Versorgung im psychiatrischen und psychotherapeutisch/psychosomatischen Bereich") in 1990 emphasized the role of psychiatric hospitals – as outlined by the expert committee – for mental health care.

Reports on the situation of psychiatry in the former German Democratic Republic (GDR)
Initiated by the Federal Ministry of Health, a report – published briefly after the reunification – reviewed the status of psychiatry in the former GDR. This document (Bericht zur Lage der Psychiatrie in der ehemaligen DDR 1991) was established by an expert group whose members personally visited or surveyed, using a postal survey instrument, all psychiatric institutions. Concerning the regulations for compulsory admissions, they criticized the six-week-period within which a court's decision had to be established as non-compliant with the German Constitutional Law. The experts' recommendations asked for a revision which would be in line with the established, German state mental health laws defining a period of no more than three days (in Baden-Württemberg – only 24 hours in many other German states, see Salize et al. 2002) for a restriction of freedom that physicians/psychiatrists can decide on.
In each of the new German *Länder*, the State Ministries of Health appointed special independent committees (mostly working in the first half of the 1990s) to assess the political misuse of psychiatry in the former GDR. Concerning the legal framework for compulsory admissions, all five committees concluded that there was no systematic political misuse. However, if there were high-ranking international political events (example: World Youth Games), political authorities tried to advise the hospitals to admit patients who might behave in a socially

disturbing way or to restrict the freedom of already admitted patients with a risk for such behaviour. Realization of these politically motivated orders was the responsibility of the directors of the hospitals and therefore not homogeneous (Abschlußbericht der Kommission zur Untersuchung von Mißbrauch der Psychiatrie im sächsischen Gebiet der ehemaligen DDR 1997, Süß 1998).
In an official statement on the "situation of the mentally ill in Germany" published in 1992 in reply to a parliamentary inquiry initiated by the opposition party after the reunification, the Federal Government did not release any comments on the above-mentioned legal issues – but the inquiry also did not include any questions in this respect (Antwort der Bundesregierung auf die Große Anfrage der Fraktion der SPD "Situation der psychisch Kranken in der Bundesrepublik Deutschland").

Report for the 75th conference of the State Health Ministers
In 2001 to 2002 a working group of experts in mental health care was appointed to the task of reviewing developments in the German mental health care system within the last 25 years and establishing recommendations for future activities in this field. Although the report (Arbeitsgruppe Psychiatrie der obersten Landesgesundheitsbehörden 2003) tries to summarize all major developments in separate chapters dealing with developments within the judicial system, financing mental health services, structural developments of mental health care, provision of mental health care in different residential and non-residential services, and the specific situation of mental health care in the former GDR, there is only a brief paragraph on involuntary admissions/coercive treatment measures within the chapter covering legal aspects. This refers to the commitment under the public law, and only outlines the fact that respective regulations have been consolidated in the State Mental Health Laws.

### 5.5.2 Most Important Reports of International Organizations

The only reports we have been able to locate expressly concerning German psychiatry from one of these organizations are the reports by the European Committee for the Prevention of Torture and Inhuman or Degrading Treatment or Punishment (CPT). No such statements could be found from the UNHCR, the European Commissioner for Human Rights or any other European or worldwide bodies. The "White Paper" by the Committee of Ministers of the Council of Europe (2000) does not mention Germany in particular.

The latest report by the CPT on Germany is dated March 12, 2003 and deals with the Committee's findings during a visit to several forensic psychiatric facilities in December 2000. General psychiatric wards were not visited on this occasion. Nonetheless, the report gives the following recommendations to German "psychiatric establishments" in general:

- That the use of instruments of physical restraint in psychiatric establishments be used only when strictly necessary and for the shortest possible period.
- That a specific register be established in psychiatric establishments for the purpose of recording the use of physical restraint.
- That medical and nursing staff be reminded of their obligation to fill in thoroughly the relevant forms each time resort to physical restraint is made.
- The CPT invites the German authorities to encourage all patients' representatives in Germany to meet patients (and not only those who specifically ask to see them) regularly in their living units, especially when patients are subject to a measure of restraint.

The report stresses that,

*"On account of their vulnerability, the mentally ill and mentally handicapped warrant much attention in order to prevent any form of conduct - or avoid any omission - contrary to their well-being. It follows that the procedure by which involuntary placement is decided should offer guarantees of independence and impartiality, as well as of objective medical expertise. Further, involuntary placement should cease as soon as it is no longer required by the patient's mental state. Consequently, the need for such a placement must be regularly reviewed."*

The report concludes that The Law on the Civil Placement of Persons (*Unterbringungsgesetz-UBG*) of the Land of Baden-Württemberg meets these criteria. The corresponding law for the Land of Saxony has not been reviewed by the Committee and no psychiatric facilities in Saxony were visited on this occasion.

Earlier visits by the European Committee for the Prevention of Torture and Inhuman or Degrading Treatment or Punishment to Germany have been made in 1998, 1996 and 1991. In 1998 and 1996, no psychiatric facilities were visited. In 1991 there were visits to two psychiatric hospitals in Saxony. The corresponding report concludes:

*"At Waldheim Psychiatric Institution, both the living conditions of patients and the treatment provided to them left a great deal to be desired. In consequence the CPT cannot but welcome the official closure of that institution on May 8, 1992.*
*The CPT has made a number of recommendations regarding the situation found in the Hochweitzschen Psychiatric Clinic, in relation to the patients' living conditions, their treatment and their rights. More particularly, it was clear that treatment was still largely governed by a philosophy based on the 'custody' of patients, despite the efforts of staff to adjust to a new professional environment focused on patient rehabilitation. It is evident that any significant progress in this area will depend upon appropriate training, both initial and in-service, and the provision of adequate resources."*

The CPT has brought together "substantive" sections of their reports that are independent of the specific situation in any country in a document titled "The CPT standards". This document gives the essential guideline the CPT uses for their reports:

> *"The Committee hopes in this way to give a clear advance indication to national authorities of its views regarding the manner in which persons deprived of their liberty ought to be treated and, more generally, to stimulate discussion on such matters".*

Section VI of the CPT standards deals with "Involuntary placement in psychiatric establishments".

### 5.5.3 Most Important Reports of Non-Governmental Organizations

No reports of non-governmental organizations (e.g. Amnesty International and Human Rights Watch) in connection with the application of coercive means in German psychiatry could be identified. Searches in the Internet with the corresponding search terms yielded only reports on psychiatry in Nazi-Germany and in the former East Germany (GDR). The Annual Report 2003 of Amnesty International (Covering events from January to December 2002) mentions for Germany e.g. police ill-treatment and alleged ill-treatment in prison, but there is no mention of detention or treatment in psychiatry. Human Rights Watch launched their German-language website on June 12, 2003. No information pertaining to German psychiatry could be found there either. The Human Rights Watch World Report 2003 does not contain a section on Germany.

## 5.6 Safeguard System

Introductory remark: We propose to subdivide safeguard mechanisms in order to clearly differentiate between the level focusing on individual persons or incidents and the level of abstract safeguards which cannot influence or revise any decisions on individual incidents/persons.

### 5.6.1 Safeguard Procedures of the Use of Coercive Measures in Psychiatric Care

The system of legal protection of the individual against measures of involuntary placement or involuntary treatment is reflected in the three-part area of mental health legislation (civil, public administrative or criminal law). Concerning measures of involuntary treatment including the use of coercive measures and the conditions and implementation of a detention, the person demanding legal intervention always has the additional opportunity to apply to the public authority or to the psychiatric institution in order to obtain review without involving a court or tribunal (extra judicial remedies). Decisions on involuntary placement like admission orders or committal sentences, however, require the judicial order of a court or tribunal as stated in Article 104 subsections 2, 3 and 4 of the German Basic Law. Therefore, only further a judicial safeguard is provided, and an internal institutional review on individual demand does not exist.

#### 5.6.1.1 Remedies Before a Court Against Measures Depriving Mentally Disordered Persons of Liberty (Involuntary Placement)

The judicial protection against any measure depriving of liberty is subordinated to the constitutional principle of Article 104 subsections 2, 3 and 4 of the German Basic Law. Therefore, only a judge may decide on the admissibility or continuation of an involuntary placement or detention. Where such placement or commitment is not based on the order of a judge, a judicial decision must be obtained without delay. If the person is provisionally detained on suspicion of having committed a criminal offence, the decision of the judge must follow no later than the following day of apprehension.

a) A person complaining about a court decision on involuntary placement (in principle the person concerned or his or her guardian/tutor) based on civil law (leave of the Guardianship Court pursuant to section 1906.2 of the German Civil Code or leave of the Family Court pursuant to section 1631b of the German Civil Code) may request review of the decision by appeal to that court. Section 70 m subsection 1 of the German Code on Matters of non-contentious Jurisdiction states that an immediate appeal is admissible against decisions which take effect from the date the decision becomes final. The period for filling an appeal is limited to two weeks beginning with the announcement of the decision (section 22 subsection 1 of the German Code on Matters of non-contentious Jurisdiction). If the Court does not grant the redress sought by appeal, the decision of the higher instance ("Appeal Court") must be sought. Furthermore the appellant has the right to file a further appeal from the decision of the Appeal Court to the Higher Regional Court of the Land, when the appeal is limited to points of law (section 27 subsection 1 of the German Code on Matters of non-contentious Jurisdiction).

b) Judicial decisions on confinement (section 10.1 and 10.2 of the Saxon Mental Health Act), preliminary confinement (section 17 of the Saxon Mental Health Act), immediate preliminary confinement (section 18.1 and 18.2 of the Saxon Mental Health Act), immediate preliminary confinement in case of imminent danger (section 18.3 of the Saxon Mental Health Act) and immediate preliminary restraint (section 18.4 of the Saxon Mental Health Act) according to public administrative law are rendered by Guardianship Courts. Section 70 subsection 1 sentence 2 no. 3 of the German Code on Matters of non-contentious Jurisdiction states that these are the competent jurisdictional bodies for decisions on a placement representing a loss of personal freedom pursuant to the legal acts of the States (*Länder*) on the placement of persons with mental disorders. Consequently, the safeguard procedures correspond to the judicial remedies described before (appeal subject to a time limit of two weeks and further appeal when limited to points of law).

c) The commitment of mentally disordered criminal offenders to psychiatric hospitals pursuant to section 63 of the German Penal Code and the commitment of criminal offenders who have a proclivity to consume alcohol or other intoxicants to excess to an institution for withdrawal treatment pursuant to section 64 of the German Penal Code are based on a decision of a penal court (County Court or Regional Court depending on the expected sentence). Therefore, the person concerned has the same rights on appeal against the judgement as delinquents sentenced to imprisonment. The admissible remedy against a sentence of the County Court is the appeal on questions of fact and law to the Regional Court, whereas a sentence of the Regional Court can be appealed only on questions and points of law to the Federal Supreme Court.

#### 5.6.1.2 Judicial Review of Measures Regulating the Conditions and the Implementation of a Placement or Detention

Measures and conditions for implementing involuntary placement or detention in psychiatric institutions mainly concern the application of medical and other therapeutic treatments of mentally disordered or ill persons particularly in form of involuntary treatment, preventive measures of protection against imminent danger of serious harm to the mentally disordered or ill person or to other persons or legally protected important interests of others and the use of coercive measures in order to enforce such measures.

a) In civil matters the Guardianship Court approves and authorizes the application of certain medical measures to persons under guardianship (section 1904 of the German Civil Code) or measures to restrain personal freedom without detention (section 1906.4 and 1906.5 of the German Civil Code). The person concerned or the guardian/tutor has the right of appeal from the decisions on those matters to the Guardianship Court in order to request review. Section 70 m subsection 1 of the German Code on Matters of non-contentious Jurisdiction provides an immediate appeal within two weeks after the announcement of the decision for those cases (section 22 subsection 1 of the German Code on Matters of non-contentious Jurisdiction). If the court does not grant the redress sought by appeal, the decision of the higher instance ("Appeal Court") must be sought. According to the right of further appeal against adjudications on measures depriving of liberty rendered by the Appeal Court, the applicant may also file a further appeal limited to points of law to the Higher Regional Court of the Land (section 27 subsection 1 of the German Code on Matters of non-contentious Jurisdiction).

b) Concerning administrative law, the ordering and the application of involuntary treatment and preventive measures of protection against imminent danger of serious harm and the use of coercive measures to enforce the implementation of those acts can be judicially reviewed by recourse to the Guardianship Court. Pursuant to section 70 l subsection 1 of the German Code on Matters of non-contentious Jurisdiction, the person concerned has the right of motion for a court decision consisting of a review of facts and points of law in so far as individual rights have been infringed. Additionally, the right of motion may comprise the demand for the court to obligate the psychiatric institution to take measures in favour of the person concerned. If the person concerned is already detained before a court decision on a placement or detention has been rendered, he or she has the same rights of motion for a court decision on review of the measures mentioned above as a person detained on the basis of a court decision (section 18.8 of the Saxon Mental Health Act). All court decisions on those matters are non-appealable (section 70 l subsection 4 of the German Code on Matters of non-contentious Jurisdiction).

c) In criminal law, mentally disordered offenders committed to psychiatric hospitals pursuant to section 63 of the German Penal Code or to an institution for withdrawal treatment pursuant to section 64 of the German Penal Code have the right of motion for a court decision on review of measures concerning the conditions and the execution of sentences before the penal court (Division for Penal Execution of the Regional Court) pursuant to section 109 of the German Code on Execution of Sentences involving imprisonment or preventive measures of rehabilitation and security[20] in so far as their individual rights have been infringed. The motion is only admissible within a period of two weeks after the decision had been announced (section 112 of the German Code on Execution of Sentences involving imprisonment or preventive measures of rehabilitation and security). Besides the right of review, the motion may also comprise the demand for the court to obligate the correctional psychiatric institution to take measures in favour of the person concerned if the institution has not acted for a period of three months despite of the request of the person concerned (section 113 of the German Code on Execution of Sentences involving imprisonment or preventive measures of rehabilitation and security). The decisions of the Regional Court are

[20] Gesetz über den Vollzug der Freiheitsstrafe und der freiheitsentziehenden Maßregeln der Besserung und Sicherung of March 16, 1976 (Strafvollzugsgesetz - StVollzG) entered into force on January 1, 1977 (Law Gazette BGBl. 1976, p. 581).

appealable within a period of one month to the Higher Regional Court only on questions and points of law if a review is necessary for further legal education or to ensure the uniformity of jurisprudence (section 116 of the German Code on Execution of Sentences involving imprisonment or preventive measures of rehabilitation and security).

### 5.6.2 Authorities for Carrying Out the Task of Abstract (Not Individual) Review and Assessment on the Adequacy and Legality of the Coercive Measures Employed

#### 5.6.2.1 Parliamentary System

Parliamentary commissions

Within the last three decades the German parliament or the Federal Ministry of Health, respectively, have appointed three commissions and assigned to these the task of reviewing the mental health care system in general. The relevant results concerning involuntary admissions to psychiatric hospitals and coercive measures are quoted in section 5.5.1 of this report.

Parliamentary petition authorities

The Federal Parliament as well as each of the State Parliaments has established authorities to which each citizen can appeal if citizen's or human rights are endangered or infringed.

#### 5.6.2.2 Administrative Authority

Inspection teams

As stated above, mental health legislation in Germany is mostly in the competence of the states (Länder). Within this legal framework, the establishment of specific arrangements for "external" inspection can be defined. For instance, the Saxon mental health law (paragraph 3 Sächsisches Psychisch Kranken Gesetz) requires the Ministry of Social Affairs to organize regular and unannounced inspection visits to all psychiatric hospitals, non-hospital residential care institutions, old-age residential homes for people with mental illness and protected rehabilitation workshops for the severely mentally ill. Such visits should be performed on an annual basis. One of their tasks is the assessment of the standard of care and documentation of all coercive measures in order to protect patients' rights.

The inspection teams are composed of a mental health professional, a non-medical professional (usually a lawyer or other legal professional) and a service user. In the states of Lower Saxony and Saxony-Anhalt, reports of inspection teams are made directly to the state parliament. This aims to introduce an element of direct legislative control of residential mental health care institutions. These rules apply to both hospital and non-hospital services. In the past, quality assurance in homes for people with severe mental illness has been considered to be deficient (Bundesministerium für Gesundheit 1998, Kunze 1981, von Cranach 2000). At present, some state mental health laws are in the process of revision, and one focus of the changes introduced is increased service user participation in the inspection and review process (e.g. in Schleswig-Holstein). Public accessibility of the inspection reports is limited (e.g. Sächsischer Landtag 1999 and 2002), and the issues are not generally widely discussed. There is no professional mental health forum which discusses these findings on a regular basis and in a systematic manner, and there is no evidence for the effectiveness of these inspections.

Patients' ombudsmen (Patientenfürsprecher)
Another arrangement for „external" inspection is the appointment of patients' ombudsmen as defined e.g. in the Saxon mental health law (paragraph 4 Sächsisches Psychisch Kranken Gesetz). Responsibility for this appointment is in the hands of the public health office for the area in which the psychiatric hospital is located. Regularly, patients' ombudsmen announce fixed hours of their presence in the hospital during which they can be addressed by the patients and try to take care of their needs and complaints. These persons have the right to visit all parts of the hospital and to directly talk with all patients. If they notice serious problems in the quality of care, they inform the director and carrier of the service and also the inspection team.

### 5.6.3 Internal Safeguard Procedures for the Correction of the Coercive Means Used

There are several widely established internal procedures in psychiatric hospitals. However, these are neither standardized nor subject to continuous quality assurance.
There is no uniform clinical safeguard system established in German psychiatric hospitals for ordering, supervising or administering coercive measures. However, there are established, uniform hierarchies which assign clinical responsibility. The most important elements within this organization are: 1. Each medical measure – including coercive ones – administered by the nursing staff has to be ordered (normally in writing) by the physician responsible for treatment of patients in the ward he is assigned to (normally a resident in psychiatry or a board-certified psychiatrist). Note: Clinical psychologists are not allowed to order these measures. Although nurses are allowed to conduct these measures according to need, in the case of any untoward events, the physician might be forced to review that he has sufficiently supervised the practise of administering the measures or agreed to delegate these tasks to the nurses after having trained them properly. 2. The head physician of the ward/hospital has to take the final

responsibility for the standard of the clinical work of his subordinates. Therefore, in routine clinical practice, each coercive measure (if possible, before administering it) is *at least* discussed with the head physician (or, often, the order legitimized by a second signature from the head physician). In most cases, this leads to a (brief) personal clinical examination of the patient concerned by the head physician. The rationale for this procedure is to guarantee (for the patient) that clinical decisions in administering or ending coercive measures are based on a clinical expertise at the minimum standard held by board-certified psychiatrists. 3. Many – but not all – of the State Mental Health Laws require this standard of clinical expertise also for decisions in the community setting aimed at bringing the patient involuntarily to the hospital. 4. The problem that night shifts in psychiatric hospitals are mostly performed by residents in psychiatry does not affect above-mentioned rules because patients can be detained for a period defined in the state laws within which the patient must be clinically examined and a report on the results of this examination be sent to the municipal authority and to the court if the hospital decides to ask for further detention of the patients. This definition enables the performance of secondary examinations involving a board-certified psychiatrist. At weekends however, personal clinical examinations performed with the standard of board-certified specialist knowledge are sometimes not conducted if the case/clinical decisions are only discussed on the phone with the senior or head physician on duty.

Another internal safeguard procedure could be the use of a standardized documentation system: 87% of all German psychiatric hospitals use a special sheet for documentation of fixation/ isolation; these sheets (ca. 50 different versions could be identified) are self-designed and do not have common items/standards. 83% of the psychiatric hospitals have established a guideline for their staff concerning administering of fixation/isolation. There is also no standard for these site-specific clinical guidelines (Steinert 1998).

## 5.7 Other Information

### 5.7.1 Information Material on Patient Rights

Most recently, two Federal Ministries published a document focusing on patients' rights in Germany which should serve as a guideline for patients and physicians (Patientenrechte in Deutschland. Leitfaden für Patienten und Ärzte, 2003). Although a broad range of national health institutions was involved in establishing this document, which aims to reinforce the autonomy of the patient (e.g. in establishing informed consent, in respecting his privacy, in establishing advanced directives, in reading his clinical records etc.) none of the national psychiatric institutions participated in this work and none of the infringements of patients' rights connected with coercive treatment in psychiatry is covered in this brochure.

### 5.7.2 Monitoring of the Mental Health Acts

In Germany, there is no official body in the Federal States assigned to this task. Nor is this task assigned to a defined non-political institution at the national or Federal State level. However, Federal States have defined periods (of several years) after which revisions of laws have to pass the regular procedure of legislation. Therefore, some mental health acts have recently been or soon will be revised in German Federal States (e.g. Saxony, Schleswig-Holstein).

## 5.8 Charts

The two following charts illustrate the timeline and different stages of the most important and frequently used procedures concerning detention/involuntary admission to a psychiatric hospital according to the Saxon mental health act (i.e. *one* of the acts in force in the German Federal States). Included in these charts is the information on the different parties/legal instances involved in these procedures and the given definitions according to which they are obliged to behave.

## Diagram 5.1: Regular Judicial Procedure Concerning Involuntary Placement of a Mentally Ill Person* According to the Saxon Mental Health Act

**General instruction:**
Legal information and written information of the patient (§ 9 Saxon Mental Health Act)

***Pre-condition (§ 10 Saxon Mental Health Act):***

1. mental disorder
2. significant and current threat to the patients' life or health

OR

3. significant and current threat for important legally protected interests of others
4. threat can not be prevented otherwise

within the preliminary/preparatory procedure (§ 13 Saxon Mental Health Act) the local public health office acts according to its officially defined tasks

⇩

Expert report written by a Public-Health specialist[+] (involving a board-certified psychiatrist or a physician experienced in psychiatry)

⇩

personal hearing/examination of the patient

⇩

Decision

⇩

local public health office officially applies to the court for involuntary placement[++]

⇩

Execution of involuntary placement is the responsibility of the local public health office which can involve the police (§ 14 Saxon Mental Health Act)

under 3 (working-days)

legally defined duration of involuntary placement

* At any time during the procedure the patient can apply for a decision of the court against any of the measures

[+] Administrative authority (i.e. local public health office) should be contacted, relatives should asked, legally appointed guardian (responsible for the place of residence and mental health care) has to be informed

[++] If there is no legally defined guardian appointed, the court also decides if and which kind of treatment can be conducted without special approval of the court (§ 16 Saxonian Mental Health Act)

## Diagram 5.2: Immediate Preliminary Confinement or Restraint[1] (Section 18 of the Saxon Mental Health Act)

Court can not take its decision within a period sufficient to prevent the imminent danger

⇨ administrative authority (i.e. local public health office) orders the immediate preliminary confinement and its execution.

⇩

Informs the court at the latest by 10.00 a.m. of the day that follows the start of the restraint

⇩

Patient has to be clinically examined immediately*,**: are the required pre-conditions for involuntary placement fulfilled?

+ Involuntary detention in hospital

− Release from hospital → immediate notification of the court and the administrative authority
OR
Remain in hospital because of a legally relevant informed consent

⇩

Court can not take its decision within a period sufficient to prevent the concrete and immediate danger

OR

patient refuses hospital care contrary to the decision of the court.

⇨ Police is authorized to bring the patient to the hospital without an order of the administrative authority; if possible a medical doctor should first be involved.

⇩

Patient has to be clinically examined immediately*,**: are the required pre-conditions for involuntary placement fulfilled?

↓

Caring admission or placement to the hospital without consent of the person concerned.

⇩

Court can not take its decision within a period sufficient to prevent the imminent danger

AND

patient stays in a hospital, but is not involuntarily admitted as defined by this mental health act

AND

administrative authority can not take its decision within an adequate time-span to prevent the danger*,**

↓

Patient can be preliminarily confined in the hospital without his consent

⇩

Release from hospital if no court decision has been rendered until the end of the day that follows the start of restraint. The court, the administrative authority and with regard to minors and to persons under guardianship the legal representative (responsible for the tasks of defining residence or taking care of the health of the patient) have to be informed immediately about the release.

[1] in reference to any measures during the process of carrying out the detention, the patient can apply to the court in advance of the court's order to confine the patient

* In these cases the hospital has to submit an expert's report (whether involuntary placement is necessary from a medical point of view or if other less burdening measures are sufficient, whether and which treatments without the consent of the patient are necessary, whether the patient is in a state to express his will, whether there are significant disadvantages for his health or an endangerment of other persons if the patient is personally examined by the court) to the court and to the administrative authority at the latest by 10 a.m. of the day that follows the start of the involuntary hospital stay of the patient.

** The patient has to be provided with the opportunity to inform relatives or a person whom he trusts. These persons shall be heard according to the patient's demand if the purpose of a placement can be served and the proceedings are not disturbed in a non-proportional manner.

## References

Aktion Psychisch Kranke e.V., Deutsche Krankenhausgesellschaft, and Spitzenverbände der Krankenkassen (eds) (1998) Bundesweite Erhebung zur Evaluation der Psychiatrie-Peronalverordnung. Schriftenreihe des Bundesministeriums für Gesundheit, Band 99, Nomos Verlagsgesellschaft, Baden-Baden

Arbeitsgruppe Psychiatrie der obersten Landesgesundheitsbehörden (2003) Bestandsaufnahme zu den Entwicklungen der Psychiatrie in den letzten 25 Jahren. Der 76. Gesundheitsministerkonferenz vorgelegt

Bauer, M. (2000) Perspektiven der Krankenhauspsychiatrie. Positionspapier. Psychiatrische Praxis, 27(2) Beilage

Bundesminister für Jugend, Familie, Frauen und Gesundheit (eds) (1998) Empfehlungen der Expertenkommission der Bundesregierung zur Reform der Versorgung im psychiatrischen und psychotherapeutisch/psychosomatischen Bereich auf der Grundlage des Modellprogramms Psychiatrie der Bundesregierung. Bonn

Bundesministerium für Gesundheit (eds) (1996) Leben im Heim. Angebotsstrukturen und Chancen selbstständiger Lebensführung in Wohneinrichtungen für Behindertenhilfe. Schriftenreihe des Bundesministeriums für Gesundheit, Band 102, Nomos Verlagsgesellschaft, Baden-Baden

Bundesministerium für Gesundheit (eds) (1996) Leitfaden zur Qualitätsbeurteilung in psychiatrischen Kliniken. Projekt 1994 – 1996. Schriftenreihe des Bundesministeriums für Gesundheit, Band 74, Nomos Verlagsgesellschaft, Baden-Baden

Bundesministerium für Gesundheit (1991) Zur Lage der Psychiatrie in der ehemaligen DDR – Bestandsaufnahme und Empfehlungen -. Gutachten

Bundesministerium für Gesundheit und Soziale Sicherung/Bundesministerium der Justiz (Eds.) (2003). Patientenrechte in Deutschland. Leitfaden für Patienten und Ärzte

Committee of Ministers of the Council of Europe (2000) “White Paper” on the protection of the human rights and dignity of people suffering from mental disorder, especially those placed as involuntary patients in a psychiatric establishment

Council of Europe - Committee for the Prevention of Torture and Inhuman or Degrading Treatment or Punishment (2003) Report to the German Government on the visit to Germany carried out by the European Committee for the Prevention of Torture and Inhuman or Degrading Treatment or Punishment (CPT) from 3 to 15 December 2000; Strasbourg

Council of Europe - Committee for the Prevention of Torture and Inhuman or Degrading Treatment or Punishment (1999) Report to the German Government on the visit to Frankfurt am Main Airport carried out by the European Committee for the Prevention of Torture and Inhuman or Degrading Treatment or Punishment (CPT) from 25 to 27 May 1998; Strasbourg

Council of Europe - Committee for the Prevention of Torture and Inhuman or Degrading Treatment or Punishment (1997) Report to the German Government on the visit to Germany carried out by the European Committee for the Prevention of Torture and Inhuman or Degrading Treatment or Punishment (CPT) from 14 to 26 April 1996; Strasbourg

Council of Europe - Committee for the Prevention of Torture and Inhuman or Degrading Treatment or Punishment (1993) Report to the Government of the Federal Republic of Germany on the visit to Germany carried out by the European Committee for the Prevention of Torture and Inhuman or Degrading Treatment or Punishment (CPT) from 8 to 20 December 1991; Strasbourg

Council of Europe - Committee for the Prevention of Torture and Inhuman or Degrading Treatment or Punishment (2002) The CPT standards - "Substantive" sections of the CPT's General Reports; Strasbourg

Deutsche Gesellschaft für Psychiatrie, Psychotherapie und Nervenheilkunde. Leitlinien „Psychosoziale Therapien“. Steinkopff, Darmstadt, in preparation

Deutscher Bundestag, Drucksache 11/8494 (1990) Stellungnahme der Bundesregierung zu dem Bericht “Empfehlungen der Expertenkommission der Bundesregierung zur Reform der Versorgung im psychiatrischen und psychotherapeutisch/psychosomatischen Bereich“

Deutscher Bundestag, Drucksache 12/4016 (1992) Antwort der Bundesregierung auf die Große Anfrage der Fraktion der SPD "Situation der psychisch Kranken in der Bundesrepublik Deutschland"

Deutscher Bundestag, Drucksache 7/4200 (1975) Bericht über die Lage der Psychiatrie in der Bundesrepublik Deutschland – Zur psychiatrischen und psychotherapeutisch/psychosomatischen Versorgung der Bevölkerung -. Verlag Dr. Heger, Bonn-Bad Godesberg

Fähndrich E (2000) Erfahrungen mit der Basisdokumentation im klinischen Bereich. Psycho 26: 381-385

Gebhardt RP, Steinert T (1998) Innere Struktur der stationären psychiatrischen Krankenhausversorgung 22 Jahre nach der Psychiatrie-Enquete. Nervenarzt 69: 791-798

Härter M, Berger M (1997) Qualitätszirkel – eine Maßnahme der Qualitätssicherung in der ambulanten psychiatrisch-psychotherapeutischen Versorgung. In: Berger M, Gaebel W (eds) Qualitätssicherung in der Psychiatrie. Springer-Verlag, Berlin, p 89-98

Jannsen B, Burgmann C, Habel U (2000) Externe Qualitätssicherung der stationären Behandlung schizophrener Patienten. Nervenarzt 71: 364-372

Kallert T, Steinert T (2003) Erfassung und Reduktion von Zwangsmaßnahmen in psychiatrischen Krankenhäusern in Sachsen und Baden-Württemberg. Research proposal submitted to the German Research Foundation

Kebbel J, Pörksen N, Aktion Psychisch Kranke (eds) (1998) Gewalt und Zwang in der stationären Psychiatrie. Tagungsberichte, Band 25, Köln: Rheinland-Verlag

Ketelsen R, Zechert C, Klimitz H, Rauwald C (2000) Entwicklung eines Kooperationsmodells zwischen drei psychiatrischen Kliniken mit dem Ziel der Qualitätssicherung bei Zwangsmaßnahmen am Beispiel der Fixierungsdokumentation. Psychiatrische Praxis 28(2): 69-74

Kunze H, Kaltenbach L (1996) Psychiatrie-Personalverordnung. Textausgabe mit Material und Erläuterungen für die Praxis. Kohlhammer Verlag, Köln

Kunze H (1981) Psychiatrische Übergangseinrichtungen und Heime: Psychisch Kranke und Behinderte im Abseits der Psychiatrie-Reform. Enke, Stuttgart

Kuster W, Schwink A, Steinert T (2002) Vergleichende Erfassung heterogener Datenstrukturen am Beispiel der Dokumentation von Zwangsmaßnahmen in psychiatrischen Kliniken. Nervenarzt 73: 188

Renker K (1965) Rodewischer Thesen. Die Rehabilitation psychisch akut und chronisch Kranker. Z ges Hyg 11: 61-65

Mitscherlich A, Mielke F (1989) Medizin ohne Menschlichkeit. Dokumente des Nürnberger Ärzteprozesses, Frankfurt a.M.

Sächsischer Landtag, 2. Wahlperiode (1999) Zusammenfassender Bericht des Sächsischen Staatsministeriums für Soziales, Gesundheit und Familie über die Ergebnisse der Arbeit der Besuchskommissionen nach paragraph 3 Abs. 2 des Sächsischen Gesetzes über die Hilfen und die Unterbringung bei psychischen Krankheiten vom 16. Juni 1994. Drucksache 2/11246

Sächsischer Landtag, 3. Wahlperiode (2002) Zusammenfassender Bericht des Sächsischen Staatsministeriums für Soziales, Gesundheit, Jugend und Familie über die Ergebnisse der Arbeit der Besuchskommissionen nach paragraph 3 Abs. 2 des Sächsischen Gesetzes über die Hilfen und die Unterbringung bei psychischen Krankheiten vom 16. Juni 1994. Drucksache 3/5789

Sächsisches Staatsministerium für Soziales, Gesundheit und Familie (eds) (1997) Abschlußbericht der Kommission zur Untersuchung von Mißbrauch der Psychiatrie im sächsischen Gebiet der ehemaligen DDR

Salize HJ, Dressing H, Peitz M (2002) Compulsory admission and involuntary treatment of mentally ill patients – legislation and practice in EU-member states. Final report of the research project. Mannheim

Schilter T (1999) Unmenschliches Ermessen. Die nationalsozialistische „Euthanasie"-Tötungsanstalt Pirna-Sonnenstein 1940/41. Gustav Kiepenheuer Verlag, Leipzig

Schmidt G (1983) Selektion in der Heilanstalt 1939-45, Frankfurt a.M.

Smolka M, Klimitz H, Scheuring B, Fähndrich E (1997) Zwangsmaßnahmen in der Psychiatrie aus der Sicht der Patienten. Nervenarzt 68: 888-895

Schneider F, Stieglitz RD, Gaebel W (2001) Qualitätssicherung in der stationären psychiatrischen Behandlung. Psycho 27: 207-210

Steinert T, Brenner R, Deifel G, Gebhardt RP, Koch K, Kohler T, Onnen V, Schmidt-Michel PO, Süss C, Vollmer E (1998) Zwangsmaßnahmen im psychiatrischen Krankenhaus: Ein Aspekt der Qualitätssicherung. Spektrum der Psychiatrie, Psychotherapie und Nervenheilkunde 27: 35-39

Steinert T, Kuster W, Hager H, Spaemann C, Fox S, Bohnet U, Pape M, Hess I (2001) Häufigkeit und Dauer von Zwangsmaßnahmen in psychiatrischen Krankenhäusern und Abteilungen. Nervenheilkunde 20: Suppl. 3, 154-155

Steinert T (1998) Chancen und Risiken der Anwendung von Dokumentationsmethoden zur Anwendung von Zwangsmaßnahmen. In: Kebbel, J, Pörksen N, Aktion Psychisch Kranke (eds) Gewalt und Zwang in der stationären Psychiatrie. Tagungsberichte, Band 25. Rheinland-Verlag, Köln, p 135-140

Süß S (1998) Politisch missbraucht? Psychiatrie und Staatssicherheit in der DDR. Ch. Links Verlag, Berlin

von Oefele K (2002) Die Entwicklung des Betreuungsrechts aus psychiatrischer Sicht. Gesundheitswesen 64: 272-277

von Cranach M (2000) Housing for psychiatric patients inside and outside of hospitals. Psychiatrische Praxis 27 (Sonderheft 2): S59-S63

Waldmann KD (1998) Die Realisierung der Rodewischer Thesen zu DDR-Zeiten – Versuch einer Analyse aus heutiger Sicht. Psychiatrische Praxis 25: 200-203

Wolfersdorf M, Stieglitz RD, Metzger R (1997) Qualitätssicherung der stationären Depressionsbehandlung. Psychiatrische Praxis 24: 120-128

**CHAPTER 6**

# Legal Report – Greece

Giorgos TRIANTAPHYLLOU

## 6.1 Preliminary Remarks

Until 1992, the involuntary hospitalization of people with mental disorders in Greece was regulated by Legislative Decree 104/73 and other relevant Ministerial Decrees. A patient could be involuntarily hospitalized following an application by a close relative or by the public prosecutor, if two psychiatrists certified that hospitalization could improve or help avoid the deterioration of her or his health. The public prosecutor then countersigned their decision. In emergency cases, if patients were considered a danger to public order, or to the safety of themselves or others, any party including the police could apply for their involuntary hospitalization. If the person in question then refused to be assessed, he could be transferred to a psychiatric hospital through the issue of a simple certificate from the police or the mayor, even without professional medical opinion. The adoption, in 1983, by the Committee of Ministers of the Council of Europe of a recommendation to member States *(Recommendation No R (83)2)* on the legal protection of persons suffering from a mental disorder placed as involuntary patients, prompted change in legislation.

Currently, mental health in Greece is regulated by the sixth section of Act 2071/92, a General Health Act entitled "Modernization and Organization of the Health System", which has brought Greek legislation in line with the aforementioned recommendation. The law is valid throughout all Greek territories and because Greece is a unitary state there is no other regional or community legislation.

The new legislative regulations set specific criteria and preconditions for involuntary hospitalization and establish a specific procedure involving the court system in order to safeguard the patients' personal rights and respect their personal freedom.

Involuntary admission can only be requested after all other available options have been considered. The procedure imposes a serious responsibility upon the caregivers, who sometimes are unwilling to accept this responsibility, fearing that the patient will later resent them for this course of action. Clinical experience unfortunately proves that in some cases this holds true. If the patient willingly accepts medication and remains in care for few days, it is common practice not to proceed with involuntary admission (Christodoulou et al. 2002).

### 6.1.1 Definition of Terms in the Greek Law

> *"Voluntary hospitalization is the patient's admission and stay for treatment in a proper Mental Health Unit with his/she/her consent. The patient must be capable of making decisions which affect his health and the Head Doctor must agree that this treatment is necessary" (article 94 of Act 2071/92).*
> *"Involuntary hospitalization is the patient's admission and stay for treatment in a proper Mental Health Unit without his/she/her consent. Involuntary hospitalization is distinct from the patient being placed under "guard" according to the Penal Code" (article 95 of Act 2071/92)."*

There is no definition of involuntary treatment or coercive measures in Greek law.
There are two levels of dispensation of justice in the Greek Court system. The first level includes *Monomeles Protodikeio* (One Member First Court) and *Polymeles Prododikeio* (Many Member First Court) which are district courts with separate competence. The second level includes *Efeteio* (Court of Appeal) which is a regional court hearing appeals against the sentences of the first level courts of its region. The *Eisaggeleas Protodikon* (District Attorney) is the public prosecutor competent for involuntary hospitalization. The *Eisaggeleas of Areios Pagos* (Attorney of the Supreme Court of Justice or General Attorney) supervises the work of public prosecutors in their implementation of the law.

### 6.1.2 Survey Methodology

For the data gathering of this report, a literature search has been done on the Web in the Greek legal database NOMOS, the Greek legal database of the Bar of Athens, the CPT database, the Greek Parliament's site, the National Printing House's site, the National Commission's for Human Rights site, the Ombudsman's site, Amnesty's International site and other related sites. Searching has been also done in the indexes of several printed Greek legal and psychiatric journals, available only in printed form.
This searching covered a period of eleven years, from 1992 when the Act 2071/92 was put in effect till today. Search terms varied depending on the special requirements for the specific literature database.

## 6.2 Applicable Laws and General Norms

### 6.2.1 Constitutional Norms

#### 6.2.1.1 General Norms

Several articles of the Constitution of Greece[1] apply to cases of involuntary hospitalization, involuntary treatment and coercive measures.

---

[1] The Greek Parliament, Resolution of April 6, 2001, Official Gazette 85 A, 2001

*"All persons shall have the right to freely develop their personality and to participate in the social, economic and political life of the Country, insofar as they do not infringe upon the rights of others or violate the Constitution or moral values. All persons living within the Greek Territory enjoy the full protection of their life, honour and freedom. Personal liberty is inviolable. No one shall be prosecuted, arrested, imprisoned or otherwise confined, except when and as the law provides. All persons are entitled to the protection of their health. Individual administrative measures restricting free movement and residency throughout the Country, and of the free entrance and exit therein of every Greek person shall be prohibited. Coercive measures of such content may be imposed only as an additional penalty following a criminal court ruling, in exceptional cases of emergency and only in order to prevent the perpetration of criminal acts, as specified by the law"* (paragraphs 1,2,3 and 4 of article 5 of the Constitution).

*"Torture, any bodily maltreatment, impairment of health, or the use of psychological violence as well as any other offence against human dignity are prohibited and to be punished, as provided by law"* (paragraph 2 of article 7 of the Constitution).

*"The State shall care for the health of citizens" and „persons suffering from an incurable bodily or mental ailments are entitled to the special care of the State"* (paragraphs 3 and 2 of article 21 of the Constitution).

Finally article 25 provides that *"the rights of a person, as an individual and as a member of the society as well as the principle of the constitutional welfare are guaranteed by the State. All state agents shall be obliged to ensure their unhindered and effective exercise. Restrictions of any kind which, according to the Constitution, may be imposed upon these rights, should be provided either directly by the Constitution or by the law, in case a reservation exists in the latter's favour, and should respect the principle of proportionality".*

#### 6.2.1.2 Specific Norms

According to an interpretative clause included in the Constitution under article 5,

*"the prohibition of coercive measures does not preclude the imposition of measures necessary for the protection of public health or the health of sick persons, as specified by the law".*

### 6.2.2 General Laws

Currently, involuntary hospitalization is regulated by the aforementioned Act 2071 / 1992[2] for the modernization of the National Health System which enhances safeguards for patients in the context of involuntary hospitalization, determines a specific procedure and covers hospitalization orders, possibilities of appeal, and reviews of placement.

#### 6.2.2.1 Involuntary Admission

Under this Act, patients can be hospitalized without their consent only if the following conditions are met:

---

[2] Official Gazette 123 A, 1992

> *"the patient must be suffering from a mental disorder; the patient must be incapable of making decisions which affect his/she/her health; failure to hospitalize the patient would cause deterioration in his/she/her state of health"* (paragraph 2. I of Article 95).

In addition, patients can be hospitalized without their consent if

> *"hospitalization of a patient suffering from a mental disorder is necessary for preventing him/her from inflicting bodily harm on him/herself or others"* (paragraph 2. II, Article 95). *"Failing to or the refusal of a person to conform to the social, moral or political values, which seem to prevail within society, is not considered to be a mental disorder by itself"* (paragraph 3, Article 95).

> *"Involuntary hospitalization of the referred patient can be requested by the spouse, a parent, a grandparent, a child, a grandchild, a brother, a sister or any person in charge of the patient, or the guardian in the case the patient is legally incapacitated. Where there are no such persons, and it is additionally an urgent case, hospitalization can be requested ex officio by the Eisaggeleas (public prosecutor) of the district in which the patient is permanently or temporarily residing"* (Article 96).

> *"The application for involuntary hospitalization should be made to the competent public prosecutor of the district where the referred patient has his permanent or temporary residence. The application must be accompanied by medical opinions from two psychiatrists or, if a second psychiatric opinion cannot be obtained, by the opinion of a psychiatrist and of a doctor specialised in a related field, referring to the conditions of paragraph 2 of Article 95 either I or II. The psychiatrists who provide the opinions should not be related to either the applicant or the referred patient"* and *"shall be from a special list drawn up by the local Physicians' Association every two years"* (paragraphs 1,2 and 3, Article 96).

> *"The public prosecutor, ascertaining that the formal preconditions are fulfilled and providing that both medical opinions agree on the need for involuntary hospitalization, orders the patient's transfer to the proper mental health unit within the Mental Health Section of the patient's residence, unless special circumstances force his hospitalization elsewhere. In case medical opinions differ, the public prosecutor may order the patient's transfer and then refer the patient's case to the district court sitting as a bench"* (paragraphs 1,2,3 and 4, Article 96).

The latter is disputed. Legal writers have strongly criticized such a power of the public prosecutor and they have proposed an interpretation of the law that dismisses it (Paraskevopoulos 1993).

> *"Upon admission, the patient must be informed of his/she/her rights, and in particular of his right to appeal, by the hospital director or by another responsible person. A written record must be made of the fact that the patient has been informed of his/she/her rights, which should be signed by the person responsible for informing the patient and by the person escorting the patient"* (paragraph 4, Article 96).

> *"If the procedure is initiated ex officio by a public prosecutor, or if it is mentioned in the application that the patient's examination had been impossible due to his refusal to participate, the public prosecutor is entitled to order the patient's transfer to a public psychiatric ward for evaluation and issue of medical opinions. The patient's transfer must be carried out in a manner, which preserves respect for his/she/her personality and dignity, and his/she/her stay there for conducting the necessary evaluation may not last for more than 48 hours"* (paragraph 5, Article 96).

*"Within three days following the hospitalization order, the public prosecutor must refer the patient's case to the district Polymeles Protodikeio (Many-member First Court), and attend at the same time to the patient's transfer to the court. The court must convene within ten days in a session closed to the public, for the protection of the patient's private life. Notice to appear at the court hearing must be served on the patient 48 hours in advance, and she/he has the right to be represented by a lawyer and by a psychiatrist acting as technical adviser. In the case where the patient is considered dangerous these time periods can be abbreviated"* (paragraph 6, Article 96).

*"In the event that the court decides that the medical opinions differ or they are not persuasive or the scientific director of the hospital, where the patient has been admitted, expresses a contradictory opinion, the court orders the patient's evaluation by another psychiatrist, registered with the country's medical associations, preferably a university professor or a scientific director of a public Mental Health Unit or his deputy"* (paragraph 7, Article 96).

*"The grounds for the court's placement decision must be specifically stated. In case the application is sustained, the patient's admission to the mental health ward is prolonged and in the event that the application is denied, his immediate discharge is ordered"* (paragraph 8, Article 96).

*"A caveat or appeal can be submitted against the court's decision within two months in accordance with the rules of civil procedure. A caveat may be submitted by the scientific director of the Mental Health Unit in which the patient is hospitalized. The appeal must come up for hearing to the Efeteio (Court of Appeal) in a session closed to the public, within 15 days. The Court of Appeal may ask for a new medical opinion or for whatever it finds expedient".* (Article 97).

*"Involuntary hospitalization must end as soon as the preconditions of paragraph 2, Article 95 cease to apply. In this case the scientific director of the psychiatric ward discharges the patient and reports in writing to the competent public prosecutor. Involuntary hospitalization shall not normally exceed six months. After the first three months in hospital, the scientific director of the psychiatric ward and another psychiatrist of the mental health section, must submit a report to the competent public prosecutor on the patient's state of health. The prosecutor may forward the report to the court with a request for extension or termination of hospitalization. The patient or his/she/her relatives mentioned in paragraph 1 of article 96 or his/she/her guardian are entitled to request the termination of the involuntary hospitalization by an application to the public prosecutor. Should the court, to which the public prosecutor immediately submits the application, deny the request, a further request may be submitted after three months. Extension of a patient's hospitalization beyond the six-month limit, due to exceptional circumstances, requires the agreement of a board of three psychiatrists, formed with the patient's treating doctor and two more doctors appointed by the public prosecutor"* (Article 99).

*"In case of recurrence, a patient who has been previously involuntarily hospitalized can be admitted to a psychiatric ward according to article 96 if the preconditions of paragraph 2, Article 94 are fulfilled"* (Article 100).

*"Two psychiatrists, or a psychiatrist and a general practitioner, in the event that a second psychiatrist cannot be found, must affirm the patient's ability to judge on his/she/her health interests, in the event that a patient who is involuntarily hospitalized "requests" his/she/her voluntary hospitalization. The patient appoints the second psychiatrist or the*

*general practitioner and she/he must not be a staff member of the Mental Health Unit in which the patient is hospitalized. A copy of the affirmation is then sent immediately to the public prosecutor who initiated the procedure of involuntary hospitalization"* (paragraph 5, Article 94)

**Remarks**

The new legislation was mostly welcomed, due to the more careful observance of the patient's rights. On the other hand, this procedure is usually not observed in full, leading to hospital staff being accused of neglect.

After the public prosecutor's order, the patient is transferred to the hospital under police escort. The police consider the task of dealing with compulsory admissions and psychiatric patients as erroneous and not as high on their list of priorities. They do not consider themselves to be sufficiently skilled in this area, but their behaviour is usually one of understanding, and reassuring to the patient. Effort is taken to prevent changing an involuntary admission to voluntary. For this, a written report by another independent psychiatrist stating that the patient is able to judge what is best for his/she/her own health is requested. A copy of this report is then sent to the Public Prosecutor (Christodoulou et al. 2002).

### 6.2.2.2 Involuntary Treatment and Coercive Measures

*"Voluntarily hospitalized patients in Mental Health Units may exercise all rights connected to their personal liberty as any patient hospitalized for reasons other than a mental disorder"* (Article 94, Act 2071/92). *"Patients are entitled to refuse or to consent to any diagnostic act or treatment. In the case of a patient with a partial or serious or full term mental disability, his or her right is exercised by a person acting for him or her, according to the law"* (Article 47, Act 2071 / 92).

*"Patients or their representatives, in the case of mentally disabled persons, are entitled to be informed a priori about the dangers due to extraordinary or experimental diagnostic measures or treatment. Implementation of such acts can only take place if patients themselves specifically provide informed consent. Their consent can be freely withdrawn at any time"* (Article 47, Act 2071 / 92). *"Any diagnostic method or treatment, which is not internationally used, is considered to be experimental and an approval from the Supreme Scientific Council of Health is required for its implementation"* (Article 5, Act 2345 / 95[3]).

According to Act 2071 / 92 a Presidential Decree which shall be issued following a proposal by the Minister of Health, after counselling with the Hellenic Medical Association, shall put in effect a Code of Medical Ethics regulating, among others, the relations between health professionals and patients.

*"The conditions of involuntary hospitalization must meet the needs of treatment. The necessary coercive measures must not exclude the necessary means for treatment, e.g. leaves of absence, organized day-outs, stay in supervised places beyond closed establishments. The implementation of these measures will be regulated by a Decree of the Minister of*

3 Official Gazette 213 A, 1995

*Health. In any case the patient's personality shall be respected. Restrictions of the patient's personal liberty must only be dictated by their health condition and by the needs of treatment"* (Article 98, Act 2071 / 92).

**Remarks**

The patient maintains his personal rights and can communicate with relatives or friends, participate in ward activities and is not kept separately from mentally ill patients admitted voluntarily. If his or her condition is well enough, the patient can go on organized day-outs and is allowed to undertake unsupervised home visits. The patient receives the same level of care as informal patients and is treated according to the same rules. The patient maintains the right to communicate with authorities or individuals, and to send and receive mail without censorship. His or her ability to complete financial transactions is not considered impaired but the court can take measures to prevent squandering of the patient's assets (Christodoulou et al. 2002).

### 6.2.2.3 Amendments

The new article 1687 of the Civil Law Code that was put in effect in 1996 (article 13 of Act 2447 / 1996[4]) provides that

> *"when the condition of a person forces his/she/her involuntary hospitalization at a mental health unit, this takes place after a preceding permission from the court and according to the terms of special laws".*

By this Act 2447 / 1996 there was, also, an amendment of the Civil Procedure Code, and its replaced article 740 provides that the involuntary hospitalization of a person is within the competence of the *Monomeles Protodikeio* (One-member First Court). According to the terms of Act 2071 / 1992 an involuntary hospitalization of a person was within the competence of the *Polymeles Protodikeio* (Many-member First Court).

**Remarks**

Act 2071 / 92 is still considered to be the special law in effect but the formulation of article 1687 of the Civil Law Code evokes scepticism on the public prosecutor's involvement and order before any sentence of the court. In practice, studies have revealed that the sentence of the court, which actually "ratifies" the involuntary hospitalization that has already taken place by the public prosecutor's order, can come far too late, beyond any legitimate time period (Georgiadou et al. 2003, Kosmatos 2002).

In the case where a person's confinement is achieved by a public prosecutor's order for assessment, the court may never be involved if there is no need for involuntary hospitalization.

---

4 Official Gazette 278 A, 1996

Deficiencies in practice, referring to the application of the provisions of Act 2071/92 (Georgiadou et al. 2003, Kosmatos 2002), and disadvantages of the procedure, such as its bureaucratic character and the lack of community involvement, lead to proposals for changes. It is suggested that the head doctor of a mental health unit should bear the responsibility for the involuntary admission monitored by on-site visits from a committee of representatives of judicial, health, community and volunteers' organizations (Leivaditis 1994). It is also suggested that the patient should be transferred to the mental health unit only after the relevant decision by the Court or, in emergency cases, only after a temporary order from the Court (Kosmatos 2002).

#### 6.2.2.4 Laws on Mentally Ill Criminals

According to the Penal Code[5], the perpetrator of a crime is not punished at all (Article 34) or a reduced punishment is inflicted on him (Article 36) if, due to disordered cognitive functioning or disordered consciousness, she/he could not have realized at all or she/he could not have clearly realized that his or her action was wrong. The reduced punishment time can be served in special psychiatric departments or branches of prisons, in the event that special care for the perpetrator is needed.

If the crime was a felony or a major misdemeanour and the perpetrator is a danger to the safety of the public, confinement can be of an indefinite time period with a minimum limit. Every two years a council of judges, after an opinion by experts, may decide upon the discharge of the confined. Confinement cannot last more than 15 years beyond the minimum time in case of a felony, or ten years in case of a misdemeanour (Article 39).

When no punishment is inflicted upon the perpetrator and his crime was a felony or a major misdemeanour and she/he is, also, dangerous for the public safety, then the court may order his guarding confinement in a public forensic unit (Article 69). The confinement lasts for as long as public safety is endangered. Every three years the court decides upon the discharge of the confined. The same court can order their discharge at any time upon an application by the public prosecutor or the head doctor (Article 70).

### 6.2.4 International Conventions and Agreements Incorporated Into National Laws

#### 6.2.3.1 Norms of the European Convention on Human Rights

The European Convention of Rome (November 4, 1950) was ratified in Greece by Legislative Decree 53 / 1974[6], and, according to Article 28, paragraph 1 of

---

5 Presidential Decree 283/85, Official Gazette A 106

6 Official Gazette 256 A, 1974

the Constitution is an integral part of the Greek state's legal system and prevails over any other term of law, including several applicable terms on the subject. Article 3 of the convention provides that

> *„no one shall be subjected to torture or to inhuman or degrading treatment or punishment".* According to Article 5 *"everyone has the right to liberty and security of person and no one shall be deprived of their liberty"*

apart from the cases mentioned in the same article, and in accordance with a procedure prescribed by law. Section (e) sets an exception for persons of unsound mind, alcoholics or drug addicts and vagrants and permits their lawful detention.
A provision is also included that

> *"everyone who is deprived of their liberty by arrest or detention shall be entitled to take proceedings by which the lawfulness of his detention shall be decided speedily by a court and their release shall be ordered if the detention is not lawful".*

### 6.2.3.2 Norms of the Council of Europe Convention on Human Rights and Biomedicine

The European Convention of Aviedo (April 4, 1997) was ratified in Greece by Act 2619 / 1998[7], and, according to Article 28 paragraph 1 of the Constitution, is also an integral part of the Greek internal Law and prevails over any other term of law, including several applicable terms on the subject.
According to the general rule included in Article 5,

> *"an intervention in the health field may only be carried out after the person concerned has given free and informed consent to it. This person shall beforehand be given appropriate information as to the purpose and nature of the intervention as well as on its consequences and risks involved. The person concerned may freely withdraw consent at any time".*

Article 6 provides that

> *"an intervention may only be carried out on a person who does not have the capacity to consent for his or her direct benefit. If according to law, an adult does not have the capacity to consent to an intervention because of a mental disability, a disease or for similar reasons, the intervention may only be carried out with the authorization of his or her representative or an authority or a person or body provided for by law. The individual concerned shall as far as possible take part in the authorization procedure. The representative, the authority, the person or the body mentioned in paragraphs 2 and 3 above shall be given, under the same conditions, the information referred to in Article 5. The authorization referred to, above, may be withdrawn at any time in the best interests of the person concerned".*

Furthermore, subject to protective conditions prescribed by law, including supervisory, check and appeal procedures,

---

7 Official Gazette 132 A, 1998

> *"a person who suffers from a mental disorder of serious nature may be subjected, without his or her consent, to an intervention aimed at treating his or her mental disorder only if, without such treatment, serious harm is likely to result for his or her health"* (Article 7).

#### 6.2.3.3 Norms of the International Covenant on Civil and Political Rights

The International Covenant on Civil and Political Rights that was ratified in Greece by Act 2462 / 1997[8], and, according to Article 28 paragraph 1 of the Constitution, is also an integral part of the Greek internal Law and prevails over any other term of law, including several applicable terms on the subject.
According to this

> *"no one shall be subjected to torture or to cruel, inhuman or degrading treatment or punishment. In particular, no one shall be subjected without his or her free consent to medical or scientific experimentation. Everyone has the right to liberty and security of person. No one shall be subjected to arbitrary arrest or detention. No one shall be deprived of his or her liberty except on such grounds and in accordance with such procedure as are established by law. Anyone who is deprived of his or her liberty by arrest or detention shall be entitled to take proceedings before a court, in order that court may decide without delay on the lawfulness of this detention and order his or her release if the detention is not lawful. All persons deprived of their liberty shall be treated with humanity and with respect for the inherent dignity of the human person. No one shall be subjected to arbitrary or unlawful interference with his or her privacy, family, home or correspondence, nor to unlawful attacks on his honour and reputation".*

### 6.2.4 Second Level of Legal Norms

The Special Committee for the Safeguard of the Protection of the Rights of Persons with Mental Disorders issued its 35 / July 14, 2003 document *(unpublished)* containing guidelines on the implementation of coercive measures for all psychiatric patients, which is addressed to the Three Member Committees for the Defence of Citizens' Rights in the Psychiatric Hospitals. The Committee considers it advisable to point out certain basic principles of right practice relating to the restraint and seclusion after having identified a number of cases of infringement of patients' rights. The Committee states that these guidelines are based on common points found within the relevant international literature on the subject, such as the "management of imminent violence" by the Royal College of Psychiatrists, "safeguards in use of restraint and seclusion" by the Bazelon Center for Mental Health Law and others. The guidelines are the following:

1. the only reason for implementing restraint and seclusion is to avoid severe bodily harm to the patient, the personnel or others. Self destructing behaviour rarely requires restraint or seclusion and it is advised that the patient should be constantly monitored to avoid such measures.

---

[8] Official Gazette 25 A, 1997

2. the decision for restraint or seclusion is a temporary measure and it should result from a collaboration and discussion within the therapeutic team. The competent psychiatrist makes the final decision.
3. restraint or seclusion should be a part of a treatment plan which should be decided upon simultaneously.
4. restraint or seclusion should not last long (hours). In the event that it lasts more than twelve hours within 48 hours, it should be supervised independently. In these cases the patient's treatment plan should be revised.
5. it is absolutely necessary that the reasons for detention or its prolonging, are recorded in detail regularly, after an examination of the patient.
6. regular monitoring of the patient should include visits by the personnel or by the competent doctor, also at meal-times. In any case, monitoring and recording should be frequent (e.g. every thirty minutes).
7. the monitoring procedure should respect the dignity of the patient. The necessary sanitary arrangements should be observed (heating, neatness, clothing, food etc).

Finally the Committee feels obliged to wish that practice of restraint or seclusion would be completely abolished.

### 6.3 Jurisprudence

i. Sentences by the competent courts for ratifying the involuntary admission usually reiterate, when grounding their decisions, the required legal preconditions and accept the provided medical opinions as valid. They also tend to use the possibility of a deterioration of the patient's health in addition to the need to prevent him or her from inflicting bodily harm on him-/herself or others, although this is not a necessity according to the law (Kosmatos 2002).

ii. According to sentence 1634 / 2002 of the *Symvoulio tis Epikrateias*[9] (the Supreme Court of Justice for administrative cases) involuntary hospitalization in a mental health unit is an administrative act, legally within the competence of the civil courts, according to paragraph 4 of article 98 of the Constitution. The public prosecutor's order for involuntary hospitalization belongs to the same administrative procedure. The medical opinions, even when given by doctors of a public hospital, are not enforceable acts of an administrative authority and are merely preconditions for the public prosecutor's order.

iii. By Circular 504 / 1996, the *Eisaggeleas of Areios Pagos*[10] (the Attorney of Supreme Court of Justice or General Attorney), in order to dissolve any doubt that the new legislation under Act 2071/92 repealed any previous legislation.

---

9 legal database NOMOS, 324589

10 journal Yperaspisi (Defence) 1996, 698

iv. According to Opinion 12 / 1999 of the *Eisaggeleas of Areios Pagos*[11] (the Attorney of Supreme Court of Justice or General Attorney), the order of the public prosecutor to the police authorities for transferring a person to a mental health unit in which they are to be involuntarily hospitalized, is not an order of arrest but an administrative order aiming to carry out the lawful procedure of involuntary hospitalization.

v. According to Opinion 19 / 1999 of the *Eisaggeleas of Areios Pagos*[12] (the Attorney of Supreme Court of Justice or General Attorney), the medical opinions must be reasoned, which means that they must contain the facts (signs of disorder, possible violent actions, place, time and reason of previous treatment, reasoning for the exclusion of treatment at home, conclusion on the disorder and scientific foundation). The transfer of the patient to the Court must follow the standards of any common transfer of a patient to a hospital for treatment. If the patient's transfer is impossible or if the patient wishes not to attend, then a member or even all the members of the court should visit him at the Mental Health Unit to listen to his views.

vi. According to Report 13218 / 2001, the *Synigoros tou Politi*[13] (Ombudsman), treating the subject of proper information of patients (although not of mental health patients) and their consent to treatment, finds that hospitals should take all the necessary measures in order to secure full and valid information of the patients and authenticity of their consent to treatment.

vii. According to Circular 633 / 2000, the *Eisaggeleas Protodikon*[14] (District Attorney or Public Prosecutor) of Thessaloniki, recommends that public prosecutors should examine the patient's past for establishing evidence of previous violent behaviour. The public prosecutors should request from the police evidence for such behaviour. The actual need for treatment should prevail over the fears associated with a manifest or supposed mental disorder.

### 6.4 Relevant Protocols and Internal Norms

No relevant protocols or internal norms regarding involuntary hospitalization or the application of coercive measures in Greece could be identified.

### 6.5 Reports

#### 6.5.1 Reports of CPT

The Council of Europe – Committee for the Prevention of Torture and Inhuman

---

11 journal Poiniki Dikaiosyni (Penal Justice) 2000, 270

12 legal database NOMOS, 176137

13 journal Poiniki Dikaiosyni (Penal Justice) 2002, 153

14 journal Yperaspisi (Defence) 2000, 630

or Degrading Treatment or Punishment (CPT) published three reports on the conditions of psychiatric care in Greece.

In the 1993 report *(Report to the government of Greece, 1993),* the CPT delegation felt there was a serious risk of isolation being used by the staff as a punishment for what they might regard as patients' misbehaviour. Such an attitude would, of course, be unacceptable.
Regarding instruments of physical restraint, at the institutions visited in Athens and Rafina, the delegation observed that they were frequently used and, furthermore, implemented in a potentially dangerous manner. As was the case for isolation, in no establishment did the delegation find evidence of guidelines issued to staff on the use of instruments of physical restraint, or of any guidance regarding the therapeutic expediency of such a measure. They were applied without medical supervision and without a written record being made. The fact that the decision to use instruments of physical restraint was left to the discretion of untrained nursing staff who were often numerically inadequate in relation to the number of patients in their care, lead the CPT to conclude that there was a serious risk of physical restraint being used in excess of requirements.
The CPT recommended to the Greek authorities that they should take the necessary measures, without delay, to ensure in the following order that:

- the requisite physical improvements are made in all isolation rooms of the Attica State Mental Health Hospital for children, to ensure that isolation from patients is carried out under acceptable material conditions and in conformity with suitable safety standards;
- a detailed medical policy on counteracting recourse to isolation and instruments of physical restraint is laid down, dealing in particular with: the types of cases in which application of these measures is permissible; their purposes; their duration and frequent review; the provision of appropriate human contact, and the staff's duty of increased attention;
- measures of isolation or physical restraint are only applied following the express instruction of a doctor or are immediately brought to the attention of a doctor for approval;
- every instance of use of such measures is recorded in the patient's file and in an appropriate register, with an indication of the times at which the measure began and ended, the circumstances of the case and the reasons for resorting to the measure;
- staff receive suitable training on control techniques (verbal communication techniques, holding techniques, etc.) vis-à-vis with agitated or violent patients.

Finally, the CPT wished to stress that isolation or instruments of physical restraint should never be used as a punishment, or their use prolonged for that purpose. The CPT delegation also ascertained that the provisions relating to involuntary hospitalization were not applied and, in most cases, not even known. The CPT recommended that the Greek authorities take, as a matter of urgency, appropriate measures to ensure that the provisions of the 1992 Act governing involuntary hospitalization of patients and guarantees available to patients – in particular as regards their admission and discharge – are duly applied. The CPT also wished to be informed of the extent to which the 1992 Act would be applied to patients hospitalized before its entry into force and, more generally, whether there is a procedure for review at appropriate intervals of placements lasting longer than six months. Regarding psychiatric patients confined under section 69 of the Penal Code, the delegation was told by doctors that the courts tend automatically to order the patient's continued hospitalization even if a medical opinion certifies that there is no further need for it and that the patient no longer shows symptoms of mental illness or dangerousness.

In the 1996 report *(Report to the government of Greece 1996),* the CPT expressed satisfaction with the positive developments regarding the hospital's nursing staff, but mentioned that further effort was needed particularly as regards qualified staff for therapeutic activities. Accordingly, it recommended that the Greek authorities should take steps to substantially increase the number of such staff. It also wished to know whether the vacant doctor's posts had then been filled. The CPT once again expressed its satisfaction with the progress made since its last visit in relation to some of the patients' living areas. It recommended the Greek authorities to actively pursue the execution of the works planned. In this context, special attention should be paid to providing a differentiated therapeutic and pedagogic environment affording stimulation to patients appropriate to their age and pathology (visual stimuli, personal possessions, entertainment items such as toys or other suitable objects). The CPT reiterated its recommendation that the basic hospital equipment appropriate to the patients' needs be made available without delay. In the light of the foregoing, the CPT recommended that the Greek authorities should intensify their efforts to develop substantially differentiated treatment activities using the full range of therapies (somato-, psycho-, socio- and occupational therapy). The CPT would also like to know whether the hospital authorities had developed a preventive policy against transmissible diseases (e.g. hepatitis). As already indicated, on its previous visit the CPT expressed serious concern about the use of isolation and physical restraint, although the situation had considerably improved since its first visit in 1993.
As for the use of physical restraint, the CPT was satisfied that its delegation no longer found the situation as described in its previous report. The delegation found that physical restraint was confined to exceptional cases. Detailed instruc-

tions were given to the nursing staff by the doctors in respect to each patient. These instructions required the staff in particular to increase surveillance if the patient was agitated and to inform the doctor on duty of the use of physical restraint. In addition, the circumstances and duration of the restraint measure were recorded in the nursing register. The CPT considered that this procedure largely met the recommendations it had made in the previous report. However, it would be desirable to provide in addition for all measures of physical restraint to be recorded in the patient's file and in a specific register established for this purpose, indicating the time of the beginning and end of the measure, the circumstances of the case, the reasons for resorting to the measure and an account of any injuries sustained by patients or members of staff. The CPT recommended that the Greek authorities take appropriate measures to realize this recommendation.

The delegation was informed that the doctors and the Administrative Board of a certain Hospital had sought several times, but in vain, to have several patients, no longer in need of hospital psychiatric treatment or whose period of observation had been completed, admitted to other appropriate institutions. The CPT recommended that the Greek authorities take appropriate measures to ensure that patients do not stay longer than their state of mental health requires. In 1993 the CPT noted that in practice the legal provisions concerning involuntary hospitalization were not applied or even generally known. It therefore recommended that the Greek authorities take appropriate measures, as a matter of urgency, to implement the relevant provisions of Act 2071/92.

During the 1997 visit the delegation found *(Report to the government of Greece, 1997)* that, although the parts of Act 2071/92 relating to involuntary hospitalization (section 96) and the length and termination of involuntary hospitalization (section 99) were now known, there were considerable difficulties in applying them. It appeared in particular that no list of doctors authorized to carry out the required assessments in accordance with the law had been drawn up. Moreover, in the two hospitals visited, conversations with psychiatrists highlighted their ambivalence towards this legislation, particularly the legal aspects, which were deemed to carry too much weight and be unrealistic. Numerous practical obstacles to the law's application were also cited, such as the difficulties of organising transport for patients to appear before the relevant court. With regard to the legal provisions concerning the length and termination of involuntary hospitalization, the delegation was told by psychiatrists in both hospitals visited that, in practice, patients were never referred to the board of three psychiatrists required under the law to rule on the continuation of hospitalization beyond six months. The CPT felt that the main reason for the difficulties in implementing Act 2071/92 was the continuing absence of the necessary regulations for the ap-

plication and interpretation of the provisions concerned. The CPT recommended that, as a matter of urgency, the Greek authorities take the necessary steps to ensure the proper application of the provisions of Act 2071/92 relating to involuntary hospitalization. The CPT delegation was also informed that in practice it was often impossible for patients placed under Act 2071/92 who were destitute or had no families to exercise their right of access to a lawyer, as provided for under Section 96 of the Act.
As regards psychiatric patients confined under Article 69 of the Penal Code, the CPT delegation again received information similar to that reported in the first report. This information confirmed that courts still tended to order patients' continued hospitalization, even after a medical report had certified that this was no longer necessary because the patients no longer showed symptoms of mental illness.

### 6.5.2 Report of NCHR

The National Commission for Human Rights (NCHR) published in 2003 its Reply to the Questionnaire on "Human Rights of persons with disabilities" of the Office of the United Nations High Commissioner for Human Rights, Research and Right to Development Branch *(Reply to the Questionnaire, 2003)* commenting on the right provided for all hospitalized patients by article 47 of Act 2071/1992 that includes all those patients' rights to respect their human dignity and to be informed about their state of health, stating that the above are not adhered to in many cases in Greek practice, as evidenced by the Greek Ombudsman *(Report 2001, 140-141)*, recipient of a significant number of relevant individual complaints.

### 6.5.3 Report of the Ombudsman

In a report in April 2004 (Report April 2004), the Ombudsman finds that

> *"involuntary psychiatric evaluation and hospitalization are extraordinary procedures within the legal system that cause a breach in the principle that no one is to be deprived of his or her freedom unless he or she has committed a crime and no one is to be subjected to medical acts without his or her consent"; therefore, "precise observance of legislation is a fundamental obligation of every authority (administrative or judicial)".*

The Ombudsman also finds that

> *"the admission of a patient in a psychiatric establishment for evaluation can not be prolonged after 48 hours and cannot be converted to involuntary hospitalization without reason. Furthermore, a court's decision must be issued within 13 days (a 3 day term for the public prosecutor to refer the case to court plus a 10 day term for the court to convene) from the moment the public prosecutor orders the involuntary admission. In any other case there is no legitimate reason for the patient's involuntary hospitalization in a psychiatric establishment".*

The Ombudsman comments that

> *"failing to observe legislation seems to be prevalent in practice and the involved services (public prosecutor, police, hospital) fail to act in concert during the procedure of the involuntary evaluation and hospitalization...common practice cannot justify the violation of rights".*

The Ombudsman recommends

> *"an all embracing examination of the subject by the Ministry of Health and Social Solidarity"*

in cooperation with the Ministry of Justice, aiming at resolving problems arising in the implementation of the law and refers his report to the Attorney of the Supreme Court for considering an intervention regarding the observance of Act 2071 / 92.

No reports of non-governmental organizations regarding involuntary hospitalization or the application of coercive measures in Greece could be identified.

**6.6 Safeguards**

i. The *Head Doctor* (scientific director) of the mental health unit bears the responsibility for treatment as long as the patient is hospitalized (Act 2071/02). *Any civil servant* involved may be checked and punished according to the regulation of the Civil Servants Code (Act 2683/1999[15]) through the disciplinary procedure. Disciplinary offence is any infringement of the civil servant's duty, by an action or a failure to act, for which the civil servant may be held responsible. Duty is defined as the civil servant's obligations set down in a law, orders and guidelines. Improper behaviour towards citizens is specifically mentioned as a disciplinary offence. The disciplinary power may be exercised by the competent disciplinary bodies of the Hospital, using preliminary investigation, sworn administrative inquiry, and disciplinary questioning.

ii. The *public prosecutor* and the *Court* are involved in not ratifying or prolonging the involuntary hospitalization, as previously described.

iii. A *Special Committee for the Safeguard of the Protection of the Rights of Persons with Mental Disorders* was founded by Act 2716 / 99[16] for the modernization of mental health services. This Special Committee consists of a psychiatrist, a child psychiatrist, two social workers, one mental health professional, two lawyers and two representatives of mental health service users or representatives of associations of families of mental health service users.

---

15 Official Gazette 19 A, 1999

16 Official Gazette 96 A, 1999

The Special Committee supervises and safeguards the protection of the Rights of Persons with Mental Disorders e.g. proper living conditions, actual implementation of rights protected by relevant laws (communication with an attorney, appeal, information etc), protection of property, social rehabilitation.
The Special Committee examines complaints and charges of citizens, associations or authorities, makes ordinary or extraordinary visits to mental health units, informs the people about the rights of the mentally ill, examines the obligatory annual reports of the officers in charge of mental health units and those of the three-member committees for the defence of citizen's rights based at each hospital (paragraph 4, Article 1, Act 2519 / 1997[17]), submits annual reports, or at any time that a violation is established, to the Chairman of the Committee for Safeguarding the Protection of the Patients' Rights (founded by Act 2519 / 1997), intervenes every time that a violation is established, makes recommendations, and submits reports to the competent authorities for pressing disciplinary or criminal charges, and also organizes, supervises and co-ordinates voluntary legal aid for persons with mental disorders in collaboration with the local Bar Associations.

iv. The *Synigoros tou Politi* (Ombudsman), an institution founded by Act 2477/97[18] may be involved following a complaint against Public Health Units, to examine a case as illegitimate behaviour of state agents.
v. The *College of Inspectors of Public Administration* has been founded by Act 2477/97[18] aiming at securing a tidy and effective functioning of the Public Administration. The inspectorate is a body for internal checks under Minister for the Interior, Public Administration and Decentralization. It is responsible for exercising inspections, extraordinary monitoring and investigations, gathering evidence, pressing criminal or disciplinary charges and pointing out cases of corruption, misgovernment, ineffectiveness, low productivity and the quality of services.

vi. Indirect monitoring of coercive measures appears when a case of *violating the criminal law* emerges during treatment. Common violations might be those of Article 259 of the Penal Code punishing the infringement of an officer's duty or, in more serious cases, the violation of Article 314 of the Penal Code punishing bodily harm arising from malpractice. In the latter case the criminal procedure against the offender can be initiated only by the victim, filing a charge, and not by the public prosecutor ex officio.

---

[17] Official Gazette 165 A, 1997
[18] Official Gazette 59 A, 1997

vii. Abstract safeguard procedures are within the competence of the *National Commission for Human Rights* (NCHR) which was founded by Law 2667/ 1998[19] and was inaugurated on January 10, 2000. NCHR is a statutory National Human Rights Institution having a consultative status with the Greek State on issues pertaining to human rights protection. The creation of NCHR emanated from the need to monitor developments regarding human rights protection at the domestic and international level, to inform Greek public opinion about human rights-related issues and, above all, to provide guidelines to the Greek State aimed at the establishment of a modern, principle-guided policy of human rights protection. Its competences include: the study of human rights issues raised by the government, by the Convention of the Presidents of the Greek Parliament, by NCHR members or by non-governmental organizations; the submission of recommendations and proposals; elaboration of studies; submission of reports and opinions for legislative, administrative or other measures which may lead to the amelioration of human rights protection in Greece; the development of initiatives for the sensitization of public opinion and mass media on issues related to respecting human rights; the cultivation of respecting human rights in the context of the national educational system; the maintenance of permanent contacts and co-operation with international organizations, similar organs of other States, as well as with national or international non-governmental organizations; the submission of consultative opinions regarding human rights-related reports which Greece is to submit to international organizations; the publicizing of NCHR positions in any appropriate manner; the drawing up of an annual report on human rights protection in Greece; the organization of a Human Rights Documentation Centre; the examination of the ways in which Greek legislation may be harmonized with the international law standards on human rights protection; and the subsequent submission of relevant opinions to competent state organs.

viii. The *National Council on Medical Morality and Ethics* has been founded, in the Ministry of Health, aiming at providing an opinion on all matters of morality and ethics and also solving disputes of the local Committees of Medical Ethics.

---

[19] Official Gazette 281 A, 1998

## Diagram 6.1: Flowchart of the Procedure for Involuntary Admission

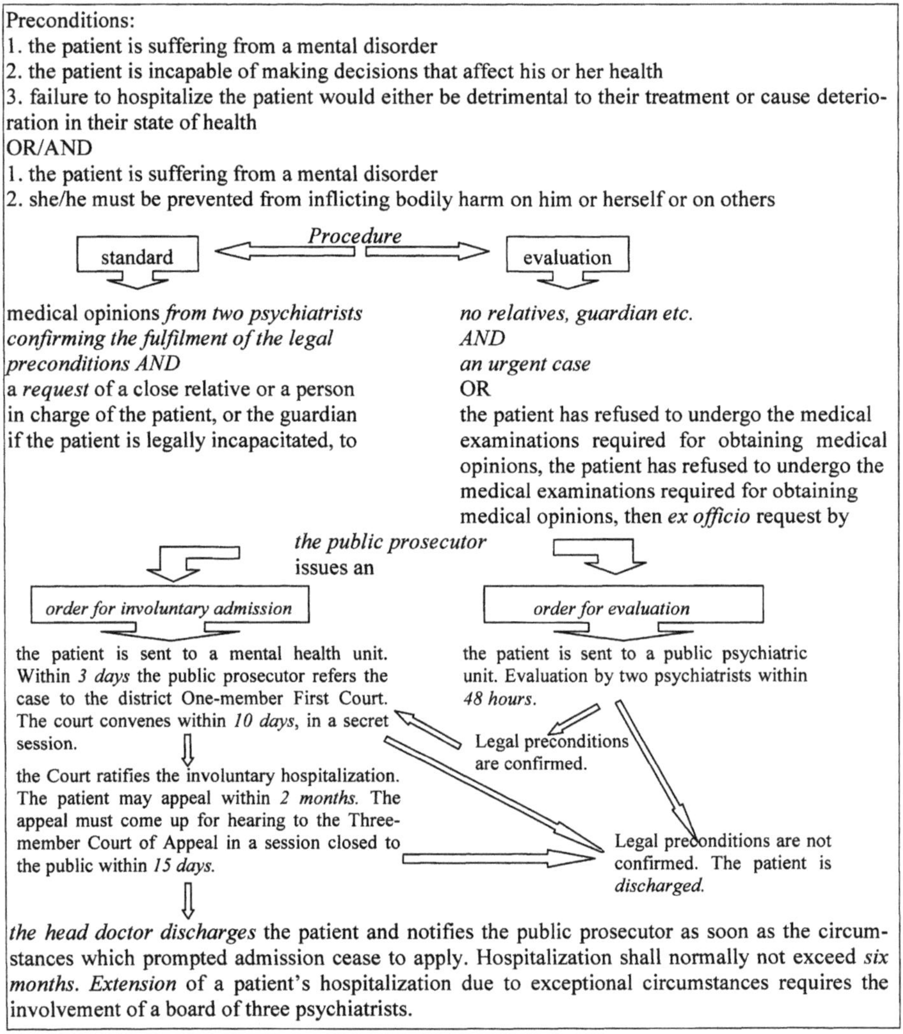


## References

Christodoulou G, Alevizos B, Douzenis A (2002) Compulsory admission and involuntary treatment in the EU-Greece. In Salize HJ, Dressing H, Peitz M (eds) Compulsory admission and involuntary treatment of mentally ill patients – legislation and practice in EU-Member States. Final report. European Commission – Health & Consumer Protection Directorate-General, pp. 87-95

Georgiadou E, Mastrogianni A, Syngelakis M, Karastergiou A (2003) Involuntary hospitalization: the legal framework and its application. Hellenic General Hospital Psychiatry 1: 24-29

Kosmatos K (2002) Involuntary hospitalization in mental health care units. Research findings and perspectives concerning the application of Law 2071/92. Athens: Ant. N. Sakkoulas Publishers.

Leivaditis M (1994) Psychiatry and Law. Athens: Papazisi Publishers.

Paraskevopoulos N. (1993). Act 2071/92 Modernization and Organization of Health System, chapter 6, involuntary hospitalization of persons suffering from mental disorder in a psychiatric unit. Yperaspisi (Defence), 199-212

Recommendation No. R (83) 2 of the Committee of Ministers to the member states concerning the legal protection of persons suffering from mental disorder placed as involuntary patients (adopted by the Committee of Ministers on 22 February 1983 at the 356th meeting of the Ministers' Deputies)

Reply to the Questionnaire on "Human Rights of persons with disabilities" of the Office of the United Nations High Commissioner for Human Rights, Research and Right to Development Branch by the National Commission for Human Rights (NCHR), (2003)

Report of the Greek Ombudsman. (2001)

Report to the Government of Greece on the visit to Greece carried out by the European Committee for the Prevention of Torture and Inhuman or Degrading Treatment or Punishment (CPT) from 14 to 26 March 1993. CPT/Inf (94) 20

Report to the Government of Greece on the visit to Greece carried out by the European Committee for the Prevention of Torture and Inhuman or Degrading Treatment or Punishment (CPT) from 4 to 6 November 1996. CPT/Inf (2001) 17

Report to the Government of Greece on the visit to Greece carried out by the European Committee for the Prevention of Torture and Inhuman or Degrading Treatment or Punishment (CPT) from 25 May to 6 June 1997. CPT/Inf (2001) 18

**CHAPTER 7**

# Legal Report – Israel

Maisam MUSALLAM

## 7.1 Preliminary Remarks[1]

### 7.1.1 Historical Development of Mental Health Legislation

In 1991, Israel enacted a new mental health law entitled the Treatment of Mental Patients Law, 1991[2]. The law of 1991 substantially revised Israel's original Mental Health Law of 1955[3], which provided that an individual with mental illness could be automatically involuntarily committed to a mental institution for an indeterminate period of time once it was determined "that the patient is likely to endanger himself or another." At the time of its enactment, the 1955 law was considered liberal since it provided some procedural protections.

The 1955 law, however, was based entirely on a medical model, meaning that psychiatrists, not the court, controlled the commitment process. Few, if any limits were placed on the discretion of psychiatrists in the commitment process. The law also failed to provide a clear definition of the level of danger required to sustain a commitment. As a result, many people were inappropriately committed to mental institutions for indeterminate periods of time. Courts and scholars criticized the 1955 law on this basis. Such criticism took the form of legislative proposals, but none were enacted into law until 1991.

Even the 1991 law did not entirely abandon the medical model in favour of the legalistic model. It sought instead to remedy the problems associated with the 1955 law by providing a better balance between individual liberties and the exercise of the psychiatrist's determination of "need for treatment". For example, the 1991 law replaces the former law's indeterminate period of commitment by imposing time limits on the duration of commitment orders.

No major changes to the current law are planned for the moment. However, some preparatory legislative work to improve the law is underway.

---

1 This information is mainly taken from A. Kanter and U. Aviram, "Israel's Involuntary Outpatient Commitment Law: Lessons From The American Experience", Israel Law Review Vol. 29 No. 4 (1995), p. 565.

2 The Treatment of Mental Patients Law, 1991, *S.H.* no. 1339, p. 58.

3 Treatment of Mentally Sick Persons Law, 1955, *S.H.* no. 187, p. 121.

### 7.1.2 Survey Methodology

This report is based on the present legislation in Israel on compulsory mental care and on the jurisprudence of the Supreme Court in Israel. It also includes an account of the reports of a non-governmental organization (ACRI)[4] and the recommendations of the Association of Psychiatry regarding the Israeli legislation on compulsory psychiatric care, as well as an account of the preparatory legislative work.

The decisions of the Supreme Court are published in the official book of the Supreme Court (IsrSC). The decisions can also be found on the court's official web site[5]. The newer preparatory work can be found on the web site of the Israeli government[6]. This literature search spans the last ten years.

## 7.2 Laws and General Norms

### 7.2.1 Constitutional Norms

Israel does not have a constitution; it has Basic Laws, which have Constitutional status. One such law that applies to our issue is the Basic Law: Human Dignity and Freedom[7]. The law opens with a declarative statement that it is designed to protect human dignity and liberty. Section 2 of this law states: *"one may not harm the life, body and dignity of a person"*. Section 4, entitled 'Protection of life, body and dignity', states: *"Every person is entitled to protection of his life, body and dignity."* Section 5 provides that human liberty cannot be limited by imprisonment, arrest or in any other way.

### 7.2.2 Specific Laws

The rights of mental patients in Israel, and the methods of forced hospitalization, were first defined in the "Mental Health Law, 1955". This law was amended in a major way in 1991 (there was also another amendment in 1995, concerning minors). The new Treatment of Mental Patients Law of 1991 is designed to ensure that forced hospitalization is used only when it is essential for the protection of society or the patient himself. The law of 1991 protects patients' rights in psychiatric hospitals, such as the right to receive a listing of their rights and obligations, to receive medical information about their condition (according to the doctor's judgment) and to treatment. In addition, the law protects the patients' rights to send and receive mail, to have visitors and to communicate with people outside of the hospital, although these rights can be limited by hospital staff. The right to keep contact with one's lawyer, guardian and governmental officials

---

4 The Association for Civil Rights in Israel, see section 7.5 of this report.

5 www.court.gov.il

6 www.knesset.gov.il

7 Basic Law: Human Dignity and Freedom, (1992) *S.H.* no. 1391, p. 150.

may not be limited (sec. 35(e)). Patients also have the right to privacy and confidentiality, although these rights may be waived under certain circumstances (sec. 42).
The new law recognizes, for the first time, both the right to refuse treatment, but only for voluntary patients (sec. 35(h)), and the procedure of involuntary outpatient treatment (ambulatory treatment), which can be used as an alternative to involuntary hospitalization.
The law also distinguishes between the civil and criminal track. The authorities that carry out all the procedures in a *civil* commitment are defined in the law: The District Psychiatrist (a government psychiatrist), The District Psychiatric Committee (which is appointed by the Minister of Health, consists of three members: one lawyer and two psychiatrists and has the power to review under certain circumstances the district psychiatrist's decisions), and finally the court (basically the District Court) which is authorized to review the committee's decisions.
The district psychiatrist controls the initial decision of forced commitment for *civil* patients (who are not hospitalized due to a criminal act), after being convinced by a psychiatric examination that the patient meets the standards for psychiatric commitment (sec. 9). But courts are directly involved in the initial commitment of individuals who are accused of a *criminal* act and considered incompetent to be punished (sec. 15-17). According to sec. 15(a), the court has the power to commit an accused person to hospital or ambulatory treatment if the court is convinced, based on the opinion of the district psychiatrist, that the defendant is unfit to stand trial due to his/she/her mental illness. The court does not decide, however, whether treatment should be provided or where such treatment shall be provided. The district psychiatrist has the power to make all treatment decisions (sec. 15 (g)).
The main criticism against the 1991 law is that there is still no court involvement during the initial civil commitment process. The district psychiatrist continues to control the initial decision of whom to commit to involuntary treatment and where such treatment will take place. The 1991 law did not fully abandon the medical model that was defined in the law of 1955. Moreover, although the district psychiatrists' decisions are subject to review by the psychiatric committee, the committee itself is not an independent body. The members of this committee, like the district psychiatrists, are all appointed by the Minister of Health[8].
Some psychiatrists claim that the law's structure, which gives the district psychiatrist power to order forced hospitalization, portrays psychiatry as a profession that limits the individual's freedom and deprives him of his right to decide

8 A. Kanter and U. Aviram, "Israel's Involuntary Outpatient Commitment Law: Lessons From The American Experience", Israel Law Review Vol. 29 No. 4 (1995), p. 565, 622.

what to do with his own body. Therefore, The Association of Psychiatry in Israel recommended that the decision of forced hospitalization on the civil track should be placed in the hands of a non-medical body, for example the court, in order to improve the image of psychiatrists in society. In this case, the court would play an active role in issuing commitment and the psychiatrists would concentrate on their medical tasks[9].

A person facing commitment on the civil track has no right to legal representation at the initial commitment hearing. Only on appeal of a commitment order to the psychiatric committee may an attorney or guardian represent the patient (sec. 26(c)). On the criminal track, on the other hand, the law grants the patient the right to be legally represented (sec. 18). In order to improve the quality of the hearing and the likelihood that the patient's rights will be protected, a proposed revision of this section suggests that the law should provide legal representation in commitment hearings before both the psychiatric committee and the court. If the patient does not have an attorney, the court must appoint one[10].

According to sec. 14, a district psychiatrist who ordered psychiatric examination, hospitalization or ambulatory treatment may authorize a person or the police forces to enter the patient's home and use reasonable force in order to execute the order. The court's hospitalization order gives the police force the authority to bring any patient to the institution determined by the district psychiatrist (sec. 20).

Under sec. 44, a doctor may face criminal punishment (detention of up to five years) if he does not follow the law when determining whether a person is sick or not, and a doctor "who knowingly orders unnecessary or illegal hospitalization of a person" may face the same punishment. A doctor "who uses coercive measures that do not accord to the law in a hospital or clinic", may also face detention punishment of up to three years.

The law concerning minors was the same until 1995. The only difference was that for minors under 18 years old, the consent of their guardians was considered as the minors' own consent. In 1995, changes were made, mainly widening the rights of minors and changing procedures. Section 4a of the Treatment of Mental Patients Law provides that minors over 15 cannot be committed involuntarily without a court order and that minors under 15 cannot be committed involuntarily (even if the parents or guardians agree) without review of the Psychiatric Committee for Children and Juveniles[11].

---

9 A. Toiv, Forced Hospitalization of Mentally Ill Patients- Legal Review, The Association of Psychiatry in Israel- www.mentalnet.org.il

10 Draft Proposal for Treatment of Mental Patients Law (amendment number 3) (forced hospitalization), June 2002. www.knesset.gov.il\Laws\Data\BillAllOld\3145\3145_All

11 See more about this in section 7.6 of this report.

### 7.2.3 General Laws

*The Patients' Rights Law* was enacted in 1996[12]. Its objective is to regulate the relationship between people who require medical treatment and members of the medical staff. The law has established, for the first time, norms and codes of conduct concerning patients' rights. The opening paragraph of the law states:

> *"This Act aims to establish the right of every person who requests medical care or who is in receipt of medical care and to protect his dignity and privacy."*

According to this law, the right to receive medical treatment is assured to all, without discrimination on grounds of religion, race, sex, nationality etc. The patient is entitled to proper medical care, which should be provided with the best professional standards and quality. No medical treatment shall be administered unless the patient has consented to it. Such consent should be "informed consent," based on all data in the diagnosis, the risks involved and the chances and risks of alternative treatment. Under this law, the dignity and privacy of the patient must be assured at all stages of his treatment. He has the right to receive information concerning his medical record, which may not be disclosed by any member of the medical staff (medical confidentiality) to a third party except under certain circumstances.

To assure the implementation of this law, three committees were established: an Investigative Committee (to investigate patients' complaints or incidents involving medical treatment), a Quality and Control Committee (an internal committee appointed to evaluate medical procedures in order to improve the quality of medical care), and an Ethics Committee (to be established in every medical facility). The law also requires the appointment of a person in charge of Patients' Rights who will advise and help patients concerning their rights and instruct members of the medical and administrative staff in the facility in all matters relating to the law.

The law concerning minors, *Youth (Care and Supervision) Law, 1960*[13], was amended in 1995 at the same time as the Treatment of Mental Patients Law. The Youth Law contains, among other provisions, new procedures regarding the commitment of minors for mental health treatment. The court will not order in-patient hospitalization

> *"unless it finds, based on an opinion of the psychiatric committee for children and juveniles which examined the child, that there is no other way to give treatment to the minor except by hospitalization (sec. 3e (2))."*

---

[12] The Patients' Rights Law, (1996) *S.H* no. 1591, p. 325.

[13] Youth (Care and Supervision) Law, (1960) *S.H* no. 311, p. 52.

*Legal Capacity and Guardianship Law, 1962*[14]: According to this law, the court has the power, under certain provisions, to appoint guardians for minors (under the age of 18) and people who, due to illness or disability (such as mental illness or retardation), are incapable of taking care of their own interests.

*The Persons in Need Law, 1966*[15]: This law applies to minors under 14 or people who, due to mental illness, retardation or older age, are incapable of taking care of themselves. It contains the required provisions for the protection of their lives and mental safety. In this case, the court may order a treatment even if the person does not consent.

### 7.2.4 Second Level of Legal Norms

Treatment of Mental Patients Regulations, 1992[16]: these regulations include the procedures for psychiatric examination, coercive psychiatric hospitalization and the patient's consent to hospitalization. It provides accurate instructions concerning the implementation of coercive measures such as isolation, restraint, and ECT.
The regulations also include the forms which must be completed for carrying out these procedures.

### 7.3 Jurisprudence

Under the Treatment of Mental Patients Law, 1991 (hereinafter The Mental Patients Law), the court is not involved during the initial commitment stage unless criminal defendants are involved or, in the subsequent monitoring and enforcement of the law, unless an appeal is submitted to the district court against a psychiatric committee decision. The district psychiatrist continues to control the initial decision of committing a patient to involuntary treatment and where such treatment will take place. Moreover, if the patient fails to comply with an outpatient commitment order, he or she may automatically be hospitalized by the district psychiatrist (The Mental Patients Law, sec. 15(e)).

In CApp 2060/97 Valinchik V. Tel Aviv District Psychiatrist, IsrSC 52 (1) 697[17], a woman was brought to criminal trial. The court found, based on the opinion of the district psychiatrist, that the petitioner was mentally ill and was unfit to stand trial. The court ordered that the woman was dangerous neither to

---

14 Legal Capacity and Guardianship Law, (1962) *S.H* no. 380, p. 120.
15 The Persons in Need Law, (1966) *S.H* no. 641, p. 150.
16 Treatment of Mental Patients Regulations, (1992) *K.T.* no. 5443, p. 1070.
17 CApp 2060/97 Valinchik V. Tel Aviv District Psychiatrist, IsrSC 52 (1) 697 (11.3.98).

herself nor to the community and should receive compulsory outpatient treatment according to section 15(b). After the woman refused this form of treatment, the district psychiatrist ordered that she be hospitalized in a psychiatric institution under section 15(e). An appeal against the psychiatrist's decision was submitted to the district court. The court ruled that a patient does not have the right to appeal against such a decision. Therefore the patient referred to the Supreme Court.

The Supreme Court discussed first a mental patient's rights and his/she/her fundamental rights according to the Basic Law: Human Dignity and Freedom. The court ruled that forced hospitalization of an incompetent criminal defendant infringes upon his constitutional rights, including his liberty, dignity, autonomy and self-image, by imposing a stigma upon the accused long after his release from commitment.

> *"These rights are not absolute. Opposite them stand the interests of protecting public safety from the accused, as well as treating the accused and protecting him from himself. We must reasonably balance the patient's rights, on one hand, and the public interests, on the other, by choosing the treatment which will limit the patient's liberty as little as possible. The outpatient treatment is adequate for achieving this goal and must be chosen whenever the patient does not cause any risk to the community or to himself."*

Regarding the patient's right to appeal against the district psychiatrist's hospitalization order issued according to section 15(e), the Supreme Court ruled that if the patient, according to section 15(f) of the law, has the right to appeal against the court's hospitalization order, then he has the same right concerning the psychiatrist's decision.

The patient also has the right to an attorney to represent him before the district psychiatrist when facing a hospitalization order under sec 15(e). According to both the Mental Patients Law and the general laws, prior to any limitation of the individual's liberty by governmental power, the patient must be given the right to be heard. The mental patient is, in most cases, incapable of understanding the procedure he faces, and needs an attorney who will protect his rights and interests.

In another case CA 3854/02 John Doe V. District Psychiatric Board for Adults[18], the petitioner had spent more than fourteen years in a psychiatric institution according to a judicial hospitalization order. Despite his medical treatment, he remained unfit for trial. The question in the appeal was: how long may hospitalization be carried out under the authority of the original judicial hospitalization or-

---

18 CA 3854/02 John Doe V. District Psychiatric Board for Adults (22.1.2003). www.court.gov.il

der? Is the judicial hospitalization order limited by time, and if so, what is that limitation?
The Supreme Court ruled that if the medical treatment is unsuccessful, the patient cannot be discharged from the hospital due to the danger he presents to himself and to others. The mentally ill defendant must remain in the psychiatric institution on the authority of the hospitalization order.
The court added,

> *"Indeed, the forced hospitalization infringes upon the liberty and dignity of the patient. Nevertheless, this infringement is justified in that it is intended both for the protection of the accused as well as for the protection of society."*[19]

The court clarified that forced hospitalization on the authority of a judicial hospitalization order issued during a criminal proceeding (Mental Patients Law, sec. 17, 16(a), 15(a)) is not the only form of forced hospitalization recognized by the law. In addition to criminal hospitalization under the authority of a judicial order ("the criminal track"), the law also recognizes hospitalization on the authority of a "civil" hospitalization order ("the civil track"). A comparative study of the criminal and civil tracks shows that the infringement upon the mental patient's liberty is more severe on the criminal track. For example, on the criminal track, the forced hospitalization, on the authority of the judicial order, continues until the psychiatric committee orders that the accused should be discharged (sec. 28). On the civil track, on the other hand, the period of hospitalization cannot exceed six months unless the psychiatric committee extends the period, and such extensions cannot exceed six months (sec. 10).

The court found that, since there is no specific legislation to deal with these issues, detailed arrangements were needed. In the court's opinion, the court must decide whether a hospitalization order should be cancelled. The court issued the original hospitalization order and is responsible for deciding whether time has brought the need for its cancellation. A hospitalization order is not automatically cancelled because it has become unreasonable. So long as the court has not cancelled the hospitalization order, it remains valid. No other official may cancel the hospitalization order, including the psychiatric committee.

How will the court become aware of the need to reconsider the reasonableness of the hospitalization order? The psychiatric patient himself is allowed to approach the court and request the annulment of the hospitalization order. How-

---

[19] Section 35(b) of The Mental Patients Law, provides that hospitalization is mainly intended for the treatment of the patient. The patient can be hospitalized only according to this law for his protection and the protection of society.

ever, due to his condition, this task must not be left only to him. An institutional arrangement which makes it possible to follow the development of the situation must be ensured. One of the institutions which may be considered is the psychiatric committee. It reviews the psychiatric patient's case every six months (sec. 28(a)). It is familiar with the psychiatric patient's condition and the chances of his recovery. However, one of the obstacles for the psychiatric committee is that it is a statutory body of limited authority. It has no authority to approach the court in such a case. Another institutional agent is the Attorney General. He charged the accused, and is aware of the hospitalization order, and has the ability to appeal the decisions of the psychiatric committee before the court (sec. 29(a)). As one who is responsible for public interests, he also has the ability to approach the district psychiatrist and encourage him to transfer the patient from the criminal track to the civil track. The psychiatric committee may be asked to report to the Attorney General regarding its decision to keep the accused in a psychiatric institution. The court must examine the defendant's case and hear the Attorney General's opinion regarding the validity of the charge and the validity of the hospitalization order. It must decide whether there is room to cancel the hospitalization order, while also taking into account the arrangements for hospitalization via the civil track.

### 7.4 Protocols and Internal Norms[20]

a) According to the Mental Patients Law, patients who are willingly hospitalized cannot be treated or medicated against their will or without their consent (sec. 4(a), 35(h)). Patients who are forcibly hospitalized can be treated (standard treatment) against their will (sec. 35(i)). In both cases, a separate consent (or ruling for involuntary patients) is needed for special treatments, such as ECT (sec. 4(a), 35(I)).

Isolation or restraint is permissible only by physician's order, and *"only when needed to prevent danger to the patient or others"* (sec. 34(b)). These measures are time limited (sec. 34(c)), and there are regulations for prolonging them (sec. 34(d)).

b) The Mental Patients Regulations, 1992, include directions on how to carry out the coercive measures of isolation, restraint, and ECT.

*"The patient can be isolated in a special room which has been designated for this purpose and has suitable safety arrangements* (sec. 27)." The restraint procedure is permissible only by physician's order and in a special room designated for this purpose (sec. 28). A restraint order is valid only for four hours (sec.

---

[20] There are no inner protocols used by national health institutions in Israel. The legal system is national.

In emergency situations and in the absence of a physician, the nurse in charge may order the restraint of a patient and must inform the physician as soon as possible in order to obtain approval (sec. 30).
Section 34(a) provides that ECT will be administered only if three physicians, including the hospital director, the ward director where the patient is hospitalized, or the clinic director where the patient is receiving his treatment, have decided this based on a physical examination (sec. 34(a)(1), 34(a)(2)). If the patient was willingly hospitalized, he must give his consent. If he has been deemed legally incompetent, his guardian must give his consent to this treatment (sec.34 (a)(3)).

**7.5 Reports of Non-Governmental Organizations**

The Association for Civil Rights in Israel (ACRI) has been dealing with the complaints of patients who were forcibly hospitalized even before the enactment of the Mental Patients Law, 1991.
The ACRI's report detailing the state of human rights in Israel, 2002[21], refers to the lack of representation in forced psychiatric commitment. According to the law, any individual who is forcibly committed is eligible to appeal the decision of the psychiatric committee before the local courts. However, in actuality, the process of appeal is available only to those who are represented by a legal counsellor: a small minority of the individuals who are forcibly committed. In cases where an appeal is filed, legal representation often brings a change in the position of the authorities, state acknowledgement that the hospitalization was not carried out according to the law, and a release of the patient without any further hearing.
According to the ACRI position (ACRI report, August 2001)[22], the judicial authority is the only institution which should be responsible for forced commitments. The psychiatric committee does not have a suitable mechanism for exploring the facts and the patient's circumstances. By contrast, the judicial authority has the power to investigate the matter and hear the patient's arguments; this would grant protection of the patients' rights. The ACRI mentioned in this report a suggestion regarding section 5 of the Mental Patients Regulations, which demanded the amendment of this section to include the patient's right to receive information about the decision concerning his/she/her outpatient com-

21 Lack of Representation in Forced Psychiatric Commitment, The Association for Civil Rights in Israel (excerpted from the State of Human Rights in Israel, 2002). www.acri.org.il

22 The Association for Civil Rights and The Forced Hospitalization Issue, The Association for Civil Rights in Israel (ACRI report, August 2001). www.acri.org.il

receive information about the decision concerning his/she/her outpatient commitment[23]. This information would give him the chance to refute the evidence against him before the psychiatric committee.
It also recommended that the law provide for legal representation in all forced commitment hearings. This would improve the quality of the hearing and the likelihood that the individual's rights will be protected. The authority responsible for the appointment of legal counsellors should be independent and trained for this purpose. Regarding non-urgent commitment and compulsory outpatient treatment, the ACRI recommended that the initial decision be placed in the hands of judicial, not medical authority. These situations might not be urgent, but they limit the individual's freedom and deprive him of his right to decide what to do with his body. The patient should also have the right to refuse treatment for the purpose of referring to institutions (such as attorneys, the ACRI) for advice. Some treatments might have severe side effects that could influence the patient's judgment and his ability to understand his rights, such as his right to appeal against the commitment decision.
Moreover, the ACRI recommended cancelling the civil commitment procedure. The grounds for civil hospitalization relate to situations that have criminal aspects (threats or violent actions towards others). Thus, there is a need for judicial review just as in all criminal offences.
The ACRI also suggested cancelling the section in the law regarding voluntary commitment. In most cases, the patient's consent to hospitalization is fictitious and is given only under severe pressure from the psychiatric system in order to avoid fulfilling the conditions for forced commitment.

## 7.6 Safeguard System

### 7.6.1 Safeguard Procedures Relevant to Individual Persons or Cases

The Mental Patients Law of 1991 includes two methods of involuntary commitment: one is the involuntary inpatient commitment, and the second is the involuntary outpatient commitment (compulsory ambulatory care). The second method allows an individual who is determined to be mentally ill to be committed to involuntary outpatient treatment as a condition of release from inpatient care, or as an alternative to involuntary hospitalization (sec. 11(a)-(b)). The law also distinguishes between civil and criminal tracks.

There are a few ways and methods of hospitalization for *civil* patients (who are not hospitalized due to a criminal act, or by the court in the course of criminal proceedings held against them):

---

[23] This section was amended in June 2001 to provide that the patient receives a copy of the outpatient commitment order.

1) Voluntary hospitalization – upon the patient's request. If the patient demands discharge, he is either discharged, or can be kept against his will for 48 hours (sec. 4(b)). If the hospital director finds that the patient meets the standards for forced hospitalization (see below), he must refer to the district psychiatrist for a hospitalization order (sec. 4(d)).

2) Urgent hospitalization – a patient arriving by any means may be hospitalized against his will for 48 hours if the hospital director considers it urgent and the patient meets the conditions for forced urgent examination (sec. 5(a), 5(b)).

3) Forced hospitalization – a patient is hospitalized against his will. Practically, there are five alternatives:

(3a) Forced urgent psychiatric examination – The district psychiatrist may order forced urgent examination when a patient is psychotic, endangers either himself or other people, and refuses to be examined (sec. 6).

(3b) Forced non-urgent psychiatric examination – same as (3a), but in cases where the danger is not so imminent; the patient may also neglect himself or annoy others (sec. 7).

(3c) Forced urgent hospitalization – Same as (3a), but in cases where the patient has already been examined and his condition confirmed (sec. 9 (a)).

(3d) Forced non-urgent hospitalization – Same as (3b), but in cases where the patient has already been examined and his condition confirmed (sec. 9(b)).

(3e) Forced ambulatory treatment – Same as (3c) or (3d), but where it is possible to treat the patient without or following hospitalization (sec. 11(a), 11(b)).

The *District Psychiatrist*, acting as an internal safeguard body, carries out the appropriate procedure after being convinced, by a psychiatric examination, that the patient meets the given legal standards. He issues a written order, which is valid for execution for ten days (sec. 9(c)). The forced hospitalization lasts seven days, and can be prolonged after that period by the district psychiatrist for seven more days (sec. 10(a), 10(b)). After the initial 14 days of hospitalization, there could first be a prolongation by the *District Psychiatric Committee* for three months, and afterwards for six months at a time (sec. 10(c)). This committee must examine the patient before deciding (sec. 10(d)).

Forced ambulatory treatment lasts six months, and can be extended for periods of six months by the district psychiatrist (sec. 11(a)-11(c)). Moreover, the district psychiatrist has the power to hospitalize a patient automatically if he or she fails to comply with an outpatient commitment order (sec. 11(d)). No hearing or court review is necessary.

All forced civil hospitalizations can be terminated at the sole discretion of the hospital director. He has the authority to release any patient (except for patients hospitalized on the criminal track), whether voluntary or involuntary, at any time, at his own discretion (sec. 30).

The patient or his relatives can appeal to the district committee against the patient's release (sec 31).
Any person can appeal to the district committee against forced hospitalization or ambulatory treatment (sec. 12). Any decision of the district psychiatrist can be appealed to the district psychiatric committee.
The patient, his relatives and the Attorney General can appeal against district psychiatric committee decisions to the district court within 45 days (sec. 29). This is the only case where the court becomes involved in the procedure of civil psychiatric hospitalization.
The patient has neither immediate access to the court nor the right to an attorney to present his case before the psychiatric committee. A person facing commitment has no right to legal representation at the initial commitment hearing. On appeal of a commitment order, however, an attorney or guardian may represent the person (sec. 26(c)).

Minors who are mentally disturbed are considered minors in need, and as such can be treated according to the Youth (Care and Supervision) Law, 1960. In 1995 The Mental Patients Law, 1991, and The Youth Law, 1960, were amended with changes to the hospitalization process for minors.
The main new issues are:
Minors can be hospitalized following general regulations similar to those valid for adults: willingly, by their custodians (sec. 4a(b), the Mental Patients Law), or forcibly, provided they are examined at all stages of hospitalization (or prior to it) by a child and adolescent psychiatrist who refers his examination to the district psychiatrist (sec. 3 of the Mental Patients Law, sec. 3e of the Youth Law).
A minor welfare officer (acting according to the Youth Law) has the right to bring a minor to be examined by a child and adolescent psychiatrist, or in a hospital (sec. 3 of the Youth Law). He has to get approval from a juvenile court, but in emergencies can act at his own discretion and apply to the juvenile court afterwards (sec. 11 of the Youth Law).
The juvenile court, according to sections 3b and 3c of The Youth Law, has the authority to refer minors to forced psychiatric examination, either ambulatory or hospitalized (somewhat in parallel to the authority of the district psychiatrist according to section 6(b) of The Mental Patients Law).
The hospitalization lasts seven days, and can be extended by the hospital director for seven more days (sec. 3c(b), the Youth Law). The ambulatory order lasts 30 days (sec. 3b(c), the Youth Law).
The juvenile court can rule on forced hospitalization for treatment of minors under section 3e of the Youth Law: 1)

> *"the minor has a mental illness and he or she meets the requirements of section 9 of the Mental Patients Law (see supra);"* or 2) *"if the minor suffers from a mental illness or se-*

*vere mental disturbance which may cause an immediate physical risk to himself or others, or may cause severe damage to his psychological development in the absence of hospitalization, the court will not order inpatient treatment unless it finds, based on the opinion of the district psychiatric committee for children and adolescents which examined the minor, that there is no way to give treatment to the minor except by hospitalization."*

The hospitalization is for 30 days. Afterwards, it can be extended by the court for periods of three months each following recommendation by the district child and adolescent psychiatric committee which proves that there is no alternative method of treatment (sec. 3e(c), the Youth Law).

Under section 3d of the Youth Law, a court may order ambulatory treatment if: 1)

*"the court finds, based on the opinion of a district psychiatrist, which is based on the opinion of a child psychiatrist who examined the minor, that the minor has a mental illness or disturbance which requires psychiatric treatment in order to prevent physical risk to himself or others, or to prevent severe damage to his psychological development"; or 2) "the court finds, based on a psychologist's opinion, that the minor's mental condition requires psychological treatment to prevent damage to his psychological development".*

The ambulatory treatment lasts three months, and may be consecutively extended by three more months by the court (sec. 3d(b), the Youth Law).

Minors who are over 15 years old, and disagree with their custodians about hospitalization (whether regarding accepting or objecting to hospitalization), are referred to a juvenile court, which must rule on their hospitalization (sec. 4a(c), Mental Patients Law). In these proceedings, an attorney must represent them (sec. 3f(b), Youth Law). Minors who are under 15 years old must be referred to the district child and adolescent psychiatric committee (sec. 4a(d), Mental Patients Law). This committee consists of five members: jurist, child and adolescent psychiatrist, clinical psychologist, educational psychologist and social worker.

The district child and adolescent psychiatric committee must review every hospitalization of a minor. A voluntary hospitalization must be reviewed after two months, and can be prolonged for three months at this time by the committee (sec. 4a(f), Mental Patients Law). The court, following recommendation by the committee, can prolong forced hospitalization for three months at this time (sec. 3e(c), Youth Law). Their main consideration should be whether there is any alternative method of treatment to hospitalization for the minor.

The juvenile court (acting as an external safeguard body) is much more active here in deciding and ruling on forced hospitalizations of minors, mainly according to the Youth law.

Courts are also directly involved in the initial commitment of individuals who are accused of a criminal act and considered not competent to be punished (sec.

15-17, Mental Patients Law). According to the Mental Patients Law, section 15(a), the court has the power to commit an accused person to hospital or ambulatory treatment if the court is convinced, based on the opinion of the district psychiatrist, that he/she is unfit to stand trial due to his/she/her mental illness.

> *"The court may not order ambulatory treatment unless the court is convinced that his/she/her release into the community poses no risk to his/she/her safety or the safety of the community (sec. 15(d))."*

The court itself does not decide, however, whether treatment should be provided or where such treatment shall be provided. The district psychiatrist has the power to make all treatment decisions (sec. 15 (g)).

Section 15(e) provides that if the accused fails to comply with an ambulatory order, he or she may be automatically hospitalized by the district psychiatrist.

In order to grant the patient the right to be legally represented in the criminal track, section 18 provides that

> *"commitment orders under sections 15-17 must be given in the presence of the patient's attorney, and if he does not have an attorney, the court must appoint one."*

This section indicates that the infringement upon the patient's rights may be more severe in the criminal track. In the civil track, on the other hand, the law does not grant the patient this right.

### 7.6.2 Abstract Safeguard Procedures

According to section 22 of the Mental Patients Law, the Head of The Mental Health Services, who is appointed by the Minister of Health, is responsible for the management of the Mental Health Services. He has the power to monitor hospitals and clinics. He may check whether the district psychiatrists carry out all procedures according to the law.

He also has the right to ask for any information related to any patient from the hospital staff, to enter hospitals and clinics, to check patients in these institutions and to carry out an investigation. The district psychiatrist, in order to carry out his duties, has the right to enter any hospital or clinic in his district, to ask for any information from any person and to carry out an investigation in order to assure the implementation of the law (sec. 23). The district psychiatrist must inform the Attorney General and the chairman of the psychiatric committee about any inpatient or outpatient hospitalization order which was issued by him or by the court (sec. 38). A hospital director also must inform the Head of The Mental Health Services about receiving a patient into the hospital or releasing him from the hospital (sec. 39). In a new legislative proposal, it is suggested that the Minister of Health be required to submit a report every year to the Labor, Welfare and Health Committee (parliamentary committee), detailing the number of forced hospitalization orders of adults and minors that were issued in the last year, and the number of hospitalized patients[24].

**References**

Basic Law: Human Dignity and Freedom, (1992) *S.H.* no. 1391, p. 150.
The Treatment of Mental Patients Law, 1991, *S.H.* no. 1339, p. 58.
Treatment of Mentally Sick Persons Law, 1955, *S.H.* no.187, 121.
The Patients' Rights Law, (1996) *S.H* no. 1591, p. 325.
Youth (Care and Supervision) Law, (1960) *S.H.* no. 311, p. 52.
Legal Capacity and Guardianship Law, (1962) *S.H* no. 380, p. 120.
The Persons in Need Law, (1966) *S.H* no. 641, p. 150.
Treatment of Mental Patients Regulations, (1992) *K.T.* no. 5443, p. 1070.
A. Kanter and U. Aviram, "Israel's Involuntary Outpatient Commitment Law: Lessons From The American Experience", Israel Law Review Vol. 29 No. 4 (1995), p. 565.
A. Tiov, Forced Hospitalization of Mentally Ill Patients- Legal Review, The Association of Psychiatry in Israel- www.mentalnet.org.il.
In CApp 2060/97 Valinchik V. Tel Aviv District Psychiatrist, IsrSC 52 (1) 697 (11.3.98).
CA 3854/02 John Doe V. District Psychiatric Board for Adults (22.1.2003). www.court.gov.il
The Association for Civil Rights and the Forced Hospitalization Issue, The Association for Civil Rights in Israel (ACRI report, August 2001). www.acri.org.il
Lack of Representation in Forced Psychiatric Commitment, The Association for Civil Rights in Israel (excerpted from the State of Human Rights in Israel, 2002).
Draft Proposal for Treatment of Mental Patients Law (amendment number 3) (forced hospitalization), June 2002. www.knesset.gov.il\Laws\Data\BillAllOld\3145\3145_All

24 Draft Proposal for Treatment of Mental Patients Law (amendment number 3) (forced hospitalization), June 2002. www.knesset.gov.il\Laws\Data\BillAllOld\3145\3145_All

## Diagram 7.1: Flowchart of Involuntary Psychiatric Commitment, Israel

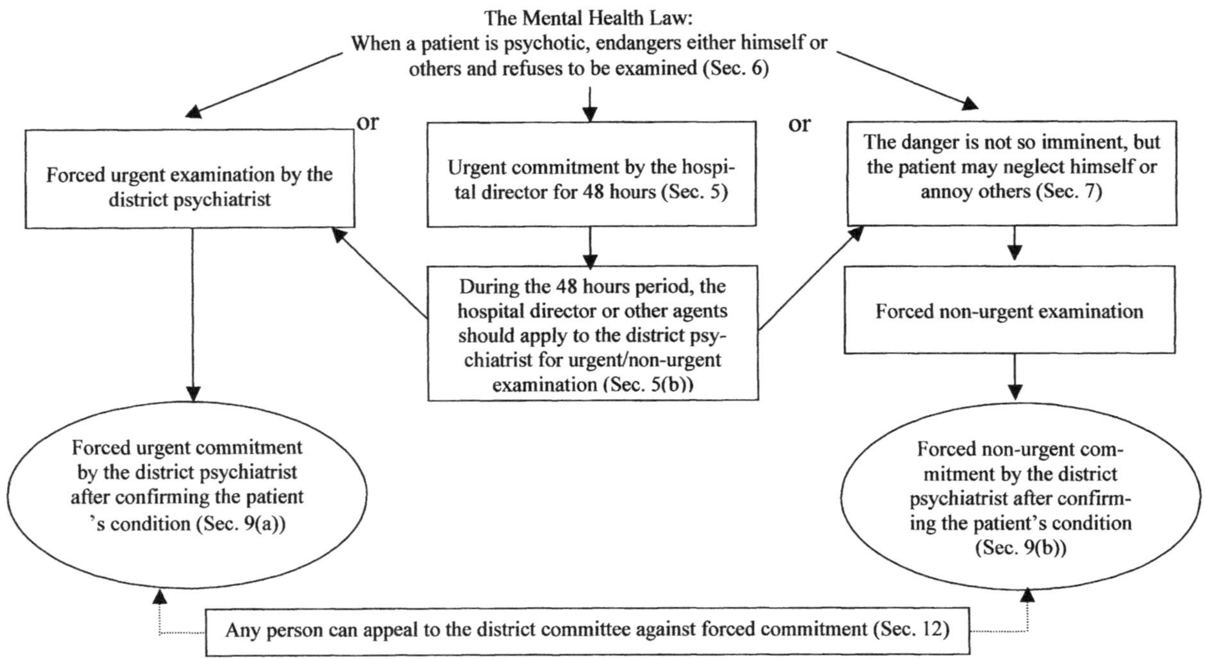


Note: Forced commitment lasts for seven days, and can be extended for another seven days by the district psychiatrist and can be prolonged by the district psychiatrist committee for three months and afterwards for 6 months at a time (Sec. 10(a)-(c)).

**CHAPTER 8**

# Legal Report – Italy

Alberto MANACORDA, Corrado DE ROSA

## 8.1 Preliminary Remarks

### 8.1.1 Historical Overview of Coercive Psychiatric Treatment in Italy

I. In Italy, until the middle of the nineteenth century, people suffering from mental illness were kept in locations deemed suitable by society, even if this accommodation was against their will. A

> *"legal norm" equivalent to the modern meaning of this term did not exist. Involuntary admission was carried out using a variety of methods, however these were only ever used following an "order from an authority".*

Italy's particular geo-political circumstances in the mid-nineteenth century resulted in different norms which were valid in each sovereign State until a unified legal system was adopted across the country. After the political unification of Italy (1861) a process of legal normalisation in different fields began. During this time, it was also deemed necessary to start a process of nationwide unification of public assistance norms relating to mental health care.

The Parliament had to work very hard, not because of substantial conflicts on the subject, but because of several political and governmental crises of generic nature.

Finally, it achieved promulgation of law February 14, 1904, n. 36 ("Dispositions on mental hospitals and ill people")[1]; later on, the executive power of its set of rules was approved by a Royal Decree dated August 16, 1909, n. 615[2].

This set of rules established the following: Article 1. – Individuals affected by any type of mental illness must be kept and treated in mental hospitals if they are a danger to themselves and their community or are responsible for public scandal and cannot be kept conventionally or treated in places other than mental hospitals.

Hospitalization in a mental hospital was of a coercive nature: it started with an initial phase of "observation", not exceeding 30 days, ordered by the *Pretore* (lower court judge) or by the police in emergency cases. If the person was not dismissed during this observation period, hospitalization continued with a "de-

---

1 Law .36/1904: "Disposizioni sui manicomi e sugli alienati". Published in Gazzetta Ufficiale n. 43, February 22, 1904

2 Royal Decree 615/1909: "Regolamento di esecuzione della legge sui manicomi e sugli alienati"

finitive admission" ordered by a court decree. Individuals who were aware of their "partial mental illness status" could request admission independently as defined by the law. If the director of the hospital ordered admission in such a case, it was then of coercive nature.
It should be noted, however, that the set of norms issued between 1904 to 1909 were largely aimed at restricting the personal liberty of the patient rather than at providing them with treatment. These norms were based on notions of "danger to themselves and their community" and "of public scandal." This was confirmed by a series of legal norms contained in the penal code that was enforced and valid until 1978.

II. The internal organization of mental hospitals changed with the issuing of law March 18, 1968, n. 431 ("Measures for psychiatric assistance")[3]. From then on, they were referred to as "psychiatric hospitals." The law established the following: Article 4. – Voluntary admission and dismissals. The patient can voluntarily request admission to a psychiatric hospital or the doctor on duty can order it or admission can take place for diagnostic assessment and treatment. In these cases, norms in force for admissions, hospitalizations and dismissals ordered by an authority are not applicable (omission).

III. With law May 13, 1978, n. 180, the system of psychiatric hospitals became outdated because norms concerning "prepared and involuntary admissions" were established. Besides norms on voluntary admissions, this law also introduced rules on involuntary admissions for mental illness, and changed the norms contained in the penal code that were not compatible with the new set of rules. In particular: Book III, title I, volume I, section III, paragraph 6 of the penal code made "monetary sanctions concerning custody of mentally ill individuals, minors or detained people" a prosecutable offence. Law n. 180/1978 (Article10)[4] eliminated the words "mentally ill."
Article 716 of the penal code dealt with cases involving "Failing to inform the relevant authorities about the escape of mentally interdicted individuals or minors". *Law n.180/1978 eliminated the words "mentally interdicted" and "billed for treatment of ills."*
With article 11 of law n. 180/1978, several earlier articles of law n.36/1904 and some others from the penal code were abrogated. These respectively dealt with: Article 714. Neglectful or unauthorized custody, in mental hospitals or reformatories, of mentally ill individuals or minors. Article 715. Neglectful or unauthor-

3 Law 431/1968: "Providenze per l'assistenza psichiatrica". Published in Gazzetta Ufficiale n. 101, April 20, 1968

4 Law 180/1978: " Accertamenti e trattamenti sanitarti volontari e obbligatori". Published in Gazzetta Ufficiale n. 133, May 16, 1978

ized private custody of mentally ill individuals. Article 717. Neglectful denunciation of mental illnesses or serious and dangerous psychiatric illnesses.
IV. Law December 23, 1978, n. 833 ("Institution of a National Psychiatric Service")[5], in its articles 33,34, and 35 reiterated the content of law n. 180/1978 concerning the involuntary admission due to mental illness.

## 8.2 Applicable Laws and General Norms

### 8.2.1 Constitutional Norms

*a. General*

Constitution of the Italian Republic (1948)[6]:
Article 13. – Personal freedom cannot be violated.
No type of detention, inspection or personal search or any other kind of limitation of personal freedom is permitted unless regulated by an order issued by the judicial authority for cases contemplated by the law.
In emergency cases, strictly indicated by the law, the law enforcement authority can carry out temporary measures of which the judicial authority must be informed within 48 hours. If the judicial authority does not validate them, the measures are revoked and nullified.
Any type of physical or moral violence against individuals whose freedom is restricted will be punished.
(omission)

*b. Specific*

Constitution of the Italian Republic:
Article 32. – The Republic guarantees health as a fundamental right of the individual, being in the interest of the community and grants free treatment to destitute people.
Nobody can be forced to undergo a medical treatment unless ordered by law. Persons may not violate the dignity of humans guaranteed by law.

### 8.2.2 General Laws

#### 8.2.2.1 Administrative Measures

**Law May 13, 1978, n. 180:**
Article 1 – Voluntary and involuntary admissions and tests
Medical treatment and tests are voluntary. In cases under subject law, and in those subject to state laws, the medical authority can order medical treatment and tests which respect the individual's dignity, civil and political rights guaran-

---

5 Law 833/1978 "Istituzione del Servizio Sanitario Nazionale", December 23, 1978
6 Decision of the Assemblea Costituente, December 22, 1947. Published in Gazzetta Ufficiale n. 298, December 27, 1947

teed by the Constitution, including, where possible, the right to choose the treating physician and the place of treatment.
Involuntary admissions and tests paid by the state and/or by public institutions or entities are to be carried out in public medical districts and when hospitalization is necessary in public hospitals or in conventional facilities.
During medical treatment, the patient can communicate with whom he/she thinks it is necessary.
Involuntary admissions and tests previously mentioned must be accompanied by initiatives which attempt to gain the consent and participation of the individual(s) coerced into assessment and/or treatment.

The mayor, acting as the local medical authority, can order involuntary admissions and tests on the condition that this is backed by the well-founded request of a physician.

Article 2 – Involuntary admissions due to mental illness
Measures mentioned in sub-paragraph 2 of the previous article can be applied to individuals referred to an authority due to impaired mental functioning.
For cases explained in the previous sub-paragraph, proposals for involuntary admission can require that treatment measures during hospitalization need only be applied if there are changes in the referred individual's psychological condition demanding urgent medical intervention. If the individual rejects these changes and if their condition or circumstance does not permit institutionalised care of this nature, appropriate medical measures can be provided outside the hospital.
The provision ordering the involuntary admission into hospitalization must be authorized (as described in the last sub-paragraph of Article 1) by the validation of a physician's proposal working in a public medical facility and must be founded in accordance with the requirements of the previous sub-paragraph.

Article 3 – Procedures of involuntary admissions and tests under hospitalization for mental illness
The provision contained in Article 2 by which the mayor orders mandatory hospitalization accompanied by a physician's proposal as defined in the last paragraph of Article 1 and by the validation process of Article 2 must be served to the local district tutelary judge within 48 hours using a city process server.
Within the next 48 hours, the tutelary judge examines the information and must issue a decree validating or rejecting the provision, and must also inform the mayor. If the provision is not validated the mayor issues another order terminating involuntary admission into hospitalization.

If a mayor from a different district issues the above-mentioned provision, he must inform the mayor from the patient's district of residence. If the provision is issued for foreign citizens or stateless people, the prefect has to inform the Ministry of the Interior and where possible the relevant consulate.
When involuntary admission exceeds seven days or more, the physician in charge of the medical unit, as explained in Article 6, must issue a proposal to the mayor ordering hospitalization. The mayor is then obliged to inform the judge, in keeping with the terms and conditions contained in sub-paragraphs 1 and 2 of this article, and has to indicate the treatment's probable duration.
The above-mentioned physician must inform the mayor when preconditions necessary for an involuntary admission are no longer met, both in cases of discharge of the individual and of prolonged hospitalization; he also communicates if the treatment cannot be continued. Within 48 hours from time of delivery, the mayor is obliged to pass on this information to the judge.
If necessary, the judge orders urgent measures to safeguard and administer the patient's property.
If during this process there is a failure to observe the provisions contained in sub-paragraphs 1, 4 and 5 of this article, this will result in the termination of the effects of the order and an investigation into whether there has been a breach of duty, unless there is evidence suggesting that the patient is involved in a serious crime.

Article 4 – Revocation and changes of the involuntary admission
Anybody can request the mayor to revoke or change the provision with which a prolonged involuntary admission was ordered.
The mayor can decide within ten days on proposals related to revocation or changes. Provisions of revocation or changes are handled following the same procedures as defined in Article 3.

Article 5 – Juridical safeguard
The individual undergoing an involuntary admission and any other interested individual can lodge an appeal to the competent territorial court against the provision validated by the judge.
Within 30 days from the deadline established in sub-paragraph 2 of Article 3., the mayor can submit a similar appeal against the non-validation of a provision ordering involuntary admission.
Involved parties can attend the trial without defence counsel. They can be represented by a person with the power-of-attorney attested in writing attached to the document of appeal or in a separate document. The document of appeal can be submitted to the court by registered mail.

The president of the panel sets the date of the hearing with a decree written on the document of appeal. The chancellor will serve it to concerned parties and to the public prosecutor.
Having both examined the provision ordering the involuntary admission and heard the public prosecutor, the president of the panel can suspend the treatment – even prior to the full hearing of the person being considered for admission.
In case of suspension, the president can decide within ten days.
Having heard the public prosecutor and acquired information and evidence as required or requested by the parties, the panel meets in the council chamber.
The appeal and forthcoming provisions are free of charge. The decision of the panel need not be entered in criminal records.

Article 6 – (omission)
Article 7 – (omission)
Article 8 – (omission)
Article 9 – (omission)

Article 10 – Changes to the penal code
In the index of book III, title I, volume I, section III, paragraph 6 of the penal code the following expression is no longer to be used: "mentally ill".
In the index of Article 716 of the penal code the following expression is no longer to be used: "mentally sick".
In the same article the following expression is no longer to be used: "in a treatment facility or".

Article 11 – Final norms
The following articles are abrogated: 1, 2, 3, and 3b,i,s of law February 14, 1904, n.36 dealing with "Dispositions on mental hospitals and ill people" and subsequent changes, Article 420 of the civil code, Articles 714, 715 and 717 of the penal code, n. 1 of Article 2 and Article 3 of the law regulating norms for the discipline of the active electorate and maintenance and revision of election lists, approved with a decree issued by the President of the Republic on March 20, 1967, n. 223 and any other dispositions not in compliance with this law.
Dispositions of this law and those contained in Articles 1,2,3,4,5,6,7,8 and 9 remain in force until the date when laws written by the Institution for National Medical Service will come into force.
Competencies of military authorities, of physicians at ports, airports and on national boarders, as well as ship and airplane commanders are excluded in provisions dealing with involuntary admissions until the dispositions currently in force and regulating the international prophylaxis of infectious and contagious

diseases (including mandatory vaccination) are amended and/or coordinated in a single document.

**Remarks**

Law n. 180/1978 has the double characteristic of a "temporary norm" and a "general policy law". As "temporary norm" it contains in sub-paragraph 2 of Article 11 the requirement to terminate the effects of most of its norms with the entry into force of the National Medical Service: this happened with law 833/1978. As "a general policy law", it gives the Regions and autonomous Provinces the authority to issue their own norms and to manage psychiatric assistance facilities, especially those involved with cases of involuntary hospitalization admission for persons with mental illness. Those institutions, in fact, need to operate in compliance with State laws, with legislative and structural appointments concerning "medical and hospital issues" (Article 117 of the Constitution). This concept has not been totally modified by the recent Constitutional law dated 8.10.2001, n.3.

In the course of time, one or more laws on psychiatric assistance have been promulgated in each of the 21 Italian Regions. The judicial mechanism of the TSO (involuntary admission) has not been changed, though, since this is regulated by State laws.

**Law December 23, 1978, n. 833: "Establishment of the National Medical Service":**

Article 33 – Norms for voluntary and involuntary admissions

Medical treatment and tests are voluntary.

In cases covered by this law and in those covered by the state, the responsible medical authority can order medical treatment. They have to respect the dignity of the individual and their civil and political rights as guaranteed by the Constitution, including if possible, the right to choose their physician and place of treatment.

The mayor, acting as the medical authority, can order involuntary admissions with a provision supported by a written proposal issued by a physician.

Involuntary admissions and tests are carried out in public territorial medical districts and when hospitalization is necessary in hospitals or in conventional facilities.

Involuntary admissions and tests, as previously illustrated, must be supported by initiatives adequate to grant the consent and participation of those who are forced to participate in the program. The local medical organization tries to reduce the costs of involuntary admissions by developing initiatives of prevention and medical education, and by improving the relationship between services and the community.

During involuntary admission the patient has the right to communicate with whom he/she thinks necessary.
Anybody can submit to the mayor a proposal to revoke or alter the provision ordering an involuntary admission.
The mayor can decide within ten days on revoking or altering the provision. Revocations or alterations are handled following the same procedures as defined for involuntary admissions and tests under hospitalization for mental illness.

**Remarks**
Article 33 generally regulates involuntary admissions (TSO), including those for mental illness. Besides mental illnesses, the current Italian juridical system orders mandatory medical treatment also for infectious and contagious diseases. This leads to the conclusion that an involuntary admission is not required in cases of cardio-vascular, traumatic, neo-plastic etc. diseases. As explained in section 8.7.1 on "Personal liberty" and "Freedom of treatment", the Italian juridical system provides for and covers the "right to treatment" but not "the obligation to receive treatment" with the exception of the right/duty of the physician to perform emergency treatment for any kind of pathologies that may endanger the life of an individual (see Emergency Treatment).
The consent or refusal of treatment must be "valid". Consent or refusal of treatment is considered valid if expressed by an individual aged above 18, and if not interdicted because of mental illnesses. The consent or refusal expressed by a mentally ill individual not interdicted is considered valid irrespective of the specific psychological pathology he/she has. For those individuals whose consent or refusal is not legally valid, the parent in the case of a minor and the guardian in the case of a mentally interdicted individual may express consent to or refusal of treatment. If the physician deems the treatment necessary for individuals whose consent or refusal is not legally valid, there are two options. If the parent or guardian expresses consent to treatment, the physician may initiate it. In contrast, if the parent or guardian does not consent to it or if the two parents of a minor are not in agreement with each other, the physician may request an intervention by a judge. Even if a judge deems treatment necessary, the physician cannot proceed with the involuntary admission apart from specific types of mental illness, infectious or contagious diseases stipulated by the law. In these cases, according to Article 33 and Article 34, the mayor always issues the provision. In all other cases, the judge will temporarily prevent parents or guardians from using the right/duty to decide on behalf of the minor or interdicted individual by giving this power to somebody else. Children in need of blood transfusions currently constitute a frequent example of such cases where parents deny their consent due to religious reasons.

Article 34 – Voluntary and involuntary admissions for mental illnesses

The regional law stipulates the institution of departmental services for the prevention, treatment and rehabilitation of mental health cases within the local medical unit area and the general services for mental health.

Measures contained in sub-paragraph 2 of the previous article can be applied to mentally ill individuals.

Interventions for the prevention, treatment and rehabilitation of mental health cases are usually carried out in private facilities in the territory as explained in sub-paragraph 1.

An involuntary admission for mental illness can require that the treatment be performed under hospitalization only if there are psychological alterations requiring emergency medical measures, or if the interdicted individual refuses the measures, or if there are no circumstances suitable for carrying out appropriate medical measures in a facility other than the hospital. An involuntary admission into hospitalization must be supported by a validated proposal as described in Article 33, sub-paragraph 3. This has to be issued by a physician of the local medical unit, and it has to demonstrate that the requirements of this sub-paragraph are met.

In cases covered by the previous sub-paragraph, hospitalization must be performed in general hospitals, in psychiatric units for diagnosis and treatment within departmental facilities specifically responsible for the safeguard of mental health – including private facilities in order to grant continuity of therapy. Hospital wards described by this sub-paragraph are equipped with beds up to a number established by the responsible regional medical authority.

Article 35 – Procedures for involuntary admissions under hospitalization for mental illness and judicial custody

A provision issued by the mayor ordering an involuntary admission into hospitalization must be validated within 48 hours according to Article 34, sub-paragraph 4, additionally it must be supported by a physician's request as mentioned in Article 33, which need be served within 48 hours from the beginning of hospitalization to the tutelary judge through a city process server responsible for the patient's district of residence.

Having acquired the information and ordered the appropriate assessments, the tutelary judge issues a decree of validation or non-validation for the provision and informs the mayor within the next 48 hours. If the provision is not validated, the mayor declares the involuntary hospitalization admission void.

If a mayor from a district other than the patient's residential district issues the provision, the mayor and the tutelary judge from the patient's district of residence must be informed. If the provision described in sub-paragraph 1 of this article is issued to foreign citizens or stateless individuals, the prefect has to inform the Ministry of the Interior and also the competent Consulate where possible.

In cases of involuntary admissions exceeding seven days or more, the doctor in charge of the local medical unit has to draft a request to the mayor who had ordered hospitalization. Furthermore, he will inform the tutelary judge respecting the terms established in sub-paragraph 1 and 2 of this article and will indicate the probable duration of the treatment.

The above-mentioned physician must inform the mayor when preconditions are no longer met for requiring an involuntary admission both in cases of dismissal of the patient or of continuous hospitalization. He will also inform the mayor of any sudden impediment to continuing the treatment. As a result the mayor must inform the tutelary judge within 48 hours.

If necessary, the tutelary judge defines the emergency measures necessary for preserving and administering the patient's property.

If during this process there is a failure to observe the provisions contained in sub-paragraphs 1, 4 and 5 of this article, this will result in the termination of the effects of the order and an investigation into whether there has been a breach of duty, unless there is evidence suggesting that the patient is involved in a serious crime.

Both the individual undergoing an involuntary admission and any other interested party can submit to the competent territorial court an appeal against the provision validated by the tutelary judge.

Within 30 days, the mayor can lodge a similar appeal against the non-validation of the provision ordering the involuntary admission.

The parties can attend the trial without a defence counsel, and can be represented by a person with a power-of-attorney attested in writing at the end of the document of appeal or in a separate document. The document of appeal can be submitted to the court by registered mail.

The president of the panel sets the date for the hearing with a decree written on the document of appeal. The chancellor will then serve it to the parties and to the public prosecutor.

Having examined the provision ordering the involuntary admission and having heard the public prosecutor, the president of the panel can suspend treatment – even prior to the full hearing of other parties concerned.

In case of suspension, the president can decide within ten days.

Having heard the public prosecutor and acquired information and evidence as required or requested by the parties, the panel meets in the council chambers.

The appeal and forthcoming provisions are free of charge. The decision of the panel is not subject to be entered in the patient's criminal records.

*Norms concerning involuntary admissions for non-mental diseases are the following:*

Royal Decree 27.7.1934, n.1265 "Single document of medical laws" (especially Article 286: isolation or hospitalization also mandatory for individuals affected by leprosy with contagious symptoms in development)[7];

Law 25.7. 1956, n. 837 "Reformation of the enforced legislation on the prophylaxis of venereal diseases"[8];

Law 5.6.1990 "Fight against AIDS";

Decree of the President of the Republic 9.10.1990, n.309: "Single document of laws concerning drugs and psychotropic substances, prevention, treatment and rehabilitation of drug-addiction cases"[9]

### 8.2.2.2 Criminal Measures

**Code of criminal procedure**[10]

Article 37 – Preventive measures

1. In cases where the mental status of the defendant seems to require psychiatric treatment, the judge promptly informs the competent authority to carry out the measures required by law for the medical treatment of the mental illnesses.
2. In case of delay, the judge orders temporary hospitalization of the defendant in an appropriate psychiatric facility. Effects of this order terminate when the authority indicated in paragraph 1 executes the provision.
3. In cases of the defendant's preventive custody, the judge orders that the measure is in compliance with Article 286.
4. (Omission)

**Remarks**

If the defendant presents symptoms of psychiatric pathology during criminal proceedings, either the judge or the public prosecutor informs the mayor, who acts as the local medical authority for administrative purposes, as it is within the major's power to order an involuntary admission (TSO) due to mental illness. If

---

7 Royal Decree 1934, n.1256: "Testo unico delle leggi sanitarie". Published in Gazzetta Ufficiale n. 186, August 9, 1934

8 Law 837/1956 "Riforma della legislazione vigente per la profilassi delle malattie venere-e". Published in Gazzetta Ufficiale n. 198, August 8, 1956

9 Decree of the President of the Italian Republic 9.10.1990, n.309 "Testo unico delle leggi in material di disciplina degli stupefacenti e sostanze psicotrope, prevenzione, cura e riabilitazione dei relativi stati di tossicodipendenza". Published in Gazzetta Ufficiale n. 255, October 31, 1990

10 Decree of the President of the Italian Republic, 447/1988. Published in Gazzetta Ufficiale n. 250, October 24, 1988

a delay in ordering involuntary admission puts the health or well being of concerned persons in question, the judge informs the mayor and issues an order for temporary hospitalization in an appropriate psychiatric facility (civil, not judiciary). However, a hospitalization order served by a judge does not establish the permissibility of compulsory treatment. According to the Italian judicial system, ordering involuntary admission accompanied by treatment is a power always reserved for the local medical authority (the mayor) and never the judge. Decisions relating to treatment must be made by the Local Health Authority (the Mayor being the highest Local Health Authority). In cases of incarceration, Article 286 applies.

Article 286 – Preventive measures instead of treatment

1. If the person undergoing preventive measures has a mental illness or their present mental condition impairs their capacity to understand proceedings, the judge can order a temporary hospitalization in lieu of preventive measures undertaken in jail to prevent escape. Hospitalization cannot be continued if the defendant has no mental illness.
2. (Omission).

**Remarks**

During the criminal proceedings the judge can, without asking the administrative authority, order a defendant requiring treatment on psychiatric grounds to undergo "temporary hospitalization" in a psychiatric hospital (civil, not judicial) where the defendant is detained in police custody. Even in this case, as explained in Article 73, the mandatory aspect concerns only the hospitalization and not the treatment.

**Penal code**[11]

Article 148 – Psychiatric incapacitation unexpectedly occurred to the convicted
If prior to beginning restrictive measures or during their execution, the convicted person is unexpectedly affected by mental infirmity, the judge can order that the patient be hospitalized in a judiciary psychiatric facility if he thinks that the infirmity can prevent the sentence from being executed. The judge can order the convicted person's hospitalization in a civil psychiatric hospital via a judiciary psychiatric facility if the sentence involves less than three years of incarceration (or arrest) and if the individual in question in not a professional criminal, repeat offender, nor proven to be inclined toward criminal activity.
This provision is revoked when the grounds for calling upon it do not exist anymore.

---

[11] Royal Decree 1398/1930. Published in Gazzetta Ufficiale n. 253, 28 October 1930

**Remarks**
Individuals sentenced to jail who are affected by a sudden mental infirmity "that would prevent the sentence from being executed" must be hospitalized in a judiciary psychiatric hospital (OPG) or in a nursing care centre (CCC). These are both penitentiary facilities. Hospitalization lasts for the duration of the impaired mental functioning and terminates with the completion of the sentence.

Article 206 – Temporary enforcement of security measures
During the trial, a minor, or a person with impaired mental functioning due to mental illness, or a person suffering from alcohol or drug addiction, or a person under chronic intoxication of drugs or alcohol can be temporarily hospitalized in a judiciary psychiatric hospital (OPG) or in a nursing care centre (CCC).
The judge revokes this order when he thinks that this individual is no longer a danger to the public.
(Omission)

**Remarks**
Individuals whose mental functioning is impaired due to mental illness, habitual alcoholics, drug addicted, or intoxicated by alcohol or drugs can be hospitalized in a judiciary psychiatric hospital (OPG) or in a nursing care centre (CCC), both penitentiary institutions, for the duration of the criminal proceedings they are involved in and for the time "they could commit new crimes."

Article 219 – Assignment to a nursing care centre
An individual convicted of wilful murder whose sentence is reduced because of impaired mental functioning, intoxication by alcohol or drug substances or because of they are deaf or cannot speak can be hospitalized in a nursing care centre for a period of one year or longer when the sentence declared by the law is over five years of seclusion.
If the law for the committed crime requires imprisonment for life, or seclusion longer than ten years, the security measure can be ordered for a period of more than three years.
For any other crime requiring imprisonment by law and in the case that the convicted individual is a person considered a danger to the public, admission to a nursing care centre is ordered for a minimum of six months; however, the judge can order probation in lieu of hospitalization. This substitution cannot take place when the sentence has been reduced on the grounds of intoxication due to alcohol, drug abuse or addiction.
(Omission)

**Remarks**

In addition to the sentence, a "security prison measure" consisting of the admission to a nursing care centre (CCC) for the entire time the defendant could commit other crimes applies to the individuals whose sentence has been reduced because of impaired mental functioning, chronic intoxication due to alcohol or drug abuse or addiction, or are deaf and cannot speak.

Article 221 – Alcoholics and persons habitually in inebriated states

In absence of other security prison measures, individuals suffering from addictive disorders who are convicted of crimes committed under the influence of alcohol or drugs are admitted to a nursing care centre.

However, for crimes punished with a sentence not exceeding three years, admission can be substituted for probation.

Admissions take place in special wards and last for at least six months.

**Remarks**

In addition to the sentence, the measure of which is augmented with respect to its statutory prediction, individuals convicted to jail for more than three years who have committed crimes under the influence of alcohol or drug substances (due to addiction) must be admitted to a nursing care centre (CCC) for the entire period of time they could commit new crimes.

Article 222 – Admission to a judiciary psychiatric hospital

In cases of impaired mental functioning, chronic intoxication through alcoholic or drug substances and for persons who are deaf and cannot speak, the defendant is always admitted to a judiciary psychiatric hospital for a minimum of two years. Exceptions to this rule are constituted by minor offences, negligent or unintentional homicides and for all other crimes for which the law establishes a monetary sanction or incarceration for at least two years. In this case the Law Enforcement Authority is to be informed.

The minimum period for admission into a judiciary psychiatric hospital is ten years if, given the committed crime, the law establishes imprisonment for life, and five years if the sentence includes a period of incarceration for a minimum of ten years.

**Remarks**

A real sentence cannot be issued for individuals acquitted of criminal charges, for persons with a mental illness, intoxication through alcoholic or drug substances and for persons who are deaf and cannot speak. Such individuals must be admitted into a judiciary psychiatric hospital (OPG) for the period of time believed necessary to prevent new crimes being committed. The minimum period required for admission is two, five or ten years based on the seriousness of the crime committed.

Article 232 – Minors or mentally interdicted individuals under probation
A minor or a mentally interdicted person cannot be under probation unless given to foster care or to institutions belonging to social services which are adequate for providing education and assistance.
If foster care is not possible or is deemed inappropriate, admission to a reformatory or care and custody centre is to be ordered.
If during the probation period, the minor does not show regret or the person with a mental illness becomes dangerous again, probation is then replaced by admission into a care and custody centre.

**Remarks**
Persons with a mental illness under probation must be admitted into a care and custody centre (CCC) for the period of time thought necessary to prevent them from committing new crimes when it is not possible to send them to other appropriate facilities.
Note: as previously explained for *Code of Criminal Procedure* norms, even for *Penal Code* norms (Articles 148, 206, 219, 221, 222, 232) involuntary admission refers only to the period of hospitalization but not to the treatment of the mental illness.

### 8.2.3 International Conventions and Agreements Incorporated into National Laws

> *"The European Committee for the Prevention of Torture and Inhuman and Degrading Treatment or Punishment (CPT) was set up under the 197 Council of Europe Convention of the same name." "The work of the CPT is designed to be an integrated part of the Council of Europe system for the protection of human rights, placing a proactive non-judicial mechanism alongside the existing reactive judicial mechanism of the European Court of Human Rights."*

CPT's activities include visits (periodical or on a case-by-case basis) to the Member States of the Convention. In these occasions, the CPT gathers necessary information from the Public Authorities, from local Non-Governmental Organizations and from private clients. It has

> *"unlimited access to any place where persons are deprived of their liberty by a public authority, including the right to move inside such places without restriction"*

(10th General Report on CPT's activities).
On November 26, 1987, Italy signed the Convention that has been ratified on December 29, 1988. It has been in force in the Italian judicial system since April 1, 1989.

**8.3 Jurisprudence**

Corte Costituzionale (Constitutional Court)

Sentence n.88/1979[12]: with reference to Article 32 of the Constitution that recognizes health as "a fundamental right of the individual" and as "in the interest of the community", this sentence affirms the supremacy of the private aspect ("right of the individual") in public law over the "interest of the community"; it emphasizes that the individual's right to health is not only "fundamental" but also primary and absolute, and it is part of the "inviolable human rights" granted by Article 2 of the Constitution.

Sentence n.307/1990[13]: as far as vaccinations are concerned, it reiterates the importance of the principle of self-determination concerning medical treatment.
Sentence n.218/1994[14]: as far as HIV tests (not treatment) are concerned this sentence declared illegitimate the norm requiring consent from individuals performing professional duties or activities with potential risks for third parties' health before they can be tested. Otherwise, the right to health as an "interest of the community" is violated.

Sentence n.258/1994[15]: the exception to constitutional legitimacy of the law imposing vaccination against B hepatitis upon certain categories of individuals is rejected.

Sentence: n. 118/1996[16]: it declares the partial illegitimacy of the norms concerning vaccinations against poliomyelitis. As a general principle, the court establishes that the law imposing an involuntary treatment is in conflict with Article 32 of the Constitution because it aims to protect the health both of the community and that of the individual subject to the treatment.

**Remarks**

The Constitutional Court is the highest level of the Italian judicial system. It examines if ordinary laws comply with the principles of the Constitution. In cases of failure to comply, even partial failures, the subject matter is removed from the legal system. As previously explained, the constitutional jurisprudence concerning involuntary admissions is focused on spreading infectious and contagious diseases and on the related preventive norms (vaccinations). On the other hand, it does not concern involuntary admissions for mental illnesses. The difference

---

12 *Nalli v. Capenti* S. 88 C. Cost. 26/7/1979, www.giuricost.org/decisioni/index

13 *Oprandi v. Ministry of Health* S. 307 C. Cost. 14/6/1990, www.giuricost.org/decisioni/index

14 *Marchioro v. O.I.C.* S. 218 1994 C. Cost. 23/5/1994, www.giuricost.org/decisioni/index

15 *Zampierin v.City of Bassano del Grappa* S.258 23/6/1994, www.giuricost.org/decisioni/index

16 *Brogini v. Ministry of Health* S. 118 18/4/1996, www.giuricost.org/decisioni/index

lies in the fact that the topic of the discussion is focused on the possible contrast between "the right of the individual" and "the interest of the community" as covered by Article 32 of the Constitution. Now, "the right of the individual" is only of judicial importance if performed in a legally valid way, i.e. the will of the subject individual is considered as "free" and "valid". Generally, this does not apply to cases pertaining to persons with mental illnesses because it is widely presumed that there is an "invalidity of expression of will" involved.

## 8.4 Protocols and Internal Norms Related to Coercive Measures or Compulsory Medical Treatment

In Italy, there are no protocols on coercive measures officially accepted at national level. Each psychiatric ward has its own rules and internal norms.

Among the coercive measures routinely applied, physical restraint is the most common one. Other measures include forced pharmacological treatment, seclusion, immobilisation in bed, limitation of external visits etc..

Often these coercive measures are administered without the patient's consent. In each case however, physicians and psychiatric staff have to protect the patient's interests and rights according to the Italian Constitution.

There are several situations in which it is necessary to apply coercive measures in psychiatric wards. The most common is in case of patients' aggressive behaviour.

In some cases, physicians can use physical restraint in order to administer forced pharmacological treatment.

In several psychiatric wards, internal rules suggest the need to use *ad hoc* records to obtain reliable information and to use strategies to prevent, when possible, the application of physical restraint.

Psychiatric staff should gradually approach a patient with aggressive behaviour: firstly, they should interact only verbally with patients. Secondly, only when all other therapeutic options failed, staff are allowed to use physical and/or mechanical restraint.

Only physicians/psychiatrists are allowed to order coercive measures. Responsibility for ordering these measures generally lies with the physicians/psychiatrists.

If physical restraint cannot be avoided, there should be as many staff members as possible available for implementing this clinical measure. This is the main reason why restrictive measures are usually applied during periods of staff rotation.

Reasons and duration of restrictive measures should be recorded in the documentation system; this documentation has to include the following details: period (date of starting and finishing), description of the application of the mechanical devices (hands, feet, abdomen), name of the responsible clinical staff,

name of the physician responsible for this measure, and the reasons and ways of ordering and applying this measure.
Mechanical restraint must be restricted for the shortest possible period. The physician must evaluate all alternative interventions before ordering a coercive measure.
During this treatment, the physician must carry out a full physical and mental examination.
Nurses must fill in *ad hoc* schedules and their official records in which they have to report on: breathing, consciousness, skin state, personal hygiene and other relevant information. Nurses also have the task of providing opportunities for patients to visit the toilet and have regular meals.
All staff members should be involved in the application of such measures, and all of them must be involved in the process of evaluation of alternatives to physical restraint.

### 8.5 Reports

The CPT has conducted four "periodical" visits to Italy and has submitted three different reports to the Italian Government. Two of these have been published.
During the 1992 visit, the CPT also visited the locations of the Judiciary Psychiatric Hospital (OPG) in Naples and found that the intensive therapy section was an "anti-therapeutic place" because of its dirty and negligent conditions, its intensive pharmacological care approach and the total lack of all kinds of physical activity for the most severely ill patients.
Subsequently, from October 22 to November 6, 1995, the CPT performed a second visit to the Naples' OPG and to the Civil Psychiatric Hospital "Leonardo Bianchi", also in Naples. The first institution was found to have improved certain objective conditions since 1992, but still displayed a lack of specific and personal treatment for the patients. The Civil Psychiatric Hospital "Leonardo Bianchi" was visited during an advanced status of patient deinstitutionalization: it was responsible for 624 patients compared with its maximum capacity of 3500 which had been reached in previous years. This hospital was found in a serious state of decay as far as its physical structure was concerned.

### 8.6 Safeguards

Safeguard procedures for coercive measures in psychiatry differ between penal coercive measures and those dictated by the involuntary admission (TSO) due to mental illness regulated by Articles 33,34, and 35 of law n.833/1978.
Safeguard procedures are of a penal and juridical nature and are laid down in the *Code of Criminal Procedure*: the present report will not extensively deal with these.

In contrast, safeguard procedures for involuntary admission (TSO) due to mental illnesses are of an administrative nature with potential interventions of a civil juridical nature. Here a distinction is to be made between "*a priori* safeguard procedures" and "*a posteriori* safeguard procedures."

### 8.6.1 A Priori Safeguard Procedures

An involuntary admission (TSO) for mental illness is activated by a "well-founded proposal" written by a physician. It is not necessary that the requesting physician is a psychiatrist and/or assigned to a public facility. Any physician, even a general practioner (GP) in a private practice can write such a proposal. It should contain the following: the name of the individual; mental alterations found; eventual clinical diagnosis; the reasons for his/she/her mental condition requiring "emergency treatment", and an annotation stating that the individual does not accept treatment.

If the medical proposal concerns "emergency treatment" not to be performed under hospitalization (i.e.: that which can be provided at home or in a day hospital of the responsible Department of Health, etc.), it should then be passed on to the mayor of the patient's district of residence (or of his/she/her current residence). The mayor, as the local medical authority, examines the proposal. If he or she finds it formally regular, because the law does not require him to assess the merits, he issues an order of "involuntary admission *not* under hospitalization."

On the other hand, if the medical proposal states that "there are no conditions and circumstances supporting appropriate and emergency measures outside an hospital", the physician proposes that "the emergency treatment" should be performed through an involuntary admission "under hospitalization." In this case, the initial medical proposal is passed on to a second physician who must be a member of the National Medical Service (ASL). They do not have to be a psychiatrist but need to examine and verify the grounds and congruence of the proposal itself.

If they deem the proposal valid and congruous, they validate it. If not, they do not validate it and the proposal loses its effects.

If validated, the proposal drafted by the first physician and then validated by the physician of the public facility is brought to the attention of the mayor from the patient's district of residence or of the district where he/she currently resides.

The mayor, always as the local medical authority, examines the proposal. If they find it regular in its form, they issue within 48 hours from the validation of the physician of the National Medical Service, an order for an "involuntary admission under hospitalization" against the individual in question.

At this point, the mayor's order enters into force and the mentally interdicted individual is hospitalized in the designated hospital.

At the same time, within 48 hours from hospitalization, the enforced mayor's order, the initial proposal and the validation issued by the physician of the public service are transmitted to a tutelary judge. Besides examining the formal regularity of the proposal, a tutelary judge, after having "acquired the necessary information and ordered eventual assessments", issues a validation or non-validation of the mayor's order.
If the mayor's order is approved by a tutelary judge, the patient remains in care for a total and maximum of seven days starting from its beginning. If care exceeds seven days, the physician in charge of the psychiatric service transmits to the mayor a proposal for the "extension" or "continuation" of the involuntary admission. The mayor examines it and, if they find it regular, they issue another order for involuntary care – always for seven day periods. Other requests and mayoral orders can be issued in the course of time without restrictions.
If a tutelary judge does not approve the mayor's order for an involuntary admission under hospitalization, the mayor immediately issues another order terminating the effects of the former one. The involuntary admission must be terminated in any case.
The mayor can appeal against the tutelary judge's decision not approving their order for the involuntary admission of the person referred for admission. The appeal needs to be presented within 30 days starting from the day the judge issued the "non-validation" decree of the mayor's order. A court will pronounce judgement on the mayor's appeal.

### 8.6.2 A Posteriori Safeguard Procedures

Article 33, sub-paragraph 6, law n. 833/1978 reads as follows:

> *"During an involuntary admission, the patient has the right to communicate with whom he thinks is necessary."*

The person referred for involuntary admission has, if necessary, the possibility of communicating in person, by telephone, by mail to anybody (a family member, a friend, an attorney, police authority, a judge, etc.) in order to request termination of the treatment itself. By these means, or independently,

> *"anybody can request the mayor to revoke or change the provision by which the involuntary admission was ordered."*

(Article 33 paragraph 7, law n. 833/1978). Please note that the term "anybody" includes not only the patient but any other person, even one who represents an organization. Within ten days, the mayor can decide on revocation orders or amendments using the same process as defined when a change or a revocation is requested. (Article 33 paragraph 8, law n. 833/1978). According to some researchers, it is possible to also verbally appeal against the mayor's decision of non-issuance of the order. The procedure described until here are *a posteriori* safeguard procedures of *administrative* nature.

*A posteriori* safeguard procedures of *judicial* nature can include, according to the general criteria of the legal system and even if this is not established by law n.833/1978, an appeal to an administrative judge submitted by any interested person against the mayor's provision ordering involuntary admission. Article 35 paragraph 8, law n. 833/1978 reads as follows

> *"the person undergoing an involuntary admission, and any interested person can submit to the responsible territorial court an appeal against the provision validated by the tutelary judge."*

A judicial proceeding begun in this manner is of civil and not of criminal nature. This is also an *uncomplicated proceeding* because it does not incorporate charges against involved parties.

### 8.7 Other Information

#### 8.7.1 "Personal Liberty" and "Freedom to Non-Treatment"

The constitutions of most modern countries provide for and cover the "right to health" and the "right to treatment", but not an "obligation to be healthy" or an "obligation to obtain treatment." The exceptions are the Constitution of Japan (1946, art. 25), of Peru (1933, art. 46), of Panama (1946, art. 92), and Uruguay (1948, art. 43).

During the constitution of the Italian National Assembly, it was proposed that the word "obligation" be inserted into the text, but the proposal was rejected.

There is however a valid prohibition in Italy against voluntary damages to an individual's health status:

a) when the damage aims to achieve an illegal advantage (i.e. a reimbursement from an insurance company or to achieve exemption from compulsory military service);
b) when the damage implies a "permanent damage to physical integrity" (art. 5 civil code)[17].

However, illegal behaviour concerning voluntary and conscious damage to an individual's health status cannot always be classified as a "punishable behaviour" and therefore as a "crime".

Generally, involuntary admissions imply a restriction of certain aspects of "personal liberty" and in particular of the "freedom to non-treatment". This restriction is covered by the Constitution (art. 32), and its terms are also specified in the jurisprudence on constitutional issues.

From a judicial point of view, the notion of "personal liberty" has a broader meaning than that of "freedom to non-treatment."

---

[17] Royal Decree 262/1942. Published in Gazzetta Ufficiale n. 79, April 4, 1942

Since according to Article 13 of the Constitution, "no types of restriction of individual liberty are permitted except when ordered by a judicial authority", involuntary admission and involuntary admission due to mental illness cannot entirely restrict the patient's "individual liberty", but only his/she/her "freedom to treatment". This is valid both for involuntary admissions under hospitalizations and not under hospitalization. Despite this, individuals hospitalized under involuntary admission are often considered as "temporarily deprived of their individual liberty". They often cannot leave their place of treatment.
As a paradox, it is noted that the Italian legislation curiously defines situations where *restriction of individual liberty* and *treatment for mental illnesses* are combined. These situations are previously mentioned as contained in the *Code of Criminal Procedure* and in the *Penal Code*. The anomaly lies in the fact that the restriction of individual liberty in those cases is legal since it's ordered by "a provision issued by the judicial authority in compliance with the law". So, it is in compliance with the Constitution as well. The psychiatric treatment, *in fact*, is often "compulsory" and "coercive" without authorization by any laws. All the cases described in section 8.2.2.2 of this report (coercive criminal measures) relate to this paradox with the exception of cases covered by Article 73 of the *Code of Criminal Procedure* as related to individuals affected by a mental illness and "subject to temporary hospitalization" ordered by a judge or a public prosecutor and to whom the mayor issued an order for involuntary admission according to Article 35 of law December 23, 1978, n. 833.

### 8.7.2 Some Specific Legal Aspects

#### 8.7.2.1 Emergency Treatment

In emergency cases, the treatment of any pathology including a mental illness represents an obligation for the physician.

Penal code, Article 593
Failure to assist is punishable with imprisonment up to three months or by a fine of up to 309 Euro. Anybody who finds a human body that seems inanimate, or a wounded person, or a person in danger, and then fails to give the necessary assistance or pass on this information to the responsible authority is also liable.
The obligation to intervene does not depend on the will of the subject in need of assistance if he/she is still in "danger" and this obligation exists even when the person in danger does not consent to assistance. The person assisting individuals in danger who do not want to be helped can invoke one of the "causes of not punishment" covered in Articles 51, 52 and 54 of the penal code:
Article 51 – Exercising a right or accomplishment of a duty
Exercising a right or accomplishing a duty imposed by a judicial norm or by a legal order issued by a public authority does not incur punishment (omission).

Article 52 – Legitimate defence
Anybody who is obliged to commit an action due to the need to defend his or her own rights or the danger of an impending attack cannot be punished. The defence, however, must be proportional to the offensive actions.

Article 54 – Necessity status
Anybody who is obliged to commit an action because of it is necessary to rescue themselves or others from a serious danger, or from a danger he/she did not voluntarily cause, and therefore considered unavoidable, cannot be punished. The action must be proportional to the danger. (omission)
This legal norm does not depend on the fact that the individual in danger could be mentally ill and therefore unable to express a valid will.
In cases of mental illness, once given assistance or emergency treatment, it is always possible, when necessary, to order a voluntary treatment or an involuntary admission according to Articles 34 and 35 of law n. 833/1978.

#### 8.7.2.2 Coercive Measures

Once the mayor issues a provision covered by art. 34 of law n.833/1978, ordering for the assessment or involuntary admission due to mental illness against a certain subject, a physician is obliged to perform the tests and treatment deemed necessary. Other individuals, however, are obliged to overcome, even with force, resistance from the individual against whom the mayor's provision has been issued. This is applicable both for involuntary admissions under and not under hospitalization.
This obligation to enforce the mayor's provisions, as "a legitimate order of an authority", even overpowering the prospective patient's resistance, is the duty of all public forces agents and officers (Police, Carabinieri) and especially of those belonging to the municipal police forces since the mayor himself directs them. Furthermore, since it is a provision relating to medical measures, an active and necessary collaboration between police forces and medical personnel is required. The use of force must be proportional to the actual resistance, given the case's circumstances. However excessive use of force in response to resistance can constitute a crime.

#### 8.7.2.3 Preventive Measures of Security and Order

All psychiatric facilities must establish structural and organizational measures to prevent damage inflicted on patients by themselves and on other people. When these rules are not respected, the medical personnel are liable from a penal point of view, and can be charged with damages that patients cause to themselves or to others. According to the penal code:

Article 40 – Principle of causality
If you do not impede an event that you are judicially forced to prevent from taking place, you cause it.

Article 43 – Psychological element of crime
The crime (omission) is negligent, or unintentional, when the event, even if foreseen, is not committed with intention and takes place because of negligence or imprudence, that results from a failure to comply with laws, rules, orders or norms.

Besides criminal liability, the medical personnel can be civilly liable from a patrimonial point of view.
In the event of threats or aggression from a patient or other people (other patients, visitors or medical personnel) measures to be used are all of a psychological (interpersonal) and/or pharmacological nature. Their aim is to reduce the aggressiveness.
Staff are permitted to temporarily isolate an aggressive patient even in places with no purpose designed infrastructure or through using measures that could potentially cause harm. It is, however, not wise to isolate a patient without first employing psychological/pharmacological measures in order to reduce his/she/her aggressiveness as a preventive measure. It is not advisable to leave an aggressive patient alone when isolated; it is always recommended that some medical staff be with him/her. Length of isolation must be as short as possible and proportional to the circumstances. Isolation must be ordered by a physician in writing for which he/she accepts direct responsibility. It cannot be ordered (not even indirectly) as a punishment.
The use of physical force is permitted for the duration of and with the methods necessary for pharmacological treatment (sufficient to reduce aggressiveness) to become effective. It is important that physical force employed need be proportional to the potential consequences of the present aggressiveness, realistically evaluated based on experience.
In some cases, the use of physical force is implemented through coercion or physical immobilization of the aggressive patient: i.e., with leather or canvas belts around the upper or lower limbs or through restraining the patient in his/she/her bed or in another appropriate bed. Physical coercion must constitute the *extrema ratio* and can be used only when other measures, appropriately used, are ineffective or require too much time to become effective.
Physical coercion cannot be of a punishable, dissuasive or preventive nature in any cases, even in an indirect manner.
Utilized within the limits described above, physical coercion can be considered as a therapy. Therefore, the physician who accepts direct and personal responsi-

bility for the case in addition to supervising the patient is the only person authorized to order the use of physical coercion. It must be prescribed in writing, be annotated in the patient's medical record, and must be signed. The starting and terminating times of coercion must also be recorded. During coercion, the physician must personally examine the patient to monitor that this treatment does not cause any alterations in their state of health. Special attention must be paid to respiratory and circulatory functions and it is advisory and prudent to avoid any compression of the nervous and vascular systems.

In psychiatry, physical coercion is not regulated by any special law, but by general norms.

From a judicial point of view, physical coercion constitutes a typical "illegal act" that could be discussed as a crime under the rubric of several laws: from "private violence" (art. 610 penal code), to "aggravated kidnapping" (art. 650 penal code). When it is used as a therapy, within the limits previously described, the "causes of non-punishment" apply to whoever ordered it as stated in Articles 51, 52 and 54 of the penal code. (see Emergency treatment).

As previously mentioned, ultimately physicians can only order the use of physical coercion with aggressive individuals who endanger their own and/or others' safety and/or life; it is never used in cases of aggression against objects.

In Italy, the above-mentioned laws are valid for all general legal cases as well as for cases involving psychiatric admission regardless of whether that admission is voluntary or involuntary. As a result physical coercion is neither specifically prohibited in the case of psychiatric patients hospitalized under voluntary admission nor is it automatically allowed for patients hospitalized under involuntary admission. In fact, the use of physical coercion is always based exclusively on a case-based clinical evaluation that must take into consideration the patient-specific conditions of therapy required.

Some analogies with physical coercion in psychiatry can be found in the penitentiary field. Law July 26, 1975, n. 354 ("Norms on the penitentiary system and on the execution of depriving and limiting freedom") reads as follows:

Article 41 – Use of physical force and of coercion tools

No tool of physical coercion can be used if it is not clearly discussed by the rules, and it cannot be used for disciplinary purposes, but only to avoid harm to individuals or objects or to guarantee that individual's safety.

The use of physical coercion must be limited to the time period necessary and must be continually monitored by a physician.

The Presidential Decree dated June 30, 2000, n. 230 ("Norms on the penitentiary system and on depriving and limiting liberty")[18] reads as follows:

Art. 82 – Means of physical coercion
Physical coercion, allowed for the purposes indicated in Article 41, subparagraph 3 of law 26, is applied under medical supervision and with the same means and aims as used in public hospitals.

**Diagram 8.1: Regular Judicial Procedure Concerning Detention of a Mentally Ill Person According to Italian Law (833/78)**

**Pre-condition:**
1.) Psychological alterations which demand urgent medical intervention;
2.) The individual rejects therapy;
3.) There are no conditions or circumstances that permit appropriate medical measures being carried out in locations other than hospitals.

**Involuntary Admission:**

Expert report written by a physician proposing the involuntary admission of a psychiatric patient
↓
Confirmation by a physician working in the National Health Service
↓
Submission of proposal to and confirmation by the mayor
↓
Mayor's order of involuntary admission[19]
↓
Notification of Mayor's order to a tutelary judge
↓
Tutelary judge's validation (within 48 hours) of the involuntary admission

---

18 Presidential Decree 230/2000: "Regolamento recante norme sull'ordinamento penitenziario e sulle misure private e limitative della libertà" Published in Gazzetta Ufficiale n. 195, August 22, 2000

19 Legally defined duration of involuntary admission: seven days (can be prolonged)

**CHAPTER 9**

# Legal Report – Lithuania

Dalia ZELECKIENE

## 9.1 Preliminary Remarks

### 9.1.1 Some Historical Notes

Coercive measures in psychiatry, involuntary admission and detention in psychiatric hospitals and compulsory treatment and care in Lithuania are regulated by the Constitution of the Republic of Lithuania, the Criminal Code, the Code of Criminal Procedures, the Civil Code, the Law on the Health System, the Law on Mental Health Care, the Law on the Rights of Patients and Compensation of the Damage to Their Health, the Law on Ethics of Biomedical Research, the Order No. 133 "On Approval of the Procedure for Primary Examination of the Person's Mental Condition" of March 7, 1996 of the Ministry of Health.

In evaluating norms of Lithuanian law, we must pay attention to historical aspects of the development the Lithuanian state and law. Independence of the Lithuanian State was restored on March 11, 1990, after long years of Soviet Union occupation. Until 1990, the laws of the Soviet Union were valid in Lithuania. After restoration of the independence, democratic processes were started, and it was necessary to regulate matters relevant for society from a new angle. Many new statutes were created during this period. In 1992, the Constitution of the Lithuanian Republic was passed. The Civil Code was passed in 2000, but really came into force on July 1, 2001.

The special Law on Mental Health care was passed in 1995, and came into force on January 1, 1996. Such a law was passed in Lithuania for the first time. Before Soviet occupation, such a law was lacking, but some aspects of mentally ill persons' rights were included in other legislation, e.g. in 1928, "The statute of mentally sick people patronage" was passed. In the period of Soviet occupation, the rights of mentally ill persons were not regulated properly. The order and conditions of forced hospitalization (involuntary admission and detention in psychiatric hospitals) were controlled by various instructions which created the possibility of misuse.

Basic changes of the Mental Health Care Law were made on July 5, 2001, aiming to coordinate its contents with the Civil Code and International Conventions. Nowadays, the Republic of Lithuania is a democratic and unitary legal state. Its political system is based on the division of power between three bodies: legislative, executive and the judicial system.

### 9.1.2. Survey Methodology

This report is based on the present legislation in Lithuania on compulsory mental care, on the jurisprudence of the Supreme Court of Lithuania and on the reports of local governmental and non-governmental organizations about the Lithuanian legislation on compulsory psychiatric care.

All legal norms are published in the official book "Valstybės žinios". All legal norms can also be found on the official web site of Parliament (Seimas)[1]. The decisions of the Supreme Court are published in the official book of the Supreme Court "Teismu praktika". The decisions can also be found on the Court's official web site[2]. This research covers the last 15 years.

## 9.2 Applicable Laws and General Norms

### 9.2.1 Constitutional Norms

*Constitution of the Republic of Lithuania*

Approved by the citizens of the Republic of Lithuania in the Referendum on October 25, 1992

*Article 20*

Personal freedom shall be inviolable.

No person may be arbitrarily arrested or detained. No person may be deprived of freedom except on the bases, and according to the procedures, which have been established in laws.

A person detained in flagrante delicto must, within 48 hours, be brought to court for the purpose of determining, in the presence of the detainee, the validity of the detention. In the case that the court does not authorize the decision to arrest the person, the detained individual shall be released immediately.

*Article 21*

The person shall be inviolable.

Human dignity shall be protected by law.

It shall be prohibited to torture, injure, degrade, or maltreat a person, as well as to establish such punishment.

No person may be subjected to scientific or medical testing without his or her knowledge thereof and consent thereto.

---

1 www.lrs.lt

2 www.lat.litlex.lt

### 9.2.2 General Laws

#### 9.2.2.1 Criminal Code

*Article 98. Coercive medical measures*

1. The court may apply the following coercive medical measures with regard to persons who have been judged by the court as not or only partly responsible for their actions, and also with regard to those persons whose mental health has deteriorated as a result of a committed crime or imposed punishment, and to those who may not understand the essence of their behaviour:

1) outpatient supervision under the conditions of primary mental health care;

2) inpatient supervision under the conditions of general supervision in mental health facilities;

3) inpatient supervision under the conditions of enhanced supervision in specialised mental health facilities;

4) inpatient supervision under the conditions of strict supervision in specialised mental health facilities.

2. Outpatient supervision shall be applied with the court's approval to a person whose risk profile based on the committed action and whose mental disorder requires no supervision, and who is in no need of inpatient treatment or who can be further treated as an outpatient after inpatient treatment has improved his mental condition.

3. Inpatient supervision under the conditions of general supervision terms shall be applied with the court's approval to a person who needs inpatient supervision and treatment as a result of his mental disorder.

4. Inpatient supervision under the conditions of enhanced supervision shall be applied with the court's approval to a person who needs specialised inpatient supervision and treatment as a result of his risk profile based on the committed action and his mental disorder.

5. Inpatient supervision under the conditions of strict supervision shall be applied with the court's approval to a person who has attempted to take somebody's life or to harm the health of another person, and who is particularly dangerous to other people and requires specialised inpatient supervision and treatment as a result of his mental disorder.

6. The court shall not define the duration of application of coercive medical measures. The latter shall be applied until the person recovers or his mental condition improves and the risk factors disappear. At least once every six months, the court must decide either to extend the application of coercive measures, change their type or terminate their application based on the findings of a health care establishment.

7. In the absence of the need to apply coercive medical measures to the person, and also if the court terminates the application of these measures, the person

may be transferred by the court to the guardianship and care of his relatives or other persons, and further medical supervision may also be established.

*Article 146. Unlawful deprivation of freedom*
1. The person who unlawfully deprives another person of his freedom in the absence of signs of being taken hostage shall be either fined or imprisoned for up to three years.
2. The person who has acted as prescribed in Part 1 of this Article by using violence or endangering the life or health of the victim, or by depriving him of his freedom for a period exceeding 48 hours shall be imprisoned for up to four years.
3. The person who unlawfully deprives another person of his freedom by placing him in a psychiatric hospital for reasons other than illness shall be imprisoned for up to five years.

#### 9.2.2.2 Code of Criminal Procedures

*Article 141. Committal to a health care establishment*
1. In the event of the need to carry out a forensic medical or forensic psychiatric examination during the investigation or examination of a criminal case, the suspect, upon the decision of the pre-trial detention judge or the court's decision, may be referred to an examination facility and kept there until the examination certificate is submitted to the prosecutor or the court. The time spent in the examination facility shall be included in the term of detention.
2. In the case that the forensic psychiatric examination produces the diagnosis that the suspect poses a risk to society as a result of his mental illness, the length of stay in the examination facility may be extended by the decision of the judge or the suspect may be transferred to another specialised facility until the court takes the decision to impose coercive medical measures.
3. If the suspect is committed to an examination facility, the length of his stay shall be prolonged in accordance with the same procedure applicable to imposing, prolonging or appealing against detention.
4. A detained suspect may be committed to the examination facility during pre-trial detention upon the decision of a prosecutor.
5. The defendant may also be committed to the examination facility, during the course of a trial.

#### 9.2.2.3 Law on the Health System

Art. 3 Item 19 of this Law provides that *only laws* shall establish conditions of mental health care and the legal framework of organising and managing this care, as well as of the safeguards on the conditions thereof.

### 9.2.2.4 Law on Ethics of Biomedical Research

*Article 7. Protection of vulnerable persons*

3. The consent of a person who suffers from a mental disorder but may provide his free and informed consent to take part in biomedical research must be attested by two witnesses and the head of the health care establishment where the research is conducted. Approval of the Medical Ethics Commission must also be obtained. The procedure of forming the Medical Ethics Commission and of conducting its activities shall be laid down in the model regulations of the Medical Ethics Commission of a health care establishment approved by the Ministry of Health.

**Remark**

Biomedical research may not be performed on persons who cannot give their informed consent hereto.

### 9.2.2.5 Law on the Rights of Patients and Compensation of the Damage to their Health

*Article 8. The right to refuse treatment*

4. The Law on Mental Health Care shall establish the nature of treatment of a mental patient who is unable to correctly assess the condition of his own health.

### 9.2.2.6 Civil Code

*Article 2.26. Impermissibility of restraining the freedom of a natural person*

1. The freedom of a natural person shall be inviolable. Any care or restraint may be applied to a legally capable person only upon his consent or in cases established by law.
2. No personal consent shall be needed for health care in the case of risk to the person's life or the need to refer him to an inpatient health care establishment in order to protect interests of society.
3. The mental condition of a person may be examined only upon his consent or the consent of the court. Consent to carry out an examination of the mental condition of a legally incapable person may be given only by his guardian or the court. In case of risk to his life, emergency mental care may be provided without the consent of the person.
4. A person may be admitted to a mental health facility only upon his consent or the consent of the court. If a person is suffering from a severe mental illness and if there is a real danger that by his actions he is likely to commit serious harm to his health or to the health, life and property of others, he may be hospitalized involuntarily, but for no longer than 48 hours. Involuntary hospitalization may be prolonged only with the consent of the court in accordance with the procedure established by law. In the case that the person is legally incapable, the con-

sent to involuntary hospitalization may be given by the person's guardian, but for no longer than 48 hours. Involuntary hospitalization of a person may be further prolonged only with the consent of the court in accordance with the procedure established by law.
5. Persons who unlawfully restrain the freedom of a natural person must compensate him for material and non-material damage.

*Article 6.729. Consent of the patient*
1. The patient may not be treated or be provided any other health and/or nursing care against his will, unless otherwise established by legislation. In cases where the written consent of the patient is required, the laws may regulate the provision of healthcare services to the patient.
3. The modalities of treatment of a mental patient who is unable to correctly assess the condition of his own health shall be established by the relevant laws.

**9.2.2.7 Law on Mental Health Care**
The purpose of the Law on Mental Health Care of the Republic of Lithuania is to establish the rights of persons who are provided with mental health care, and to regulate the procedure and supervision of mental health care.

*Article 16.* No treatment shall be given to a patient without his consent, except when he is an involuntary patient hospitalized by reason of circumstances specified in Article 27 of this Law. In such cases the psychiatrist shall inform the patient and his representative of the prescribed involuntary treatment. The information must be recorded in the patient's clinical record.
In the cases specified in paragraph 1 hereof, consent for the patient's involuntary treatment must be obtained in accordance with the procedure laid down in Article 28 of this Law. Until the court's consent is obtained, the patient, upon the decision of two psychiatrists and one medical doctor representing the administration of a mental health facility, may be subjected to involuntary treatment for a period not exceeding 48 hours.
A patient may be treated involuntary only if he is involuntarily hospitalized to an inpatient mental health facility.

*Article 22.* The patient or his representative shall have the right to be present and to be heard out by the administration of the mental health facility, the Ministry of Health, and in court when the issues concerning his involuntary hospitalization and involuntary treatment, mental health care, etc. are being decided.

*Article 23.* The primary examination and assessment of the patient's mental condition may be performed by a psychiatrist on reasonable suspicion of a se-

vere mental illness the symptoms whereof are identified in Article 27 of this Law. Primary examination of the person's mental condition shall be carried out in accordance with the procedure established by the Ministry of Health.
A medical doctor, the patient's representative, his close relatives, and the police may request his primary examination.

*Article 24.* If a request to be hospitalized is directed towards a patient, he may only be hospitalized provided that:
1) at least one psychiatrist, upon examining the patient, recommends that he should be treated as an inpatient at a mental health facility;
2) he has been informed about his rights at a mental health facility, the purpose of hospitalization, the right to leave the psychiatric facility and restrictions of his rights as specified in Article 27 of this Law.

*Article 25.* Patients who are minors may be hospitalized only with the consent of one parents or guardian except under the circumstances specified in Article 27 of this Law. In case of involuntary hospitalization of a minor by reason of circumstances specified in Article 27 of this Law, involuntary hospitalization and involuntary treatment conditions prescribed by this Law shall be applicable to him.
If the patient who is a minor is under the age of ten years, one of the parents or guardians shall have the right to enter the hospital with him.
In the event of hospitalization of a patient who is a minor and over the age of ten years, one of the parents or guardians, should he so request, may stay at the mental health facility along with the minor. The decision on the issue shall rest with the psychiatrist who shall have to take into account the character of the illness and the minor's mental condition. If the parents or guardians object to the psychiatrist's decision, they may appeal against it to the administration of the mental health facility, the Ministry of Health or the court.

*Article 26.* Patients hospitalized in compliance with the requirements of Article 24 of this Law shall have the right to leave the mental health facility at any time, provided that there are no circumstances specified in Article 27 of this Law.

*Article 27.* A person who suffers from a severe mental illness and refuses hospitalization may be admitted involuntarily to the custody of the hospital only if there is real danger that by his actions he is likely to commit serious harm to:
1) his health and/or life;
2) to the health and/or life of others.

*Article 28.* When the circumstances specified in Article 27 of this Law do exist, the mentally ill person may be involuntarily hospitalized and administered treatment in a mental health facility for a period not exceeding 48 hours without the consent of the court. If such consent is not obtained within 48 hours, involuntary hospitalization and involuntary treatment must be terminated. The administration of the mental health facility must forthwith notify the patient's representative of the involuntary hospitalization.
In the event of an involuntary hospitalization, the administration of the mental health facility must promptly take the case to court within no less than 48 hours. Upon considering the findings of the mental health facility, the court shall have the right to take a decision regarding the extension of the patient's involuntary hospitalization and involuntary treatment period but for no longer than one month from the day of the involuntary admission to the mental health facility. Following the psychiatrist's recommendations, the mental health facility administration shall have the right to terminate the patient's involuntary hospitalization and involuntary treatment prior to the expiry of the term.
Should it be necessary to prolong involuntary hospitalization and involuntary treatment, the administration of the mental health facility must take the case to court again. The court may, based on the findings of the mental health facility, either prolong or terminate the patient's involuntary hospitalization and involuntary treatment, though each extension may not exceed 6 months. On the recommendation of the attending psychiatrist, the administration of the mental health facility shall have the right to terminate the patient's involuntary hospitalization and involuntary treatment prior to the expiry of the prescribed period.

*Article 29.* If the circumstances specified in Article 27 exist, the patient shall be taken to involuntary hospitalization by the police at the request of the mentally ill person's representative, on instructions of the physician or by the order of the court judge in the presence of a medical doctor. The procedure for involuntary hospitalization shall be established by the institutions authorized by the government.

*Article 30.* A mentally ill person who is being involuntarily admitted to a mental health facility as a patient must acknowledge by his signature that he has been informed by the mental health facility administration about his involuntary hospitalization and his rights at the mental health facility. If the mentally ill person refuses or is unable to write his signature, the fact of his having been informed about his involuntary hospitalization shall be testified in writing by two witnesses who must be mental health facility staff members, but need not be psychiatrists.

*Article 31.* A person's hospitalization in violation of the requirements of this Law shall be illegal. Persons through whose fault a person was illegally hospitalized shall be held liable in the manner established by the laws of the Republic of Lithuania.

*Article. 36.* The court must decide with reference to Article 27 and to Criminal Code on the involuntary hospitalization and compulsory treatment of mentally ill persons who have committed actions dangerous to society and who have been judged as not responsible for their actions.

*Article 37.* On the recommendation of a mental health facility and having decided, based on the findings of the mental health facility, that a person must undergo treatment after being involuntarily hospitalized, the court must indicate the mental health facility to which the person must be admitted and determine the length of involuntary hospitalization as well as the conditions of health care. After the lapse of six months, or earlier if necessary, and upon the recommendation of the mental health facility, the court must consider, based on the findings of the mental health facility, the issue of involuntary hospitalization and involuntary treatment and either prolong hospitalization and the above treatment – each time, however, for a period not exceeding six months – or must terminate the same.

**Remarks on the Civil Code and Law on Mental Health Care**

1. The Civil Code came into force on July 1, 2001. Aiming to coordinate the Mental Health Care Law with the Civil Code, the Mental Health Care Amendment Law was passed on July 5, 2001. The Mental Health Care Law of 1995 established the institution of mental health committees in local government, which rule on questions dealing with forced hospitalization. Article No. 28 of the 1995 Mental Health Care Law provided that patients could be forcibly hospitalized and forcibly treated in mental institutions for no longer than 72 hours without the consent of the mental health committee of the local government. The administration of a mental institution was obliged to take the case to the committee without any delay and the committee discussed psychiatrists' recommendations and then had the right to decide on patients' forcible hospitalization and treatment, but for no longer than one month after the beginning of forcible hospitalization. After one month, if forcible hospitalization and treatment were still needed, the administration of the mental institution was obliged to take the case to court for prolongation of forcible hospitalization and treatment. All those regulations, after having been coordinated with the Civil Code, were changed.
2. The application of the law in practice demonstrates that regulation of statutes is not sufficiently clear:

a) It remains unclear if a real threat to the property of the patient or surrounding people could be sufficient for constituting an independent ground for forcible hospitalization. Mental Health Care Law doesn't provide such a ground. Though Civil Code provides such ground, there are doubts about its independence. Authors of the Civil Code comment in favour of constituting an independent ground. Until now, there is no judicial precedent on this question.
b) Adoption of a decision on forcible hospitalization is a special judicial procedure. It is cause for concern that the Code of Civil Procedures does not provide individual judicial regulations for such procedure.

### 9.2.3 International Conventions and Agreements Incorporated Into National Laws

a) European Convention for the Protection of Human Rights and Fundamental Freedoms, ratified on April 27, 1995.
b) Convention for the Protection of Human Rights and Dignity of the Human Being with Regard to the Application of Biology and Medicine and its Additional Protocol on the Prohibition of Cloning Human Beings, ratified on September 19, 2002.

### 9.2.4. Second Level of Legal Norms

Order No. 133 *"On Approval of the Procedure for Primary Examination of the Person's Mental Condition"* of March 7, 1996 of the Ministry of Health:

*"- primary examination of the person's mental condition may be performed by a psychiatrist on reasonable suspicion of a severe mental disorder, and that there is a real danger that by his actions the person is likely to commit serious harm to his health, life, health and/or the life of others.*
*- if a person consults a psychiatrist concerning primary examination of his mental condition upon his own initiative (or that of his relatives and the person does not object), he must be examined by the psychiatrist and, where needed, he must be provided with all required mental assistance.*
*- in case relatives consult a psychiatrist concerning the primary examination of the person's mental condition and that person objects to the examination, the psychiatrist shall make a decision on the examination of mental condition of such a person if he suspects a severe mental illness. The relatives must consult a psychiatrist or a health care establishment in writing by indicating specific symptoms of the person's mental disorder.*
*- minors below the age of 16 years may be examined by a psychiatrist only in the presence of their parents or guardians (excluding emergency cases).*
*- minors who request to be examined without the presence of parents or guardians may be examined without the consent of the parents or guardians upon the decision of a psychiatrist.*
*- in the case of suspicion of a severe mental illness, police officers must call for the assistance of a mental health service or deliver the person to a mental health facility themselves.*

*- if the person believes that primary examination of his mental condition has been carried out in the absence of reasonable grounds, he shall have the right of appeal to the senior psychiatrist of the Republic of Lithuania, the Ministry of Health of the Republic of Lithuania, and the court."*

### 9.3 Jurisprudence

The court system of the Republic of Lithuania consist of courts of general jurisdiction and administrative courts. Local courts, district courts, the Court of Appeal and the Supreme Court are courts of general jurisdiction. The administrative courts system of Lithuania consists of regional administrative courts and the Supreme Administrative Court of Lithuania. The system of administrative courts in Lithuania is separated from the courts of general jurisdiction. Administrative courts consider complaints (applications) against administrative enactments adopted by the entities of public and internal administration and their acts or omissions (i.e., neglect to perform their duties).
No decisions or jurisprudence of the Supreme Court are available on the aforesaid issues.

### 9.4 Protocols and Internal Norms Related to Coercive Measures or Compulsory Medical Treatment

The individual coercive measures are not regulated by general or second level legal norms.

### 9.5 Reports

European Committee for the prevention of Torture and Inhuman or Degrading Treatment or Punishment (CPT) visited Lithuania in February 2000. During the visit The Prison Hospital was visited. The report says:

*"The psychiatric unit accommodated patients with substance abuse problems, organic brain diseases (including epilepsy), and reactive disorders. The unit was in a poor state of repair; the concrete floors were cracked and uneven, the decor was drab, and the area was draughty. Patients were locked in cells and there did not appear to be any routine association. No rehabilitative facilities were available; instead, staff relied principally on pharmacotherapy and, to a much more limited extent, psychotherapy. Due to the lack of an observation or seclusion room, suicidal patients were "managed" by placing them in a cell with other patients. The situation at the unit could fairly be described as antitherapeutic.*
*The CPT recommends that the Lithuanian authorities accord a high priority to the completion of the new premises for the Prison Hospital. In the interim, it recommends that genuine efforts be made to reduce overcrowding in the existing facilities, in particular in the tuberculosis unit. The CPT also recommends that staffing levels at the hospital be reviewed."*

European Committee for the prevention of Torture and Inhuman or Degrading Treatment or Punishment (CPT) carried out a second visit to Lithuania in February 2004. This time the delegation visited Kaunas Psychiatric Hospital. The report on this visit is not yet published.

**9.6 Safeguard System**

Safeguards on the application of involuntary treatment and involuntary hospitalization are the responsibility of the court that issues consent to involuntary hospitalization and involuntary treatment.

A patient may be involuntarily hospitalized and involuntarily treated without the consent of the court for a period not exceeding 48 hours. If such consent is not obtained within 48 hours, involuntary hospitalization and involuntary treatment must be terminated. The consent of the court specifies the mental health facility in which the patient has to be hospitalized and establishes the duration of involuntary hospitalization and the circumstances of health care. The duration of involuntary hospitalization may not exceed one month.

Involuntary hospitalization and involuntary treatment of the patient may be extended only with the consent of the court for a period not exceeding six months. The administration of the mental health facility must take the case concerning consent to the court.

The court decision on the issue of consent shall not be appealed against.

A person's hospitalization in violation of the aforesaid requirements shall be illegal. Persons through whose fault a person was illegally hospitalized shall be subject to both criminal and civil liability.

On the recommendation of the attending psychiatrist, the administration of the mental health facility shall have the right to terminate the patient's involuntary hospitalization and involuntary treatment prior to the expiry of the prescribed time period (Law on Mental Health Care 28 article).

A representative of the involuntarily hospitalized and treated person may appeal to the court according to the general procedure concerning the application of unlawful coercive measures or preventive measures of security and order.

Civil code, the Law on Mental Health Care and Law on the Rights of Patients and Compensation of the Damage to Their Health provide for two types of representatives of the person involuntarily hospitalized: representatives according to law and authorized representatives. Representatives according to law of children up to 16 years of age are parents, foster-parents or guardians. Representatives according to law of adult patients who can't reasonably estimate their interests and don't have a guardian are persons who have the written warrant of attorney of the patient. If such a person does not exist, the representatives according to law are the spouse of the patient, parents of the patient or children of the patient. Authorized representatives must have a notarized warrant of attorney of the person involuntarily hospitalized.

**Diagram 9.1: Regular Judicial Procedure Concerning Involuntary Admission to a Psychiatric Hospital in Lithuania**

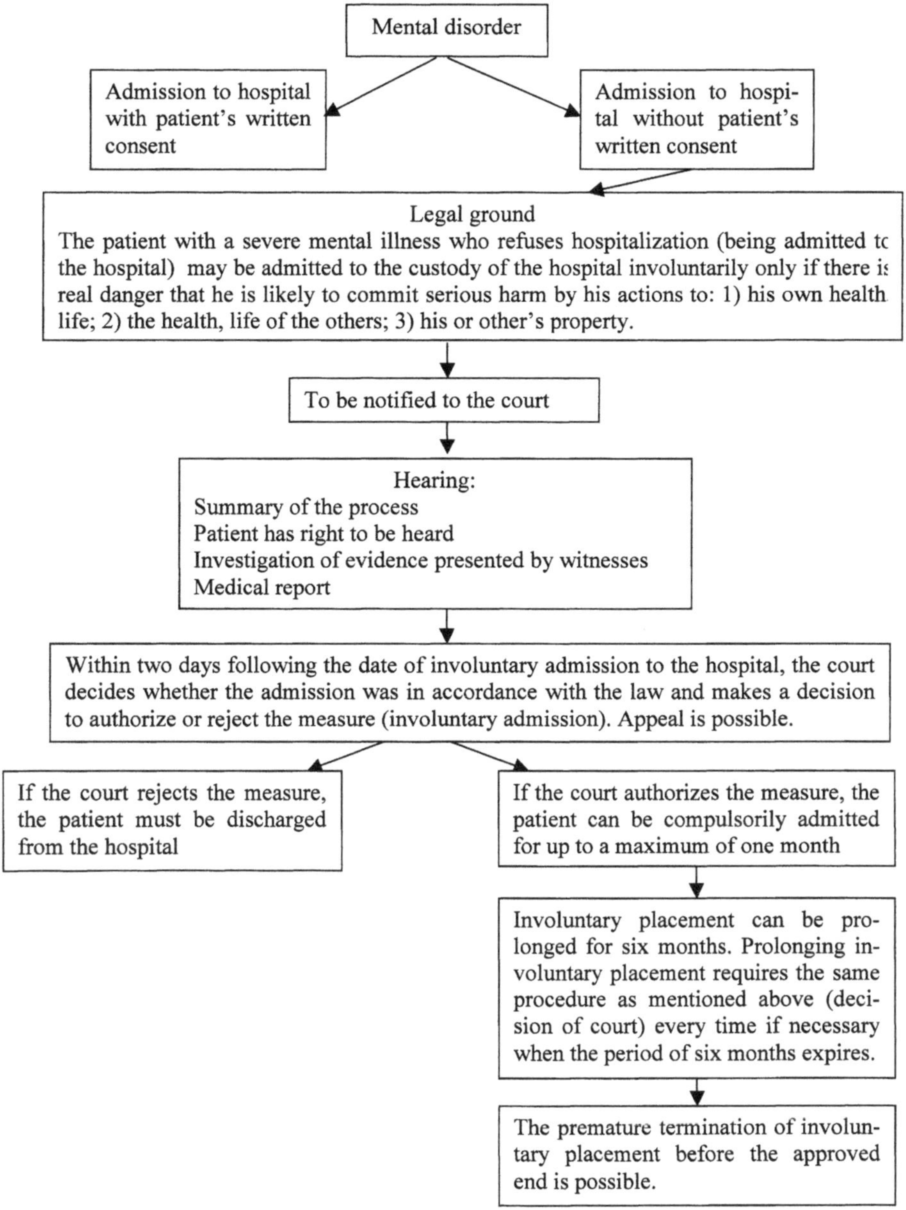

**CHAPTER 10**

# Legal Report – Poland[1]

Stanislaw DABROWSKI, Andrzej KIEJNA, Joanna RYMASZEWSKA

## 10.1 Introduction

### 10.1.2 General Explanation

The Republic of Poland is a democratic and unitary legal state founded on the principles of social justice. Poland's political system is based on the division of power between three bodies: legislative, executive and judicial. Poland has always had a legislative system characteristic of a continental European state, i.e. the civil law system is derived from the concepts of Roman law.

Polish medical law, which also pertains to psychiatry, distinguishes between the sources and principles of law. The most important categories of these sources are:

- The Constitution of the Republic of Poland,
- The Medical Ethical Code,
- The European Convention on Human Rights and Dignity of Human Beings Regarding Applications of Biology and Medicine.

Regardless of the dispute between lawyers on whether the Medical Ethical Code is an actual legal act or not, it regulates almost all the essential issues of medical law, such as patients' rights and informed consent.

The European Convention of November 11, 1996 contains complex regulations for all the relevant medical and psychiatric issues, such as the principle of free and informed consent and protection of persons incapable of expressing it.

The principles of medical law, similarly to the sources, do not have a normative character, but are contained in sources and serve as generalizations of detailed norms. The most important principles associated with psychiatric proceedings are:

- the principle of the patient's good (salus aegroti suprema lex est) and its specific directives: equal access to medical health care services, and appropriate medical care,
- the principle of protecting a patient's dignity, which is regulated in detail in Art. 19 § 1 pt. 4 from the Health Care Facilities Act -HCFA (the right to privacy and the respect of dignity) and Art. 40 from the Physician's

[1] Acknowledgements: the authors would like to thank Dr Tomasz Hadryś for the translation.

Profession Act-PPA (the obligation to keep patients' medical information confidential),
- the principle of protecting a patient's autonomy by related, detailed directives, such as a patient's right to express free and conscious consent (Art. 32 PPA) and the conditions under which medical intervention is to be carried out without a patient's consent (Art. 30 § 2, Art. 33 and 34 PPA).

### 10.1.2 Methodology of the Survey

This report considers all the acts and second level legal norms (i.e. ordinances) regulating the issue of coercion and physical restraint used on persons with mental disorders.
The report consists of two parts:
- The first deals with the Constitution and other general laws
- The second considers the Mental Health Act (MHA)

All juridical texts beginning with „Art." and "§:" are literal translations of Polish regulations into English. Comments are only provided for the Mental Health Act itself. This review covers the period of the last 25 years.
For the purpose of reviewing High Court verdicts, "LEX" software has been used.

## 10.2 Applicable Laws and General Norms

### 10.2.1 Constitutional Norms

The main constitutional regulations in medical and psychiatric matters are cited in various paragraphs in the second chapter of the Constitution ("Freedoms, Rights and Obligations of a Person and Citizen"):
Text passed on the April 2, 1997 during The National Assembly (Acts Register No. 78, pos. 483)

#### 10.2.1.1. General Principles

*Art. 30.*
The inherent and inalienable dignity of any person shall constitute a source of freedoms and rights of persons and citizens. It shall be inviolable. The respect and protection thereof shall be the obligation of public authorities.

*Art. 31.*
1. The freedom of any person shall receive legal protection.
2. Everyonc shall respect the freedoms and rights of others. No one shall be compelled to do what is not required by law.
3. Any limitation upon the exercise of constitutional freedoms and rights may be imposed only by statute, and only when necessary in a democratic state

for the protection of its security or public order, or to protect the natural environment, health or public morals, or the freedoms and rights of other persons. Such limitations shall not violate the essence of freedoms and rights.

*Art. 32.*
1. All persons shall be equal in the eyes of the law. All persons shall have the right to equal treatment by public authorities.
2. No one shall be discriminated against in political, social or economic life for any reason whatsoever.

**10.2.1.2. Specific Principles**
*Art. 39.*
No-one shall be subjected to scientific experimentation, including medical experimentation, without his or her voluntary consent.

*Art. 41.*
1. Personal inviolability and security shall be guaranteed to everyone. Any deprivation or limitation of liberty may be imposed only in accordance with the principles and procedures specified by statute.

**10.2.2 General Laws**
General laws sanctioning the use of compulsory measures:

Note: it appears there are no English versions of the Criminal and Civil Codes, therefore the translation of articles and provisions presented below is informal and not authorized and as such should only be regarded as purely informative, not as a source of law.

**10.2.2.1 Criminal Code**
(of August 2, 1997, Acts Register No. 88, pos. 553)
*Art. 31.*
§ 1. Anyone who, due to mental illness, mental retardation or other disturbance of mental functioning, is unable to apprehend the meaning of his/her action or control his/her behaviour during a criminal action, commits no crime.
§ 2. If, during a criminal act, the ability to apprehend its meaning or control one's behaviour is limited in a considerable way, the Court shall have the privilege of extraordinary commutation of the penalty.
§ 3. Provisions § 1 and 2 are invalid if the perpetrator was in a state of drunkenness or intoxication leading to an inhibition or diminishment of responsibility which could have been expected or anticipated.

*Art. 72.*
[Obligations]
§ 1. In giving sentence, the Court may oblige the convict to:
1) inform the Court or probation officer about the course of probation,
2) apologize to the aggrieved,
3) place upon the perpetrator the obligation of paying for subsistence of the aggrieved,
4) be gainfully employed, attend school or vocational training,
5) abstain from abusing alcohol or other intoxicants,
6) undergo specific treatment, especially detoxification or rehabilitation,
7) refrain from contact with specified groups of people or visiting specified places,
8) refrain from, in the course of probation, specified behaviour which could lead to recurrent criminality

*Art. 93.*
[The fundaments]
The Court may adjudicate any preventive measures mentioned in this chapter associated with compulsory commitment to a closed psychiatric facility only when they are indispensable to preventing the perpetrator from committing another illicit act resulting from his or her mental illness, mental retardation or addiction to alcohol or other substances. Before giving a verdict, the Court shall consider the opinion of psychiatrists and/or psychologists.

*Art. 94.*
§ 1. If the perpetrator, being in a state of irresponsibility defined in Art. 31. § 1, commits a prohibited action of considerable public harmfulness and there is a high probability that such an action might be repeated, the Court shall adjudicate the compulsory commitment of the perpetrator to an appropriate health care facility.
§ 2. The duration of compulsory stay in such an institution is not initially defined; the Court shall adjudicate the dismissal of the perpetrator, if further hospitalization is no longer necessary.
§ 3. Should the conditions specified in § 1 or in Art. 93 be fulfilled, the Court may adjudicate to commit the perpetrator to another appropriate health care facility after the initial commitment. Such a verdict cannot be given if more than five years have passed since dismissal from the initial compulsory hospitalization.

*Art. 192.*
§ 1. Anyone who carries out medical procedures without a patient's consent shall be subjected to a fine, penalty of limited freedom or imprisonment up to two years.
§ 2. Prosecution shall be initiated at the motion of the aggrieved.

**10.2.2.2 Code of Penal Proceedings**
(of August 2, 1997, Acts Register No. 88, pos. 553)

*Art. 202.*
§ 1. In order to gain an expert report on the mental condition of the accused, the Court, and in the preparatory proceedings the prosecutor, shall appoint at least two professional psychiatrists.
§ 2. At the motion of professional psychiatrists, another expert or experts from different professions may be appointed to participate in an expert report.
§ 3. Experts cannot be married to one another or related with each other in any way that could raise justified doubt about their independence.
§ 4. An expert's opinion should contain statements pertaining both to the perpetrator's soundness of mind at the time of the criminal act as well as to his/her present mental condition and ability to participate in the legal proceedings. If it proves necessary, the report should also contain statements pertaining to the conditions listed in Art. 93 of the Criminal Code.

*Art. 203.*
§ 1. If experts find it necessary and make a motion, psychiatric examination may be expanded to observation in a health care facility.
§ 2. Any decision regarding the place where observation is to be conducted is made by the Court. In the preparatory proceedings, the Court adjudicates at the motion of the prosecutor.
§ 3. The observation period should not exceed six weeks; at the motion of the health care facility, the Court may prolong this period to a defined duration necessary to conclude observation. The Court has to be notified promptly by the experts as soon as observation concludes.
§ 4. Complaints regarding failures to observe the rules stated in § 2 and 3 may be filed.

**10.2.2.3 Penal Executive Code**
(of August 2, 1997, Acts Register No. 88, pos. 553)
*Art. 201.*
§ 1. In executing the sentence of preventive measures associated with commitment to a closed health care facility or detoxification unit, the Court shall send

the transcript of the verdict, together with the order to escort the perpetrator, to the health care facility, police department and/or corresponding military organ, as appropriate. The transcript of the verdict, together with the order to admit to the corresponding facility, shall be sent to its director.
§ 2. If the perpetrator is held in penitentiary or in custody, the Court shall send the escort order and the transcript of the verdict to the governor of the penitentiary or place of custody, as appropriate.
§ 3. The Health and Social Welfare Minister, in cooperation with the Minister of Justice, decrees the list of health care facilities and detoxification units selected to execute preventive measures, specifies their capacity, rules of referral and handling of perpetrators committed there, as well as the principles of securing such institutions.

**10.2.2.4 Civil Code**

(of April 29, 1964, Acts Register No. 16, pos. 93)
Art. 23. Personal rights, especially health, liberty, honour, freedom of conscience, surname or pseudonym, image, confidentiality of correspondence, protection of home and family and scientific, artistic, inventive and rationalizing activities are protected by the rules of the Civil Code, regardless of other legal provisions providing such protection.
Art. 82. Any statement given by a person, who for whatsoever reason was in a state excluding the possibility of conscious or free decision making and expression of will, is invalid. This pertains in particular to mental illness, mental retardation or other, even temporary, disturbances of mental functioning.

**10.2.2.5 Civil Procedure Code**

(of November 17, 1964, Acts Register No. 43 pos. 296)

*Art. 553.*
Any person who is to be deemed legally incapacitated has to be examined by one or more appointed expert psychiatrists.

*Art. 554.*
If the court finds it necessary, based on the experts' opinion of two psychiatrists, it may decide to commit a person who is to be deemed legally incapacitated to a health care facility for observation for no longer than six weeks. In exceptional situations the duration of the observational period may be prolonged up to three months.

*Art. 556.*
§ 1 The person who is to be deemed legally incapacitated has to be heard and according to actual needs such a hearing should take place in the presence of a doctor.
§ 2 For this purpose, the Court may order the compulsory escort of the person to the court trial or, if this were inadvisable, hear this person by the appointed judge or by court at another appointed place.

**10.2.2.6 Act on Police**
(of April 6, 1990, Acts Register No 30 pos. 179)

*Art. 14.*
§ 3 Policemen on duty are obliged to respect the dignity of citizens and to obey and protect human rights.

*Art. 15.*
§ 1 Policemen on duty referred to in Art. 14 have a right to:
3) arrest any person who in a clear way directly endangers the life or health of others, or their property.
§ 3 Arrest may be implemented only if other means have proven to be pointless or unsuccessful.

*Art. 16.*
§ 1 In cases of disobedience towards legally justified commands of police organs or officers, policemen are allowed to use physical restraint.

**10.2.2.7 Physician's Profession Act**
(of December 5, 1996, Acts Register 1997, No 28 pos. 152)

*Art. 32.*
§ 1 A physician may conduct an examination or provide other medical services, with the exception of conditions stated within this Act, only after obtaining a patient's consent.
§ 2 In cases of minors or those incapable of expressing conscious consent, the consent of their legal representative is required. If a subject has no such representative or communication with him/her is impossible, consent is given by the Guardianship Court.

*Art. 33.*
§ 1 Examining or providing a patient with any medical service without his/her prior consent is allowed only when immediate medical attention is required and,

due to his/her medical condition or advanced age, the patient is incapable of expressing his/her will and contact with that patient's legal or de facto representative is impossible.

### 10.2.2.8 Act on Upbringing in Sobriety and Counteracting Alcoholism

(of October 26, 1982, Acts Register 2002, No. 147 pos. 1231)

*Art. 24.*

Persons who due to alcohol abuse cause the disintegration of family ties, demoralize minors or systematically disturb the public peace or order are compulsorily subjected to an expert examination aimed at diagnosing dependence on alcohol and choosing the appropriate health care treatment, if required, for such a problem.

*Art. 25.*

Persons are referred to such an examination, mentioned in Art. 24, by a district committee for solving alcohol-related problems, appropriate to the place of residence or home of the person concerned, based on his or her own motion or on the committee's initiative.

*Art. 26.*

§ 1. Persons referred to in Art. 24 may be obliged to submit to treatment in an in- or outpatient medical alcohol facility, if they are found to be alcohol dependent.

§ 2. The decision to submit a person to obligatory treatment in an alcohol treatment facility is taken during a non-adversarial proceeding in the district court appropriate to the place of residence or home of the person concerned.

§ 3. The Court takes action on any motion filed by the district committee for solving alcohol-related problems or by a public prosecutor. Such a motion shall be accompanied by all the documentation gathered as well as expert reports if expert examinations took place.

*Art. 27.*

§ 1. In cases when there is no expert opinion on the question of alcohol dependence on the part of the person concerned, the Court shall order such an examination.

§ 2. If the Court, based on an expert opinion, deems it essential, it may order observation of the person concerned in a health care facility for no longer than 2 weeks. In exceptional circumstances, at the motion of the health care facility, the Court may prolong this period to six weeks.

§ 3. Before giving its decision, the Court shall hear the person concerned.

§ 4. Complaints may be filed against a Court's decision regarding medical observation.

*Art. 30.*
§ 1. In cases of unjustified failure to appear at a hearing or evading expert examination or observation in a health care facility, the Court may order a compulsory police escort.

### 10.2.2.9 Act of Counteracting Drug Addiction

(of April 24, 1997, Acts Register No. 75 pos. 468)
*Art. 17.*
§ 1. At the motion of a legal representative, blood relative, sibling, representative, de facto or ex officio, the family court may commit a dependent minor of less than 18 years of age to compulsory treatment and rehabilitation.
§ 2. The duration of compulsory treatment is not initially defined, although it may not exceed two years.
§ 3. If a dependent minor reaches 18 years of age before the treatment or rehabilitation process concludes, the family court may prolong it for any time necessary to achieve the goals of treatment and rehabilitation. However, the total period may not exceed the duration defined in § 2..
§ 4. Proceedings in cases defined in § 1 are run in accordance to provisions for proceedings in cases of minors.

*Art. 56.*
§ 1. If any dependent minor has been convicted of a crime related to the abuse of intoxicants or psychotropic drugs and imprisonment has been conditionally deferred, the Court shall oblige the convict to undergo treatment, rehabilitation or re-adaptation in an appropriate health care facility or in facilities run by entities named in Art. 3 § 3 and places him/her under the supervision of an appointed person, institution or association.

### 10.2.2.10 Act of Proceedings in Cases of Minors

(of October 26, 1982, Acts Register 1982, No. 35 pos. 228)

*Art. 12.*
When a mental retardation, mental illness, other disturbance of mental functioning or chronic abuse of alcohol or other substances leading to intoxication has been diagnosed in a minor who has committed a crime, the family court may adjudicate the commitment of the minor to any relevant health care facility. If it is only necessary to secure educational care, the Court may adjudicate the commitment of a minor to any appropriate educational institution.

**10.2.2.11 Mental Health Act (MHA)**

(of August 19, 1994, Acts Register 1994, No. 111 pos. 535) updated in 1997 and 2005

The passage of the Mental Health Act by Parliament concluded a nearly 20-year long period of legislative work on the last project of this act, which closes the legal loophole felt painfully by psychiatrists and patients. Not everyone knew that Poland was one of the very few countries in the world which had no legal regulations, even of an elementary kind, on the most dramatic aspects of psychiatric treatment, such as compulsory admission to a mental hospital with use of physical restraint. This long-lasting loophole meant that some psychiatrists did not realize the specific legal and social aspects of a patient-psychiatrist relationship and therefore tended to apply coercive treatment, broadly assuming that the criteria for the implementation of treatment should be arbitrarily and solely defined by psychiatrists themselves. The need for legal regulation was implied by Art. 87 of the Constitution in force at the time, which was later kept in force by Art. 77. of the Constitution of the Republic of Poland of October 17, 1992 (Acts Register No. 84, pos. 426). It was also implied by the provisions of the Health Care Facilities Act of August 30, 1991 (Acts Register No. 91, pos. 48), which stated that a patient had the right to express his/her consent or refusal to receive specific services (Art. 19 § 2 pt. 3). Moreover, this need also resulted from international agreements that Poland had ratified, including the European Convention on Human Rights. It was stated therein that depriving of freedom an individual with mental disorders must be legally regulated (Helsinki Foundation for Human Rights 1996).

Provisions stated in the law are divided into three categories, each with different aims.

- The aim of the provisions in the first category is to secure promotion of mental health.
- The aim of the provisions in the second category is to secure comprehensive and generally available care and help essential to living in a family and the community for persons with mental disorders. Thanks to these provisions, 370 community self-help houses were established capable of serving 10,000 mentally ill and mentally retarded persons. Also, a network of social care services, serving patients in their homes, was organized.
- The aim of the provisions in the third category is to protect the civil rights of patients being treated, with or without their consent, in mental health care facilities (Dąbrowski, Pietrzykowski 1997, 1998).

The legal definition of "a person with a mental disorder" is of great value:

*Art. 3.*

Whenever the provisions of this Act refer to
a mentally disordered person, they shall apply to a person:

a) Who is mentally ill (i.e. demonstrates psychotic disorders),
b) Who is mentally retarded, or
c) Who demonstrates other disturbances in mental functioning which, according to current medical knowledge, are classified as mental disorders, and who needs health services or other forms of assistance or care in order to live in the family or social environment,

A clear distinction between these three types of subjects, defined in the broader concept of a "person with a mental disorder", is indispensable, since individual provisions may apply to only certain types of subjects.

Definition of the principal legal terms, in compliance with the Mental Health Act:

- Emergency admission without consent to a psychiatric facility – stands for the legal procedure of admitting to a psychiatric facility a mentally ill (psychotic) patient presenting imminent danger to his/her own life or the life or health of others.
- Emergency admission without consent to a psychiatry facility for ten-day observation – stands for the legal procedure of admitting to a psychiatric facility a mentally disordered patient presenting an imminent danger to his/her own life or to the life or health of others in a situation when there are doubts as to whether that person is mentally ill.
- Non-emergency admission without consent at the motion of legitimized persons – stands for the legal procedure of admitting to a psychiatric facility a mentally ill (psychotic) patient:
  - whose behaviour to date indicates that not admitting him/her to the hospital would cause considerable deterioration to that patient's mental health or
  - who is incapable of sufficiently satisfying his/her basic needs, and whose treatment in a psychiatric hospital may be justifiably expected to improve that person's state of health.
- Emergency treatment without consent – stands for the non-consensual medical treatment of a patient admitted to an emergency department with the aim of removing the condition resulting in the admission.
- Non-emergency treatment without consent – stands for the treatment of a mentally ill (psychotic) patient in non-emergency conditions,
- Physical restraint – stands for manual restraint, compulsory medication, mechanical immobilization or seclusion of a mentally disordered patient, mainly in order to:

- prevent attempts against his/her own life or health or the life or health of others, threats to public safety and the violent destruction or damage of objects,
- administer necessary treatment procedures, referred to as emergency and non-emergency treatment, or to prevent a patient from escaping from the psychiatric facility.

The main provisions of the Act, pertaining to psychiatric procedures performed without a patient's consent and under coercion with or without physical restraint, will be partially presented here in the order in which they are applied to patients (referral, transportation, admission, treatment, discharge, psychiatric legal expertise).

1. Referral, transportation and admission to a mental hospital
Art. 10b, 11, Art. 18.1.2.3, Art. 21.1.2.3, Art. 22.1.2, Art. 23.1.2.3.4.5, Art. 24, Art. 25.1.2, Art. 28, Art. 29.1.2., Art. 30.1.2.3.4.5
Art.10b.
1. Protection of persons' rights belongs to the tasks of personal advocates of psychiatric hospitals.
2. Particularly, such tasks of the personal advocate are:
1) Help in investigation of alleged infringements of patients' rights related with admission, treatment, conditions of stays and discharge from psychiatric hospital,
2) Explaining or assistance in explaining oral and written complaints of these persons to the court,
3) Cooperation with the family, legal representative or legal or natural guardian of the patient,
4) initiation and conducting of educational and informative activities about the range of health services offered by psychiatric hospital.

*Art. 11.*
The physician may issue a certificate of health or medical opinion concerning a mentally disordered person, or refer that person to another physician, psychologist or health care facility only following a personally conducted examination of that person. A written referral to a psychiatric hospital shall be issued on the day of examination and its validity shall expire after 14 days.

*Art. 18.*
§ 1. Mentally disordered persons may be subjected to physical restraint, in the course of activities covered by this Act, only when it is warranted by special regulations of this Act or such persons:

1) make an attempt against:
   a) their own life or health, or the life or health of another person, or
   b) public safety, or
2) when such persons violently destroy or damage surrounding objects, or
3) they disturb seriously or they make impossible the functioning of units of mental health care or social care units.

§ 2. The decision to use physical restraint shall be made by a physician, who shall determine the manner of physical restraint to be applied and shall supervise its implementation in person. In psychiatric hospitals and social care units, if the immediate decision of a physician is not available, the decision to use physical restraint and personal inspection of the use shall be made by a nurse, who must notify the physician immediately. Every case of the application of physical restraint and warning about the possibility of it's application (according to § 4) shall be entered in medical records.

§ 3. Physical restraint towards persons mentioned in § 1.1 and § 1.2 may consist of manual restraint, compulsory medication, immobilization and seclusion, and towards persons mentioned in § 1.3, manual restraint and compulsory medication only.

§ 6. The legitimacy of implementing physical restraint:
1) by a physician of a health care service must be evaluated by the chief of the service or physician authorized by him within three days,
2) by any other physician or by a nurse of a social care unit must be evaluated by a psychiatrist authorized by the governor of the province within three days.

*Art. 21.*

§ 1. A person whose behaviour indicates that, due to mental disorders, he/she may pose an imminent danger to his/her own life or the life or health of others, or a person incapable of satisfying his basic vital needs self-sufficiently, may be subjected to a psychiatric examination without his/her consent; if the person is a minor (under 18 years of age) or totally incapacitated, the consent of his/her legal representative shall not be required either. In this case Art. 18 shall be appropriately applied.

§ 2. The necessity of conducting the examination referred to in § l shall be ascertained by a psychiatrist or – if the assistance of a psychiatrist is unavailable – by another physician. Prior to the examination of the person concerned, his/her legal representative shall be informed of the reasons for the non-consensual examination.

§ 3. If necessary, the physician conducting the examination shall order immediate transfer of the examined person to a hospital. If physical restraint is applied, the patient should be transferred to hospital in the presence of a physician or nurse.

*Art. 22.*

§ 1. A mentally disordered person shall be admitted to a psychiatric hospital after his/her written, informed consent based on valid referral to the hospital if the authorized physician has ascertained, following a previous personally conducted examination of that person, that reasons for admittance to the hospital exist.

1a. In emergency cases, particularly in case of lack of the ability to obtain medical assistance before reporting to a hospital, a person with mental disorders can be admitted to the psychiatric hospital after written consent, without referral, as laid out in § 1.

§ 2. Admission to psychiatric hospital of a mentally ill or mentally handicapped person who is incapable to give informed consent or his/her opinion about the admission and treatment in psychiatric hospital may take place after obtaining the acceptance of the appropriate welfare court according to the residence of this person.

2a. In emergency cases, the person mentioned in § 2 can be admitted to the psychiatric hospital without the previously obtained acceptance of the welfare court. In such cases, during admission, the physician has the duty to consult, if possible, the written opinion of another physician, if at all possible of a psychiatrist, or the written opinion of a psychologist.

2b. In such cases as described in § 2, the chief of the psychiatric hospital immediately informs the Guardianship Court appropriate to the location of the hospital in order to obtain authorization for hospitalization.

2c. If the person mentioned in § 2 opposes admission to psychiatric hospital and his/her behaviour to date indicates that he/she poses an imminent danger to his/her life or to the life or health of others, the regulations of art. 23 § 3-5 and art. 25 and 27 apply accordingly.

*Art. 23.*

§ 1. A mentally ill person may be admitted to a psychiatric hospital without the consent required under Art. 22 only when that person's behaviour to date indicates that, due to the illness, he/she poses an imminent danger to his/her own life or to the life or health of others.

§ 2. The decision regarding the admission of the person referred to in § 1 shall be made by the appointed physician following a previous, personally conducted examination of that person and, if possible, following consultation with another psychiatrist or psychologist.

§ 3. The physician referred to in § 2 is obliged to explain to the patient the reasons for his/her admission to hospital without his/her consent and to inform the patient of his/her rights.
§ 4. Admission to hospital under the conditions referred to in § 1 shall be confirmed by the head of the ward within 48 hours of admission. The head of the hospital shall notify the Guardianship Court appropriate to the seat of the hospital of this fact within 72 hours of admission.
§ 5. Proceedings referred to in § 2, 3 and 4 shall be recorded in medical records.

*Art. 24.*
§ 1. A person whose behaviour to date indicates that, due to a mental disorder, he/she poses an imminent danger to his/her life or to the life or health of others, and there are doubts as whether that person is mentally ill, may be admitted to hospital without the consent required under Art. 22, in order to settle any doubts.
§ 2. The stay in the hospital on the conditions referred to in § 1 shall not exceed ten days.

*Art. 25.*
§ 1. On the grounds of such notification, the Guardianship Court shall institute proceedings concerning the admission to a psychiatric hospital of any person referred to in Art. 23 and 24.
§ 2. The Guardianship Court may adjudicate the matter also on a motion filed by this person or by his/her legal representative, spouse, blood relatives, siblings or guardian, de facto or ex officio.

*Art. 28.*
If the behaviour of the person admitted to a psychiatric hospital with the consent required under Art. 22 indicates that circumstances referred to in Art. 23, § 1 are present, and consent has been withdrawn, the regulations referred to in Art. 23, § 2-5 and Art. 25-27, respectively, shall be appropriately applied.

*Art. 29.*
§ 1. Admission to a psychiatric hospital without the consent required under the provisions of Art. 22 is also possible in the case of a mentally ill person:
1) whose behaviour to date indicates that not admitting him/her to hospital would cause considerable deterioration to that person's mental health, or
2) who is incapable of self-sufficiently satisfying his/her basic vital needs, and whose treatment in a psychiatric hospital may be justifiably expected to improve that person's state of health.

§ 2. The necessity of admission of any person referred to in § 1 to a psychiatric hospital without his/her consent shall be adjudicated by the Guardianship Court

appropriate to that person's place of residence at the motion of that person's spouse, blood relatives, siblings, legal representative, or de facto guardian.
§ 3. With respect to a person receiving social care, as referred to in Art. 8, such a motion may also be filed by the welfare organ.

*Art. 30.*
§ 1. The motion referred to in Art. 29 § 2 and 3 shall be accompanied by a psychiatrist's certificate, justifying in detail the need for treatment in a psychiatric hospital. In the absence of such a certificate, or when it has been issued earlier than 14 days prior to the date of lodging the motion, the Guardianship Court shall reject the motion; in this case the provisions of Art. 130 of the Civil Proceedings Code shall not be deemed applicable.
§ 2. The certificate shall be issued by a psychiatrist employed in a public psychiatric facility at the substantiated request of a person or agencies authorized to bring a motion to institute legal proceedings in that case.
§ 3. If the psychiatrist employed in a public psychiatric facility recognizes the need for issuing a psychiatrist's certificate, he/she shall appoint the date of examination and notify the person referred to in Art. 29 § 1 informing him/her about the possibility of a police escort should this person not report for the examination.
§ 4. If the person referred to in § 3 does not report for the examination, a psychiatrist employed in a public psychiatric facility may ask for a police escort for this person to an examination in a public psychiatric facility. Under justified circumstances such an examination may be conducted in that person's place of residence.
§ 5. If the person referred to in Art. 29 § 1 refuses to submit himself/herself to examination, such an examination may be conducted without that person's consent: Art. 21 shall be appropriately applied.

**Comments**
Consequences:

- Despite the Health Minister's decree issued in Art. 49 of the MHA, a large proportion of those referred to mental health facilities (27%) are admitted there without having the appropriate referral form and also not in accordance with Art. 11 of MHA and Art. 42 of PPA (Physician's Profession Act). Similarly, a large proportion of patients (30%) are not personally assessed by the referring doctor. This concerns patients admitted without consent (41%) more often than those admitted with consent (25%).
- Physical restraint during transportation is applied more often in cases of patients admitted without their consent (53%) than with it (13%). Despite

the requirements set by Art. 21 § 3, physical restraint applied during the transportation of patients most often takes place without the attendance of a doctor or nurse.

- 25% of admissions to mental health facilities of patients giving their consent violates the provisions of Art. 22 § 1 (no date of admission, signature under an illegible stamp, often substituting informed consent to another treatment, which is a sad example of the routine handling of patients and has no power in the eyes of the law). The obligation described previously (1997) in Art 22 § 2 to identify and register patients who raise serious doubts as to whether or not they are able to express conscious consent (according to patients' beliefs 17% grant their consent to admission only because of coercion) is often not obeyed, which is an unacceptable practice. After update of Mental Health Act in 2005, the Art 22 § 2 was changed.
- Admissions without consent constituted 8.4% of all admissions in 2002 (8.9% in 1999 and 10% in 1997); 9.5% to mental health facilities and 5% to psychiatric wards affiliated with general hospitals. 80% of such admissions were on the basis of Art. 23 of MHA, 13% under Art. 24, 5% under Art. 28 and 2% under Art. 29. Among medical reasons for admission, schizophrenia and delusional disorders were the most frequent, dominating other reasons, such as affective and alcohol-related psychoses. Among behavioural reasons for admission, aggression against others (44%) and aggression against oneself (21%) were most prevalent.

Criticism: The obligation to record in medical files as to whether or not a patient was informed of the reasons for compulsory admission and reasons for using physical restraint upon him/her and the obligation of identifying patients whose consent is doubtful in the medical records are both deemed by some psychiatrists unnecessary and bureaucratic procedures (Dąbrowski 2001, in press a).

2. Stay in the ward
Art. 26, Art. 33.1.2, Art. 34

*Art. 26.*
§ 1. If a patient admitted to psychiatric hospital without consent subsequently gives his consent to his/her hospitalization in that facility, the Guardianship Court shall terminate the proceedings instigated following the notification or motion referred to in Art. 25, if, in the Court's opinion, that person has given his informed consent.
§ 2. Prior to the termination of the proceedings, the Court is obliged to hear the person referred to in § 1.

*Art. 33.*

§ 1. Indispensable treatment procedures may be applied to a person admitted to psychiatric hospital without his/her consent in order to remove the reasons for admission without consent as provided for by this Act.

§ 2. A physician appointed to carry out these procedures shall inform the person referred to in § 1 about the planned treatment.

§ 3. The Minister of Health and Social Welfare, in consultation with the General Medical Council, shall determine, as a legally binding ordinance, the list of treatment procedures involving increased risk to the patient; their application shall require the informed consent of the person referred to in § 1 or of that person's legal representative.

§ 4. The provisions of § 1 and 2 shall not be deemed applicable to persons admitted to psychiatric hospital according to the provisions of Art. 24.

*Art. 34.*

Physical restraint may be applied to a person admitted to psychiatric hospital without his consent under the circumstances specified in Art. 18 and also when such restraint is necessary in order to administer indispensable treatment procedures referred to in Art. 33. Physical restraint may also be applied in order to prevent that person from wilfully leaving the psychiatric facility.

**Comments**

Consequences:

- About 30% to 33% of those admitted to mental health facilities without consent later express such consent in hospital.
- The issue of consent to treatment is regulated by the provisions of Art. 32 of the Physician's Profession Act. Studies show that 36.5% of those admitted to mental hospital with consent have expressed their consent consciously, 12.5% consented but in the opinion of examiners were not capable of expressing such consent and the remaining 51.0% did not consent to treatment, because they were not asked at all.
- Physical restraint, mainly in the form of immobilization, was administered to 12.4% of those treated over a period of six months. The reasons for implementing such restraint were concordant with Art. 18 and 34 of the MHA in 54.2% of cases; in 33.7% of cases the reasons were only formally concordant and not sufficiently justified, in 3.8% of the cases the reasons were contrary to regulations, in 4.1% of cases doubtful and in 4.2% of cases restraint was administered on demand from the patient. The physician ordering physical restraint and the head of the hospital automatically accept responsibility for using this kind of measure.

- Many patients, admitted with or without their consent, are not asked for their consent to treatment associated with a high risk.

Criticism from the side of psychiatrists: the acts introduce too much bureaucracy; from the side of patients: there are many complaints about not obtaining their consent and lack of information about treatment (Dąbrowski 2001).

3. Discharge from hospital
Art. 35.1, Art. 36.1.2.3
*Art. 35.*
§ 1. The decision concerning the discharge from psychiatric hospital of a person hospitalized without his/her consent shall be made by the head of the ward if he acknowledges that the reasons for that person's admission and hospitalization without consent have expired.

*Art. 36.*
§ 1. A person hospitalized in a psychiatric hospital may submit in this hospital, in any form, a request for discharge from the hospital. This request shall be recorded in medical records.
§ 2. A person hospitalized without consent in a psychiatric hospital, that person's legal representative, spouse, siblings, blood relatives, or de facto guardian may request the discharge of that person from the psychiatric hospital not earlier than 30 days after the validation of the decision of the Guardianship Court concerning the admission or further treatment of that person in that hospital without the person's consent. Such requests may be submitted in any form. They shall be recorded in the medical records.
§ 3. If discharge is denied, the hospitalized person and, appropriately, other persons listed in § 2 may appeal to the Guardianship Court appropriate to the seat of the hospital, requesting a discharge warrant. This request shall be submitted within seven days of informing that person about the discharge denial and about the term and manner of submitting the request.

**Comments**
The discharge procedure has been maximally debureaucratized and decision-making in this respect has been handed over to the head of the ward.
Consequences: a hospital rarely observes the obligation of informing the Court about a patient's discharge.
Criticism: Some lawyers think the decision regarding discharging should lie within the Court's competencies.
Planned revision: none expected.

4. Admission without consent to a nursing home
Act. 38, 39.1.2.3, Art. 40
*Art. 38.*
A person who, due to mental illness or mental retardation, is incapable of self-sufficiently satisfying his/her basic, vital needs, has no possibility of obtaining care from others and needs continuous care and nursing services but does not require hospital treatment, may be admitted to a nursing home with his/her own or his/her legal representative's consent.

*Art. 39.*
§ 1. If the person referred to in Art. 38 or that person's legal representative does not give consent to admission to a nursing home and lack of care poses a risk to that person's life, a social welfare agency may apply to the Guardianship Court appropriate to the person's place of residence and file a motion for his/her admission to a nursing home without that person's consent.
§ 2. The motion referred to in § 1 may also be filed by the head of a psychiatric hospital if a hospitalized person is incapable of self-sufficiently satisfying his/her basic vital needs, requires continuous care and nursing but does not require further treatment in that hospital.
§ 3. If the person in need of referral to a nursing home, due to his/her mental state, is incapable of giving his consent, the Guardianship Court shall adjudicate the referral of such a person to a nursing home.

*Art. 40.*
§ 1.When implementing the Guardianship Court decision on admission to a nursing home, the provisions of Art. 18 shall be applied.
§ 2. Physical restraint may be also implemented to prevent this person from wilfully leaving the nursing house.

**Comments**
Aim: Prior to 1994 a mentally ill person could be placed without consent in a nursing home by a decision of the provincial court. At present, a regional guardianship court may adjudicate such an admission.
The consequences of these acts have not as yet been examined.
Criticism: without objections so far.
Planned revision: none expected.

5. Psychiatric expertise in a matter of admission without consent
*Art. 45.*
§ 1. In matters defined in Art. 25, 29, 36 § 3 and Art. 39, the Guardianship Court shall adjudicate with a bench composed of one Judge following a hearing; the

hearing shall take place no later than 14 days after the filing date of the request or receipt of the notification referred to in Art. 23 § 4.
§ 1a. In cases justified by the needs of the person this legal action directly concerns, the Court shall adjudicate that the hearing takes place in the hospital.
§ 2. The Judge visiting the hospital shall hear the person admitted to the psychiatric hospital in accordance with the provisions of Art. 23, 24 or 28 no later than 48 hours following the receipt of the notification referred to in Art. 23 § 4. If the Judge ascertains that hospitalization of that person in the psychiatric hospital is evidently unjustified, the Judge shall order immediate discharge of that person from the hospital and shall file a motion for discontinuance of legal proceedings.

*Art. 46.*
§ 1. In matters concerning the admission of a mentally ill person to a psychiatric hospital and his/her discharge from such a hospital, the following persons, apart from the petitioner himself, shall be participants in legal proceedings by virtue of the law: that person and his legal representative. Should it be necessary, the Court shall inform the spouse of the person concerned and de facto guardian about the hearing; they may participate in the hearing at any time, and then become participants.
§ 1a. The person whom the hearing directly concerns may be escorted to the hearing by virtue of a Court decision. In such a case Art. 556 § 2 of the Civil Proceedings Code is accordingly applied.
§ 2. Prior to issuing the essential decision, the Court shall obtain the expert opinion of one or more psychiatrists. A person participating in the decision on the admission of a mentally ill person to a psychiatric hospital or in the denial of his/her discharge from there shall not be appointed as a court expert.
§ 2a. If a mentally ill person, who is to be subjected to examination by an appointed expert, refuses to attend, or in any other way evades examination, the Court may order a police escort for this person to the relevant public psychiatric facility.
§ 2b. Assuring the execution of the Court's decision of admission to a mental hospital of a person referred to in Art. 29 § 1 is the governor's obligation.
§ 3. The provisions of § 1 and 2 shall be appropriately applied to the proceedings concerning admission to a nursing home: necessary assistance should be provided to the person referred to in Art. 39 by a social welfare agency until his/her admission to the nursing home.
§ 4. The Court shall notify the public prosecutor of the need for his/her participation in the proceedings, if such participation is deemed necessary.

*Art. 46a.*
The police escort referred to in art. 46 takes place in the presence of a doctor or nurse employed in a public psychiatric facility.

**Comments**
Consequences: A study on psychiatric expertise in 436 cases of admissions without consent showed that the quality of such expertise is very poor. The main irregularities are as follows: in emergency admissions (according to Art. 23 and 24) 11.3% of expert opinions were issued without personal examination of a patient and 37.5% lacked justification of the reasons (imminent danger) for admission; for 124 cases of admissions based upon motions referred to in Art. 29, 45.0% of certificates referred to in Art. 30% and 8.3% of expert opinions were not supported by a personal examination of a patient (Dąbrowski 1998, 2000).
Criticism: At present, these provisions have caused no objections.
Planned revision: Some articles will be altered in concordance with the 2003 Law on Health Insurance.

### 10.2.3. Second Level of Legal Norms (Ordinance, Executive Regulation)

#### 10.2.3.1 The Ordinance of the Minister of Health of February 26, 2001 to Art. 201 § 3 of the Penal Executive (Acts Register No. 26, pos. 297) Specifying the List of Psychiatric Facilities and Alcohol Treatment Services Appointed to Carry out Preventive Measures, the Number of Beds Available there, Rules of Referring and Handling Mentally Disturbed Perpetrators, as well as the Security Requirements for such Facilities

*§ 12.*
Physical restraint shall be used in concordance with the ordinance of the Minister of Health of August 23, 1995 on the way physical restraint is to be applied.

#### 10.2.3.2 The Ordinance of the Minister of Health of May 6, 1983 (Acts Register 1983, No. 25, pos. 115) on the Matter of Regulations of Alcohol Treatment Services and Medical Care for Persons Dependant on Alcohol

*§ 11.*
1. If, during a patient's stay in a ward, a condition or occurrence which is hazardous to his/her life, or in which a patient directly endangers the life or health of others is confirmed, the head of the ward, or other medical employee appointed by him, may order, should all other means be insufficient, the implementation of measures limiting a patient's movements, such as manual restraint or the application of a straitjacket or immobilization belt.
2. If any of the means mentioned in pt.1 are used, a protocol shall be written with a description of the measures applied, justification of their use and signatures of the persons who took the decision regarding restraint.

3. After each instance of applying restraint, a patient should be immediately seen by a doctor.

**10.2.3.3 The Ordinance of the Cabinet of December 11, 1996 (Acts Register 1996, No. 154, pos. 746) on the Matter of Detailed Conditions under which Physical Restraint may be Exercised Upon Minors Held in Borstals and Youth Shelters**

The text of this ordinance is very similar to the ordinance of the Minister of Health of August 23, 1995.

**10.2.3.4**

Some of the provisions from the Principles for the Protection of Persons with Mental Illness and for the Improvement of Mental Health Care, United Nations G.A. Resolution 119, December 17, 1991 (e.g. informed consent) were incorporated into the Physician's Profession Act.

**10.3 Jurisprudence**

The Supreme Court:

- Decision II CRN 201/95 regulated that, in order to confirm „the state of menace to…", it is obligatory to ascertain objective and rational circumstances implying the possibility of a threat to someone's life or health.
- Resolution III CZP 6/96 clarified that the discharge from mental hospital of a patient admitted there without consent and in an emergency does not justify the abandonment of adjudication by the Guardianship Court in this particular case and may not be the cause of its dismissal.
- Decision II CRN 81/96 ruled that – according to Art. 29 – the justified anticipation of an improvement in the health of a mentally ill person resulting from his/her treatment in mental hospital shall be the basis for admission without consent only when this person is incapable of independently satisfying his/her basic vital needs. This justified anticipation may not be the basis for admission without consent when the motion is based solely on the provision of Art. 29 § 1 pt. 1.
- Resolution III CKU 22/97 deemed that Art. 578 of the Civil Proceedings Code is not applicable to a Guardianship Court decision given in cases based on the provisions of MHA. As a result, all decisions based on MHA provisions are only applicable after their legal validation. There is, however, one exception: a decision based on Art. 27 (no justified reason for admission without consent to mental hospital) is applicable immediately, prior to legal validation.
- Resolution II CKU 72/96 stated:

*„a Guardianship Court decision to admit a mentally ill person to a mental health facility under Art. 29 of the MHA of August 19, 1994 (Acts Register No. 111, pos. 535) may be taken only if the relevant expert opinion referred to in Art. 30 of MHA is not questioned during the hearing. The explanation of doubts as to whether the person concerned is mentally ill or not and whether other conditions of Art. 29 § 1 of MHA are fulfilled or not cannot be in themselves the premise for such a decision".*

- Resolution I CKN 571/97 clarified that:

  *„a Guardianship Court decision to admit a mentally ill person to a mental health facility according to Art. 29 § 1 of the MHA of 19 August 1994 (Acts Register No. 111, pos. 535) does not imply that this person may be committed to the hospital for an unspecified period of time. The duration of such a stay in hospital depends on whether the reason, for which the decision for admission was taken, continues to exist (Art. 35 § 1 and Art. 36 of MHA)".*

## 10.4 Protocols Related to Coercive Measures

In matters of documenting any physical restraints applied, there are several obligatory protocols (i.e. a description of the procedures executed and affirmed facts) defined in appendices to ordinances of the Minister of Health.

1. An immobilization and seclusion sheet (a flow sheet for recording the reasons and duration of restraint, observations at regular time intervals and other data). This sheet is an appendix to the Ordinance of the Minister of Health of August 19, 1995.
2. Notification to the head of the hospital that physical restraint has been applied (an appendix to the ordinance mentioned above).
3. Notification to the psychiatrist authorized by the local authorities to assess the grounds for any physical restraint applied (an appendix to the ordinance mentioned above).
4. The form on the referral of a mentally ill person to a mental hospital with the application of physical restraint (an appendix to the Ordinance of the Minister of Health of November 23, 1995).
5. Notification to the Guardianship Court on admission to a mental health facility without a patient's consent (an appendix of the ordinance mentioned above).
6. Notification to the Guardianship Court regarding the discharge from a mental health facility of a patient admitted there without consent.

There are no other internal regulations pertaining to coercion and physical restraint in a mental health facility.

## 10.5 Reports

1. Report of the Institute of Psychiatry and Neurology on the Implementation of the Mental Health Act in 1997, 1999 and 2002, prepared on the request

of the Parliamentary Health Commission (IPiN 1999, Ministry of Health 2002).
2. Report of the Helsinki Foundation for Human Rights "The right to humanitarian treatment in closed institutions", Warsaw 1996.
3. Report of the Helsinki Foundation for Human Rights "Human rights in psychiatric hospitals and social welfare homes", Warsaw 1996.

Studies performed by the Helsinki Foundation in 1996 (i.e. one year after MHA came into effect) in ten randomly selected mental health facilities and psychiatric wards in general hospitals showed that none of the hospitals' internal regulations contained any information about effective appeal procedures. Theoretically, a patient was always allowed to complain about anything to a nurse, physician, head of the ward or head of the hospital, but no patients nor any of the staff ever filed a complaint.
In one huge mental hospital a patients' rights spokesman had already been employed for two and a half years. Newly admitted patients were informed about this upon their admission. Whenever a patient wanted to complain about anything, he was taken to the spokesman by staff members. The spokesman did not visit wards on his own initiative.
Cooperation with courts took various forms: hearings in cases of compulsory treatment were held in the hospital with the patient concerned present. There was only one exception: in the mental health facility in L., all hearings took place exclusively in a court building and patients were brought in by two orderlies. Such a procedure had a negative influence on patients and disorganized the work of the staff (orderlies had to leave the hospital for the hearing). In the opinion of psychiatrists, legal proceedings were far too sluggish and courts did not keep deadlines. One of the patients treated in the mental health facility in R. stayed there for four months after being admitted under Art. 23 of MHA (i.e. without consent) and all that time was regarded as such. At the end of this period the Court discontinued the case. Patients were afraid of the court and sometimes were threatened with it ("...you either consent or we go to the court..."). A patient with alcohol-induced psychosis was informed that if he consented he would be treated for only five days and if he refused he would be treated involuntarily and the decision would then be taken by the court, which would last up to five weeks. The patient finally consented.
Immobilization (using belts) was usually applied to patients in rooms with many beds, even though there were empty rooms in the ward more appropriate for this kind of restraint. This practice was strongly criticized by immobilized patients themselves, as well as their room-mates. The first felt humiliated and the latter felt embarrassed and helpless.

Patients reported that immobilization had been used against them as a sort of penalty for "being disobedient" (one patient repeatedly switched lights on and off) or as a form of „prevention" (a patient had drunk some alcohol and the nurse was afraid he would „mess around"). In some cases anxiety or motor hyperactivity were used in the immobilization and seclusion sheets as reasons for physical restraint. These are not sufficient justifications according to Art. 18 § 1 of MHA.

**10.6 Safeguard System**

1. Protection of the rights of patients with mental disorders, particularly in the matter of admission and stay in mental hospital and application of physical restraint in that hospital or a nursing home, is directly regulated by legal acts and provisions of the Minister of Justice, who in cooperation with relevant ministers specifies the means and procedures of safeguarding the care of mentally ill persons in these ordinances.
   - In the case of a perpetrator of an illicit act of considerable public harmfulness who is subjected to the preventive measure of placement in a mental health facility or in a maximum security forensic psychiatric regional centre, this inspection is carried out by a penitential judge according to Art. 32 and 33 § 1 of the Penal Executive Code.
   - In the case of a minor held in a mental health facility on the basis of a Court decision (Art. 12 of the Act on Proceedings in Cases of Minors), this inspection is carried out by a judge of the Family Court according to Art. 77 and 78 of the Act on Proceedings in Cases of Minors of October 26, 1982 (Acts Register No. 35, pos. 228).
   - In the case of an alcohol-dependent person obliged by the court to receive treatment in a mental health facility or alcohol treatment centre, this inspection is carried out by the judge of the Family Court according to Art. 36 of the Act on Upbringing in Sobriety and Counteracting Alcoholism and Ordinance of the Minister of Justice of May 7, 1983 (Acts Register No. 25, pos. 111).
   - In the case of a mentally ill or mentally retarded person admitted to a mental health facility or nursing home with or without consent, this inspection is carried out by the judge of the Guardianship Court according to Art. 43 of the Mental Health Act of 19 August 1994 and Ordinance of the Minister of Justice of February 22, 1995 (Acts Register No. 23, pos. 128). Inspections are carried out at least once a year, more often when necessary. It is a judge's obligation to evaluate the necessity of any further stay in the hospital of every patient hospitalized there for longer than six months.

2. Another form of safeguard for the legitimacy of medical decisions made by a doctor on duty is the hearing of each person admitted without consent in accordance with the provisions of Art. 23, 24 or 28 of MHA no later than 48 hours following the receipt of notification referred to in Art. 23, § 4. If the judge ascertains that hospitalization of such a person is evidently unjustified, the judge shall order the immediate discharge of that person from hospital. In 1995 to 1996 the percentage of those immediately discharged was 1.5% and now it is .25% of all emergency admittances without consent.
3. Each decision by a psychiatrist to admit a patient to hospital without his/her consent, either an emergency admission or admission based on a motion, has to be verified by the Guardianship Court, which adjudicates after taking into consideration the opinion of the psychiatric expert appointed. However, such a safeguard may raise a lot of doubts, due to the court's exaggerated deference to expert opinion. This expresses itself in the following facts: short average length of hearing, witnesses rarely being present, lack of adequate behavioural justification for admission (no imminent danger to others) in 37.0% of opinions, insufficiently clear, cogent and convincing evidence in a large proportion of the remaining opinions. This pertains mainly to opinions issued in cases of emergency admissions and less to opinions on admissions based on a motion.
4. Courts very rarely appoint a defence lawyer and patients very seldom appoint one on their own initiative.
5. In 1996/1997 the Supreme Inspection Chamber inspected the implementation of the Mental Health Act in the whole country (information on the results of the implementation of the mental health act, Warsaw, October 1997) (NIK 1997) and in 2002 it inspected hospitals in Lower Silesia (information on the results of the inspection, Wroclaw, March 2002) (NIK 2002).

### 10.7 Other Information

The Institute of Psychiatry and Neurology in Warsaw evaluates the realization of provisions of the MHA grouped in the third category (the aim of these provisions is to protect the civil rights of patients treated both with and without consent in mental hospitals), which encompasses administrative-medical and some judicial-lawsuit warranties. This evaluation is carried out by a small team monitoring:

- a few administrative-medical provisions regulating admissions without consent, using a simple questionnaire filled in once quarterly by almost all mental health facilities, excluding detoxification services,
- a wide spectrum of provisions pertaining to consent, physical restraint, judicial-psychiatric expertise and others, using complex questionnaires

filled in by scientists themselves and evaluating randomly selected target groups of several hundred patients.

All data illustrating the process of implementation and realization of the provisions of MHA presented here come from the monitoring procedures mentioned above.

## References

Dąbrowski S (1998) Specjalistyczne usługi opiekuńcze- jako forma oparcia społecznego. [Specialist community social services as a form of community social support]. Psychiatria Polska 32: 443-451

Dąbrowski S, Brodniak WA, Welbel S (2000) Projekt standardów środowiskowych domów samopomocy. Postępy Psychiatrii i Neurologii 9: 443-454

Dąbrowski S (2001) Ocena przestrzegania przepisów ustawy o ochronie zdrowia psychicznego dotyczących przymusu bezpośredniego. Postępy Psychiatrii i Neurologii 10: 375-382

Dąbrowski S, Brodniak WA, Welbel A (in press) Ocena przestrzegania przepisów o zgodzie na leczenie w szpitalu psychiatrycznym. Postępy Psychiatrii i Neurologii

Dąbrowski S, Pietrzykowski J (1997) Ustawa o ochronie zdrowia psychicznego. Komentarz. [Mental Health Act. Commentary]. Warszawa: Instytut Psychiatrii i Neurologii

Dąbrowski S, Pietrzykowski J (1998) Ustawa o ochronie zdrowia psychicznego. Suplement do komentarza. [Mental Health Act. Supplement to Commentary]. Warszawa: Instytut Psychiatrii i Neurologii

Dąbrowski S, Brodniak WA, Welbel A (in press) Wstępne wyniki badań nad opiniami psychiatrycznymi w sprawie przyjęcia bez zgody do szpitala psychiatrycznego. Postępy Psychiatrii i Neurologii

Helsinki Foundation for Human Rights (1996) Report Helsinki Foundation for Human Rights "Human rights in psychiatric hospitals and homes of social welfare". Warsaw

Instytut Psychiatrii i Neurologii (1999) Sprawozdanie z realizacji ustawy o ochronie zdrowia psychicznego (1998 r.). Warszawa: IPiN

[Ministry of Health] Ministerstwo Zdrowia (2002) Sprawozdanie z realizacji ustawy o ochronie zdrowia psychicznego (1999-2001). Warszawa: Ministerstwo Zdrowia

Naczelna Izba Kontroli (1997) Informacja o wynikach kontroli realizacji ustawy o ochronie zdrowia psychicznego. Warszawa: NIK

NIK, Delegatura we Wrocławiu (2002) Informacja o wynikach kontroli sprawdzających realizację ustawy o ochronie zdrowia psychicznego. Wrocław: NIK, Delegatura we Wrocławiu

Ustawa z dnia 20 maja 2005 o zmianie ustawy o ochronie zdrowia psychicznego. [Act from 20 of May 2005 changing the Mental Health Act]. http://ks.sejm.gov.pl

**Diagram 10.1 Admission to Psychiatric Facility without/with Consent**

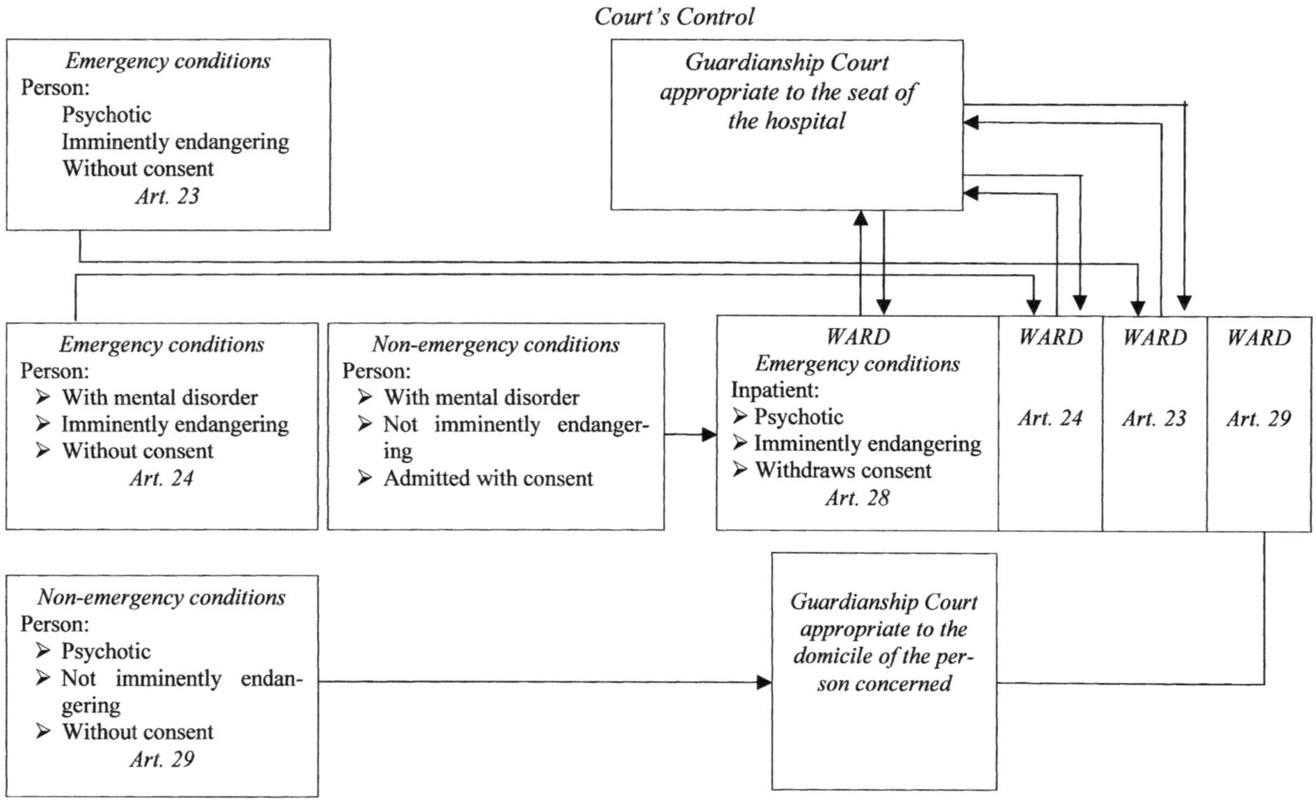

**CHAPTER 11**

# Legal Report – Slovak Republic

Jan FARKAŠ, Jana ELIÁŠOVÁ, Juraj BIL'O

## 11.1 Preliminary Remarks

### 11.1.1 Historical Development of the Slovak System of Law

In the Slovak legal system no single law regulates coercive measures in psychiatry, involuntary admission and detention in psychiatric hospitals, compulsory treatment and care.

These aspects of mental health care are regulated by Constitutional Laws, Laws of the National Council (Národná rada) as well as by departmental public notices from the Ministry of Health of the Slovak Republic (Ministerstvo zdravotníctva Slovenskej republiky), and all of these vary in their legal force.

Even before World War One, within the framework of the unified Austro-Hungarian state, there was a so-called "detention procedure" (adopted from the Austrian legal system) in force throughout the territory of Slovakia. Through this procedure the court could comment on the permissibility of both a prospective patient's admission to hospital and of keeping them in hospital care without their consent (21).

This law was adopted as a constitutional law for the territory of the Slovak Republic for the first time through Constitutional Law No. 150/1948 Coll. of the Constitution of the Czechoslovak Republic (22) in Article 29. According to Article 29 paragraph 1:

> *"Everybody is entitled to the protection of his or her health. All citizens have the right to medical care."*

The right to health protection was recognized for the second time by Constitutional Law No. 100/1960 Coll. – the Constitution of the Czechoslovak Socialist Republic (23). According to Article 23 paragraph 1:

> *"All working people are entitled to health protection and medical care as well as to the right to be financially assured in old age and in disability for work."*

According to Article 30 paragraph 1 of the above constitution "Personal integrity shall be guaranteed."

Despite Article 30 paragraph1 of the Constitution of the Czechoslovak Socialist Republic the Law No. 20/1966 Coll. pertaining to health care remained, for many years, the major source of law for regulation of mental health care.
This situation was both a consequence and illustration of juridical thinking. At that time, the Constitution was being formally taught and declared at ceremonial occasions as the corner stone of the Czechoslovak legal system, but in fact the Constitution stood in a "juridical vacuum". In practice, the real source of law and basis of the legal system was not derived from the Constitution, but it was the law which constituted the foundations of all social relationships and was continually modified by politically acceptable regulations. This juridical mentality still prevails. It also contributes to deficiencies in effective jurisdiction and is one of the causes for the cyclically repeating amendments to laws of fundamental importance.
Mental health care's instructing parameter, according to Law No. 20/1966 Coll., was Article 23 paragraph 4, which regulated patients' admission to hospital care with or without the consent of the person afflicted by a mental disorder. The basic precondition for a person to be admitted to hospital care in this case was that he/she posed a direct threat to him/herself or others in his/her community. Psychiatric practice adjusted this provision to "threatening offence," under which ill people who had not threatened anybody were sometimes admitted to hospital care without consent and their personal liberty restricted as a preventive measure because they "potentially" posed a threat to themselves or their community if they were left free.
Hospital treatment including admitting patients without their consent enabled further holding in care without their consent – according to Article 23 paragraph 4 nursing care treatment could be carried out regardless of the manifestation of the ill person's will. This was supported by other concepts of legal amendment in force, created by "private persons" to whom no right to "interpret the law" or to "standardize the application practice" was actually provided by an authority or law. However, the violation of socialist law and order by private persons aiming to standardize the interpretation of the law prevailed unchallenged (7).

As an example we cite a passage of the article by Kolibaš-Fleischer-Čaplova-Tuža published in Lekársky obzor, 1998, No. 5, page 309, named "Legal and psychiatric issues of decision making process on treatment" (11):

> *"A treatment without a patient's consent is justified because of the fact that, in consideration of his or her health, it is not possible to seek his or her consent. It is possible also in the initial stage of the illness which corresponds to modern and prospectively conceived health care. In mental retardation (oligophrenia) we do not speak about psychosis, even if it is the case that a high number of mental symptoms and the disorder of critical faculties are at a level comparable with psychosis, and as such a patient's placement in a psychiatric hospital without his or her consent is fully justified if needed."* (Page 310). *"For exam-*

*ple in the case of a suicide attempt in the sense of a rash action, and if it is not certain whether the suicidal tendencies have been fully vented, it is possible to place the patient into a psychiatric establishment without his or her consent even if he or she is not suffering from psychosis, but maybe from a pathological condition in the common sense of the term. The psychotic patient can also be treated for somatic illness without his or her consent. Refusal of treatment (a signed declaration) can not be accepted.“*

A radical step toward increasing the protection of personal freedom was made by the change of the system of law in the early nineties of the last century.
The following laws became sources of the new legal regulation: Constitutional Law N. 23/1991 Coll., Law No. 519/1991 Coll. as an amendment to the Code of Civil Procedure and the Notarial Code, Act of the Slovak National Council No. 419/1991 Coll. amending some regulations in the area of public health and the Act of the Czech National Council No. 548/1991 Coll. amending the Law No. 20/1966 Coll. and the Act of the Czech National Council No. 425/1990 Coll.

In the Constitutional Law No. 23/1991 Coll. Article 16 paragraph 6 was adopted according to which

*"The law will stipulate in which cases a person may be admitted or detained in inpatient health care without his or her consent. This measure shall be communicated to the court which shall make a decision on this placement within seven days."*

According to Article11 of the Constitution of the Slovak Republic

*"International agreements on human rights and basic freedoms which were ratified by the Slovak Republic and were proclaimed in the manner stipulated by the law will take precedence over the national laws - provided that they guarantee greater basic rights and freedoms."*

According to the Article 2 of the Constitutional Law No. 23/1991 Coll. (Charter of Basic Rights and Freedoms)

*"International agreements on human rights and basic freedoms ratified and proclaimed by the Czech and Slovak Federal Republic are generally binding for the whole national territory and take precedence over the law."*

Agreement on Protection of Human Rights and Fundamental Freedoms in the wording of Protocols No. 3 and 8 was signed in the name of the Czech and Slovak Federal Republic on February 21, 1991. It was ratified by the President of the Czech and Slovak Federal Republic in accordance with Article 7, paragraph 1 Lett. a) for the Law No. 131/1989 Coll. on protection of human rights and fundamental freedoms in the wording of Protocols No. 3, 5 and 8 and proclaimed in Part 41 of Collection of Laws No. 209/1992 Coll.

According to Article 153 of the Constitution of the Slovak Republic

> *"to the Slovak Republic shall pass all rights and obligations, by which the Czech and the Slovak Republic have been bound, in extent stipulated by the constitutional law of the Czech and Slovak Federal Republic or in extent stipulated between the Czech Republic and the Slovak Republic."*

Therefore, the International Treaty on Civil and Political Rights, the International Treaty on Economic, Social and Cultural Rights as well as the Agreement on Protection of Human Rights and Freedoms have the character of the source of law also throughout the Slovak Republic.
On May 28, 1993 the notification of succession of the Slovak Republic into multilateral treaties took place, to which the Secretary General of the United Nations was a signatory, with validity starting on January 1, 1993. As a consequence, on the day on which Czech and Slovak Federal Republics divided, the following treaties, among others, came into effect for the Slovak Republic: International Treaty on Civic and Political Rights, International Treaty on Economic, Social and Cultural Rights (Notice of the Ministry of Foreign Affairs of the Slovak Republic on accomplishment of the notification of succession of the Slovak Republic into multilateral treaties, a signatory to which was the Secretary General of United Nations, No. 53/1994 Coll.L.). On June 30, 1993, the Board of Ministers of the Council of Europe confirmed, with validity from January 1, 1993, the succession of the Slovak Republic into multilateral treaties undersigned by the Secretary General of the United Nations and to which the Czech and Slovak Federal Republic had been a contracting party .

The legal position of the patient in its basic form includes:

1. the right to be a patient,
2. the right to decide, with the knowledge of the cause, if he or she undergoes a curative procedure proposed by the physician or another health care worker,
3. procedural guarantees of the powers granted to him or her by the law for asserting the right to health protection.

The extent of the constitutional health protection law in accordance with the present-day legal regulations detailed in our report can be seen as defined by these rights.

Essentially, political changes in Slovakia, which has been an independent country and unitary state since January 1, 1993, did not have any impact on the legal regulation in these mental health matters because Slovakia had ratified and subsequently adopted all laws and treaties concerning these issues from the former Czech and Slovak Federal Republic (7, 21, 22, 23, 24, 25).

### 11.1.2 Comment on the structure of this report

In an effort to clarify aspects of the law, judicial decisions made by supreme courts, a selection of verdicts and opinions, as well as a collection of verdicts given by Supreme Courts have been incorporated into individual legal norms.

**Comments:**

R = Collection of judicial verdicts and opinions (the so-called "blue collection"). This mark has been used to indicate judicates (judicial decisions) made public by Supreme Courts of Czechoslovak Socialist Republic, Czech and Slovak Federal Republic, Czech Republic and Slovak Republic until December 31, 1992 and judicates made public by the Supreme Court of the Slovak Republic from January 1, 1993.

V = Selection of verdicts and opinions by Supreme Courts (so-called "white collection")

Z = Collections of opinions, reports and decisions by courts and of judicial proceedings by Supreme Courts I 1965 – 1967, III 1964 – 1969, IV 1970 – 1983

Zb = Collection of Laws until December 31, 1992
Z.z. = Collection of Laws of the National Council of the Slovak Republic after January 1, 1993

### 11.2 Applicable Laws and General Norms

The problems of coercive measures like involuntary admission, detention in a psychiatric hospital, compulsory treatment and guardianship in the Slovak system of law are regulated by:

I. Constitution of the Slovak Republic
II. Health Care Act
III. Code of Civil Procedure
IV. Penal Law and Code of Penal Procedure
V. Civil Code
VI. Charter of Patient's Rights in the Slovak Republic
VII. Protection of the right to personal freedom against restraint because of health reasons in proceeding before Constitutional Court (Ústavný súd).
VIII. Public Guardian of Rights Act (Ombudsman)

### 11.2.1 Constitution of the Slovak Republic

The Constitution of the Slovak Republic from September 1, 1992 and the amendments 244/1998 of the Collection of Laws and 90/2001 of the Collection of Laws (hereinafter Constitution) is the fundamental law and the pillar of the Slovak legal system from which all laws and acts unfold.

According to Part Two, Chapter Two of the Constitution, "Fundamental Rights and Freedoms":

Article 16, paragraph, Constitution

> *"The right of every individual to integrity and privacy shall be guaranteed. This right may be limited only in cases specifically provided by law."*

Article 17 paragraph 7, Constitution

> *"A person may be committed to or held in a medical institution without his or her consent only in cases stipulated by law. Such cases shall be reported to the court within twenty-four hours and the court shall make a decision regarding such placement within five days."*

Article 17 paragraph 7, Constitution

> *"A psychological examination of the person charged with an offence is permissible only by a written court order."*

*Notes:* The Constitution of the Slovak Republic also regulates the takeover of generally accepted international treaties and agreements, constitutional concepts, postulates on human rights and freedoms, on legislative, executive powers and the force of laws.
The Constitution shall adhere to such important documents as the Universal Declaration of Human Rights from December 1948, the Rome Convention on Protection of Human Rights and Freedoms, the Treaty on Civil and Political Rights, the documents of the Helsinki process and, finally, in the interest of the perspective development of the Slovak Republic, also to the documents pertaining to the processes of European Union integration.
The quality of a democracy depends not only on the quality of its legislation but also on the degree to which the protection of rights and freedoms are guaranteed by its Constitution.
The following comes under the ensemble of these guarantees: constitutionality, rule of law, court institutions, freedom of confession of faith, freedom of speech, inviolability of mail, personal immunity, presumption of innocence, presumption of bravery of the citizen, strict time limits prescribed by law for unavoidable limitation of personal freedom, for body search and house search, as well as a limited interference by authorities and health institutions with personal freedom whilst examining a mental state (25).

### 11.2.2 General Laws

#### 11.2.2.1 Health Care Act

From the point of view of material law, Article 17 paragraph 6 of the Constitution shall be executed by Health Care Act No. 277/1994 from August 24, 1994 in the wording of its amendments 98/1995, 110/1996, 222/1996, 140/1998, 241/1998, 80/2000, 416/2001, 553/2001, 118/2002, 131/2002, 219/2002, 450/2002, 457/2002, 138/2003, 445/2003 (hereinafter Health Care Act).

According to § 14 "Care without patient's consent"

(1) Examination and treatment measures, including residential health care, may also be carried out if it is not possible to ask the patient for their consent because of his or her state of health or if it is not possible to ask for consent from his or her representative because of his or her absence, but their consent can be taken for granted.

(2) Patients may be taken into residential care without their consent if
   a) there are illnesses on which compulsory treatment may be imposed,
   b) the patient, because of his or her mental illness or with symptoms of a mental disorder or a mental illness, poses a direct threat to him or herself or his or her community or if there is a danger of a grave deterioration of his or her state of health.
   c) the patient is in a state where his or her vital functions are threatened and life saving actions and the uninterrupted monitoring of vital functions are necessary.

(3) It is an obligation of the health care institution to inform the court in the district where the health institution is situated that the patient has been taken into residential care without his or her consent, within 24 hours. The court shall make a decision on the lawfulness of the action's grounds. Until the decision of the court is available, only examinations and treatments necessary to save the life and health of the patient or to provide safety to his or her community may be performed.

(4) If the reasons for taking a patient into residential care without his or her consent cease to exist, it will be the obligation of the health care institution to release the patient or to obtain from the patient or his or her legal representative consent in a written form or in the form of a written record of a declaration made orally that the provision for health care should be continued.

(5) If the patient who, due to his or her state of health is likely to pose a threat to himself /herself or his/her community, leaves the health care institution without the consent of the physician, it is the obligation of this institution to inform the police immediately of the case.

(6) It is the obligation of the health care institution to inform the public prosecutor, investigator or police authority of:
   a) suicide, suicide attempts and cases where there is a justified suspicion that a third person could have participated in damaging a patient's health or causing death,
   b) admission of a patient whose identity can not be determined or who has been injured by a firearm or other types of weapons,
   c) suspicion of cruelty to, or abuse of a child, or another person who does not have legal capacity or whose legal capacity has been limited.

§ 38 Condition of mental health care

(1) Persons with symptoms of a mental disorder or a mental illness shall be provided with outpatient or inpatient mental health care.

(2) Examination and treatment measures within the mental health care process shall be performed with the consent of the patient or his or her legal representative or guardian. It shall be the obligation of the physician to provide patients with adequate information about their illness. Otherwise the physician will provide the patient's legal representative or guardian with full information.

(3) To perform particularly important mental health care or surgical interventions which could substantially alter the personality of either a patient under 18 years of age, a patient with a limited legal capacity or an incapacitated patient, beside the consent of the legal representative or guardian granted on the recommendation of a professional council, the consent of the court is also necessary.

(4) The methods to be used for treatment of homosexual patients shall be set down by a generally binding legal regulation to be issued by the Ministry of Public Health.

(5) A patient may be admitted into residential mental health care without his or her consent in cases set forth under § 14 paragraph 2 letter b).

(6) If a patient who poses a threat, due to his or her state of health, to members of his or her community should leave the health care institution without the consent of a physician, it will be the obligation of this institution to notify the responsible police unit of this event so that they can attempt to find out where the patient may be staying. If possible, the health care institution shall also inform the persons potentially at risk from the patient.

(7) According to § 14 paragraph 3, health care institutions are obliged to report to the court cases where patients with symptoms of a mental disorder or illness are admitted with consent but during the course of treatment it is deemed necessary to restrict their free movement. Until the court reaches a decision the only examination and treatment measures which are permissi-

ble are those necessary for saving the patient's life, preventing a serious deterioration in the patient's health or protecting the patient's community.

*Notes:* Health Care Act entered into force on January 1, 1995. On the same day the previous act numbered 20/1966 on people's health care, through which problems relating to health care without patient's consent were regulated in a similar manner, became void.

Commentary on Health Care Act (Zákon o zdravotnej starostlivosti)
As far as the provision on health care is concerned the legal literature (17, 18) says:

> *"Assessment of circumstances under which the patient threatens him or herself appears to be free of problems. Cases will be considered where the patient acts, due to his or her mental disorder, in a way that threatens his or her health or life. This can include an excessive use of medication, ingestion of poisonous substances and liquids, handling of substances and materials which can bring about a deterioration in health and danger to life (such as the handling of sharp objects, weapons). We can consider a patient to be posing a threat to their SELF in the case when such behaviour is directed by the ill person at him or herself even in the presence of other people. The definition of 'poses a threat to his or her community' appears to be much more problematic. COMMUNITY – the notion can be understood in a narrower sense, but also in a very broad one. Different meanings can be given to this notion also in connection with a more detailed definition of the way he or she is posing a threat to his or her community.*
> *It can be assumed that the lawmaker had mainly PHYSICAL THREAT in mind, linked directly to the protection of life or health. But because physical threat usually involves verbal threat too, cases cannot be excluded where the ill person due to his or her disorder is threatening the community verbally by mail as this may entail, although indirectly, injury to health.*
> *In this case, an independent enquiry would be used to assess to what degree a threat to a community can be considered as dangerous in order to justify the admission of the ill person into hospital care without his or her consent."*

### 11.2.2.2 Code of Civil Procedure

From the point of view of procedural law, Article 17 paragraph 6 of the Constitution shall be executed by the Act No. 99/1994 from December 4, 1963 in the wording of its amendments numbered 37/1967, 158/1969, 49/1973, 20/1975, 133/1982, 180/1990, 328/1991, 519/1991, 263/1992, 5/1993, 46/1994, 190/1995, 232/1995, 233/1995, 58/1996, 281/1996, 211/1997, 359/1997, 124/1998, 144/1998, 169/1998, 187/1998, 225/1998, 233/1998, 235/1998, 331/1998, 46/1999, 66/1999, 166/1999, 185/1999, 223/1999, 303/2001, 501/2001, 215/2002, 232/2002, 424/2002, 451/2002, 620/2002, 480/2002, 75/2003, 353/2003 of the Collection of Laws – Code of Civil Procedure (hereinafter "C.C.P.").

Procedure on vote of permissibility of an admission or holding in a health care institution

§ 191a

(1) It is the obligation of the health care practising institution (hereinafter "institution") in which persons are placed for the reasons set forth in special regulations to notify the court in whose district the institution is situated. This must be done within 24 hours of the admission of every person placed in the institution without his or her written consent (hereinafter "ill").

(2) If the person admitted to health care with his or her written consent has their freedom of movement limited or is limited in his or her outside contact in the course of the treatment, it will be the obligation of the institution to make note of this according to paragraph 1 within 24 hours after the occurrence of such a limitation.

*Notes:* The above legal situation has been valid since the amendment of C.C.P. number 519/1991 came into force on January 1, 1992.

In order to keep the coercive-treatment and handling practices under control and to prevent the abuse of constitutional care, the so-called "detention procedure" had already been introduced before World War One. Through this procedure the court could comment on the admissibility of detention and on the permissibility of keeping the patient in residential care without his or her consent. This procedure was reused by the C.C.P. from 1950 onwards but was modified by number 20/1966 of the people's Health Care Act so that this paper could play a role for national committees, and that decisions of national committees would be controlled by the court in proceedings pursuant to Article 244 and following articles of C.C.P.: However, this was only the case if the patient or persons close to him or her specifically requested it. Thus, control of detention proceedings became a problem.

Using the word "hold" the lawmaker argues that this can also refer to those cases where the patient will be admitted to residential care with his or her consent but he or she need be excluded from having or have limited access to outside contact.

The above stated principles shall be valid for both citizens of the Slovak Republic as well as foreign nationals in the Slovak Republic.

§ 191b

(1) For each person the health care institution receives, formal notification pursuant to Article 191a shall be given to the court requesting that the court shall start a proceeding voting on the permissibility of admission to this institution unless the admission and holding was ordered by the court in another proceeding.

(2) If the person admitted to the institution does not have any other representative, the court shall appoint to him or her a guardian for this proceeding.
(3) The court shall collect evidence necessary to consider if the admission of the patient (Article 191a paragraph 1 and 2) took place on legal grounds, shall hear the patient and his or her attending physician. Generally, it is not necessary to order a trial.
(4) Within five days from the day when the time limitation according to paragraph 191a began the court shall decide, in a decree, whether the admission took place on legal grounds (Article 191a paragraph 1).

*Notes:* The above proceeding shall be conducted by the court in a so-called "help registry NcU" and because of this, office work in first level County Courts of primary jurisdiction will be done by junior judges as a rule.
The court shall decide on the beginning of the proceeding by a decree in which a guardian will also be appointed to the patient. They are simply collision guardians, i.e. guardians appointed for this proceeding only and whose function will finish on the day court decisions enter into force. The appointment of a collision guardian will be a formal proceeding. As a guardian the court will often appoint someone from the staff of the County Court (Okresný súd). This is due to the fact that the time it takes to deliver the appointment decree will be significantly shortened and the guardian status will be validated quicker. As a rule, the collision guardian will not go to see the patient in his or her institution but will only formally receive papers from the court. In practice there will be no cases where the guardian would appeal against decisions of the court.
The courts will observe interviews with the patient and the attending physician. These interviews will take place directly in the institution.
The court will make a decision on the matter of admission in a decree. The diction of the provision of Article 191b means that the court will have to make a decision within five days starting from the day on which the restriction took place i.e. regardless of the fact that the last day is a Saturday, Sunday or a public holiday. In practice, the courts will observe the term of five working days. The reason for this is a financial one. If the courts had to make decisions strictly within the limit of five days from the day of patient's restriction, in County Courts (Okresné súdy) services of judges, as well as of recording secretaries would have to be established in the manner typical for criminal cases. This would increase the financial exigency to be borne by the state pursuant to Article 191g.
The courts will not order a proceeding in these cases although it is possible to order a proceeding.

§ 191c

(1) A decree according to Article 191b paragraph 4 will be served to the placed person, but if according to his or her attending physician he or she will not be able to understand the contents of the decision, then it will be served to his or her legal representative (guardian) and to their institution. To the placed person and to the institution the decree shall be served within 24 hours from the decision, but at the latest, within the limit of five days from the day on which the restriction took place pursuant to Article 191a. If the decree is not served to the placed person, it shall be served to his or her representative (guardian) within the fixed time limit.

(2) The appeal against this decree will not have any suspending effect. The institution may also appeal if it was said that the admission had not taken place in accordance with the legal system.

(3) The institution may also release the placed person if the court says that the admission took place in accordance with the legal system.

*Notes:* An appeal against the decree may be lodged by the guardian *ad litem*, or the institution which is also an involved party in the case that the decree will be delivered to the patient. This appeal may also be lodged by the patient him or herself, provided that he or she has legal capacity.

All general provisions of the Code of Civil Procedure, Article 201 and the following will apply to the appeal within a time period of thirty days from the day on which the decree was served.

The time period of 30 days will pass for each involved party independently.

The court of appeal (Odvolávací súd) shall be the responsible Regional Court (Krajský súd).

For the Regional Court (Krajský súd) there will be no time limit to deal with the appeal.

Lodging an appeal will not have any suspending effect, i.e. after lodging an appeal the patient will remain in the health care institution.

§ 191d

(1) If the court confirms that the admission took place in accordance with the legal system and the placed person is restrained or excluded from having outside contact, the court will continue the proceeding by voting on the admissibility of further detention in an institution.

(2) An expert shall be appointed by the court to find out the state of health of the placed person. The task of the expert is to say if it remains necessary to keep the person placed in an institution under restraint or excluded from having outside contact. A physician who is employed in the same institution where the placed person has been held may not be appointed as expert.

(3) The court shall order a hearing to which the placed person (provided the placed person, according to his or her attending physician or to a written attestation from a medical health expert, is able to understand the course and the importance of the hearing) and his or her representative (guardian) shall be invited. In the hearing, the expert and, as the case may be, also the attending physician, and the placed person shall be heard, and other adequate evidence collected by the court shall be reviewed.

(4) In the judgement to be pronounced within three months from the verdict on permissibility of admission into the institution the court shall decide whether further detention is or is not admissible and if it is so for what period of time. Correspondingly, the dispositions of paragraph 191c paragraphs 2 and 3 will be valid also here.

*Notes:* Here, the law differentiates between "admission" and "detention" in a health care institution. Admission is regulated by § 191a, § 191b, § 191c C.C.P., holding by § 191d, 191e and § 191f C.C.P.

Before a three-month period of time from the sentence on permissibility of admission into an institution is over, the court will decide, *ex officio*, whether further detention in an institution is admissible and for what period of time. To do so, the courts shall demand reports from the relevant institutions. In this proceeding an expert shall be appointed by the court to find out the state of health and shall order a hearing due to the fact that, in this stage, a decision on the case shall be made by a sentence. In practice, courts will observe the above dispositions. The proceeding will be conducted under the same reference number as the admission.

Regular remedies and structure of courts

To make a decision on admissibility as well as on holding in a health care institution is the responsibility of County Courts (Okresné súdy) as courts of first instance, i.e. the lowest components within the judicial system of the Slovak Republic. Courts of appeals (Odvolacie súdy) are Regional Courts (Krajské súdy) as courts of second instance. Appeals against a decree on admission as well as against a sentence on detention in a health institution belong to so-called "regular remedies".

An appeal against a sentence may be lodged by a guardian *ad litem* (kolízny opatrovník), a health institution being involved in the case and, if the sentence is delivered to the patient, the appeal may be lodged also by the patient him or herself provided he or she has legal capacity.

To an appeal all dispositions of C.C.P. § 201 ff will apply within a 13-day period of time from the day of delivery of the sentence.

The 13-day period of time will pass for each involved party individually.

The court of appeal (Apelačný súd) is the responsible Regional Court (Krajský súd).
There will be no time limit for the Regional Court (Krajský súd) to deal with the appeal.
Lodging an appeal will not have any immediate suspending effect, i.e. also in the case of an appeal being lodged by any of the involved parties the patient will still remain in the health care institution.

Special remedies
The law will exclude the possibility of lodging a remedy – reopening the case – because of the reason that pursuant to § 229, letter b) C.C.P.

> *"...reopening will not be admissible in cases where the abolition or modification of a sentence may be reached by other means."*

Against the decision of a Regional Court (Krajský súd) as a court of appeal, a special appeal may be lodged, pursuant to § 236 following C.C.P. as a remedy. Here, the decision will be made by the Supreme Court (Najvyšší súd).
In practice, there will not be any extraordinary appeals in these cases due to high demands of time because an extraordinary appeal may be lodged within one month from the validity date of the Regional Court's decision, i.e. these time periods will be, in real time, over one year from the time of the first instance of a County Court's decision (prvostupňový okresný súd).
Another remedy pursuant to paragraph 243e C.C.P is an extraordinary appeal, which will be also excluded in these cases. The exclusion is due to the provision paragraph 243e, paragraph 1, last principle, C.C.P.

> *"it will not be possible to reach this protection by any other legal action."*

It is to the case's advantage that the public prosecutor will not be allowed to enter this proceeding.
Pursuant to § 35, paragraph 2, C.C.P.

> *"The public prosecutor will be allowed to enter a started proceeding a) in the cases of legal capacity, b) in the cases of declaration of death, c) in the cases of undersigning with Register of Companies, d) in the cases concerning the education of minors, e) of guardianship, f) of insolvency proceedings and settlement."*

Obviously, if the public prosecutor would enter into the proceeding it would not be possible, in practice, to observe the short five-day time period or the three month time period for solving the case.
As these cases will not come before the Supreme Court (Najvyšší súd), there is an absence of jurisdiction concerning these provisions of C.C.P. in the Slovak legal system.

§ 191e

(1) The force of the sentence pursuant to § 191d, paragraph 4 will expire after a one-year time period beginning from its pronouncement – provided that no shorter period of time has been fixed. Should the detention in the health care institution be prolonged over this time limit, a new investigation should be undertaken and the court will have to make a new decision on the permissibility of continuing to hold the patient. Correspondingly, the provisions § 191c paragraph 2 and 3 will also apply here.

(2) The sentence pursuant to paragraph 1 will hinder neither the health care institution to release the person held in the institution before the time period, set under paragraph 1, is over, nor the Guardian Court (Opatrovnícky súd) to take other measures.

*Notes:* The force of the sentence will expire *ex lege* one year after it has been pronounced while a shorter period of time may be fixed in the sentence. When this period of time has passed, the patient held in a health care institution should be released. If his or her state of health has not improved and it is still necessary to hold him or her in a health care institution even after the sentence is not in force, a new investigation should be held and the court will have to make a new decision on the permissibility of continuing to hold the patient in a health care institution.

§ 191f

The person held in a health care institution, provided that he or she has legal capacity, or his or her legal representative (guardian) and persons close to him or her may ask, even before the maximum time period for holding a patient in a health institution is over, for a new investigation and a decision on their release – provided that the opinion is justified and that further holding in a health care institution is not well-founded. If the court rejects the proposal for release, the court may decide not to undertake any further investigations before the maximum time period is over.

*Notes:* The Law takes into account the fact that the state of health of the patient may improve and it will not be necessary to hold the patient in a health care institution any longer. The right to lodge a proposal for a release decision belongs to the person being held in a health care institution, provided that he or she is not incapable of doing so i.e. has ceded legal rights to his or her appointed guardian or to persons close to him or her, i.e. next of kin relatives, such as a brother, sister, husband or wife. By lodging the proposal the above persons will become involved in the proceeding with all respective rights and responsibilities. But there is a danger of unfounded and recurrent proposals by the patient and persons close to him or her. This has been taken into account by the law. As a result the court has been invested with the power to decide, when it has rejected the release proposal, not to carry out any further investigations before the time period allowing to hold the patient in a health care institution is over.

§ 191g
The costs of the proceeding shall be borne by the state. The state shall not pay the costs of attorneys except for the cases under § 30, paragraph 2 of this law.

*Notes:* It is just and logical that the costs of the proceeding (which amongst others includes the costs of medical-health expert's counsel) not be borne by the health care institution, or the patient. These shall be paid for by the state with the exception of the case where an attorney has been appointed to the patient or chosen by the patient. The investigated patient should then pay for this attorney by him or herself.

*Commentary to Code of Civil Procedure (Občiansky súdny poriadok)*
The admission of an ill person into hospital care without his or her consent is a two-phase process.

The first phase involves the transport of the ill person into a medical establishment i.e. to the place where "admission" can take place. Legal basis for the restraint of personal freedom in the first phase of "admission" is given by Article 19 paragraph 1 Lett.a) of the Law No. 171/1993 Coll.L. on Police Force according to which

> *"a policeman has the right to detain a person who is posing a direct threat to his or her own life or health or the health and life of other persons."*

The wording of the law makes it possible for litigation on the basis of restraint of personal freedom to originate even in this initial phase. A policeman may restrain the personal freedom of the person posing a direct threat to his or her own or another's life or health. What kind of threat must the life or health of other persons be exposed to by the action of the ill person? Does it have to be a direct threat or is any kind of menace to the health and life of other persons sufficient? One objection to potentially unconstitutional restraint of personal freedom will be followed by another if a policeman detains an ill person because he or she poses a threat to their own life or health, but subsequently it turns out that the detention does not comply with the condition of "direct threat."

The second phase of the process of restraint of personal freedom due to health reasons is the "admission" itself of the ill person into hospital care.

The law regulates material and procedural conditions for “admission” due to health reasons.

Material conditions for admission into hospital care are regulated by the Law No.277/1994 Coll.L. on health care. According to Article 38 paragraph 1 of this regulation

> *“Outpatient or inpatient psychiatric care shall be provided to persons with symptoms of mental disorder or mental illness.”*

The law does not allow for the provision of psychiatric care to persons not showing symptoms of mental disorder or illness. These symptoms are the first material condition for providing psychiatric care in any form i.e. also in the form of restraining personal freedom throughout hospital care.

The second condition provides information on the ill person’s state of health. According to Article 38 paragraph3 the physician shall give the ill person appropriate information on his or her illness and shall also completely inform his or her legal representative or guardian.

The third material condition specified by the law is the consent to the examination, and treatment measures entailed in psychiatric care. In accordance with Article 38 paragraph 2 of the Law No. 277/1994 Coll.L. consent shall be given by the patient or his or her representative or guardian. In accordance with Article 38 paragraph 3 of the Law 277/1994 Coll.L. (3, 8, 19)

> *“To carry out particularly important psychiatric or other surgical interventions which might seriously alter the personality of a patient younger than 18 years, or of a patient with limited legal capacity or a patient under restraint, in addition to the consent of his or her legal representative or guardian given upon the opinion of a panel meeting, the consent of the court is also needed.”*

**11.2.2.3 Penal Law and Code of Criminal Procedure**

From the point of view of material law, the problems of compulsory treatments in the Slovak system of Law, also called “protective treatments”, are regulated by the Law No. 140/1961 from November 29, 1961 in the wording of its amendments numbered 120/1962, 120/1962, 53/1993, 184/1964, 56/1965, 56/1965, 81/1966, 148/1969, 45/1973,43/1980, 10/1989, 159/1989, 47/1990, 84/1990, 175/1990, 457/1990, 545/1990, 490/1991, 557/1991, 1/1992, 177/1993, 248/1994, 102/1995, 233/1995, 100/1996, 13/1998, 129/1998, 10/1999, 183/1999, 399/2000, 253/2001, 485/2001, 38/2002, 237/2002, 421/2002, 448/2002, 448/2002, 553/2002 of the Collection of Laws – Criminal Law (hereinafter C.L.)

§ 72

*"Protective treatment:*
*(1) The court will impose protective treatment in the case under § 25 and § 32, paragraph 2 or if the person committing an act, normally classified as a criminal act, is without penal responsibility because of his or her insanity and his or her free movement proves to be dangerous.*
*(2) The court will be allowed to do so when:*
*a) The offender has committed the criminal act in the state of diminished responsibility and his or her free movement proves to be dangerous; or*
*b) The offender is addicted to the use of a habit-forming-substance and has committed the criminal act under the influence of this substance or in connection with its abuse. But, the protective treatment shall not be imposed if it is, due to the offender's personality, obvious that the treatment aims cannot be achieved; or*
*c) The offender has committed a violent criminal act toward a close person or an entrusted person and if it may be, on a founded basis, supposed, due to the offender's personality, that he or she will continue with such violent acts.*
*(3) Protective treatment may be imposed by the court in addition to punishment or in the case of remission of punishment.*
*(4) If a sentence of imprisonment has been pronounced, the protective treatment, generally, will start after the convicted person has entered the prison. Generally, in other cases the treatment shall be carried out in a health care establishment. If due to the nature of the illness and the existing treatment possibilities, a conclusion can be made that the aims can be achieved also with outpatient treatment, the court may also order this type of treatment, or, as the case may be, subsequently exchange the residential treatment for outpatient treatment or vice versa. If the duration of the stay in a prison is not long enough to achieve the aims of the treatment, the court may decide on the continuation of the treatment in a residential or other curative establishment.*
*(5) Protective treatment will last until the aims are achieved. The duration of the protective treatment imposed pursuant to paragraph 2 letter b) may be finished, however, if it is established during the course of the treatment that it is not possible to achieve the aims of the treatment.*
*(6) The court shall waive the execution of the protective treatment when the conditions because of which the protective treatment was imposed disappear before the treatment starts."*

*Notes:* Protective treatment may be imposed only by a court. The court may impose it in addition to other punishment, or independently, as the sole action to reach the aims of Penal Law. But in practice, there shall be no explicitly imposed protective measures without any other punishment being imposed as well. There will be no time limit for the execution of a protective measure. It can be neither expunged nor remitted on the basis of presidential amnesty.
Protective treatment pursuant to paragraph 1 will be imposed obligatorily. A criminal act committed by an ill/insane offender will not be sufficient itself for the court to be allowed to impose protective treatment. To be allowed to do so, a condition must be satisfied, namely that the offender's free movement poses a

threat to society. The court will always order a protective treatment on the basis of a medical assessment, simultaneously submitted by two psychiatric experts. In practice, there will be 4 types of protective (= compulsory) treatment: 1. treatment for alcoholism; 2. treatment for addiction; 3. treatment for sexual disorders/offenders; and , 4. mental health treatment.

According to paragraph 2 the court will impose an optional compulsory treatment, mainly to those offenders who are addicted to and abuse habit-forming-substances and have committed a criminal act under the influence of this substance or in connection with its abuse. If compulsory treatment is imposed in addition to imprisonment, the sentenced person may start compulsory treatment in prison provided that facilities for such treatment are available. If the duration of the stay in the prison is not long enough to achieve the aims of the treatment, the court may make a decision to prolong the sentence in a curative or outpatient establishment. The Secretary of Justice of the Slovak Republic (Minister spravodlivosti Slovenskej republiky) issued a generally binding regulation which allows compulsory treatment to be carried out during imprisonment, depending on the duration of a prisoner's sentence, following a minimum of: two months for mental health treatment; eight months for addiction treatment; eight months for the treatment of alcoholism; and two months for the treatment of sex offenders.

When imposing a compulsory treatment the court will not fix the duration of the treatment in its decision because treatment must take as long as necessary to achieve its aims. Waiving the execution of the compulsory treatment will be considered only before the execution of the treatment has started. The court shall decide on waiving the execution of the compulsory treatment on the basis of a medical report or expert counsel.

§ 25

> *"The court may waive a punishment when the offender has committed a criminal act in the state of diminished responsibility and the court believes that compulsory treatment (paragraph 72) being imposed by the court shall secure an improvement for the offender and protection of the society more efficiently than a punishment. This provision shall not be used if the offender has induced their state of diminished responsibility by him or herself, even due to carelessness, under the influence of a habit-forming-substance."*

*Notes:* To waive punishment under the above mentioned conditions is optional. The fact that the criminal act was committed in the state of diminished responsibility will not exclude the penal responsibility but will only diminish it and justify a particular approach to the offender.

§ 32

*"(2) If the court holds that in consideration of the state of health of such an offender it would be possible, when imposing a compulsory treatment (paragraph 72) simultaneously, also to achieve the aims of punishment with a shorter punishment, it will reduce the imprisonment time under the minimum sentence without being bound to the limitation under paragraph 40 paragraph 4, and it will impose compulsory treatment."*

*Notes:* If an offender is in a state of diminished responsibility not caused by him or herself at the time of committing a criminal act, this will justify the particular method by which the type and scope of the punishment is decided upon. Diminished responsibility shall not be considered an attenuating circumstance. Generally, the state of diminished responsibility will have a double consequence: on the one hand it will diminish the degree of the offender's culpability and, generally, on the other hand it will increase the dangerousness of the offender's person (R 41/1976). When using the method under this provision the courts will always have available two expert testimonies from psychiatrists on the offender's mental health. From these expert testimonies types and forms of the most suitable compulsory treatment to be imposed simultaneously with the punishment must be deduced.

The problems of compulsory treatments from the point of view of procedural law are regulated by Law No. 141/1961 from November 29, 1961 in the wording of its amendments numbered 57/1965, 173/1968, 58/1969, 149/1969, 156/1969, 48/1973, 29/1978, 43/1980, 159/1989, 178/1990, 303/1990, 558/1991, 6/1993, 156/1993, 178/1993, 247/1994, 222/1998, 256/1998, 272/1999, 173/2000, 366/2000, 253/2001, 182/2002, 215/2002, 422/2002, 457/2003 of the Collection of Laws on penal procedure – Criminal Law (hereinafter C.C.P.)

§ 36

*"(4) The person charged must have a barrister (attorney) also in the extradition proceeding in which a decision will be made on imposing compulsory treatment except in the case of compulsory treatment for alcoholism."*

*Notes:* In this case there is a so-called compulsory defence, i.e. defence *ex officio*, the costs of which will be paid by the state.

R 7/36: If in consideration of the charged person's mental disabilities the court questions his or her capacity to defend him or herself properly, a barrister must be appointed to the charged person.

§ 142
"Authorized persons"

*"(2) A complaint on behalf of the charged person against the decree on punishment and compulsory treatment may be filed also by persons authorized to file an appeal on his or her behalf."*

*Notes:* The above persons are listed under § 246 C.C.P., as stated hereinafter.

§ 143

*"(1) A complaint about a decree shall be filed with the responsible authority within three days from the communication of that decree's passing. Shall the decree also be forwarded to the charged person as well as to his or her legal representative or barrister, the three day time period will start from the time of the latest communication.*
*(2) The period of time provided to persons authorized pursuant to provision § 142, paragraph 2 to file a complaint on behalf of charged persons finishes on the same day as the time period allocated for complaints to be filed by the charged person. However, the time period for the public prosecutor is otherwise determined."*

*Notes:* Complaints may be filed in writing, by dictation, or may be wired. The name given to the complaint will not matter. Its content will always be considered. The lawmaker says that the time period of three days is short in order to avoid useless delays of penal procedure.

§ 146
Procedure before an authority against which the complaint is directed

*"(1) The authority, on receiving a complaint about its decision, may meet the complainant provided that a modification of the original decree will not interfere with the rights of any other party involved in the penal proceeding. If it is a decree issued by an investigator or by a police authority after the previous consent of a public prosecutor or by his advice, the investigator or the police authority may deal with the complaint only after the consent of the public prosecutor has been obtained.*
*(2) If the time period to file a complaint has already elapsed for all authorized persons and the complaint was not allowed according to paragraph 1, the case shall be submitted for decision by:*
*an investigator or a police authority to the public prosecutor who will supervise the preparatory proceeding, and, if it is a complaint against a decree to which this public prosecutor had given his or her consent or advice, through him or her to the superior public prosecutor,*
*the public prosecutor to the superior public prosecutor or court,*
*the presiding judge of a County Court (okresný súd) to the superior Regional Court (nadriadený krajský súd), by the presiding judge of a Regional Court (krajský súd) to the Supreme Court (najvyšší súd). At the same time he shall, if necessary, serve a copy of the complaint to the public prosecutor and the person who could be directly affected by the decision reached regarding the complaint."*

*Notes:* In this provision, the need for the speed of the penal proceeding will be asserted to an important degree so that the authority against which the complaint is directed will be authorized to deal with the complaint by itself if the above mentioned preconditions are fulfilled. This procedure is called "*autoremedura*" (app. writ of error *coram nobis*, reconsideration).

§ 178

> *"(1) During the process of charge, the public prosecutor shall make a proposition for the court to impose compulsory treatment or compulsory education or seizure of property, provided the public prosecutor thinks this remains within the due course of law."*

*Notes:* The proposition of the public prosecutor is an option. The public prosecutor may also make this proposition during the hearing on the substance of the case. The court may impose a compulsory measure even without any proposition. Besides the hearing on the substance of the case, in a public hearing, the court may impose a compulsory measure either with or without the proposition of the public prosecutor.

§ 239

> *"(1) If it is not a case where the court had reserved the right to the decision on compulsory treatment or seizure* of property *according to § 230, paragraph 2, it may impose on them a public hearing only if the public prosecutor makes the proposition to do so.*
> *(2) Against the decision on compulsory treatment and seizure of* property *a complaint may be filed with a suspending effect."*

*Notes:* In the law, efforts to secure fair decisions on compulsory treatment are expressed in a number of ways. Either by making the decision a public hearing or open court, but only if the court has reserved the right to hear the content of the case, or if the imposition of compulsory treatment was proposed by a public prosecutor. An alternative measure to ensure fair decisions on compulsory treatment are reached is that remedies are always admissible (i.e. In the form of an appeal, if the decision made in the hearing is a sentence, as stated hereinafter, or in the form of a complaint, if the decision is a decree issued in a public session). Decisions on compulsory treatment are singularly within the jurisdiction of the court.

§ 351
Compulsory treatment execution order

> *"(1) The presiding judge shall order the execution of compulsory treatment for the curative institution in which the compulsory treatment should be carried out. If the compulsory treatment is imposed in addition to an unsuspended imprisonment sentence and in the prison there are conditions for such compulsory treatment to be carried out, the presiding*

*judge may order that compulsory treatment be carried out during the execution of the imprisonment sentence.*
*(2) If the person to whom the compulsory treatment is imposed remains dangerous for his or her community during his or her stay at liberty, the presiding judge shall arrange for his or her immediate delivery to a curative institution; otherwise, the presiding judge may grant him or her an adequate time to organize his or her affairs.*
*(3) If the person is a member of armed forces or armed corps discharged from his or her active service, the presiding judge shall ask the responsible commander or head to arrange for his or her deportation to a curative institution.*
*(4) The presiding judge shall ask the curative institution to inform the court which imposed the compulsory treatment of the beginning of the execution of the compulsory treatment. At the same time, the judge shall ask the institution to immediately inform the County Court (okresný ssúd) of the district in which the compulsory treatment is taking place if the reasons for continuation of compulsory treatment cease to exist."*

*Notes:* The court shall include in the sentence or decree *ex lege* the assertion whether the compulsory treatment should be carried out as in- or outpatient treatment. But in the sentence or in a decree no decision shall be made as to whether compulsory treatment is to be carried out in prison during the execution of the imprisonment sentence. Execution of compulsory institutional treatment shall be ordered by the presiding judge to the institution appropriate for the residence or stay of the person on whom compulsory treatment shall be imposed. Here, so-called regionalization shall be applied. Although the law always refers to a "presiding judge," in practice, in accordance with Administration Code (Spravovací poriadok) for County and Regional Courts (krajské a okresné súdy), this activity (calls for compulsory treatment to be started) will be carried out by senior judicial officials and may be also carried out by probationers.

§ 351a
Modification of compulsory treatment execution mode

*"(1) The decision to modify the mode of compulsory treatment shall be made on a public hearing by the court with jurisdiction for the curative institution in which the compulsory treatment is taking place. Against this decision a complaint with suspending effect may be launched."*

*Notes:* In this case, the court with jurisdiction for the institution shall make the decision, not the court that ordered compulsory treatment. When changing the mode of treatment courts will always decide on the basis of expert mental-health advice, and according to results obtained during the treatment it will be possible, as the case may be, to again change the method of carrying out compulsory treatment.

§ 352
Withdrawal of the execution of compulsory treatment

> *"The decision to cancel compulsory treatment execution before it starts shall be made by the court which imposed the compulsory treatment, at a public hearing at the public prosecutor's request or at the request of the charged person or without such requests. Against this decision a complaint may be launched with a suspending effect."*

*Notes:* In practice, the court will cancel the execution of compulsory treatment only if the circumstances for which the treatment was ordered cease to exist before treatment starts. This occurs predominately in cases when the state of health of the person on whom the compulsory treatment was imposed improves so much that he or she ceases to be a danger to society. The court's new decision shall always be made only on the basis of expert mental-health counsel. If compulsory treatment has already started, cancellation will be out of question. Decisions pertaining to the cancellation of compulsory treatment shall be made by the court which made the initial decision to impose compulsory treatment. The court may also make this decision without the application of a public prosecutor or charged person, for example at the request of other persons or on the basis of the knowledge obtained by the court itself.

§ 353
Release from compulsory treatment and its termination

> *"Decision on the release from compulsory treatment or on the termination of such treatment shall be made, at the request of the public prosecutor, by the charged person or curative institution, or even without any request, by a public hearing, by the County Court (okresný súd) with jurisdiction for the treatment. Against this decision a complaint may be lodged with a suspending effect."*

R 6/72: *"Compulsory treatment shall not be ordered for a certain period of time but it shall last as long as necessary to achieve its aims."*

R 36/79: *"Communications on behalf of a mental hospital stating the termination of the compulsory treatment will not be considered sufficient proof of the fact that the treatment has served its purpose and that the court may make a decision according to § 72, paragraph 5, second sentence of Penal Law on release of the charged person from this treatment."*

*Notes:* Decisions on release will be made by the courts, in practice, on the basis of the interviews with an expert psychiatrist and of the charged person. The courts shall always take into consideration the opinions of the expert psychiatrist as far as the mode and the duration of compulsory treatment are concerned. The public prosecutor him or herself may also request the release of the charged person from compulsory treatment if he or she believes that the objective of compulsory treatment has been reached and if this request has not been made by the administration of the institution itself.

Paragraph 358
Public prosecutor's supervision

*"The public prosecutor in whose judicial district compulsory treatment or compulsory education will take place shall supervise the execution of this treatment and education. The administration of the institution in which compulsory treatment and compulsory education will take place shall have to execute the orders of the public prosecutor relative to observing the regulations in force for the execution of compulsory treatment or compulsory education."*

*Notes:* The County Public Prosecutor (okresný prokurátor) in whose judicial district the mental institution is situated shall be competent for execution of supervision. The public prosecutor shall pay attention to the fact that compulsory education is to be executed in accordance with regulations in force. This activity shall be carried out by specialized public prosecutors who know the cases in question well. When carrying out the supervision the public prosecutor will be authorized to visit, at any time, places where compulsory treatment takes place, to talk to the charged persons in the absence of other persons, and to ask the staff of related institutions for explanations, translation of files and documents. The public prosecutor shall exercise this responsibility through regular inspections, at least once every three months on the basis of internal regulations issued in the form of orders by the general prosecutor.

The public prosecutor shall execute the supervision pursuant to Law No. 153/2001 on prosecution:

The public prosecutor's supervision of observance of the law in institutions where persons whose liberty has been taken away or where persons whose personal liberty has been restricted are being held.

§ 18

*"(1) The public prosecutor shall supervise that in all places where retention, imprisonment, disciplinary punishments of soldiers, compulsory treatment, compulsory education, institutional treatment or education takes place on the basis of a court's decision, as well as in cells of detention, that persons are being held only in accordance with the decision on loss or restriction of personal liberty made by a court or by another authorized state authority and that laws and other generally binding legal norms are observed in these places.*

*(2) The public prosecutor is obliged to:*

*a) carry out all inspections of legal observance in places under paragraph 1,*

*b) release immediately, by a written order, any person held in a place specified under paragraph 1 illegally without any decision or in contradiction with the decision of a court or another authorized state authority,*
*c) cancel or stop the execution of a decision, decree or measure of authorities performing administration of towns listed under paragraph 1 or of their superior authority, if they are in contradiction with the law or other generally binding legal norms,*
*d) supervise that all complaints and communications, reports and notes concerning persons held in places specified under paragraph 1 are sent immediately to those authorities or officials to which they have been addressed.*
*(3) The order of the public prosecutor issued under paragraph 2 letter b) or c) must comprise:*
*a) The name and grade of service of the public prosecutor who issues the order,*
*b) date and place of order's issuance,*
*c) explicit designation "prosecutor's order" ("príkaz prokurátora")*
*d) name of administration performing authority for the place under paragraph 1 to which the order is addressed,*
*e) first and last name, date of birth, personal birth number and place of birth of the person held in the place under paragraph 1 to which the order refers,*
*f) the verdict of the order with legal provision on the basis of which the order has been issued,*
*g) the decision against which the order is addressed or which has been violated,*
*h) justification of the order,*
*i) first and last name, signature of the public prosecutor and official seal with the emblem of the state.*
*(4) The public prosecutor shall serve the order he has issued to the administration performing authority for the institution specified under paragraph 1 and to the person concerned. In the case of his or her release the public prosecutor shall deliver the order also to the court or other state authority if it made a decision regarding the case. If there is an imminent danger of default, the public prosecutor shall issue the order orally and serve its written form to the administration performing authority for the place specified under paragraph 1 within 24 hours.*
*(5) While performing the supervision the public prosecutor shall be authorized to:*
*a) Visit places specified under paragraph 1 at any time having direct access to all premises and areas of these places,*
*b) have access to all documents related to the loss of or restriction of personal liberty,*
*c) talk to persons held in places specified under paragraph 1 without the presence of other persons,*
*d) verify if decisions and measures of the administration performing authority for places specified under paragraph 1 correspond to acts and other generally binding legal norms,*
*e) require from the administration performing authority for the staff of the places specified under paragraph 1 to provide all necessary explanations and to submit files and decisions concerning the loss of or restriction of personal liberty of the person held in the place for which the administration is responsible.*
*(6) The staff of the administration performing authority for places specified under paragraph 1 shall be obliged to carry out the orders of public prosecutor, to facilitate the fulfilment of his or her duties and the application of his or her competencies.*
*(7) None of the provisions of special laws will be touched upon by the provisions of paragraph 1 to 6."*

*Structure of courts:* Compulsory treatments will always be ordered by County Courts (okresné súdy). Courts of appeal (odvolacie súdy) will be Regional Courts (krajské súdy) (§ 16 C.C.P.). Regional Courts (krajské súdy) will be courts of first instance also in making decisions regarding compulsory treatment if the case concerns a criminal act for which the law will stipulate details concerning punishment through imprisonment, with a minimum duration of eight years if a supreme punishment may be imposed for the criminal act. In this event, Supreme Court (najvyšší súd) shall be the court of appeal (§ 17 C.C.P.). In the event of compulsory treatment being ordered in the main hearing (hearing on the substance of the case), an appeal with suspending effect shall be a remedy against the decision of the court of first instance (§ 245 C.C.P.). In support of the charged person the sentence may also be contested with an appeal, in addition to the accused person, by his or her next of kin relatives, his or her brother and sisters, adoptive parent, adoptive child, husband, wife, unmarried husband or wife. If the charged person is without legal capacity or if his or her legal capacity is limited, an appeal may be filed by his or her legal representative, or his or her barrister – even against his or her will on his or her behalf (§ 247 C.C.P.). An appeal must be filed with the court responsible for the decision being appealed within eight days from the delivery of a copy of the sentence.
When the above conditions have been met, the courts shall order execution of compulsory treatment in accordance with the Public Notice of the Ministry of Justice of the Slovak Republic number 66/1992 in the wording of its amendments numbered 18/1993 and 163/1995 on Administration Code for County and Regional Courts (Spravovací poriadok pre okresné a krajské súdy).

§ 41
Execution of institutional compulsory treatment

*"(1) The order to execute institutional compulsory treatment shall be sent by the presiding judge (one judge) to the health care institution appropriate for residency or lodging the person for the purpose of undergoing compulsory treatment. It shall be sent in duplicate with one copy of expert testimony or expert medical opinion with one copy of the decision stating the imposition of compulsory treatment. Upon agreement with the administration of the health care institution, the presiding judge (one judge) shall fix the starting date for the execution of the compulsory treatment. At the same time, the judge shall draw the attention of the administration of the responsible health care institution to the fact that change of the institutional form of compulsory treatment to outpatient form of compulsory treatment or the release from compulsory treatment under conditions pursuant to § 72, paragraph 5 of Penal Law may be done only on the basis of a valid decision of a County (district) Court with jurisdiction over the compulsory treatment which is taking place, and shall demand for a report to be sent immediately to this court, if grounds for one of the above measures start to exist.*
*The judge shall also demand that the health care institution inform the court which ordered the execution of a compulsory treatment if the person upon whom compulsory treat-*

*ment was imposed presented him or herself for the execution of compulsory treatment on the day fixed.*
*(2) The presiding judge (one judge) shall invite the person upon whom compulsory treatment was imposed to present him or herself for the execution of the treatment in the relevant health institution on the fixed day. If this person has no legal capacity, the judge shall do so through his or her legal representative. If the person to undergo compulsory treatment is not dangerous to his or her community, the necessary time period for arranging his or her affairs may be granted to him or her.*
*(3) If the invited person does not present him or herself for the execution of compulsory treatment within the fixed time limit or if he or she is dangerous to his or her community, the presiding judge (one judge) shall ask the county headquarters of the Police Corps of the Slovak Republic (Policajný zbor Slovenskej republiky) responsible for the area of residency of the person to bring the person to the health care institution."*

## § 42
## Execution of outpatient compulsory treatment

*"(1) The order to execute outpatient compulsory treatment shall be sent by the presiding judge (one judge) to the health care institution responsible for the area of residency of the person to undergo the compulsory treatment. It shall be sent in duplicate with one copy of expert testimony or expert medical opinion and one copy of the decision stating the imposition of compulsory treatment. Upon agreement with the health care institution's administration the presiding judge (one judge) shall fix the starting date for the execution of compulsory treatment.*
*(2) The presiding judge (one judge) shall ask the administration of the health care institution to request the County Court from the district in which the institution is situated to change the form of treatment to institutional care, if the person to be cured refuses to undergo the compulsory treatment or if the person's further stay in liberty has been shown to be dangerous or if it has been found out additionally that, due to the nature of the illness and related curative possibilities, the aims of compulsory treatment can not be achieved through outpatient care. The court shall also call the attention of the health care institution to the fact that the release from compulsory treatment under conditions pursuant to paragraph 72, paragraph 5 of Penal Law may be done only on the basis of a valid decision of a County Court with jurisdiction over the compulsory treatment which is taking place. At the same time the court shall demand from the health care institution that they inform the court which ordered the execution of compulsory treatment if the person upon whom compulsory treatment has been imposed presented him or herself for the execution of the compulsory treatment by the fixed time limit.*
*(3) The presiding judge (one judge) shall invite the person to which outpatient compulsory treatment was imposed to present him or herself for the execution of this treatment in the relevant health care institution no later than the fixed time limit. At the same time, the judge shall draw this person's attention to consequences for him or her in case that he or she does not do so. If this person has no legal capacity, the judge shall do so through his or her legal representative."*

## § 43
## Execution of compulsory treatment whilst serving a term of imprisonment

*"(1) If during the course of serving a term of imprisonment, no decision on the remission of the execution of compulsory treatment which is supposed to be executed has been made, or the sentenced person has not been released from this compulsory treatment, the penal institution shall present immediately, three months before the proposed end of jail sentence, and in the case of a termination of the jail situated compulsory treatment before scheduled, a report on the results compulsory treatment has achieved. If the treatment's objectives were not reached due to the duration of jail situated compulsory treatment, the court shall make a decision on the continuation of the treatment in a health care institution even before the termination of jail situated compulsory treatment.*
*(2) If, after termination of the service of a term of imprisonment, the sentenced person is supposed to be delivered to a health care institution for the continuation of compulsory treatment, the court which decided on the continuation of compulsory treatment shall fix together with the respective health care institution the starting date of the compulsory treatment to be the same as the day of termination of jail confinement. If the delivery of the sentenced person to the institution responsible for further execution of compulsory treatment does not take place, the penal institution shall release him or her, and send the compulsory treatment order back to the court. Otherwise, the penal institution shall hand over to the health care institution the order with all appropriate appendices, including expert testimony and the report on previous progress and results of the treatment."*

*Notes:* If the sentenced person avoids the ordered compulsory treatment by not presenting him or herself or otherwise by ignoring it, he or she will be committing a criminal act of obstructing execution of an authoritative decision pursuant to

§ 171, paragraph 1 letter d) C.C.P.

*"A person who obstructs or makes substantially difficult the execution of a decision of the court or other state authorities by committing activities in order to obstruct the objective of compulsory treatment or compulsory education imposed on him or her by the court, or otherwise, by escaping from the institution makes the execution of the treatment substantially difficult, shall be punished either by the loss of liberty for up to 6 months or by a financial penalty."*

*Commentary to Penal Law and Code of Criminal Procedure*
Provisions of Article 72 of the valid legal regulations have been applied in judicial practice by decisions published in the Collection of Judicial Decisions and Opinions. According to these decisions (1, 2, 12, 13, 16)

*"the court, when making a decision on imposing compulsory treatment in accordance with Article 72, paragraph 1 of Penal Law, shall have to prove the compliance with all these legal conditions, if the perpetrator of an act being otherwise criminal is not criminally responsible because of insanity and his or her liberty is dangerous."*

*"The mere perpetration of an act being otherwise criminal in the state of insanity is not sufficient for compulsory treatment in accordance with Article 72, paragraph 1 of the Penal Law to be imposed. The stay of such a person at liberty shall also have to be, for the future, dangerous to interests protected by Penal Law. This condition can be accepted as in*

*compliance with the law if it is very likely that the insane person who has perpetrated an act, being otherwise criminal, again commits a grave assault on interests protected by the Penal Law and does so under influence of a mental disorder."*

*"As to whether the stay of a perpetrator at liberty, in accordance with Article 72, paragraph 1 of Penal Law (Trestný zákon), is or is not dangerous, mainly as regards a threat to the life, health and or property of persons, should be judged upon concrete assessment of his or her behaviour and nature, based on the opinion of psychiatric experts, as to what extent it is his or her illness which may make his or her stay at liberty dangerous for the community in the future. The request by experts to impose compulsory psychiatric treatment on the perpetrator is alone not a sufficient basis for the court to make a decision on this issue. This claim needs to be considered in conjunction with a report on knowledge acquired during the examination of his or her mental state. This report concerns specifically the behaviour which became the object of the criminal prosecution and any other behaviour which experts used to reach their conclusion."*

*"The condition for compulsory hospital treatment to be imposed in accordance with Article 72, paragraph 1 of Penal Law (Trestný zákon) stating that the perpetrator's stay at liberty is dangerous for the community must be fulfilled during the time the court is making the decision on compulsory treatment. It is not sufficient to comply with the above condition at the time when the criminal prosecution has been stopped for reasons stated in Article 712, paragraph1 Lett.a) of Code of Penal Procedure (Trestný poriadok)."*

*"The dangerousness of the stay at liberty of a person who has perpetrated an act being otherwise criminal but who is not criminally responsible because of his or her insanity does not per force mean that the imposed compulsory treatment is to be carried out only in a closed hospital ... if it is to be expected that, in view of the nature of the illness and the curative possibilities, the aims of treatment will also be achieved through using the outpatient method of treatment, the court may order this method of treatment."*

### 11.2.2.4 Civil Code

The problems of guardianship from the point of view of material law are regulated by Act No. 40/1964 in the wording of its amendments numbered 58/1969, 131/1992, 94/1988, 87/1990, 105/1990, 116/1990, 87/1991, 501/1992, 278/1993, 249/1994, 211/1997, 252/1999, 218/2000, 261/2001, 281/2001, 23/2002, 34/2002, 95/2002, 215/2002, 184/2002, 526/2002 of the Collection of Law – Civil Code (hereinafter C.C.)

§ 27

*"(2) As a legal representative of a person who has been deprived of his or her legal capacity by a decision of the court or whose legal capacity has been limited by a decision of the court, a guardian shall be appointed by the court.*
*(3) If it is not possible for a relative of the person nor any other person who meets conditions for appointment as a guardian to be appointed, the court shall appoint as a guardian an authority of the local government or from one of its offices - provided it is authorized to appear on their behalf (Article 18, paragraph 1)."*

*Notes:* With the validity of the new Code of Civil Procedure No. 99/1963, i.e. since April 1, 1964, in Slovak law, the terms "tutorship" and "tutor" have not been used. The terms "guardianship" and "guardian" are used instead. The term "tutorship" only appears in Slovak law after April 1, 1964, and only in international treaties signed by the Czechoslovak Socialist Republic or Czech and Slovak Federal Republic with other countries.
In practice, the courts will prefer to appoint, as a guardian, a relative or another citizen willing to assume the function of guardian and exercise this role responsibly and reliably.
The courts will appoint local administrative authorities, i.e. a so-called public guardian, only to persons for whom neither a relative nor another suitable person can be found to be appointed guardian. The courts will appoint a so-called public guardian only if such an authority has a legal character.

*R: 14/1967:* It will be necessary to gain the consent of the person recommended as a potential guardian before they can assume the role of guardian. In the procedure of being appointed as guardian, they will become participant in the proceedings.

*From IV: (page 424)* Despite the possibility of appointing an authority from the local administration or, as the case may be, its establishment, a citizen's guardian will not be bound to the consent of these organizations.

*From IV: (page 352)* If a citizen has been legally disqualified and a guardian appointed to him or her, then the pension of such citizen shall be delivered to his or her guardian. The settlement with the court shall be a responsibility of the guardian.

*From III: (page 276)* The guardian of a person legally disqualified by a decision of the court (or partially disqualified) may, with consent of the Guardian Court (opatrovnícky súd), file for divorce on behalf of the guarded person.

From the point of view of legal procedures the guardianship is regulated by the Code of Civil Procedure Act No. 99/1963 in the wording of its amendment under Article III (hereinafter "C.C.P.").

§ 29

*"(1) If a person without legal capacity (a person who is not allowed to act individually) is not represented, the presiding judge shall appoint him a guardian provided there is a danger of default.*
*(2) If the presiding judge does not take any other measures, he or she may appoint a guardian in the case where the place of abode of the involved party is not known, to whom*

*no documents could be delivered or if the delivery of documents abroad involves unavoidable difficulties, or if the person afflicted by a mental disorder is not able to express him or herself in a comprehensible manner."*

*Notes:* A guardian appointed because of one of the reasons under § 29 shall be active as long as the initial grounds for their appointment remain. When these grounds cease to exist, the guardian's role will also cease to be valid.
In this case, the function of the guardian is the so-called guardian *ad litem* (kolízny opatrovník) who will be a guardian only for one concrete proceeding. In most cases, upon the validation of a decision in the case itself, this guardianship will cease to exist. The court shall appoint a guardian by a decree to be delivered to the guardian and the involved party against which an appeal may be filed with Appeal Regional Court (Odvolací krajský súd) within a time limit of 15 days.

§ 56

*"The time limit shall not be applicable to a person who has lost the capacity to be an involved party in a proceeding or the capacity to appear before a court.*
*At the moment another involved party (legal representative or guardian of an involved party) presents him or herself to the proceeding, a new time period shall start for them beginning from the time they presented themselves to face the proceeding."*

*Notes:* By the above provision individuals shall be protected who, in the course of the proceeding, have lost their legal capacity. Therefore, the time limits shall be observed only when a guardian is appointed on their behalf.

§ 192
(1) The presiding judge shall be obliged to provide for a guardian to be appointed to persons who are supposed to have one *ex lege*.
(2) In the decree by which a guardian is appointed the court shall also specify the extent of guardian's rights and duties.

*Notes:* Each guardianship proceeding shall be preceded by a proceeding divesting the concerned person of legal capacity. This is explained in the following. If a person has been divested of his or her legal capacity or this capacity has been limited, it is necessary for a court to appoint a guardian on their behalf. Therefore, when the sentence divesting legal capacity has entered into force, the proceeding on appointment of a guardian shall start *ex officio*. The sentence divesting legal capacity shall be pronounced in an auxiliary register NC. After the person is divested of his or her legal capacity and they are without a guardian the court shall act *ex officio* in the registry P where an individual file shall be established. In practice, the time period between the validation of the sentence divesting the person concerned of legal capacity and the beginning of guardianship proceedings will be about three months. Due to these factors, persons who have lodged a proposal for divesting an individual of legal capacity shall also lodge, after the validation of the sentence, the proposal for the guardianship proceeding.

A guardian shall be appointed by the court by a decree in which both the ambit of rights and duties shall be specified. The proceeding will take place without any hearing and the guardian shall take a vow. It is necessary to repeat that, as this proceeding will take place only in auxiliary registers, this will usually be executed by junior judges.

*From IV: (page 760)* In the proceeding concerning legal capacity the court shall not be allowed to decide on the appointment of a guardian pursuant to paragraph 192 C.C.P.. The court will be allowed to do so only in a guardianship proceeding after the validation of a decision on divesting or limiting legal capacity.

§ 193

Provisions § 176 to 180 are valid accordingly.

*Notes:* In a guardianship proceeding the court shall proceed correspondingly with the procedure on court's care on behalf of the minor. This means that the court shall decide on important acts on behalf of the guarded person in the following way: the courts will approve these acts if these acts are in favour of the guarded person, for example if the guardian person wants to buy a flat in his or her name, or will not approve these acts, for example if the guardian wants to sell the guarded person's house. The court shall direct the guardians as to how to fulfil their care duties for the guarded person, handle recommendations and reminders by citizens and legal persons concerning guardianship and take appropriate measures. The guardian appointed by the court shall take a vow before the presiding judge, obliging him or herself to fulfil his or her duties properly respecting the instructions given to him or her by the court. After the vow the guardian will receive from the presiding judge the document comprising the appointment to educate and represent the guarded person and the definition of the range of his or her rights and responsibilities resulting from this appointment. The court shall supervise the administration of property of the guarded person and shall take all necessary and appropriate measures to ascertain and secure his or her property. After the termination of his or her function the guardian shall submit to the court the balance account of the administration of property. The guardian may be required by the court to submit regular reports on his or her activity.

The same rules (as stated under article III of the present declaration) will apply to remedies and structures of the courts.

Any guardianship proceeding shall be preceded, as already stated, by a proceeding divesting the person concerned of legal capacity as regulated under § 186 to 191 C.C.P.
The court shall divest a citizen of his or her legal capacity if he or she is not capable of performing legal acts because of a mental disorder which is not temporary. It will not be possible to pronounce a person either divested of or limited in his or her legal capacity because of a temporary mental disorder. If a citizen with a mental illness, or due to the abuse of alcohol or drugs or other substances, is capable of performing some legal acts, the court shall limit his legal capacity.
Proposal to start a legal capacity divestment proceeding (divestment, limitation or return of legal capacity) may also be filed by a health care institution, which will then become an involved party in the proceeding.
The court may also start the proceeding without a proposal as soon as the court learns that there is a person in the court's district who it can be reasonably assumed has a mental disorder. The courts will learn about these cases not only from their own activity but also from information provided by other parties. In order to avoid unfounded and malicious proposals there are provisions in § 186 paragraph 2 allowing for the court to ask the plaintiff to submit a medical certificate regarding the mental health of the investigated person, provided that the plaintiff is not a state authority or themselves a health institution. If the medical certificate is not submitted within the time period fixed by the judge, the court shall stop the proceeding.
The court shall make a decision in form of a decree against which the appeal may be filed.
Proposal to start a legal capacity return proceeding may also by filed personally by the legally disqualified citizen. (§ 186 paragraph 3 C.C.P. – it is a provision on the exception from the rule that the legal representative shall act for a legally disqualified citizen).
The questioning of the examinee shall be done always in person. However, it may happen that this interview is not possible due to the nature of the illness (aggressive-agitated state, unconsciousness). These cases are covered by disposition § 187, paragraph 2 C.C.P. where permission is given to refrain from questioning. A medical-health expert shall always be interviewed by the court on the state of health of the examinee. If the case is complicated, the court may ask for opinions from several experts.
If a citizen, because of his or her mental disorder which is not merely temporary, is capable of performing only a limited number of legal acts, the court shall limit his or her legal capacity and positively or negatively fix the degree of limitation in the decision. The presiding judge shall not have to order a hearing due to feasibility reasons.

The sentence which either divests or limits a citizen of his or her legal capacity shall be delivered only to the parties involved in the proceeding. The court may decide to refrain from the delivery of the decision on legal capacity due to a mental disorder if the delivery could have negative implications or if the addressee is not capable of understanding the meaning of the decision (§ 182, paragraph 2 C.C.P.). Such action must rely on an expert opinion. The decision to refrain from a delivery will have the nature of a decision handed down by the court and will be delivered to the guardian.
The particular nature of the legal capacity proceeding is shown in a particular provision on legal costs in § 191 C.C.P. according to which these costs will be paid for by the state even if the proceeding has started following a proposal made by a health institution or another party. The state will predominately support the costs of expert evidence and the costs of delivery of the examinee to a health institution (§ 187, paragraph 3 C.C.P.).
The costs of attorney or barrister shall be borne by the one who has pleaded. This regulation is due to the fact that there is no need to have an attorney or a barrister in this proceeding because, here, questions to be addressed are specifically medical-health expert concerns. This is the reason why the state will not enter a plea on behalf of clients in guardianship proceedings.

Relative dispositions C.C.P:
- § 35, paragraph 2 letter a)

*"A public prosecutor may join a started proceeding in the matter of legal capacity."*

In practice, proposals for the deprivation of legal capacity will usually be filed by relatives of the person who has the mental disorder. There are also cases of speculative proposals, typically where a person with a mental disorder owns a significant amount of property or also if this person draws a pension. This is because of the fact that the pension shall be transferred by the Social Security Department to the guardian when a guardian is appointed.
Because of the above reasons the law will make it possible for the public prosecutor to join this proceeding *ex lege*.
In practice, public prosecutors will often become involved in these proceedings, and their role will be exercised by specialized and competent public prosecutors.

- § 81, paragraph 1

*"Even without a proposal the court may start a legal proceeding, such as: for matters concerning child welfare, a proceeding on admissibility of admission and holding a person in a health care institution, a proceeding on legal capacity, a guardianship proceeding, a proceeding on declaration of death, a proceeding on inheritance and other proceedings."*

The court will start acting *ex officio* only exceptionally, and only in the case where the person with a mental disorder does not have any relatives and the court learns about his or her activities only through recommendations from citizens or organizations.

- § 187, paragraph 1

  *"The person whose legal capacity is in question shall be appointed by the presiding judge a guardian for the proceeding."*

- § 190

  *"Any pronounced sentence shall be annulled if it is later proved that there were no conditions for the deprivation or limitation of legal capacity."*

- § 214, paragraph 2 letter d)

  *"No proceeding will need to be ordered if the question regards a decision on legal capacity, the pronouncement of admissibility of admission and holding in a health care institution or the declaration of death."*

*Note:* This provision will be also applied to courts of appeal (2, 5, 6, 15).

**11.2.3 Charter of Patient's Rights in the Slovak Republic**

The Charter of Patient's Rights in the Slovak Republic was adopted in a cabinet meeting on April 11, 2001.

Article 3 – Right to information

1. The patient has the right to be informed, in a way comprehensible to him or her, of his or her state of health, including the nature of their illness and of the necessary corollary medical care, even in a written form when he or she requires it. In the case of patients who are minors or patients deprived of or with a limited legal capacity, an adequate form for the information provided should be chosen with the patient's legal representative.

Article 4 – Patient's consent

*"3. If patient's consent can not be obtained and medical care is necessary and urgent, this activity may be carried out also without the consent of the patient."*

Article 5 – Consent regarding patients who are not capable of deciding alone.

1. On behalf of a minor patient or a patient with limited legal capacity or a patient who has been deprived of legal capacity, consent regarding legal acts shall be given by his or her legal representative or guardian or the person in whose foster care the minor is.

2. If the consent of a patient with a limited legal capacity or a patient who was deprived of legal capacity cannot be obtained, a panel's consent will be needed to carry out medical care such as operations. These may be also carried out without this consent if patient's life is endangered.

Article 9 – Filing complaints
1. A patient will have the right to file a complaint if he or she believes that his or her right to be given health care has been violated.
2. A patient may file a complaint with the director of the public health establishment (štátne zdravotné zariadenie) in which health care was given, to the state county physician, to the state regional physician (štátny krajský lekár), to the Ministry of Public Health of the Slovak Republic (Ministerstvo zdravotníctva Slovenskej republiky), to professional organizations or to other institutions.

### 11.2.4 Protection of the Right to Personal Freedom Against Restriction Because of Health Reasons in the Proceeding Before the Constitutional Court (Ústavný súd)

The right to personal freedom is a right with protection subdivided into two phases according to the current system of law. In the first phase the task of protecting this right belongs to general courts in accordance with dispositions of the Article 191a to 191g of the Code of Civil Procedure. The task of General Courts (všeobecné súdy) is to examine whether the state of health of the ill person justifies the restriction of his or her personal freedom due to health reasons. In the second phase the task of protecting the right to personal freedom passes from the General Courts (všeobecné súdy) to the Constitutional Court (ústavný súd). The duty of the Constitutional Court (ústavný súd) then, is not to examine the state of health but to supervise if personal freedom was or was not restricted in accordance with the law. Regardless of the state of health of the ill person the constitutional right recognised in Article 17, paragraph 6 will be violated by the restriction of personal freedom carried out otherwise than in accordance with the law.
A constitutional right may be restricted only under law (Article 13, paragraph 2 of Constitution). The right of inviolability of personal freedom following admission into residential health care may be restricted in accordance with the law (Article 17, paragraph 6 of Constitution). As long as personal freedom is restricted in the manner stipulated in the law, an individual's constitutional rights according to Article 17, paragraph 6 are not violated. In the case of the constitutional right according to Article17, paragraph 6 no violation of this right will occur as long as a general court acts in accordance with the Civil Procedure Code. If a general court discontinues acting in accordance with provisions of

Article 191a to Article 191g of Civil Procedure Code, or a General Court does not start proceedings in accordance with these provisions, a violation of constitutional rights has occurred. There is only one authority responsible for the protection of constitutionality which can be applied to for protection of constitutional rights in this case: the Constitutional Court (ústavný súd). The Constitutional Court's (ústavný súd) duty to protect the right to personal freedom will also be called into action when the health establishment violates Article 17, paragraph 6 of the Constitution and does not inform the court of the constriction of personal freedom or if the health institution completes its responsibilities at too late a date.

The constitutional conditions created to protect personal freedom against restriction in form of residential health care without consent does not consist only of legal norms specifically stated in the Constitution of the Slovak Republic (Ústava Slovenskej republiky). In accordance with Article 11 it also consists of rights recognized in the Agreement on Protection of Human Rights and Fundamental Freedoms. A person whose personal freedom has been restricted because of health reasons has primarily the right to ask the court to order, in accordance with Article 5, paragraph 4 of the above agreement, an individual's release from residential health care provided that the restriction of his or her personal freedom is unlawful. Article 2, paragraph 2 of Constitution "*State authorities are allowed to act only in accordance with the Constitution, within its limits and in a manner stipulated by the law,*" does not allow the Constitutional Court (Ústavný súd) to refuse a citizen the protection of rights which the law does not entrust under the protection of other state authorities regional authorities (orgány územnej samosprávy). Agreement on Protection of Human Rights and Fundamental Freedoms recognizes more subjective rights related to the constitutional right to protection of personal freedom and therefore these rights have priority over application of procedures allowed according to the Law No.38/1993 Coll.L. on the setup of the Constitutional Court of the Slovak Republic, on proceedings before this court and on the position of its judges in the wording of the Law No. 293/1995 Coll.L. The Constitutional Court may act even beyond this framework provided that it is indispensable for application of a larger extent of rights than recognized by the Slovak law that are comprised in the international agreement complying with conditions of Article 11 of the Constitution.

When protecting the right to personal freedom guaranteed by the Constitution, the Constitutional Court (ústavný súd) must consequently see that, under no circumstances, personal freedom is restricted in another manner other than the manner allowed by the law.

*Commentary on the protection of the right to personal freedom against restriction due to health reasons in the proceeding before Constitutional Court (Ústavný súd)*

Protection of personal freedom after admission into residential health care is not just an academic issue. Proceedings in accordance with Article 191a to 191g of the Civil Procedure Code have taken place before the general courts, and two proceedings pertaining to claims objecting to the violation of constitutional rights recognized by Article 17, paragraph 6 of the Constitution have taken place before the Constitutional Court of the Slovak Republic (Ústavný súd Slovenskej republiky).

In the case of I.ÚS 128/93 the claim was rejected when the Constitutional Court (Ústavný súd) found out that the claim had not been filed by a person designated as plaintiff. According to Article 130, paragraph 3 of the Constitution a claim may be filed only by a person objecting to the violation of his or her rights. The person bringing the claim before the court in the case of I.ÚS 128/93, whose identity remained undisclosed, objected to the violation of the rights of a third party who had been detained in a psychiatric hospital.

In another case I.ÚS 79/93 a patient retained in a psychiatric hospital objected to the violation of the constitutional right according to Article 17, paragraph 6 because he or she had been admitted to psychiatric hospital health care without his or her consent and even five months after his or her admission into psychiatric health care the County Court (Okresný súd) had not decided whether his or her additional detention in hospital health care was or was not permissible. Therefore, the citizen objecting with a claiming that there was a violation of their rights asked the Constitutional Court to order their release from the care institution.

The Constitutional Court (Ústavný súd) took into consideration Article 5, paragraph 4 of the Agreement on Protection of Human Rights and Fundamental Freedoms and issued an order to release the person who brought the claim before the court from the care institution (7, 25).

### 11.2.5 Public Guardian of Rights Act (Ombudsman)

The Public Guardian of Rights was introduced into the Slovak system of law with Article 151 of the Constitution of the Slovak Republic.

Article 151 a

> *"(1) The Public Guardian of Rights is an independent authority which will participate, within the range of and in the manner regulated by the law, in protection of fundamental laws and liberties of physical and juridical persons in their activities, decision-making or failure to act by authorities of public administration in their activities, decision-making or when they act in conflict with the system of law or with principles of a democratic state."*

The above article of the Constitution shall be executed by Act No. 564/2001 from December 4, 2001 in the wording of its amendment No. 411/2002 regarding the Public Guardian of Rights.

§ 1 Object of regulation

*"a) The Public Guardian of Rights' methods and extent of involvement are;*
*(1) as an independent authority they will participate in the protection of fundamental rights and liberties of physical and juridical persons in their activities, decision-making or failure to act by authorities of public administration,*
*(2) if their activities, decision-making or failure to act are in conflict with the system of law or with principles of a democratic state."*

§ 3

*"(1) The field of competence of the Public Guardian of Rights includes:*
*a) authorities of state administration,*
*b) authorities of local government,*
*c) legal and natural persons who, according to a special act, will decide on the rights and duties of physical and juridical persons in the area of public administration.*
*(2) The field of competence of the Public Guardian of Rights does not include the National Council of the Slovak Republic (Národná rada Slovenskej republiky), President of the Slovak Republic (prezident Slovenskej republiky), Government of the Slovak Republic (vláda Slovenskej republiky), Constitutional Court (Ústavný súd Slovenskej republiky), Supreme Audit Authority of the Slovak Republic (Najvyšší kontrolný úrad Slovenskej republiky), Intelligence Corps (spravodajské služby), decision-making field competences of investigators in the Police Corps (Policajný zbor), State Prosecution Office (prokuratúra) and the courts (súdy) with the exception of state administration of courts (štátna správa súdov) and on the grounds of suspicion of the disciplinary transgression of a judge.*
*(3) The field of competence of the Public Guardian of Rights does not refer to matters of an operational and mobilizational nature."*

*Notes:* Traditionally, there has been no institutional ombudsman in the Slovak legal system. As resulting from the above, the Public Guardian of Rights is not allowed to interfere with the procedure of involuntary admission and holding in a mental health care institution because these problems are dealt with by courts, not by state administration, local administration, or public administration authorities (2, 7, 25).

### 11.3 Jurisprudence

For the sake of clarity, judicates (judicial decisions) made by supreme courts, a selection of verdicts and opinions, as well as a collection of verdicts given by Supreme Courts have been incorporated into individual legal norms.

### 11.4 Protocols and Internal Norms Related to Coercive Measures and Compulsory Medical Treatment

In the Slovak system of law, internal norms relating to coercive measures in psychiatry, preventative security measures and status assurance measures, i.e. special measures or special treatment used for maintaining the desired security status of psychiatric institutions (in the cases of patients attacking the staff or damaging the furnishings), coercive measures, and forms being used to enforce involuntary treatment or preventive measures to overcome the will and the behaviour of the opposing patient by physical force have not been legally regulated.

These measures have not been regulated by jurisdiction either.

Their use will depend only on the physician's professional ethics, directives and instructions by his or her superior.

### 11.5 Reports

No reports on this topic issued by national or international organizations are known at this point.

### 11.6 Safeguard System

The safeguard system can be subdivided as follows:

1. Control carried out by the court within the framework of procedures of civil law in the decision-making process on involuntary admission into a health care establishment:

a) in proceedings on admissibility of admission into a health care establishment in accordance with dispositions of Articles 191a, 191b, 191c of Civil Procedure Code.

b) in proceedings on admissibility regarding the further holding of a patient in a health care establishment according to dispositions of Articles 191d, 191e, 191f of Civil Procedure Code.

2. Control carried out by the prosecutor within the framework of proceedings of penal law in the form of the prosecutor's supervision of observance of the law in places where persons whose liberty has been taken away or persons with restricted personal liberty are held in accordance with Article 358 of Penal Procedure Code and Article 18 of Prosecution Act No.153/2001 Coll.L.

*Notes to 1 and 2:* Both systems of control are described in detail in section 11.2.2 of this report.

3. Control carried out by the Ministry of Health of the Slovak Republic (Ministerstvo zdravotníctva Slovenskej republiky) as a State administration body in accordance with the Law No. 10/1996 Coll.L. with control of the State admini-

stration in form of supervision of health care establishments. Within this framework the ministry of health will carry out:

a) supervision of supervised subjects, establishment of their objective condition and other important facts, primarily deficiencies in their activity, causes for the found deficiencies, harmful consequences and persons responsible for the found deficiencies.

b) supervision of observance of Health Care Act No.277/1994 Coll.L.

c) supervision of quality conditions and extent of health care provided in health care establishments.

*Notes:* This kind of control does not work as part of decision-making processes but works on the basis either of a concrete claim (filed by a concrete person) to be examined through this kind of control mechanism or on the basis of a claim by the Ministry of Health of the Slovak Republic (3, 8, 19).

**References**

Antonín Ružek (1973) Trestní řád – komentář. Orbis. Penal Code –Commentary
ASPI – Automatizovaný súbor právnych informácií /Automated Legal Information File
Bajcura A et al. (1996) Občiansky súdny poriadok. Eurounion. Civil Procedure Code
Benčík M et al. (1985) Právnícká príručka. Obzor Bratislava. Law Manual
Bičovský J, Holub M (1984) Občiansky zákonník. Panorama. Civil Code
Češka Z et al. (1997) Občinasky zákonník – komentář. Panorama. Civil Code – Commentary
Dronec J (1996) Ústavné práva a zdravotníctvo. Archa. Consititutional Rights and Public Health
Handl V, Rubeš J et al. (1985) Občanský soudní řád – komentář. Panorama. Civil Procedure Code – commentary
Hlavsa P (1980) Predpisy z oblasti organizácie justície a prokuratúry. Panorama Praha. Regulations from the Area of Organization of Justice and Prosecution
Holub M 1986 Zákon o rodine. Panorama. Family Law
Kolibaš-Fleischer-Čaplova-Tuža, in Lekársky obzor, 1998, No. 5, page 309
Madara Z et al. (1988) Právnický slovník. Panorama Praha. Law Dictionary
Matys K et al. (1975) Trestný zákon. Orbis Praha. /Penal Law
Matys K et al. (1978) Trestný zákon – komentár. Obzor Bratislava. Penal Law – Commentary
Občiansky zákonník č. 141(1950 Zb) /Civil Code No. 141/1950 Coll.
Stiffel H et al. (2001) Trestný zákon. Iura Edition. Penal Law
Svoboda J et al. (1994) Občiansky zákonník. Eurounion. Civil Code
Svoboda J et al. (1998) Občiansky zákonník Komentár. Eurounion. Civil Code – Commentary
Team of authors (2004) Občiansky súdny poriadok. Nová Práca Bratislava. Civil Procedure Code
Tolár J et al. (1985) Trestný poriadok. Panorama Praha. Criminal Procedure Code
Ústava ČSR (1920) /Constitution of the Czechoslovak Republic/
Ústava ČSR (1948) /Constitution of the Czechoslovak Republic/
Ústava ČSSR (1960) /Constitution of the Czechoslovak Socialist Republic/
Ústava ČSFR (1990) /Constitution of the Czech and Slovak Federal Republic/
Ústava SR (1992) /Constitution of the Slovak Republic/

## Diagram 11.1 Flowchart of the Process of Involuntary Admission in the Slovak Republic

Mental disorder

↓

Admission to hospital

↙ ↘

With patient's written consent (the patient becomes restrained in his/her free movement or contact outwards during the treatment)

Without patient's written consent

↘ ↙

legal ground
(due to the disorder patient is a threat to him/herself or others)

↓

The court responsible for the district in which the hospital is located is to be notified within 24 hours of admission or restraint

24 hours

↓

Judicial proceeding on admissibility of an admission
(generally without ordering a hearing)
- giving of evidence
- examination of the patient
- examination of the attending physician

↓

Within 5 days from the date of restraint the court decides whether the admission was in accordance with the law (appeal is possible)

5 days admis-sion

↙ ↘

If admission was not in accordance with the law, the patient leaves the hospital.

If admission was in accordance with the law, the court continues with the procedure on admissibility of further detention (ordering a hearing)
- appoints and hears an expert
- invites and hears the patient
- hears the attending physician

↙

The hospital may release the patient even if the court's decision is that admission was on legal grounds

↓

3 months

Detention

Court decides whether further detention is admissible and for how long. The decision must be proclaimed within 3 months from the decision on admission. The decision remains in force for 1 year.

↙

The hospital may release the detained patient even before the time period determined by the court expires.

↓

*After 1 year a new examination and a new decision on admissibility of further detention takes place.*

1 year

# Chapter 12

# Legal Report – Spain

Luis Fernando BARRIOS FLORES, Francisco TORRES-GONZÁLEZ

## 12.1 Preliminary Remarks

The Spanish Constitution of December 27, 1978 (hereinafter SC) was a milestone in the regulation of coercive measures in psychiatry. Prior to the SC, this matter had always been governed by administrative regulations (Royal Decrees, May 12 and 19, 1885 and Decree, July 3, 1932 – amended on May 27, 1932). Their emphasis was on the role of doctors, and the control exercised by the courts was merely formal (Bercovitz 1976). In this period, there were some references to the use of coercive measures other than confinement, such as isolation and physical restraint (s.91 of Royal Decree 12.5.1885 and s.3 (2) of Decree 3.7.1931).

Once the SC came into effect it was obvious that the regulation of these measures needed to be adapted to the principles enshrined therein (Mena 1985). In formal terms, the nature of the regulation changed from administrative to civil. First, under Act 13/1983, 24 October, a new provision, section 211, governing the confinement of an "allegedly incapable person", was included in the Civil Code (hereinafter CC) (Cobreros 1981, Bercovitz 1986, Ramos 1988, Ribera 1991, Roca 1991, Dolz 1992, Lacaba 1993, Marín 1999). Subsequently, this provision was amended by Act 1/1996, 15 January, to omit the reference to any kind of alleged incapacity and to lay down that confinement due to mental disorders shall take place simply when the person involved is not in a condition to make the decision himself. Finally, the rules governing psychiatric confinement were incorporated into civil procedural law, specifically in rule 763 of the Civil Procedure Rules (Act 1/2000, 7 January) (hereinafter CPR) (Barrios 2003a, 2003c, Barrios & Barcia 2005, Ferreirós 2001).

Basically, Act 13/1983 stipulated the control of the courts over involuntary confinement (Bercovitz 1989). Admission must always be authorized in advance or subsequently ratified by the courts. Under the CC, a patient needed the authorization of the courts to leave the confinement centre. Nowadays, however, under the CPR, this depends on the decision of the doctor, of which the judge must be notified, or on the decision of the court itself after considering the periodical medical reports. At present there is no explicit reference whatsoever to any coercive measure other than confinement; therefore, it is necessary to refer to constitutional or even criminal provisions in order to define the scope and limits of the applicable coercive measures.

The SC introduced another fundamental change since it envisaged a State with a different structure. The traditional unitary State was replaced by an autonomic one, resembling a federal rather than a regional State. Each Autonomous Community has its own executive and legislative powers. The fact that such powers are shared between the State and each individual Autonomous Community has implications for the matter dealt with in this report. In addition to the State administrative legislation, there are different autonomous legislations that govern a patient's autonomy and the need for his informed consent prior to any medical intervention. In the field of criminal law however, the State has retained exclusive and complete competence. There is only one Penal Code (hereinafter PC) and one "Criminal Procedure Rules" (hereinafter CrPR).

## 12.2 Applicable Laws and General Norms

### 12.2.1 Constitutional Norms

#### General

*"Section 1(1). Spain is a social, democratic State governed by the rule of law, in which freedom, justice, equality and political pluralism are the supreme values of its legal system."*

*"Section 10(1). A person's dignity, his inherent inviolable rights, the free development of his personality, respect for the law and the rights of others are the foundation of political and social order.*
*(2). The norms concerning fundamental rights and freedoms recognised by the Constitution shall be interpreted within the meaning of the Declaration of Human Rights and international conventions and agreements on this subject ratified by Spain".*

*"Section 17(1). Everyone has the right to freedom and security of person. No one may be deprived of his/her freedom except in accordance with the provisions of this section and in the cases and manner envisaged by law.*
*(2). Preventive custody shall last no longer than is strictly necessary to carry out the pertinent investigations to solve the crime, and in any case, the person detained must be released or brought before a law court within seventy two hours.*
*(3). The person detained must be informed immediately and in a way that he can understand of his rights, including his right to remain silent, and the reasons for his detention. He is entitled to legal advice during the police inquiry and court proceedings, in the terms laid down by law.*
*(4). The law shall regulate the 'habeas corpus' procedure to ensure that any person unlawfully arrested is brought before a law court. Likewise, the maximum term of custody while awaiting trial shall be determined by law."*

*"Section 43(1). The right to the protection of health is guaranteed.*
*(2). The authorities are responsible for organizing and protecting public health by means of preventive measures and the provision of the necessary care and assistance. The rights and duties of all interested parties in this respect shall be laid down by law."*

*"Section 49. The authorities shall implement a policy of prevention, treatment, rehabilitation and integration of the physically and mentally handicapped, providing them with the*

*specialized care that they require and affording them enhanced protection so that they may avail themselves of the rights granted to all citizens under this title."*

**Specific**
There are no specific constitutional norms.

**Remark**
The SC regulates freedom at three levels. Firstly, as a general principle, section 1(1) envisages freedom as a supreme value of the legal system that acts as the preferential criterion for interpretation of the entire legal system. Secondly, freedom and dignity are considered fundamental rights (ss. 10(1) and 17 of the SC) whose legal development must be carried out by means of a "public general act" (s.81.1 of the SC), that is, an act of Parliament that requires a qualified majority to be passed. Moreover, as fundamental rights, they enjoy enhanced protection (appeal for legal protection may be brought before the law courts and even before the Constitutional Court) (s. 53(2) of the SC). Thirdly, protection of health in general (s. 43(1) and (2) of the SC) and the treatment of the mentally disordered in particular (s 49 of the SC) are envisaged as guiding principles of economic and social policy. These principles influence the current legislation, judicial practice and the actions of the authorities. However, they are not directly applicable since they can only be evoked before the jurisdictional bodies in accordance with the provisions of the implementing legislation (s 53(3) of the SC ) (Aznar 2000).

### 12.2.2 General Laws

#### 12.2.2.1 Administrative Legislation

**State**
Act 41/2002, 14 November, which is the basic act governing patients' autonomy, as well as the rights and obligations relating to information and clinical documentation (hereinafter PRA)

*"Section 1. Scope. The purpose of this Act is to regulate the rights and obligations of patients, users and professionals, as well as of the health centres and services, both public and private, regarding the autonomy of patients and clinical documentation and information."*

*"Section 2. Basic principles.*
*(1) Respect for a person's free will, dignity and privacy shall guide all activities involving obtaining, using, filing, keeping and transferring clinical documents and information.*
*(2). As a general principle, any intervention relating to health care requires the prior consent of the patient or user. Consent, which should be obtained after providing the patient with the necessary information, shall be given in writing in the cases envisaged in the Act.*
*(3). A patient or user has the right to freely choose, after receiving the necessary information, between the clinical options available.*

*(4). A patient or user has the right to refuse treatment, except in the cases laid down in the Act, and such refusal shall be given in writing.*
*(6). A professional who provides health care and assistance is obliged not only to carry out the techniques correctly, but also to fulfil his duty in relation to clinical documents and information, and to respect the decisions freely adopted by the patient."*

*"Section 8. Informed consent.*
*(1). Prior to any action being taken in relation to a patient's health care, his consent must be freely given after having received the information envisaged in section 2 and evaluated the options available.*
*(5). A patient is free to withdraw his consent in writing at any time."*

*"Section 9. Limits to informed consent and consent given by legal representative.*
*(2). A doctor may perform clinical interventions that are indispensable for a patient's health without the latter's consent in the following cases:*
*b) When a patient's physical or mental well-being is in serious, immediate danger and it is not possible to obtain his consent, by consulting members of his family or those close to him when circumstances permit.*
*(3). Consent shall be given by a patient's representative in the following situations:*
*a) When, in the opinion of the patient's doctor, the patient is not capable of making a decision or when his mental or physical state prevents him from understanding the situation. When the patient has no legal representative, consent may be given by a member of his family or a person related to him* de facto.
*b) When the patient is legally incapacitated.*
*(5). When recourse is made to consent given by a representative, it shall be in keeping with the circumstances, in proportion to the patient's needs and in his favour, while respecting his personal dignity. The patient shall participate as much as possible in the decisions taken throughout the health care process."*

## General Health Care Act (Act 14/1986, 25 April) (hereinafter GHA)

*"Section 10. Everyone has the following rights in relation to the various public health care services:*
*(1). Respect for their personality, human dignity and privacy and the right not to be discriminated against on the grounds of race, gender, morals, ideology, political or trade union affiliation, financial status or social class.*
*(15). While respecting the specific financial system of each health care service, the rights enshrined in paragraphs (1), (3), (4), (5), (6), (7), (9) and (11) of this section shall also be exercised in relation to private health services".*

*"Section 20(2). Patients who require hospitalization to treat their conditions shall be admitted to the psychiatric units of general hospitals."*

### Autonomous communities

The Autonomous Communities have passed their own legislation on patients' rights. Thus, in Catalonia, Act 21/2000, 21 December, deals with the right of patients to receive information related to their health care, their autonomy and public documents (s 7); in Galicia, Act 3/2001, 28 May, relates to informed consent and patients' clinical records (s 6 and 11); in Navarre, Regional Act

11/2002, 6 May, concerns patients' rights to have their prior wishes respected, and to receive information and clinical documents (s.8); and in Valencia, Act 1/2003, 28 January, deals with patients' rights including the right to receive information (ss. 8-11).
Each Autonomous Community also has its own legislation on the organization of health care (usually called "the Health Care Act", "Health Service Act" or "Health care Organization Act").

**Remark**
State administrative legislation on coercion in psychiatry covers two aspects: on the one hand a patient's rights and the decision regarding which centre he is to be confined in, and on the other the organization of the care given.
Patients' rights are regulated in the PRA and the GHA (Cobreros 1988). Both acts are considered fundamental (Additional Provision 1 of the PRA and s. 2(1) of the GHA) and are applicable throughout Spain (149(1)(16) of the SC). Both the State and the Autonomous Communities must adopt the necessary measures to ensure they are enforced. Some legislation of the Autonomous Communities precedes the PRA and some is more recent. However, given the "fundamental" nature of this Act, their legislation must be in accordance with and construed in the light of this national Act. In addition, patients' rights are applicable in the case of both public and private institutions (s.1 of the PRA and s.10(15) of the GHA).
The dignity of a person and his right to privacy (s.2(1) of the PRA and s.10(1) of the GHA), respect for his freedom of will (s. 2(1) of the PRA), respect for his personality and the right not to be discriminated against (s. 10(1) of the GHA) are considered fundamental rights. In principle, the patient's informed consent must be given to any health care action (ss. 2(2) and 8 of the PRA), and the patient has the right to refuse treatment (s.2(4) of the PRA). However, when the patient is legally incapacitated or can not make his own decisions, the consent of his representative is required (s. 9(3) of the PRA). Moreover, medical intervention is possible when there is "grave danger to the patient's mental or physical well-being and it is not possible to obtain his authorization" (s. 9(2)(b) of the PRA).
Section 20 of the GHA provides that mental patients shall be hospitalized, whether voluntarily or involuntarily, in psychiatric units of general hospitals rather than in special psychiatric hospitals.

The Autonomous Communities have two different types of legislation. On the one hand, the health care legislation relating to a patient's rights (the Acts cited above), and on the other, legislation concerning organization of the care provided by the health services of each Autonomous Community. Nowadays, practically all the powers in matters of health care have been transferred to the Autonomous Communities and so the latter are responsible for the organization and characteristics of the care and assistance given, providing of course that they respect the "basic acts" that are applicable and the Spanish Constitution. Each Autonomous Community has its own health authorities and the legislative power to determine how its health service should be organized.

#### 12.2.2.2 Civil Legislation

**State**

The Civil Procedure Rules (Act 1/2000, 7 January)

*"Rule 763. Involuntary confinement due to mental disorders.*

*(1). The confinement due to mental disorders of a person who is in no condition to decide for himself shall require authorization of the court in the area in which the person resides, even if someone else holds his custody or guardianship.*

*Authorization must be obtained prior to confinement, except in the case of an emergency when it is necessary to carry out such a measure immediately. In such a case, the head of the centre in which the patient is confined shall inform the competent court of the fact as soon as possible and, in all cases, within a period of twenty four hours, so that the confinement may be legally ratified. Such ratification must take place within a maximum of seventy two hours from the time the court was notified of the confinement.*

*In the case of an emergency confinement, the court in the area in which the confinement centre is located has the competence to ratify the measure. Said court shall act, where appropriate, pursuant to the provisions of rule 757.3 of these Rules.*

*(2). The confinement of minors shall always take place in a mental health centre appropriate to their age and based on the medical report of the services giving assistance to the minor.*

*(3). Before granting authorization or ratifying a confinement that has already taken place, the person involved, the public prosecutor and any other person whose appearance the court considers opportune or is requested by the person involved shall be given a hearing. Moreover, in addition to hearing any other evidence it might consider relevant to the case, the court itself shall examine the person whose confinement is the issue and hear the opinion of the doctor designated by the court. Throughout the proceedings, the person involved is entitled to legal advice in accordance with rule 758 of these Rules.*

*In any case, an appeal may be lodged against the court's decision in relation to the confinement.*

*(4). The decision that confinement should take place shall also set out the obligation of the doctors in charge of the person confined to inform the court periodically whether it is necessary to maintain the measure, in addition to providing any other report that the court may require at its discretion.*

*The periodical reports shall be issued every six months, unless the court, taking into account the nature of the disorder that led to confinement, stipulates a shorter period.*

*On receiving the aforementioned reports and, where appropriate, subsequent to any action it deems necessary, the court shall decide whether the confinement shall continue or not.*

*Subject to the provisions of the above paragraphs, the doctors caring for the patient may discharge him when they consider that his confinement is no longer necessary, and immediately notify the competent court."*

**Autonomous communities**

The Family Code of Catalonia (Act 9/1998, 15 July) (hereinafter FCC)

*"Section 219.Prior authorization.*
*(1). The person exercising the wardship requires authorization of the courts to:*
*a) Confine an incapacitated person in a suitable centre.*
*b) Administer medical treatment to the incapacitated person that may seriously endanger his life, or his mental or physical well-being.*
*(2). The measures referred to in paragraph 1 may be taken without prior authorization when obtaining such authorization may involve a delay or imply a serious danger for the ward himself, other persons or property.*
*In this case, the relevant court should be notified, as well as the wardship board, if there is one, of the decision adopted within a maximum of twenty four hours."*

*"Section 255.Authorization of the courts and notification of confinement.*
*(1) A person's confinement due to mental disorder in a suitable, closed institution requires the prior authorization of the courts when the person, whatever his age, is not in a condition to decide for himself. Said authorization is not required when, in the case of a medical emergency, it is necessary to adopt this measure. However, in such a case, the director of the centre in which the person is confined shall notify the judge of the court in whose jurisdiction the centre is located, within a maximum of twenty four hours. The director must do the same when the person who is voluntarily confined is not in a condition to decide for himself that he should continue to be confined.*
*(2) Once the application for confinement has been presented or the confinement has been notified, the judge shall make a reasoned decision to authorize or disallow the confinement or its prolongation after examining the person involved and hearing the expert opinion of the doctor assigned by the court and the public prosecutor's report. Every two months, the judge shall review the situation of the person confined.*
*(3) In the case it is intended to administer medical treatment that may endanger the life or physical or mental well-being of the patient, the provisions laid down in s 219 for such treatment shall be applied, and the powers given under s. 219 to the guardian are exercised in this case by the relatives of the person confined or, in their absence, by the judge."*

**Remark**

At the State level, r. 763 of the CPR governs the regulation of confinement. The existence of specific civil legislation in Catalonia concerning confinement (s. 255 of the FCC) is justified by the fact that this territory is recognized to have its own legislative power (s.149(1)(8) of the SC) (Chimeno 2001). The legal system for confinement in Catalonia is basically the same as the system in force in the rest of Spain, although the periodic inspection by the courts is exercised more often (the patient's situation must be reviewed every two months) and the powers of guardians are regulated in more detail (s.219 of the FCC).
Authorization of the courts for admission to hospital and the judicial control exercised during confinement belongs to the civil jurisdiction (s. 22 of the Judiciary Act (Act1/1985, 1 July)) and specifically to the courts of first instance. Nevertheless, when the court of first instance is closed, authorization for admission

may be given by the senior judge or, in his absence, the night court. The competent judge is the one in whose jurisdiction the patient resides, in the case of ordinary admissions, or the judge in whose jurisdiction the hospital is located, in the case of emergency admissions (r.763.1 of the CPR). The decision of the court may always be appealed against before the Civil Division of the Provincial Court (r. 763.3 of the CPR), and an appeal may even be made to the Civil Division of the Supreme Court (r. 477 of the CPR).

Any person (as well as the social, health, or law and order services) may notify the public prosecutor or court of the existence of a reason for confinement (r. 757.2 of the CPR); however, it lies with the court to make the decision.

A person (civil or military) who, due to a mental disorder, "is not in a condition to decide for himself" may be involuntarily confined (r. 763.1 of the CPR) (Santos 2002). Minors may only be admitted to "a mental health institution that is appropriate for their age, and in accordance with the prior report of the social services attending the minor" (r. 763.2 of the CPR).

Ordinary admission, which in practice is the least common, takes place with the prior authorization of the courts (r.763.1 (2) of the CPR). When an application for admission is filed, the judge must initiate the following proceedings: a) Notify the person involved of the initiation of the proceedings so that he may appoint a defence counsel; should he not do so, the public prosecutor will represent him; b) give a hearing to the person affected by the decision, the public prosecutor and any other person the judge deems appropriate or whose appearance was requested by the interested party; c) examine for himself the person involved (r. 763.3 of the CPR); d) hear the expert opinion of a doctor, and e) consider any other evidence he deems relevant.

An emergency admission must be subsequently ratified by the courts. The director of the hospital must inform the court of the admission within a period of 24 hours and the court must reach a decision within 72 hours (r.763.1 of the CPR). If this is not done, the person admitted must be discharged. Before the court ratifies the admission, the judge must carry out the same proceedings as in the case of ordinary confinement.

Regarding the court proceedings that the judge must carry out before authorising/ratifying the confinement, it should be pointed out that: A) Examination of the person involved by the judge himself is an "essential requirement" (Judgment of the Number One Division of the Supreme Court, 20.2.1989) whose purpose is to determine his true clinical condition and the absence of confabulations. Moreover, the examination must be performed personally by the judge (Judgments of the Number One Division of the Supreme Court, 20.2.1989, 2.6.1989 and 20.3.1991). This examination may take place simultaneously with the medical examination. B) Although the CPR refers to "hearing the expert opinion of a doctor", in practice this is given in writing. The doctor involved is usually the forensic surgeon – attached to the court – or a specialist in psychiatry other than a forensic surgeon. Examination may be carried out by more than one doctor or even by an institution or a team of various specialists. The expert opinion given shall deal with the causes that justify the need or advisability of the confinement; it must be up to date and not based exclusively on the testimony of family members or the patient's medical history.

The procedure is brought to an end when the court reaches a decision (a court order), and this decision must be issued within a certain period (72 hours) in the case of an emergency admission; whereas in the case of an ordinary admission there is no such time limit. However, in the latter case, it is understood that the court will issue its decision as soon as possible.

The patient may be transported to hospital against his will and even with the help of the police, although there are no explicit statutory provisions on the matter. Intervention of the police occurs in accordance with ss. 5(1)(e); 5(2)(a)(b) and (c); 5(4); 11(1)(.b), (e) and (f); 38(3)(a) and 53(1)(i) of the National Security Forces Act (Act 2/1986, 13 March) (Chamorro & Clusa 1995, Barrios 2002).

Once confinement (either ordinary or emergency) has been decided, this measure is subject to judicial control. Thus, the doctors in charge of the patient must provide the judge with reports on the necessity of maintaining the measure as often as is specified in the authorizing/ratifying decision or, if not specified, at least every six months (r. 763.4 (1) and (2) of the CPR).

Confinement terminates either by the decision of the doctors attending the patient, who must notify the court of their decision (r.763.4 (4) of the CPR), or by the decision of the judge based on the medical reports r. 763.4 (3) of the CPR).

#### 12.2.2.3 Criminal Legislation

The Penal Code (Act 10/1995, 23 November)

*"Section 20. The following have no criminal liability:*
*(1) A person who when he commits a criminal offence is not capable of understanding the unlawfulness of his act, or of acting according to such understanding, due to any type of mental disorder or anomaly.*
*A transitory mental disorder shall not exonerate from punishment when it is provoked by the individual for the purpose of committing the offence, or when he had foreseen or should have foreseen the commission of the offence."*

*"Section 96. (1). The security measures that may be implemented under this Code are custodial and non-custodial.*
*(2) The following are custodial measures:*
*(a) Confinement in a psychiatric hospital.*
*(b) Confinement in a detoxication centre.*
*(c) Confinement in a special education centre."*

*"Section 97. During execution of the sentence, the sentencing judge or court may, by means of an indictment procedure and based on the prior proposal of the prison judge:*

*a) Order the cessation of any security measure imposed as soon as the individual ceases to be criminally dangerous.*
*b) Replace one security measure by any other deemed appropriate of those envisaged for the case in question. Should it be decided to substitute a measure and as a result the individual progresses poorly, the new measure shall be discontinued.*
*c) Suspend implementation of the measure, due to the result already obtained, for a period no longer than that which remains to complete the maximum term specified in the sentence that imposed the measure. Suspension is conditional on the individual not committing an offence during a fixed period of time, and may be annulled if any of the circumstances envisaged in s 95 of this Code were once again accredited.*
*For this reason, the prison judge shall be obliged to present at least once a year a proposal for maintaining, ceasing, replacing or suspending the custodial security measure imposed."*

*"Section 101(1). A person declared exempt from criminal liability under s.20 (1) may, if necessary, be confined in order to receive medical treatment or special education in an institution specialising in the type of mental disorder involved, or any other of the measures envisaged in s. 96 (3) may be applied. The period of confinement shall not exceed the custodial sentence the individual would have received had he been declared liable, and to this effect, the judge or court will lay down this term as the maximum in the sentence.*
*2. The person subjected to this measure may not leave the institution without authorization of the sentencing judge or court, pursuant to s. 97 of this Code."*

*"Section 104. Where there is an incomplete defence in relation to s. 20 (1), (2) and (3), the judge or court may impose, in addition to the corresponding sanction, the measures envisaged in ss. 101, 102 and 103. However, confinement shall only be applicable when a custodial sentence is imposed and it shall not last for longer than the sentence envisaged in the Code for the offence committed. The measure shall be implemented in accordance with the provisions of s. 99."*

*"Section 105. In the cases envisaged in ss. 101 to 104, the judge or court may make a reasoned decision, either at the beginning or during execution of the sentence, to implement one or more of the following measures:*
*1. For a maximum term of five years:*
*a) External treatment in a medical centre or specialist social health care institution."*

**Remark**

All the Spanish Penal Codes since 1822 have envisaged the defence of mental abnormality. All criminal legislation after the 1848 Code has included the provision (s. 8(1)) that those considered to be exempt from criminal liability for psychiatric reasons must be admitted to a hospital/institution specialising in this type of patient, and may not leave without authorization of the courts. Historically, criminal psychiatric confinement in Spain lasted indefinitely, until the present Code was passed.
The current Penal Code, passed by Act 10/1995, 23 November, also provides a defence based on psychiatric reasons (s 20(1) of the PC). When the defence is complete (non-imputability), the measure adopted is confinement for a certain period of time which may not exceed the term of the custodial sentence the indi-

vidual would have received had he been considered liable (s.101(1) of the PC). When the defence is incomplete (semi-imputability), together with the custodial sentence, the measure of confinement may also be applied (s.104 of the PC). During confinement, the judge has the discretion to replace this measure by another such as outpatient treatment (s. 105(1) of the PC).
Spanish criminal legislation also contains some provisions that could potentially be related to the use of coercive measures. If a person is deprived of his freedom and the requirements laid down in r.763 of the CPR are not fulfilled, then an offence of illegal detention is committed (ss.164 and 165 of the PC). When a person's freedom is suppressed without lawful authorization, this amounts to an offence of coercion (s.172 of the PC). Moreover, the use of coercive measures might result in offences (murder or bodily harm) against an individual's personal safety (his life or physical well-being) being committed by an act or failure to act (s.1(1) of the PC), with malicious intent (ss. 138 and 147 of the PC) or due to negligence (ss. 142 and 152 of the PC) (Delgado et al. 1994, Gómez 1997). In Spain, unlike in other countries, so-called "arbitrary medical treatment" is not typified.

#### 12.2.2.4 Prison Legislation

The General Prison Act (Act 1/1979, 26 September) (hereinafter GPA)

*"Section 3. All prison activities shall be carried out respecting the human condition of the prisoners as well as their legal interests and rights that are not affected by the sentence. No differences shall be established on grounds of race, political opinion, religion, social status or the like.*
*Therefore:*
*(1) Prisoners shall be entitled to exercise their civil, political, social, economic and cultural rights, including the right to vote, except where such rights are incompatible with the purpose of their detention or the serving of their sentence.*
*(2) The necessary measures shall be adopted to enable the prisoners and their families to conserve their right to social security benefits acquired prior to admission to prison.*
*(3) Under no circumstance shall prisoners be prevented from proceeding with any legal action that may be underway when they were admitted to prison, and they may also initiate further legal action.*
*(4) The prison service shall be responsible for the prisoners' health and safety.*
*(5) A prisoner has the right to be called by his name."*

*"Section 7. Penitentiary institutions shall include:*
*a) Prisons in which to await trial.*
*b) Prisons in which to serve sentence.*
*c) Special institutions."*

*"Section11. Special institutions are those which primarily provide care and attention and shall be of the following types:*
*b) Psychiatric centres."*

Prison Regulation (Royal Decree 190/1996, 9 February) (hereinafter PR)

*"Section 72. Coercive measures.*

*(1) Under section 45(1) of the General Prison Act, coercive measures are temporary solitary confinement, physical force, rubber truncheons, appropriate aerosols and handcuffs. The use of these measures shall be proportional to the desired result, shall never take the form of a punishment in disguise, shall only be applied when no other less drastic measure exists to obtain the desired result, and only for as long as is strictly necessary.*

*(2) The above coercive measures shall not be applied to the inmates referred to in section 254(3) of this Regulation or to patients that are reconvalescing after a serious illness, except where their behaviour poses an immediate danger to their own safety or the safety of others. When the inmate is in temporary solitary confinement, he shall be visited daily by the doctor.*

*(3) The use of coercive measures shall be previously authorized by the Director of the centre, except in the case of an emergency when this is not possible, in which case he shall be notified immediately that such measures have been used. The Director shall immediately notify the prison judge when coercive measures have been adopted and when they have ceased, providing full details of the events leading up to their use and circumstances that make it advisable to keep such measures in force.*

*(4) The material coercive means used shall be deposited in the place considered appropriate by the Director, and their number and condition shall be recorded in the official records.*

*(5) In cases of serious disturbance of the peace and imminent danger for people or installations, the Director may, as an interim measure, obtain the help of the security forces on duty in the centre, who, should they need to make use of firearms, shall do so with the limitations set out in the legislation concerning the national security forces, subject to the first final provision of the General Prison Act."*

*"Section 183. Object. Prison Psychiatric Units or Institutions are special centres with the facilities necessary to enforce the custodial security measures imposed by the competent courts."*

*"Section 184. Admission. Admission to these Psychiatric Units or Institutions shall take place in the following circumstances:*

*a) Prisoners or persons who have been arrested while suffering from psychiatric disorders, when the judicial authority decides they should be admitted for observation, in accordance with the provisions of the Criminal Procedure Rules, for the time necessary to carry out such observation and prepare the relevant report.*

*Once the report has been issued, if the judicial authority decides not to release the inmate, the management of the centre may decide to transfer him to the appropriate centre.*

*b) Persons to whom, as a result of the application of exonerating circumstances laid down in the Penal Code, confinement in a prison psychiatric centre has been applied as a security measure.*

*c) Prisoners on whom, since they have become mentally unstable, a security measure that must be carried out in a prison psychiatric unit or institution has been imposed by the sentencing court in accordance with the provisions of the Penal Code and the Criminal Procedure Rules."*

*"Section 188. Regime for Psychiatric Units or Institutions. (1). Admission to any of the different departments making up the Units or Institutions shall be carried out in accordance with the care needed by the individual patient.*

*(2). Restrictions on the personal freedom of a patient shall be limited to those that are necessary with regards to his state of health or the success of the treatment.*
*(3). The use of coercive means is an exceptional measure that shall only be allowed on a doctor's recommendation for the minimum period of time until treatment with the drugs prescribed takes effect, and always respecting the person's dignity. Even when medically speaking there is considered to be no alternative to the use of coercive means, the judicial authority responsible should be notified immediately of the measure taken for the patient, and written evidence provided of the doctor's recommendation that physical force be used.*
*(4) The provisions concerning the disciplinary system contained in this Regulation shall not be applicable to patients confined in these institutions."*

**Remark**

Spain has taken longer than other countries to dispense special treatment to mentally abnormal offenders. Only one national hospital- not specifically a prison hospital – the Saint Isabel Mental Hospital in Leganés (Madrid), provided care during the second half of the 19th century for a large number of such prisoners. The first explicit legislation on the separation of sane and mentally abnormal prisoners was a Decree passed on September 1, 1897 (Barrios 2000).
Current legislation classifies prison psychiatric institutions as "special" (ss. 7 and 11 of the GPA). Nowadays, there are two psychiatric prison hospitals – one in Alicante and the other in Seville – and a private hospital block, which receives a state subsidy, for psychiatric admissions in Catalonia (competence in prison matters has been transferred to this Autonomous Community). Moreover, the Prison Regulation of 1996 governs the existence of "Psychiatric Units" in prisons (s.183 of the PR), although it has not yet been implemented (Barrios 2003b).
Persons subjected to confinement as a disciplinary measure, prisoners who develop a mental illness, as well as prisoners or persons under arrest will be admitted to these hospitals or future units, although in the case of the latter only for forensic evaluation (188 of the PR).
Coercive measures are only used in prisons in Spain in exceptional circumstances and their use must be proportional to the desired result (s. 72(1) of the PR). Prior authorization of the Director must be obtained and subsequently notified to the prison court (s.72(3) of the PR). A person kept in solitary confinement must be visited daily by the doctor (s.72(2) of the PR).
In the case of patients in ordinary centres, coercive measures may only be used in highly exceptional circumstances, and are limited to cases in which there is imminent danger to the patient's safety or that of other persons (s.72(2) of the PR). In psychiatric units and institutions, the use of coercive measures must be considered necessary by a doctor. They should be used for as little time as possible and, again, the court must be notified (s.188(3) of the PR).

A curious problem arises in relation to the type of measures to be used in psychiatric units or institutions. Section 72(1) of the PR lists the following as the only coercive means recognised by the legislation: "temporary solitary confinement, physical force, rubber truncheons, suitable aerosols and handcuffs". Mechanical restraint is not mentioned, although this is the measure used in the psychiatric prison hospitals in Alicante and Seville.

### 12.2.3 International Conventions and Agreements

- The Universal Declaration of Human Rights of December 10, 1948, ratified by Spain. Pursuant to s.10(2) of the Spanish Constitution, the rules concerning human rights and fundamental freedoms shall be construed in agreement with said constitution and the international conventions and agreements ratified by Spain.
- International Covenant on Civil and Political Rights of December 19, 1966, ratified by Spain on April 13, 1977.
- International Covenant on Economic, Social and Cultural Rights of December 19, 1966, ratified by Spain on April 13, 1977.
- Convention for the Protection of Human Rights and Fundamental Freedoms of November 4, 1950, ratified by Spain on September 26, 1979. Article 5 dealing with the right to freedom and guarantees in cases of loss of freedom is of special interest.
- European Convention for the prevention of torture and inhuman or degrading treatment or punishment of November 26, 1987, ratified by Spain on April 28, 1989.
- Convention for the protection of Human Rights and dignity of the human being with regard to the application of biology and medicine (Oviedo Convention) of April 4, 1997, ratified by Spain on October 20, 1999.

**Remark**

In addition to their interpretive value (s.10(2) of the SC), all these agreements and conventions form part of the Spanish domestic law (s. 96 of the SC).

### 12.2.4 Second Level of Juridical Norms

**State**

No such regulation exists.

**Autonomous communities**

Some Autonomous Communities have their own second level administrative rules. Thus, the Autonomous Community of Andalusia passed Resolution 261/2002, 26 December, of the Managing Director of the Andalusian Health

Service, whereby rules are laid down concerning the procedure for involuntary admissions and transfers within Andalusia's health care network.

### 12.3 Jurisprudence

#### 12.3.1 Constitutional Court

Judgment of the Constitutional Court (hereinafter JCC) (16/1981, 18 May). Criminal psychiatric confinement does not contravene s. 17 of the SC, but indefinite deprivation of freedom is not admissible. The guarantees enshrined in the European Convention for the Protection of Human Rights and Fundamental Freedoms must be respected, and the minimum conditions specified by the European Court of Human Rights in the *Winterwerp* case, 27.10.1979, and subsequently in the cases *X versus the United Kingdom*, 5.11.1981 and *Luberti*, 23.2.1984 must be fulfilled.

JCC 112/1988, 8 June. The court is not bound by the medical reports on the patient's condition when deciding whether to release him or not. However, the court's refusal to release the patient must always be reasoned, since *"confinement can not be validly prolonged when the mental disorder no longer exists that, due to its nature and severity, justified confinement."*

JCC 104/1990, 4 June. The court refuses a *habeas corpus* petition in the case of a confinement that lasted 42 years. It allows the court hearing the *habeas corpus* petition to refer to the competent court's grounds for confinement which were based on the *"necessary objective medical confirmation of the mentally abnormal state"* of the patient which *"justifies the continuation, with no changes, of his confinement"*.

JCC 129/1999, 1 July analyses a "constitutional question" (a lower court consults the Constitutional Court concerning whether a certain legal provision is constitutional) concerning s. 211 of the CC. It holds that this provision – currently r. 763 of the CPR does indeed guarantee the personal freedom enshrined in s. 17 of the SC as well as the right to be heard and defended. It does not consider it necessary that confinement should be regulated by a public general act of Parliament. The court considers that the doctrine expressed in its judgment (JCC 112/1988) on criminal psychiatric confinement is applicable in essence to civil psychiatric confinement, since

> *"in both cases, provision is made for the deprivation of a person's freedom due to a mental disorder such as is beneficial to both the mentally abnormal person himself and society as a whole".*

All the conditions for confinement laid down by the European Court of Human Rights (in the cases *Winterwerp, X v. the United Kingdom and Luberti*) are respected in s. 211 of the CC. This judgment was passed with the dissenting vote of one of the presiding justices who held that the legal level of the regulation on civil psychiatric confinement is inadequate and that such confinement should be regulated by a public general act of parliament.

### 12.3.2 Supreme Court

Criminal jurisprudence:

Judgment of the Supreme Court (hereinafter JSC), Number 2 Division[1], 8.10.1982. The court holds that reclusion of an elderly woman at the request of her son was fraudulent, since she showed no signs of mental or neurological disorders, and typifies it as unlawful detention.

JSC, Number 2 Division, 2.10.1992. The Court typifies the admission to an old people's home of a patient who was kept there in isolation and prevented from leaving the home and even communicating with her lawyer as unlawful detention.

Civil jurisprudence:

JSC, Number 1 Division[2], 10.2.1986.

> *"A person is presumed to be mentally capable unless there is conclusive evidence to the contrary, and this implies clearly demonstrating his incapacity by means of adequate direct evidence."*

Confinement is a measure to be used only in exceptional circumstances and when indicated:

> *"any limitation of a person's freedom, such as confinement in a psychiatric centre, may not be determined «a priori» and in general terms, but only when faced with a specific situation that requires such an exceptional measure ." "Confinement in a Psychiatric Institution is not the normal outcome of the said incapacity",*

concludes the court (García-Ripoll 1992, García 2000, Sancho 2000, Ramos 2001).

JSC, Number 1 Division, 20.2.1989. An appellate court that amends the judgment of an inferior court shall examine the incapacitated/confined person personally.

---

1 Number 2 Division of the Supreme Courts hears criminal appeals in the last instance.

2 Number 1 Division of the Supreme Court hears civil appeals in the last instance.

### 12.3.3 High Courts of Justice[3]

Contentious-Administrative Jurisprudence:

Judgment of the High Court of Justice of Asturias, 13.5.1999. The health authorities are held responsible in the case of a patient who commits suicide when, despite the latter's agitation, anxiety and repeated threats of suicide, no mechanical restraining measures were taken and the patient was not moved to another ward equipped with the necessary security means.

### 12.3.4 Provincial Courts

Order of the Provincial Court[4] (hereinafter OPC) of Saragossa, 20.1.2003 . This order was declared invalid since the procedures envisaged in r. 763.3 of the CPR 2000 were not followed (the Public Prosecutor was not given a hearing, no judicial examination was carried out and no medical report was issued).

OPC of Toledo, 16.1.2003. This order recognizes that there are two conflicting points of view as regards whether authorization of the courts is necessary or not in order to admit elderly persons suffering from degenerative conditions (Alzheimer's). This order defends the need for authorization of the courts, since involuntary confinement is a *"clear limitation of the principle of personal freedom enshrined in s. 17 of the SC"*. This type of confinement

> *"not only differs in no way from confinements envisaged within the literal meaning of the old s. 211 of the CC, nowadays r. 276 of the CPR, but, quite the opposite, combines all the essential characteristics of the latter (deprivation of the freedom of a person who is not in a condition to decide for himself) that justify the intervention of the courts, as well as many others that serve to reinforce the demand for greater control and guarantees in confinement."*

OPC of Barcelona, 5.4.2001. There is no reason to revoke confinement if, during the judicial examination and in the presence of the forensic surgeon, the symptoms of a schizophrenic disorder are seen to persist, and it is advisable to prolong hospitalization.

OPC of Barcelona, 19.3.2001. Confinement is an interim measure to protect the patient's own safety, and must be considered on the indication of a doctor. It implies a closed environment, irrespective of the name given thereto.

---

[3] Each Autonomous Community has its own High Court of Justice which has three divisions: Civil-Criminal, Contentious-Administrative, and Social.

[4] The Provincial Courts (one in each of the 50 provinces) have a Civil and a Criminal Division.

OPC of Santa Cruz de Tenerife, 29.11.2000. Confinement may take place in both psychiatric hospitals and geriatric or general hospitals.

OPC of Segovia, 27.3.2000. Confinement in an old people's home is not equivalent to psychiatric confinement. However, in the case of the admission to an old people's home of persons who suffer from mental disorders, authorization of the courts is also necessary.

OPC of La Rioja, 27.10.1998. Confinement in an old people's home is different from psychiatric confinement.

OPC of Lleida, 1.6.1998. The court may be notified of the need for confinement by the psychiatrist himself.

OPC of La Rioja, 17.3.1998. Confinement is a therapeutic health care measure, and the function of the judge is to exercise control and guarantee the rights and freedoms of the patients.

OPC of Barcelona, 10.2.1998. Admission to an old people's home due to an irreversible, degenerative condition cannot be classified as psychiatric confinement.

Order of the High Court of Justice of Catalonia[5], 15.9.1994. Follow-up of the incapacitated person is not something separate from or unconnected to confinement, but constitutes a phase or part of the confinement itself.

**Remark**
There is very little case law on confinements and none has been found on the use of other coercive measures despite having consulted 4 different databases.

### 12.4 Protocols and Internal Norms

#### 12.4.1 Identification and Description of the Contents of these Protocols

In this study we have taken into consideration the protocols received from 20 psychiatric hospital units[6] belonging to the various autonomous health systems (Ramos 1999). The following points are worth mentioning:

---

5 Each Autonomous Community (there are 17) has its own High Court of Justice.

6 We examined the protocols from the following hospitals: Autonomous Community of Andalusia: the Carlos Haya Hospital, Malaga. Autonomous Community of Castile and Leon: Nuestra Señora de Sonsoles Hospital of Avila, Provincial Hospital of Avila, Yagüe General Hospital of Burgos, Hospital Complex of Leon, Santa Isabel Hospital of Leon, Bierzo Hospital of Ponferrada, University Hospital of Salamanca, Hospitalization Unit of

The differences between them: In some Autonomous Communities there is an abundance of protocols and in others there are none that we know of. There are institutions in which there are no protocols as such, only simple forms for confinement or giving consent.
The protocols deal almost exclusively with physical restraint, and there are no protocols for forced medication and practically none for isolation. There are also a few protocols for involuntary confinement.

In particular, with regard to the protocols for physical restraint (therapeutic immobilization), the following could be mentioned:
Justifications: In general the justification for physical restraint is a patient's violent behaviour or the need to prevent harm to the patient or others or to property, as well as extreme agitation on the part of the patient. In a few cases, physical restraint is indicated in order to facilitate the forced medication of a patient when he puts up resistance and the psychiatrist requests this measure; to reduce sensory stimuli; in cases of an organic pathology that requires special care in administering medication; to avoid serious disruptions in the patient's own therapy or in that of others ( removal of vials, catheters or other life support systems); in cases in which rapid sedation is not produced with drugs; when the patient refuses to rest, eat or drink and such conduct may endanger his physical safety; as negative reinforcement forming part of programmes of behavioural therapy; in cases in which the patient requests this measure, provided that there is clinical and/or therapeutic justification. In the Carlos Haya Hospital in Málaga, a detailed list is made of general, explicit and relative justifications.
Counter-justifications: There are many protocols that expressly prohibit the use of immobilization as a punishment due to dislike of the patient or for the staff's convenience. Some include the following counter-justifications: refusal of treatment, substitution of treatment already being given, cases of encephalopathy and state of confusion, unawareness of the patient's general state of health, experiences of the patient which worsen his violent behaviour, if the violence is intentionally criminal (which would be the competence of the police), situations that may be resolved by reasoning with the patient, in cases of staff shortage, behavioural therapy, the request of the patient himself.

---

the Hospital Consortium of Salamanca, Nuestra Señora de la Fuencisla Hospital of Segovia and the Dr. Villacián Health care Centre of Valladolid. Autonomous Community of Madrid: San Carlos Clinical Hospital and Ramón y Cajal Hospital. Autonomous Community of Valencia: University Clinical Hospital of Valencia, Hospital i Centre d'Especialitats Francesc Borja, Regional Hospital of Vinarós, Hospital of la Ribera, Provincial Hospital of Castellón, University Hospital Doctor Peset. Autonomous Community of the Basque Country: Psychiatric Hospital of Alava.

Prescriber of the imposition/end of the measure: In general it is the doctor (the patient's psychiatrist or the psychiatrist on duty) who takes the decision regarding both the start and end of the measure. In the Ramón y Cajal Hospital, both the prescription and end of the measure are signed by the psychiatrist and the nurse.

Description of the means/mechanism of restraint: Immobilization straps are always used, fastened by means of magnets (models available on the market), that immobilize the chest, wrists and ankles. Some protocols describe the manoeuvres to be used in order to immobilize the patient, the role of each staff member taking part and the precautions to be taken to avoid any possible harm to the patient (dangerous objects within his reach, articles of clothing of the staff or patient himself, etc.). The optimum number of people involved is 5 and the minimum is 4.

Observation and safeguards during implementation of the measure: In this respect, there is wide variation, from detailed provisions on periodic revisions and the participation of different members of staff to hardly any indications at all.

The nursing activities in the most detailed protocols are focused on: the checking of vital signs, help with personal hygiene and after defecation, regulating the conditions of the room, changing the patient's position, periodically releasing each limb in turn, looking out for any possible erosions or injury to his limbs, offering food and drink, and talking to the patient. The interval between the visits of the nursing staff varies considerably, i.e 10, 15 or 30 minutes. Some protocols specify that the patient should be visited by the psychiatrist in the first or first few hours (two to three hours), and his condition should be reviewed every twelve hours. In another protocol, the first revision is to be carried out as soon as the measure is implemented and subsequent revisions after four and six hours.

Place: Except in the odd case, there are no provisions concerning the ideal place in which to implement the immobilization measure.

Duration: Most of the protocols do not mention any maximum term for duration of the measure, although they do refer to its exceptional, temporary nature. Those that do deal with the matter of its duration indicate the following: a maximum of eight hours, which may be extended to 72 hours, or a maximum of 24 hours. In some cases, different periods of time are established depending on the age of the patient.

Records: In general, although there are some exceptions, it is necessary to record the following: the reason for the measure ("medical instructions book"), observations during implementation (progress sheets) and when the measure is discontinued. In a few cases, a specific record for the use of coercive measures is mentioned. However, frequent reference is made to immobilization forms. Other protocols explicitly mention the medical records.

Legal and ethical aspects
Only certain protocols contain provisions concerning the advisability of seeking the consent of the patient himself in order to adopt this measure.
Not all the protocols refer to the information that must be given to the patient. Some indicate that such information is to be given in advance (inform him of the reasons for the measure), others during implementation (explain to the patient the temporary nature of the measure and the care he will receive while it is in effect) and when it has ended (justification of the measure). In a few specific cases, reference is made to the need to inform the patient's family. Also some protocols refer to the need to inform the other patients who are witnesses to the manoeuvres of the reasons why the patient is being immobilized, so that they may appreciate that the measure was necessary.
Only rarely does a protocol refer to the need to inform the courts of the use of coercive measures.
There is an abundance of references to respect for the patient and his dignity.

### 12.4.2 Identification and Description of the Contents of any Internal Rules in Relation to National Hospitals

A few Autonomous Communities do have this type of administrative rule, which is inferior to an act of Parliament, on this matter (Autonomous Community of Andalusia passed Resolution 261/2002, 26 December, of the Managing Director of the Andalusian Health Service laying down rules on the procedures for transfer and involuntary admission in the health care network in this region), but it is not common.

## 12.5 Reports

### 12.5.1 National Organs

The Ombudsman[7] presents annual reports to Parliament which always contain a section dedicated to mental health care. Almost every year, some deficiency in the mental health care services is pointed out, especially in relation to the shortcomings of the facilities (state of the institutions), staff shortages, scarcity of therapeutic activities and excessive duration of confinement.
The *Monographic report "Health care and legal situation of mental patients in Spain"* in (Defensor del Pueblo 1991) was particularly important and dedicated exclusively to this matter. This detailed report prepared by the Ombudsman's office, despite focusing on the health care of mental patients, makes very little reference to the use of coercive measures other than confinement.

---

7 This figure was created by s.54 of the Constitution and is governed by Act 3/1981, 6 April. Each Autonomous Community has its own analogous figure.

*Confinement* is dealt with in paragraph 7 ("confinement and intervention of the legal authorities", pp. 517-656), chapter 8 ("Conclusions", pp. 657-662) and chapter 9 ("Recommendations", pp. 677-683). The report states that it is necessary to put civil and criminal confinements on the same level so as to guarantee the rights of the persons involved (p. 527). It emphasizes the need to review concepts such as "dangerous" and to relegate the use of confinement to clearly exceptional circumstances (p.528). The report basically focuses on an analysis of the civil legislation in force at the time: s.211 of the CC for civil confinement and s. 8.1 of the old PC for criminal confinement. Regarding the former, the report recommends a complete reform of the legislation, the creation of special courts, coordination between the different bodies in order to facilitate transfers, intervention of the prosecution service in matters of retirement on health grounds, organization of the wardship system by the health care authorities, and generalization of periodical visits to the centres. The report is also in favour of the judge personally examining the person involved before deciding whether emergency involuntary confinement is necessary, as well as recommending the revision of all confinements that took place before Act 13/1983 came into force. With regard to criminal confinements, the report favours a significant reform of the legislation to limit confinement both for objective reasons and in terms of its duration. The report also recommends limiting confinement during committal proceedings, and not allowing confinement when there is an order to discontinue the proceedings or when there is no case order.

Regarding the measure of *isolation*, the 1991 report makes specific recommendations in relation to certain establishments:

Amenities of the isolation rooms. It criticizes the use of rooms without natural light and ventilation (p. 276), and the use of rooms with inadequate windows (p. 454); in another case, it criticizes the general state of an isolation room (p. 695).

Sufficient furniture. The report criticizes some rooms with very little furniture and the fact that a patient had been kept in one such room with only a simple metal recipient serving as a toilet for about a year. The patient had only been allowed to leave the room to eat, bath and shave, and when his relatives visited him (p. 411).

Situations of unjustified isolation or isolation of doubtful justification. The report criticizes the fact that four patients were kept in a locked room; the justification being that it was a temporary measure (p. 412). More interesting is the case of a person kept in a locked room situated outside the nursing unit as such, who "continually tried to lift the latch and get out of the room". When the door was opened, it was seen that the room was used to store a number of articles in cardboard boxes. The management of the centre ordered the boxes to be removed and the report indicates that "patients' rooms must not be used as store rooms". The justification for isolating the patient in question was that it was a temporary measure "together with the fact that the patient was conflictive and had that very afternoon left the hospital to go for a walk" (p. 412).

Regarding *immobilization* measures, the report describes some situations such as the following:

- Patient in a locked single room with one leg tied to the bed. "According to the nursing staff in the centre this measure was only used at night due to the patient's aggressiveness" (Psychiatric Hospital of Palma de Mallorca (p. 410). In this case, the report recommends that the patient's condition be reviewed "in order to determine possible alternative clinical treatment, which, in any case, should be started by the doctor responsible for the patient or the doctor on duty" (p. 735).
- Two patients kept in the psycho-geriatric ward "who were immobilized by means of strait jackets. The justification given by the staff was that they were likely to harm themselves and so it was necessary to prevent them causing self-inflicted wounds" (San Rafael Psychiatric Hospital of Castro de Riberas de Lea) (pp. 410-411).
- The use of mechanical means to restrain patients was found "more often than was desirable" and justified by "shortage of staff". This measure "could be avoided if there were more staff, thereby enabling sufficient control to be exerted by other less coercive means" (Román Alberca Hospital, Murcia) (p. 411).

There is no mention of forced medication, although mention is made to electroconvulsive therapy, which in one specific case is used occasionally and always therapeutically, although without anaesthesia. To apply this therapy "consent of the patient himself or, where appropriate, of his nearest relative is usually obtained" (p. 410).

### 12.5.2 International Organizations

The European Committee for the Prevention of Torture and Inhuman or Degrading Treatment or Punishment (hereinafter CPT), created under the European Convention of the same name on November 26, 1987 has carried out two visits to Spanish psychiatric centres that are or particular interest:

The visit from April 10 to 22, 1994 was made to the Psychiatric Hospital of Santa Coloma de Gramanet, and resulted in the following recommendations: a) A detailed medical policy should be drawn up on the use of coercive measures, particularly in psychiatry. The situations in which such measures are to be used, their duration and frequency of revisions should be specified. In addition, the patient should be given adequate human contact while such measures are in force, as well as greater medical attention. b) The instruments of coercion should only be applied when expressly indicated by a doctor or, where appropriate, when the doctor intervenes to ratify application of the measure. c) Whenever

coercive measures are used, this should be reflected in the medical records of the patient and in an *ad hoc* record, indicating when the measure is implemented and discontinued, the circumstances of each particular case and reasons for resorting to such a measure.
The second visit, from November 22 to December 4, 1998, was made to the Psychiatric Hospital of San Juan de Dios (Ciempozuelos, Madrid). No evidence was found during the visit of incorrect use of medication or cases of overmedication. Concerning coercive measures, the CPT stated that these were used in accordance with the recommendations of this body, following guidelines known as "Protocolised Action in Immobilization". Only one case was found of a room used for immobilization that was very small and contained only a chair fixed to the floor to which agitated patients were tied. The CPT recommended that this room should no longer be used.

In 2004, the CPT has visited another psychiatric establishment, the Prison Psychiatric Hospital in Alicante, but to date there is no information available regarding the contents of the report.

### 12.5.3 Non-Governmental Organizations

There are no reports from these organizations.

## 12.6 Safeguard System

### 12.6.1 Safeguard Procedures

#### Special Habeas Corpus procedure

This procedure is envisaged in the Constitution (s. 17(4)) and governed by Act 6/1984, 24 May. Its purpose is to *"ensure that a person detained illegally is brought before a competent court immediately"*. An unlawfully detained person is understood to be a person detained by authorities or their agents when the necessary legal circumstances do not exist, a person detained in any establishment or place for longer than the maximum period laid down by law without being brought before a court and a person in custody whose rights guaranteed by the Constitution and other laws are not respected (s. 1 Act 6/1984).
The proceedings may be initiated by the person deprived of his freedom, the prosecution service, or the Ombudsman, and the examining justice hears the case. The intervention of a lawyer is not necessary. When the *habeas corpus* petition is presented in the place where the person has been deprived of his freedom, staff at the centre shall notify the judicial authority immediately. The procedure usually takes between 12 and 48 hours.

**Ordinary criminal proceedings**
The criminal courts deal with proceedings for offences or misdemeanours committed during or as a result of confinement or the use of any type of coercive measure (Criminal Procedure Rules).
The proceedings may be initiated by the person deprived of his freedom, his legal representative or the prosecution service. The examining justices are competent to investigate the case, while the criminal courts of first instance, or in a particularly serious case, the provincial courts, are competent to hear the case. The intervention of a barrister and a solicitor is necessary, and legal aid may be granted when the patient's income does not exceed twice the minimum wage (minimum wage in 2003 is 451.20 Euros/month).

**Safeguards in Civil jurisdiction**
Confinement proceedings envisaged in r. 763 of the CPR. The safeguard includes: authorization of the courts for admission in the case of involuntary confinement, examination of the patient by the judge, periodical review (at least every 6 months) of the state of the patient based on the doctors' obligatory reports, and the decision to bring confinement to an end (although doctors may discharge patients themselves, provided they notify the courts).

**Safeguards in contentious-administrative jurisdiction**
In the case of public establishments, it is theoretically possible to resort to two safeguard procedures (although in practice they are not used), both governed by Act 29/1998, 13 July, regulating contentious-administrative jurisdiction (hereinafter CAJA): a) Ordinary contentious-administrative appeals against the action of public bodies (s. 1(1) of the CAJA) including refusal of claims for damages attributable to them (s. 2(e) of the CAJA in relation to ss. 139-144 of Act 30/1992, 26 December, regulating the legal system for the civil service and ordinary administrative procedure) b) Contentious-administrative appeal against infringement of fundamental rights (s. 2(a) in relation to ss. 114-122 of the CAJA). It is the "ordinary appeal" envisaged in s. 53(2) of the SC that guarantees summary, preferential, special proceedings.
Both require the intervention of a barrister and solicitor, and legal aid is available if the patient has a low income. An ordinary appeal usually takes one to two years; whereas an appeal against the infringement of fundamental rights takes just a few weeks or months. The competent courts are usually the Contentious-Administrative Divisions of the High Courts of Justice.

## 12.2 Authorities

### Prosecution Service[8]

The Prosecution Service Statute (Act 30/1981, 30 December) (hereinafter PSS) provides:

> *"In order to fulfil the missions laid down in s. 1, the prosecution service is responsible for: (7) Taking on or, where appropriate, arranging the defence and legal representation, both during the trial and outside of court, of those who, since they lack the capacity to act or to represent themselves legally, cannot defend themselves, as well as to promote the creation of wardship bodies, laid down by civil law, and to form part of other bodies whose purpose is the protection and defence of minors and the mentally handicapped"*

(s.3). Moreover, in the fulfilment of its functions, it is recognized to have the power to

> *"visit at any moment the centres or detainment establishments, whether penitentiary or of any other type of confinement in the region within its jurisdiction, to examine the records of the inmates and gather as much information as it considers necessary"*

(s. 4(2) of the PSS).

The Attorney General, the head of the prosecution service (s. 124(2) of the SC)

> *"is responsible for giving the orders and instructions he considers appropriate to the prosecution service, for the internal organization of the institution and, in general, for the management and inspection of the prosecution service"*

(s.22(2) of the PSS). Concerning psychiatric confinement, he issued Instruction 6/1987, 23 November on inspection by the prosecution service of psychiatric confinement, ordering that 1) the previous Circular 2/1984 should be implemented, 2) Confinement shall be reviewed at least every six months, 3) Periodical visits shall be made to public and private establishments to review the records in order to avoid the possibility of people being wrongly confined, and 4) Individual records shall be created in order to effect a special follow-up so as to prevent people who may be reintegrated in society from remaining in the establishments.

### Court of first instance (criminal)

- It is empowered to process Habeas Corpus petitions (s. 2 of Act 6/1984) and to initiate investigations into either information laid before it or private criminal charges brought as a result of allegedly criminal acts committed involving the illegal treatment or detention of confined persons (rr.159 and 272 of the CrPR).

---

8 In addition to fulfilling the functions of public prosecution in criminal proceedings, the prosecution service is also responsible for protecting certain groups, as explained below .

**Court of first instance (Civil)**

- Authorizes/ratifies emergency/ordinary involuntary confinement (r.763.1 of the CPR)
- Examines the person admitted, receives the periodical medical reports and declares the end of confinement (r.763.3 and 4 of the CPR).

**Ombudsman and analogous autonomous figures**

- High Commissioner of Parliament for the defence of fundamental rights. He supervises the activity of the Administration and reports to Parliament (s.54 of the SC). Governed by Act 3/1981, 6 April.
- There are analogous bodies in all the Autonomous Communities, and their actions are limited to their own particular territory.
- The relationship between the Ombudsman and similar figures in the Autonomous Communities is governed by Act 36/1985, 6 November.

**Health authorities**

Complaints may be made, as well as requests for compensation for financial liability, to the Departments of Health of the Autonomous Communities, since practically all health care competencies have been transferred to them.

## 12.7 Other Information

In the search for jurisprudential and legislative information, we used the usual databases, mainly "El Derecho", which is used in all courts in Spain, together with the complementary database on legislation and case law called "Aranzadi". As far as legislation is concerned, we took into consideration all enactments on the subject from 1885 (first administrative regulation of psychiatric confinement in Spain) to date. For case law, we carried out searches in the period 1978 to 2003.

The information concerning the Ombudsman was obtained from official publications of this institution, most of which are also available on its web page (www.defensordelpueblo.es).

Information on the CPT was obtained from this Committee's web page (www.cpt.coe.int/en/).

The information on protocols was obtained by asking all the Autonomous Communities to send us copies of the models implemented in their hospitals. Only the ones mentioned in the foot note on section 12.4.1 responded.

## References

Aznar M (2000) Internamientos civiles y derechos fundamentales de los usuarios de centros sanitarios, sociales y sociosanitarios, Granada

Barrios LF (2000) Un siglo de psiquiatría penitenciaria. Revista Sanidad Penitenciaria 1: 23-30

Barrios LF (2002) Policía y urgencia psiquiátrica. I. La intervención policial en la urgencia psiquiátrica. Servicios de la Policía Municipal 46: 12-17

Barrios LF (2003a) Coerción en psiquiatría. Anales de Psiquiatría 2 (19): 55-63

Barrios LF (2003b) La Psiquiatría Penitenciaria: perspectiva histórica y problemas presentes. Newsletter Sociedad Española de Psiquiatría Legal, Feb. URL: www.psiquiatrialegal.org

Barrios LF (2003c) Uso de medios coercitivos en Psiquiatría: retrospectiva y propuesta de regulación. Derecho y Salud 11 (2): 141-163.

Barrios LF, Barcia D (2005) El marco jurídico de las urgencias psiquiátricas. You & Us, Madrid

Bercovitz R (1976) La marginación de los locos y el Derecho. Taurus, Madrid

Bercovitz R (1986) Comentario al artículo 211 CC. In: Comentarios a las reformas de nacionalidad y tutela. Tecnos, Madrid

Bercovitz R (1989) El examen por el Juez del presunto incapaz en el procedimiento de incapacitación. Revista Poder Judicial 15: 141ss

Chamorro A, Clusa D (1995) Intervención policial en los ingresos psiquiátricos: algunas reflexiones. Psiquis 16 (4): 27-33

Chimeno M (2001) El internamiento psiquiátrico forzoso en Cataluña: análisis del art. 255 del Código de familia y la ley 1/2000 de enjuiciamiento civil 100 (2): 321-343.

Cobreros E (1981) Aspectos jurídicos del internamiento de los enfermos mentales. Revista de Administración Pública 94: 135-172

Cobreros E (1988) Los tratamientos sanitarios obligatorios y el derecho a la salud (Estudio sistemático de los ordenamientos italiano y español). Oñati: HAAE/IVAP.

Defensor del Pueblo. Situación jurídica y asistencial del enfermo mental en España. Informes, Estudios y Documentos. Madrid, 1991

Delgado S, Rodríguez F, González JL (1994) Aspectos médico-legales de los internamientos psiquiátricos. In: Delgado S (ed.) Psiquiatría Legal y Forense Colex (II), Madrid: pp 635ss

Dolz MJ (1992) El internamiento psiquiátrico civil en España. Justicia, 881-909

Ferreirós CE (2001) Enfermedad y deficiencia mental: aspectos legales no vinculados al patrimonio. Alicante: Caja de Ahorros del Mediterráneo, 2001

García L (2000) Marco jurídico de la enfermedad mental. Incapacitación e internamiento. Valencia: Revista General de Derecho

Garcia-Ripoll M (1992) La protección jurídica del enfermo mental no incapacitado. Bosch, Barcelona

Gómez P (1997) Los tratamientos médicos: su responsabilidad penal y civil. Bosch, Barcelona

Lacaba F (1993) Internamiento de incapaces: problemática del artículo 211 del Código Civil. La Ley 4: 1012-1017

Marín JJ (1999) Los locos y su libertad. El artículo 211 del Código Civil (Sobre la Sentencia del Tribunal Constitucional 129/1999, de 1 de julio), Derecho Privado y Constitución 13: 183-234.

Mena JM (1985) Sobre la inconstitucionalidad del internamiento psiquiátrico. In Estudios Jurídicos en honor del Profesor Octavio Pérez Vitoria Bosch, Barcelona: pp 469-499

Ramos E (1988) El internamiento de incapaces presuntos. Revista General de Legislación y Jurisprudencia 3: 479-540

Ramos E (2001) Los procesos sobre capacidad y estado en la nueva LEC. Actualidad Civil I-10: 339-388

Ramos JA (1999) Contención mecánica. Restricción de movimientos y aislamiento. Masson, Barcelona

Ribera EA (1991) Algunas cuestiones sobre el internamiento de enfermos mentales. Revista Jurídica de Cataluña 1: 171-182

Roca J (1991) Comentario al artículo 211 CC. In Comentario del Código Civil. I. Ministerio de Justicia, Madrid

Sancho I (2000) Incapacitación y tutela (Conforme a la Ley 1/2000 de Enjuiciamiento Civil). Tirant lo Blanch, Valencia

Santos MJ (2002) El supuesto de hecho del internamiento involuntario en el artículo 763 LEC 1/2000. Tirant lo Blanch, Valencia

**Diagram 12.1: General Regulation for the Process of Involuntary Confinement**

MENTAL DISORDER
(Person is not in a condition to decide for himself regarding confinement, r.763.1 of the CPR)

↙ ↘

*Potential intervention of the police*
(ss.5(2)(b) and (c). and s.11(1)(b) of the National Security Forces Act (NSFA))

↓ ↓

*Ordinary confinement*
Petition for authorization of the courts
(r.763.1 (I) of the CPR)

*Emergency confinement*
Admission by medical indication
↓ 24hours
*Court notified of admission*
(r.763.1 (2) of the CPR)

↘ ↙

*Actions (r. 763.3 of the CPR)*
- Court hearing of patient
- Hearing of the public prosecutor
- Court examination of the patient
- Medical opinion
- Other pertinent actions

↙ ↘ 72 hours

*Authorization of the courts*
(Court where patient resides,r.763.1 (III) of the CPR)
Possibility of appeal ↵
(s. 763(3)(II) of the CPA)
↓
*Potential intervention of the police*
(s.5(2)(b) and (c), and s.11(1)(b) of the NSFA)

*Ratification of the courts*
(Court where establishment is located, r. 763.1 (1) of the CPR)
↳ Possibility of appeal
(r.763.3(2) of the CPR)

↘ ↙

*Periodical medical reports*
(At least every six months or more often if the court deems necessary, r. 763.4 of the CPR)

↓

*END OF CONFINEMENT*

↙ ↘

*Decision of the courts*
(r.763.4 (3) of the CPR)

*Decision of the doctors (Discharge)*
(r.763.4 (4) of the CPR)
↓
*Court is notified*
(r.763.4(4) of the CPR)

### Diagram 12.2: Flowchart of an Involuntary Admission Process

***Process 1***
**Involuntary ordinary admission**

*Mental disorder*
↓
*Request for judicial consent*
↓
*Hearing:*
Statement by the patient
Statement by the public prosecutor
Judicial examination of the patient
Medical report
Other advisory statements
↓
*Consent* (appeal is possible)
↓
Periodic medical reports
(at least every six months)
↓
*Medical/Judicial decision to discharge*

### Diagram 12.3: Flowchart of an Involuntary Admission Process

***Process 2***
**Urgent involuntary admission**

*Hospital admission (24 hours max.)*
↓
*Submit the information about the admission to the judicial authority*
(by the hospital administrator)
↓
*Hearing*
Statement by the patient
Statement by the public prosecutor
Judicial examination of the patient
Medical report
Other advisory hearings
(72 hours max.)
↓
*Ratification/Rejection of the measure*
(appeal is possible)
↓
*Periodic medical reports*
(at least every six months)
↓
*Medical/Judicial decision to discharge*

# CHAPTER 13

# Legal Report – Sweden

Gustav SVENSSON, Lars KJELLIN

## 13.1 Preliminary Remarks

### 13.1.1 Some Historical Notes[1]

Legal rules about mentally ill persons have existed in Sweden since the middle ages. Characteristic of these rules was that they expressed the opinion that society had the right to take charge of people who were mentally ill. If the sick person could not stay at home, he or she was placed in an asylum[2]. The hospitals, originally built for the care of persons suffering from leprosy, were often situated in isolation outside the big cities. The purpose of the isolation was to protect the surrounding society from these persons. Beginning in the 19$^{th}$ century the isolation was also intended for the individual's own interest. Through isolation, the patient's sense of order and industry was stimulated, which was considered an important part of the care of the sick person.

At the end of the 19th century, a discussion started about the legal security of the mentally ill patient. In 1913 a committee was appointed with the task of examining the current legislation. The examination resulted in the *sinnessjuklag* of 1929 ("Act on mentally ill persons"). With this act, the old asylums disappeared and were replaced by *mental hospitals*. The act declared that admission to a mental hospital should be based on whether the individual had a need for care in such a hospital. The individual himself could request admission. But even if admission occurred on a voluntary basis, the patient ran the risk of being detained by force. This right of detention of voluntarily admitted patients was not abolished until 1959.[3]

The *sinnessjuklag* was replaced in 1967 by *lagen (1966:293) om beredande av sluten psykiatrisk vård i vissa fall, LSPV* ("Compulsory Mental Care (Certain Cases) Act"). With LSPV the legal security of the patients was improved further. A central criterion for compulsory care was that the individual should be suffering from a *mental illness*. In 1982 Sweden passed a general *hälso- och*

---

1 The information about the legal development in Sweden is mainly taken from L Grönvall/L Holgersson, *Psykiatrin, tvånget och lagen*, Norstedts Juridik, Stockholm 2001.

2 The Swedish name of these asylums was "*hospital*", but this had a somewhat different meaning than the English word hospital.

3 In 1983 another new possibility was introduced for detaining a voluntarily admitted patient by force – *konvertering* ("conversion") – see more about this concept in section 13.2.2.1 of this report.

*sjukvårdslag* ("Act on Health and Medical Care"). In that act it is emphasized that the basis of all medical care is voluntariness and consent. *Socialberedningen* (a governmental committee), which was appointed in 1980, did, however, notice that the use of the concept, "mental illness", within psychiatry implied that compulsory care was regarded as quite normal. *Socialberedningen* objected to this and chose to use the term "mental disturbance" instead of mental illness. Through the use of "mental disturbance", it was indicated that the reduction of psychic ability could have a quite complex explanation (not just a medical one) and last only for a limited time, rather than permanently as implied by the concept, "mental illness".

The work of the *Socialberedningen* resulted in *lagen (1991:1128) om psykiatrisk tvångsvård, LPT*, ("Act on Compulsory Mental Care"), which came into force in 1992. According to LPT the most important criterion for compulsory care is that the patient is suffering from a *serious mental disturbance*. Compulsory care must only be given to relieve acute needs of care. (More about the criteria in section 13.2.2.1 of this report). LPT underwent quite great changes in the year 2000. The objective of these changes was to strengthen the patient's legal security with respect to care measures during ongoing compulsory care.

LPT is aimed at persons who will receive involuntary psychiatric care only because they have a *need* for psychiatric care which cannot be met voluntarily. For persons who have committed a crime, and besides that have a need for psychiatric care, there is a special legal regulation. These persons can be *sentenced by a court* to the criminal sanction *forensic mental care*. The forensic mental care is carried out according to the provisions in *lagen (1991:1129) om rättspsykiatrisk vård, LRV*, ("Act on Forensic Mental Care"). LRV is built in the same way as LPT and its content is similar to that of LPT.

### 13.1.2 Upcoming Changes

No major changes to LPT are planned for the moment, but the National psychiatry coordinator, appointed by the government, is expected to propose some alterations in the near future The provisions on sanctions for criminals with a mental disturbance will possibly be reformed in the future.[4] As already outlined, such a person, at present, will be *sentenced* to forensic mental care and not to jail. The new provisions will, if they come into force, imply that the criminal person in such a situation should be sentenced to jail (and not to care), but receive the necessary mental care during imprisonment.

4 See the report SOU 2002:3, *Rättspsykiatrisk vård* ("Forensic Mental Care").

### 13.1.3 Survey Methodology

This report is based on the present legislation in Sweden on compulsory mental care and on the preparatory works of the legislation. There is also an account of the jurisprudence of *Regeringsrätten, RR,* ("the Supreme Administrative Court") in Sweden and of reports (governmental and international) on the Swedish legislation referring to compulsory psychiatric care.

The decisions of RR are published in *Regeringsrättens årsbok, RÅ*, ("the yearbook of the Supreme Administrative Court"). The decisions can also be found in the data-base *"Rättsbanken"*. The newer preparatory works can be found at the web-site of the Swedish government.[5] For both the jurisprudence and the reports, the search covered the period of the last twenty years.

Local instructions on compulsory mental care have been gathered from the six psychiatric clinics in the county of Örebro. We have also searched for investigations of this issue carried out by non-governmental organizations representing the patients and their relatives. However, no such investigation was found.

## 13.2 Applicable Laws and General Norms

### 13.2.1 Constitutional Norms

General norms

Norms with relevance to the use of coercion in Swedish mental health care are found in *the second chapter of the Swedish Constitution*, which has been in force since 1975. This chapter is called "The catalogue of rights", because this chapter comprises the provisions for the rights of the citizens in relation to the society.

*Section 8 of the second chapter* of the Constitution says that every citizen in relation to the society is protected against deprivation of liberty. Deprivation of liberty means that the individual's freedom to move is limited. The scope of the limitation can vary. The most far-reaching is defined as arresting the individual and locking him up in a confined space. A prohibition on leaving the country or a part of the country can also be seen as a deprivation of the person's liberty, though not as far-reaching as being arrested.

However, the protection against deprivation of liberty is not absolute. According to *the first paragraph of section 12 of the second chapter* of the Constitution, the freedom to move can be restricted by law. Such a restriction may, as stated in *the second paragraph of the same section*, be employed only to provide for purposes that are acceptable in a democratic society. The limitation is never allowed to exceed what is necessary to fulfil its purpose, nor may it be employed due to political, religious, cultural or other such views.

The provisions in section 12 of the second chapter of the Constitution are the constitutional grounds for the criminal law with its regulations for punishments

---

5 www.regeringen.se/propositioner/index

which imply deprivation of a person's liberty. However, these provisions are also the constitutional grounds for acts that allow deprivation of liberty, for example, for reason that the individual abuses alcohol or drugs, or is the bearer of an illness dangerous to the public. Provisions for deprivation of liberty due to psychiatric illness belong to the last category of constitutional grounds. The Swedish act on this, LPT, we shall describe in detail in section 13.2.2.1 of this report.

Deprivation of liberty as a punishment due to a criminal act is always a decision taken by a court, even if at the base level of the court system. Deprivation of liberty due to e.g. abuse of alcohol or psychiatric illness is, however, sometimes (but not always) a decision taken by an authority other than a court (e.g. a board to which laymen are appointed, or by a physician). *Section 9 of the second chapter* of the Constitution says that a citizen in these cases is entitled to have his case examined by a court without any delay. This provision is fulfilled by the fact that the first decision, made by a board of laymen or a physician, can be taken to court.

Specific norms

Another constitutional provision of importance for the question of compulsory psychiatric care is *section 6 of the second chapter of the Constitution.* This provision says that every citizen in relation to the society is protected against "a forced corporal interference". The "forced corporal interference" includes not only surgical operations but also milder interference like medication, blood samples and vaccination. Furthermore, an examination of the patient's body carried out by a physician is regarded as a "corporal interference". There have been divided opinions about the question as to whether a *psychiatric examination* shall also be considered a "corporal interference". Most arguments lean in favour of this position. The aim of section 6 is to provide protection for personal integrity. From this perspective, a psychiatric examination is as infringing as taking a blood sample, for example.

Another question that has risen in interpreting section 6 is what is meant by the word "forced". That an action is forced if threat of violence is used is clear. However, it is more uncertain whether or not the concept "forced" also assumes that the action is taken against a person's expressed will, i.e. that an action is forced only if a person's resistance has to be overcome. The question has arisen in the case of medicine mixed in a drink without the patient's knowledge. Most arguments lean in the direction that this form of medication is also forced.

Foreigners staying in Sweden are, regarding the protection from corporal interference and deprivation of liberty, equal to Swedish citizens barring circumstances that comply with special provisions in an act of law. This means that it is possible to deprive foreigners of their freedom on grounds other than those relevant to Swedish citizens provided that those different grounds are mentioned in an act of law.

### 13.2.2 General Laws

In this part of the report, an account shall be presented of the provisions that are of importance for persons who will be subjected to compulsory psychiatric care. The account will mainly deal with situations where care is provided because of the patient's need for care. The legal situation when a mentally disturbed criminal is sentenced to psychiatric care – Forensic Mental Care – will only be outlined in a more general survey.

#### 13.2.2.1 Compulsory Mental Care due to the Patient's Need of Care (Only)

In Sweden, it is a principle that involuntary psychiatric care may be given only if it is grounded in an act of law. As mentioned above, the *Compulsory Mental Care Act,(1991:1128), LPT*, is this legal ground. In the following paragraphs there will be an overview of the most important content of LPT.

a) Preconditions for compulsory care

Perhaps the most important provisions in LPT are those that state the preconditions under which involuntary psychiatric care may be given. The provisions for this are found in *section 3*, which has the following wording:

> *"Compulsory care may only be given if*
> *1. the patient is suffering from a serious mental disturbance,*
> *2. the patient, on account of his mental state and his general personal circumstances, has an absolute need of mental care which cannot be provided other than by admitting the patient to a medical institution for comprehensive care available 24 hours per day, and*
> *3. the patient objects to such care as defined in paragraph 2, or, due to the patient's state of mind, there is grounded reason to assume that the care can not be given with his consent.*
> *Compulsory care may not be given if the patient's mental disturbance, as outlined in subsection one, paragraph 1, only constitutes a mental developmental disturbance.*
> *When the care need, as outlined in subsection one, paragraph 2, is assessed, it shall also be considered if the patient, due to his mental disturbance, is dangerous to the personal security or physical or mental health of others."*

Thus, according to section 3, there are principally three preconditions for compulsory mental care. In the following paragraphs, some comments will be given on each of these preconditions.

*(1) The patient is suffering from a serious mental disturbance*

*"Serious mental disturbance"* is a new concept introduced with LPT. In the old act, LSPV, the corresponding criterion was "psychiatric illness", and "psychiatric abnormalities on a par with psychiatric illness". The aim of LPT is to estab-

lish that the need for mental care and not a specific state of illness should determine if compulsory care shall be given or not. The concept "serious mental disturbance" shall therefore refer to medical, psychological and social factors, though the medical state of illness is still of great importance. According to the regulations presented in section 13.2.4.2, serious mental disturbances include psychosis (i.e. a state of mind with a disturbed vision of reality), depression with risk of suicide, severe personality disorder with an impulsive breakthrough of psychotic character or severe psychological disturbances with strong obsessive – compulsive behaviour. Also kleptomania, pyromania and sexual perversions can sometimes be seen as serious mental disturbances. The seriousness of a mental disturbance may be judged both by nature and extent. By nature is meant the type of illness, and extent refers to the psychosocial level of functionality and severity of symptoms.

*(2) The patient has an absolute need for qualified psychiatric all-day care*
This precondition means that the patient's life or health will be in danger if the care is not given. The assessment of the need of care shall not only consider the state of mental disturbance but also the patient's living conditions and his relationship to his surroundings. The need must be absolute for the immediate present and need not be long-term. Further, there must be a need for psychiatric care 24 hours per day. This means that a careful investigation must be made of the alternatives. If outpatient psychiatric care would be successful, a good cooperation with the local welfare committee must generally exist.
In principle, only the patient's need for mental care shall be decisive if the question of compulsory care is discussed. Some considerations for people in the surroundings shall however be made. Section 3 of LPT says that in the decision about the need of psychiatric care, it shall also be taken into account if the patient, due to his mental disturbance, is dangerous to other people's life or physical or mental health.

*(3) The patient objects to such care or there is a grounded reason to assume that the care can not be given with his consent.*
The main rule is that compulsory psychiatric care may be given only if the patient objects to the care that is needed. If the patient consents to the necessary care, the care will be given voluntarily. However, sometimes it occurs that the patient consents to the proposed care only to avoid compulsory care. In these cases the care might not take place because the patient refuses to coopcrate. If there is precedent in the patient's case history for this, it's possible to disregard the given consent and nonetheless decide about compulsory care.

The three preconditions commented above are applicable even for *adolescents*. The precondition which in those cases causes the most problems is the third one. The main principle is that it is the adolescent's opinion on the care that shall be asked for. In other words, mental care can never be given to an adolescent only because his or her guardian has consented. Of course there must be a lowest age under which the child lacks the right to determine. However, it is impossible to define this "border" clearly as a general rule, and therefore it must be defined in each specific case. However, in practice there are cases where the care institutions have allowed children as young as eleven to twelve years old to exercise their right of self-determination. Many arguments speak in favour of this, because this position reflects respect for the autonomy of the child.

b) The proceeding
Compulsory psychiatric care can occur in several ways. In general four proceedings can be differentiated.

*(1) Compulsory psychiatric care after decision of physicians*
The most common way to be admitted is a proceeding in which the crucial decisions are taken by physicians. This proceeding is started by a physician who, when examining a patient and finding that the preconditions of compulsory care are likely to be fulfilled, issues a *vårdintyg* ("care certificate"). When the *vårdintyg* is issued, the patient should immediately be transported to the care institution; there, the question of admission for compulsory care shall be settled. The question of admission shall be settled by a psychiatrist quickly after the patient has been examined and not more than *24 hours* after the patient's arrival to the care institution. The *vårdintyg* must *not be older than four days* by that time. The admission order may not be taken by the physician who has issued the *vårdintyg,* which is to be seen as a guarantee for the patient's legal security. This proceeding is in other words a "two-doctor-proceeding".
Normally, coercive measures can not be taken until it has been decided that the person shall be admitted to the care institution. However, if necessary the patient can be detained up to 24 hours at the care institution by support of the *vårdintyg* only. If such a detention decision has been taken, the patient can be subject to an intimate or superficial body search, he or she can be constrained by means of a belt, secluded or, if there is an imminent danger to the patient's life and health, be medicated by force.[6]

*(2) Continued compulsory care after decision by a court*
If the *chefsöverläkare* ("the Deputy Chief Doctor") at the patient's psychiatric

---

6 More about these coercive measures in the paragraph on *"The care measures"*.

care institution finds that compulsory care must be provided for more than four weeks after the day on which the admission order was made, the physician, before the end of this four-weeks-period, shall apply to *länsrätten* ("the county administrative court"), *LR*, for permission for continued care.[7] If LR sanctions this application, the care may proceed for a maximum of up to four months from the day on which the admission order was made. If the care period must be further prolonged, the *chefsöverläkare* shall make another application to the court before the end of the care period. LR may on that occasion consent to another six-month care period, beginning from the day of the court's examination.

*(3) Konvertering, i.e. transfer from voluntary to compulsory care*
With *konvertering* ("conversion") is meant the transfer from voluntary to compulsory care. In Sweden there has been a debate as to whether *konvertering* should be allowed or not. The most important argument against k*onvertering* is that a patient who voluntarily seeks contact with the psychiatric care should not risk being detained against his will.
The institution of *konvertering* was introduced into Swedish law during the time of LSPV. When LPT came into being, it was also decided that this institution should be kept, but the protection for the patient was strengthened. Therefore, *konvertering* can be used in Sweden today only if the preconditions for compulsory care are fulfilled together with another condition, namely that the patient, due to his mental disturbance, might hurt himself or somebody else. Moreover, a *vårdintyg* is nowadays also a requirement in cases of conversion. Within 24 hours from when the *vårdintyg* is issued, the *chefsöverläkare* must make a care decision. This care decision shall be submitted to the LR by the next day at the latest. If the *chefsöverläkare* finds that the care must continue, he or she shall, within four days from the day of the decision on compulsory care, apply to the LR to prolong this care. After that, the care period can be prolonged in the way that is described in paragraph (2) above.

*(4) Transfer from forensic mental care to compulsory care under LPT*
Forensic mental care is given to persons who have committed crimes. However, forensic mental care can also be given to other groups, e.g. persons who not yet have been convicted of the crime, but already arrested. An arrested person shall be released if there are insufficient grounds for the arrest. However, if the arrested person suffers from a serious mental disturbance, the *chefsöverläkare* at the institution where the person is being given care may decide on compulsory

---

[7] The *chefsöverläkare* may entrust this duty to an experienced physician at the caring institution with specialist qualifications in some branch of psychiatry.

care under LPT. A care certificate is not necessary in these cases, but the same time limit as in the case of conversion shall be respected (see (3) above).

c) The care

Compulsory psychiatric care shall be provided in a medical institution run by a county council. By "medical institution" is meant a unit at a hospital. This implies that compulsory psychiatric care in Sweden can never be given in outpatient settings.[8]

*(1) General provisions about the use of coercion*

When LPT was accepted in 1991, the main intention was to reduce the use of coercion within psychiatric care. This is expressed e.g. in *section 2 of LPT* which says that the compulsory care should aim at enabling the patient to take part in voluntary care. Compulsory care decreased during the 1990s in the sense that the number of care episodes went down.[9] However, the use of individual coercive measures increased. The government found this development alarming.[10] To decrease the use of coercive measures, new provisions were introduced in LPT which emphasize that such measures are allowed only in special cases. Thus, *section 2a* says that coercive measures may be used only if they are motivated by the aim of the measure. If a less far-reaching measure is sufficient, that one shall be used. The patient must be informed about the measures, in a manner adjusted to his facility for comprehension, before they are employed, the purpose of which is to convince the patient to take part in voluntary care. The coercion shall also be exercised with as much lenience as possible and with the greatest regard for the patient.

*(2) The care measures*

As soon as the patient is admitted to compulsory care a treatment plan shall be drawn up for him or her. The plan, that as far as possible shall be drawn up in consultation with the patient and his relatives, contains the care measures and other actions that are required to achieve the aim of the compulsory care and to make the results of the care sustainable. The care measures that are allowed to

---

8 Because of some tragic events in Sweden during the autumn of 2003, there has been a discussion about introducing the possibility of implementing some compulsory care measures, e g medication, in the psychiatric outpatient settings as well. However no decisions on that issue have yet been taken.

9 SOU 1998:32, *Rättssäkerhet, vårdbehov och samhällsskydd vid psykiatrisk tvångsvård* ("Legal security, need for care and protection of society in coercive psychiatric care"), p 131 ff.

10 Prop 1999/2000:44, *Psykatrisk tvångsvård och rättspsykiatrisk vård* ("Coercive psychiatric care and forensic mental care"), p 81.

be given by coercion are mentioned in LPT. This enumeration is necessary because no Swedish citizen – and no foreigner visiting Sweden – is allowed to be deprived of his liberty or made to suffer corporal interference without provisions in an act of law legitimizing these procedures.

A natural precondition for effective compulsory care is that it is possible to prevent the patient from leaving the care institution. This right to detain the patient must of course include the option of force. The act also says that coercion may be used to maintain order at the care institution and to guarantee security during the care process.

An important care measure which may be given by force is medication. Surprisingly, LPT does not say under which preconditions it is acceptable to treat with medication by coercion. Demands for specifications on this subject were rejected during the preparatory work of the act, among others by psychiatrists, who claimed that the patient then risked not receiving the best available medical care. LPT now only says that the care measures (including medication) shall be adjusted to what is needed to fulfil the aim of the compulsory care.

A severe measure of coercion is to restrain the patient by means of a belt or similar device. Restraint by a belt may be used only for a short time and only if there is an immediate danger that the patient will hurt himself or someone else. "A short time" is defined as not more than four hours.[11] If there are particular reasons, the patient may be restrained for a longer time. In that case, *Socialstyrelsen* ("the National Board of Health and Welfare"), SoS, should be notified without delay about the decision.

Seclusion must be used only if the patient behaves in such an aggressive or disturbing way that this aggravates the treatment of other patients. A seclusion order is valid for up to eight hours. If the seclusion period must be prolonged for more than these eight hours, the SoS must be notified. During the whole period of seclusion the patient must be kept under continuous supervision by care personnel.

Two more care measures under LPT are intimate and superficial body searches. These measures may be used in order to ensure that the patient is not carrying property that he is not allowed to possess under the law. Such property includes alcoholic beverages, narcotic drugs, steroids, and objects that can hurt himself or someone else at the care institution. Mail addressed to the patient may also be examined. However, the right to read the content of a letter or other written message is not included as part of this examination. Censorship, in other words, is not allowed.

---

[11] Chapter 4 section 5 in the regulations (SOSFS 2000:12 (M)) from SoS on compulsory mental care and forensic mental care, see section 13.2.4.2 of this report.

d) Termination of compulsory care

If the preconditions for compulsory care no longer exist, a decision shall immediately be taken on the termination of the compulsory care. The decision shall be made by the *chefsöverläkare* or, after delegation, by another experienced psychiatrist. The personnel shall always have in mind the issue of terminating the compulsory care. The patient himself can at any time demand the termination of the care. Such a demand can be expressed verbally. If the psychiatrist then decides that the compulsory care shall continue, the patient can appeal against this decision to the LR. If the LR decides that the compulsory care shall be terminated, the *chefsöverläkare* is not allowed to appeal against that decision.

e) The possibilities for the patient to appeal. Provisions for proceedings in a court.

As mentioned earlier, many decisions of great importance to the patient are taken by physicians. To secure a decent degree of legal security, the patient is allowed to appeal against many of those decisions.

Primarily, the patient is always allowed to appeal against every decision related to admission, no matter if it is in the case of a care certificate or some other situation. The patient can also appeal against decisions which have, for example, rejected a demand for termination of care. Other decisions that can be appealed against are, for example, decisions on conditions for permission to leave the care institution. However, decisions on the content of the care can not be appealed against. If the patient considers himself the victim of malpractice, he or she can submit a report to *Hälso- och sjukvårdens ansvarsnämnd* ("the Board of Liability in the Health and Medical Care"), HSAN, or the SoS, which are in charge of the medical care personnel.

Only the patient has the right to appeal, not the relatives. While there may be a contrast between the positions of the patient and his relatives, it has not been considered advisable to give the right to appeal to relatives as well.

Since LPT came into force in 1992 the lengths of the care episodes of compulsory care have decreased. If the possibility to appeal against a decision is to be of any importance to a patient, it is important that the cases are handled rapidly. The LR shall have hearings with the patient present if this is not deemed unnecessary. Out of respect for the patient, the personal conference is held at the institution where the patient receives care. The patient is entitled to a legal representative. In order to broaden the scope of evidence, the LR shall normally hear an expert during the conference. The expert has the right to put questions to the *chefsöverläkare* as well as to the patient.

f) Other provisions

Beyond the provisions mentioned above, LPT contains regulations addressing some specific issues. An important rule is that the patient has the right to be assisted by a *supportive person*. The patient shall be informed about this right. The supportive person shall be appointed if the patient demands this and otherwise, so long as he does not disagree to this. The supportive person shall support the patient in personal matters as long as the patient is receiving compulsory care but also for some time thereafter, if the patient so wishes.

LPT is valid for youngsters as well as adults. A specific provision says that if the young person is more than 15 years old, he has the right to represent himself in judicial and other proceedings under the Act.

Among these other provisions, there are also regulations about the participation of the police authority. If a person suffers from a serious mental disturbance and is dangerous to his own life or the personal security of another person, the police may take him into temporary custody. This measure will last until health service and medical personnel are able to provide him with the help needed. The police shall also in some cases lend assistance at the request of physicians, to enable an examination for a care certificate, for example, or to return a patient who has left the care institution without permission or who has overstayed an authorized leave beyond the perimeter of the institution.

A patient who is being cared for by authority of LPT shall, as soon as possible, through the *chefsöverläkare* be informed of, among other things, his right to appeal against certain decisions and to obtain a legal representative. LPT shall be posted in the care institution, where it shall be clearly visible to the patients.

### 13.2.2.2 Compulsory Mental Care as a Criminal Sanction

Contrary to many legal systems on the European continent, the Swedish law contains no general rule about lack of criminal responsibility for mentally ill persons who have committed criminal actions. Instead, if a person has committed the action intentionally, the person is under penalty of law even if he or she is mentally ill. However, a person who has committed a crime under the influence of a serious mental disturbance must not be sentenced to jail[12]. If the criminal person at the time of the court proceedings is still suffering from a serious mental disturbance, the court shall, under certain conditions, sentence him or her to forensic mental care.[13] The conditions are: (1) the crime is so severe that it is not possible to use only a fine as a criminal sanction, and (2) the mental state and other circumstances of the person are such that it is necessary for him or her to stay in a hospital for mental care.

---

[12] 30 chapter 6 paragraph of the criminal code.

[13] 31 chapter 3 paragraph of the criminal code.

The forensic mental care is carried out according to the *lag* (1991:1129) *om rättspsykia-trisk vård*, LRV, ("Act on Forensic Mental Care"), which is built on and has a content that in great parts corresponds to LPT. If the patient who is subject to forensic mental care is no longer suffering from a serious mental disturbance, the *chefsöverläkare* of the unit which provides care for the patient shall decide that the care shall be terminated. The question whether the forensic mental care shall be terminated or not shall be considered regularly by the *chefsöverläkare*. If the *chefsöverläkare* finds that the forensic mental care must continue for more than four months following the court's decision, the *chefsöverläkare* shall apply to the LR to prolong the care period. The LR can prolong the care period for six months. After that another application must be lodged.
If the criminal has committed the crime under influence of a serious mental disturbance, the court may decide that a *särskild utskrivningsprövning*, SUP, ("special discharge test") shall be applicable to the forensic mental care. One prerequisite is that there is a risk that the criminal, due to his mental disturbance, will relapse into criminality which is serious. In the case of a *Särskild ut skrivningsprövning*, it is the LR and not the *chefsöverläkare* who will examine whether the forensic mental care shall be terminated. But, even if *särskild utskrivningsprövning* is applicable to the care, the *chefsöverläkaren* is obliged at regular intervals to let the LR review the issue of terminating the forensic mental care.

### 13.2.3 International Conventions and Agreements Incorporated into National Laws

Since 1995 the European Convention on Human Rights has been part of the Swedish legislation. Some of the articles in the convention are relevant in this context. *Article 3* says that nobody may be subjected to torture or inhuman or humiliating treatment or punishment. The Convention also guarantees the right to liberty and security. According to *article 5* nobody may be deprived of his liberty except in certain cases according to law. The *first paragraph e)* provides as one such case that somebody may be legally deprived of his freedom because he is mentally ill. In that case, according to article 6, the person shall be entitled to a fair and public trial in front of an independent court, established according to law.

### 13.2.4 Second Level of Juridical Norms

#### 13.2.4.1 The Government's Ordinance on Compulsory Mental Care

If compulsory mental care is to be consistent with the provisions in the Constitution for protection of the citizens against deprivation of liberty and corporal interference, the regulations about this must be given in an act of law. Supplemental provisions about compulsory care are found in *the Government's ordinance (1991:1472) about compulsory mental care (and forensic mental care).* Compared to the act, the provisions in this ordinance deal only with questions of detail. The ordinance says, for example, that the *chefsöverläkare* is responsible for maintaining a list of the patients who are subjected to compulsory psychiatric care. The *chefsöverläkare* is also responsible for ensuring in every patient's medical record, besides information that is mandatory according to *Patientjournallagen* ("the Patient's Medical Record Act") (1985:562), there is also information about matters related to the compulsory care. In the medical record, there shall be kept the *vårdintyg* (or a copy of it), information about the time when the patient arrived at the care institution, the treatment plan, information about coercive measures, confiscation of property or refusal of a demand for permission to leave the care institution. In the Government's ordinance you will also find provisions about an obligation of Swedish authorities, on request of a foreign citizen, to inform the consulate of his native country if he is deprived of his liberty, and about an obligation for SoS, on request of the foreign citizen, to send him home on condition that he will get sufficient care in his native country.

#### 13.2.4.2 Regulations and General Advice on Compulsory Mental Care from the National Board of Health and Welfare (SoS)

SoS is the central authority in Sweden for questions of medical care. SoS has the right to impose regulations for medical care in order to protect individuals and to define obligations for the medical personnel. According to this competence, SoS has imposed *regulations and general advice on compulsory mental care.*[14]

In this decree there are, for example, *binding provisions* that every caregiver shall provide instructions in writing in order to secure that the compulsory care is given in accordance with LPT. There are also regulations for treatment plans. The decree says that the treatment plan shall comprise a concise picture of the medical, psychological and social problems and needs of the patient and that it shall point out the aims of the care measures. Other questions that are also regulated in the decree concern reporting of coercive measures to the SoS, the possibilities of permission to leave the care institution, and the possibilities for the *chefsöverläkare* to delegate decisions about the notification to the SoS.

Beside those provisions there are also in SOSFS 2000:12 some *allmänna råd* ("General advice"). The most important of these have already been mentioned in this report, namely the explanations of what is considered to be a serious mental disturbance.[15]

---

[14] SOSFS 2000:12 (M)

[15] See section 13.2.2.1 of this report.

### 13.3 Jurisprudence

In Sweden, the courts' examination of the compulsory mental care is made by *allmänna förvaltningsdomstolar* ("general administrative courts"). The court of first instance is *länsrätten (LR),* i.e. the county administrative court. There are 23 LR in Sweden. The decision of the LR can be appealed to some of the five *kammarrätter, KR,* i.e. the regional administrative courts. The final court of appeal is *Regeringsrätten,* RR ("the Supreme Administrative Court"). To have his case examined in RR (and in some cases in KR) the applicant must obtain *prövningstillstånd* ("permit of examination"). To get *prövningstillstånd* in RR, the case has to deal with a matter of principle. Therefore, on average only a few cases on compulsory mental care are examined by the RR a year.

#### 13.3.1 Regeringsrätten ("The Supreme Administrative Court")

Since LPT came into force on the January 1, 1992, many of the cases in RR about compulsory mental care have dealt with quite "technical" questions while just a few have been about the central concepts of the act.

*RÅ 1998 n:o 51* is an important decision since it elucidates the meaning of the condition in section 3 first paragraph p. 2 of LPT that the patient shall have an absolute need of psychiatric care. In this case the patient had been under compulsory care for more than three years but, besides the first 2,5 months, had been permitted to stay outside the care institution in his own home. In his home he was given "depot injections" with neuroleptics every second week. The request of the *chefsöverläkare*for prolonging the mental care for another six-month-period was granted by LR and KR. The patient appealed to RR.

RR stated that the patient objected to mental care and that his testimony indicated that he was not willing to go on with his medication. If he did not take his medication, this could lead to a serious deterioration of his health. However, according to medical statements, it was not clear that this would happen within six months, i.e. the maximum length of one care period according to the act. Because of that, RR ruled that the condition of an absolute need of psychiatric care was not fulfilled. Therefore, the appeal of the patient was granted.

Also in *RÅ 1999 n:o 64* one of the basic conditions for compulsory care was examined, namely that compulsory care shall be used only if it's not possible to provide care voluntarily. This condition was, at the time of the verdict, expressed by the formulation that the patient objects to the necessary care "or, on account of his mental state, is manifestly incapable of expressing a properly grounded statement in the matter." RR's verdict was – in line with the preparatory works of the act – that the latter expression should be given a very restrictive interpretation. Since the July 1, 2000, the expression of the condition of informed consent in section 3 of LPT is different; thus, the importance of RÅ 1999 n:o 64 is not as great now as it was then.

As already mentioned, the SoS must be notified of the use of a coercive measure if it has been very far-reaching in the given case. This applies, for example, to cases of restraining a patient by means of a belt for more than four hours. In *RÅ 1998 n:o 14* this happened, but nonetheless, SoS was not notified. The *chefsöverläkare* in charge was considered by RR to have broken a provision of direct importance for safety in the care process, which meant that the *chefsöverläkare* was liable to disciplinary action.
*RÅ 2000 n:o 6* is mainly about the obligation to maintain secrecy. Generally, in medical care the confidentiality of information about the individual's state of health and other personal matters is protected. However, a decision about a measure of deprivation of the patient's liberty according to the LPT is not covered by the obligation to maintain secrecy. In RÅ 2000 n:o 6 a person requested permission to read all decisions from a certain period and in a certain district of a county about persons taken in charge with the support of a *vårdintyg*. RR ruled that the requested decisions were to be seen as decisions about deprivation of liberty and therefore not covered by secrecy.

### 13.3.2 The European Court of Human Rights

If the Swedish legislation is not consistent with the European convention on Human Rights, it's possible to bring a case in front of the European Court of Human Rights in Strasbourg. However, there has been no case in front of this court in which the Swedish legislation on compulsory psychiatric care has been involved.

## 13.4 Protocols and Internal Norms

### 13.4.1 Protocols

The Swedish Psychiatric Association has worked out clinical guidelines for investigation and treatment in different kinds of compulsory care. The guidelines consist of comments in connection with the presentation of the sections in the different compulsory acts. The guidelines are under revision on account of the new regulations in LPT from 2000.

### 13.4.2 Internal Norms

In section 13.2.4.2 of this report, we mentioned that in the decrees and general advice on compulsory mental care from SoS it is stated that every caregiver shall give instructions in writing in order to secure that the compulsory care is given in accordance with LPT.
The content of the *local instructions* is often of two kinds. On one hand there are parts in the instruction which only *repeat the content of central provisions in the Act*: for example, the conditions for compulsory care or conversion or the conditions under which coercive measures can be used.

On the other hand there are provisions which contain *complements to the rules in the Act*. The local instructions can thus contain specifications of the coercive measures which are allowed to be used before the admission order has been established. For example, it is not allowed to give the patient medication in the form of "depot injection" during the first detention period of maximum 24 hours.
In the local instructions for the general psychiatric clinic at the university hospital of Örebro it is stated that a daily examination of the patient's need of care shall be carried out. The need of care is judged by a scale with seven degrees: the most intensive degree requires that someone from the personnel must follow the patient at all times and the lowest degree permits the patient to stay outside the care institution even during the night.
It is common that the local instructions contain *rules of order*. Those rules can be about the possibility for the patient to use a telephone and for friends to visit the patient. In the local instruction at the university hospital of Örebro it is stated that the patients shall have the right to communicate with their social networks and with authorities; therefore, a telephone shall always be available. The patients shall also have the right to use the fax machines of the clinic. Mobile phones on the other hand are not allowed within the hospital, but this rule applies to everyone at the hospital and not exclusively to the psychiatric patients. The patients shall eventually be given opportunity to use e-mail and internet.
The local instructions can also contain *provisions on the rights of the patients*, e.g. the right to a supportive person or the right to use an interpreter. At the psychiatric clinic at the university hospital of Örebro the patients of foreign origin shall have the right to a professional interpreter at crucial discussions about the care and when the patient receives information about his or her rights. The legislation shall be made available in Swedish, English and – if possible – also in the patient's native language.
Of great importance is *the way in which the complaints of the patients are handled*. In the local instructions for the psychiatric clinic of the university hospital of Örebro there is a detailed provision on the ways in which complaints should affect the work at the clinic.
Furthermore, provisions can be found in the local instructions for measures that can be used in order to prevent the patients from leaving the care institutions. In connection with that, the instructions also often define the preconditions for requesting help from the police.

## 13.5 Reports

### 13.5.1 Governmental Reports

The most important governmental reports in Sweden on compulsory mental care are those that were made during the preparatory work on LPT and the changes made to that act later on. Those reports are published in the governmental series *"Statens offentliga utredningar", ("Swedish Government Official Reports"), SOU.*

In 1984 *socialberedningen* (a governmental committee mentioned in the introduction of this report) presented its report *"Psychiatry, coercion and legal security".*[16] In that report there was a proposal for completely new legislation on compulsory mental care. Three new acts were proposed. The new proposal represented in many ways a departure from an older view. Most important was perhaps that the basic precondition for compulsory care no longer would be mental illness, but the more complex concept of "mental disturbance".[17] Compulsory care should normally no longer be used for a long period, but only in case of urgent need of care. The legal security of the patients should be strengthened in that the legal control of the psychiatric care should increase. The legal control should be exercised by the administrative courts.

This proposal served as a basis for the governmental bill 1990/91:58, *"Psykiatrisk tvångsvård*", ("Psychiatric compulsory care"*),* which gave rise to the two acts LPT and the Act on forensic mental care, LRV. Both acts came into force on the January 1, 1992.

In the same year SoS was given the task of evaluating the Acts. The evaluation was to answer the question whether the aim of the reform was fulfilled and whether the intended effects of the acts had resulted. SoS stated two years after the reform that the investigation provided insufficient evidence to evaluate if the aims of the legislation were achieved, and that this was especially the case for the question about the legal security of the patients.[18] The investigation did show that the use of compulsory care had decreased. However, this referred only to the numbers of patients and care occasions as well as to the length of the care episodes. On the contrary, the use of individual coercive measures had increased. The legal security of the patients had improved in some respects. The practise of LPT was however not without problems, and "legal losses" could have happened to patients in instances where *konvertering* had been conducted for vague and erroneous reasons, the keeping of medical records had been faulty and the information from the physician in charge had been incomplete.

In 1995 *tvångspsykiatrikommittén* ("the Committee of Compulsory Mental Care") was appointed the task – once again – of evaluating LPT and LRV. Above all, the committee was to investigate whether the use of compulsory care

16 SOU 1984:64, *Psykiatrin, tvånget och rättssäkerheten* ("Psychiatry, coercion and legal security").

17 Regarding the meaning of this concept, see section 13.2.2.1 of this report.

18 See the report *Psykiatrisk tvångsvård. Effekter av ny lagstiftning. Socialstyrelsen följer upp och uvärderar*, 1994:2 ("Compulsory mental care. Effects of the new legislation. The SoS follows up and evaluates").

and coercive measures had decreased to the intended level and whether the legal security of the patients had been strengthened. In its final report, the conclusion of the committee was that the compulsory care had decreased to the extent that was possible until then, but that a further decrease was desirable.[19] On the other hand, an investigation made by SoS also showed that the use of individual coercive measures had increased, above all the use of forced medication. The legal security had, according to the committee, been strengthened by the new legislation though further improvements could be made. The legal changes proposed by the committee aimed at reducing the use of coercive measures as well as improving legal security for the patients. The proposals were to a great extent accepted by the government and the changes came into force on the July 1, 2000.
The consequences of the changes in LPT and LRV in 2000 have been evaluated by SoS in a report from 2001.[20] The report stated that the compulsory care has continued to decrease in the sense that the care episodes are fewer than before, that the length of the care periods has been reduced and that *konvertering* is used to a lesser extent than before. Also, forced medication was used to a lesser extent in 2001 than in 1996/97, while the use of mechanical restraint remained at the same level as before. Important deficiencies that still existed included that in 30% of the care occasions no treatment plan was made, and that nearly 25% of the patients had not been offered a supportive person at all. SoS found it urgent that each of the *chefsöverläkare* should be sufficiently informed of his obligation to inform patients of their right to a supportive person.
Another report from the SoS contains also a follow-up and an evaluation of the changes to LPT and LRV in 2000.[21] Among other things, an investigation was made of local instructions and routines on measures related to legal security. Local instructions were found at 70% of the examined units. On the other hand, instructions about the use of coercive measures before admission order were missing at the most units. This issue was not regulated in LPT until the year of 2000. The result of the evaluation showed that the individual support for patients who were given compulsory care ought to be revised. This referred also to the decrees and general advice of SoS on the patients' possibility to make phonecalls or to communicate via internet or by other technical means of assistance.
One more task that SoS was given in 2001 was following up on and evaluating the new provisions on leave of absence in LPT and LRV. The evaluation showed that, as far as LPT is concerned, the numbers of leaves of absence had increased and that the leaves were given for longer periods, sometimes one year

---

19 *Rättssäkerhet, vårdbehov och samhällsskydd vid psykiatrisk tvångsvård*, SOU 1998:32 ("Legal security, need of care and protection of society in compulsory mental care")

20 "*Effekter av ändringar i de psykiatriska tvångsvårdslagarna*", SoS 2001.

21 *Psykiatrisk tvångsvård. Resultat av nationell tematisk verksamhetstillsyn (*"Compulsory psychiatric care. Result of a thematic work supervision*")*, Socialstyrelsen 2001.

or more.[22] The physicians had claimed that compulsory care in these cases had been necessary to guarantee a long-term treatment with neuroleptics. SoS on the other hand claimed that this proceeding was not consistent with the intentions behind the provisions. According to SoS, such a patient no longer meets the preconditions for compulsory care as defined in LPT.[23]

### 13.5.2 International Reports

The legislation on compulsory mental care in the 15 EU-member states has been assessed in a recently completed study. The result is accounted in the report *"Compulsory Admission and Involuntary Treatment of Mentally Ill Patients – Legislation and Practice in EU-Member States"*.[24] The report gives a good impression of how the Swedish legislation is related to the legislation in other EU-countries. The report shows, for example, that the Swedish legislation is pronouncedly paternalistic in the sense that the only criterion for application of the Swedish act LPT is (besides a mental disorder) simply "need for treatment". In many of the other EU-member states there is also a criterion concerning the danger represented by the patient, either to others or to him- or herself. In Sweden, a specific "danger-criterion" exists only in *konvertering*, i.e. the transfer from voluntary to compulsory care. Compared to other EU-members, the medical influence on the proceedings in Sweden is quite high since the patient can be given compulsory care for four weeks solely due to decisions by physicians. Like in most other EU-countries, involuntary placement without treatment is not possible in Sweden.

### 13.5.3 Reports from Non-Governmental Organizations (NGOs)

In Sweden there are some non-governmental organizations representing patients and their relatives. Most of them have policy programmes which present – among other things – their views on compulsory psychiatric care. We have searched for investigations on compulsory mental care made by these organizations. However – as we already mentioned in the "Survey methodology" (see 13.1.3) – no such investigations have been found.

## 13.6 Safeguard Systems

The intention of a safeguard system is to prevent coercive measures from being used without indication. From that perspective, however, it is also important that the preconditions of the coercive measures are mentioned in an act of law. As

---

22 See the report *Permissioner vid psykiatrisk tvångsvård. En uppföljning och utvärdering av ändrad reglering, ("Leaves of absence in compulsory mental care. A follow-up and an evaluation of changed regulations")*, Socialstyrelsen 2002.

23 Compare RÅ 1998 n:o 51.

24 Mannheim, Germany, May 15, 2002.

described in section 13.2.2, this is the case in Sweden. An exception to this rule is forced medication, in reference to which the act only says that the treatment shall be adjusted to what is necessary to reach the goal of the compulsory care. Below we shall give an account of the possibilities that exist in Swedish law to safeguard coercive measures applied within psychiatric care.

### 13.6.1 Safeguarding Through Authorities

*a) Obligation for the personnel to let certain decisions on coercive care be examined by the courts*

As mentioned in section 13.2.2, physicians in Sweden are authorized to decide alone on compulsory mental care during the first four weeks. If the *chefsöverläkare* finds that the patient must be given compulsory care more than four weeks beginning with the time of the admission order, he or she must apply to LR for the court's assent to such care before the end of this four-week-period. If this does not happen, the compulsory care must be terminated. The same happens if the LR rejects the application of the *chefsöverläkare*. If, on the other hand, LR grants the application, the compulsory care may continue for up to four months beginning with the day of the admission order. If the *chefsöverläkare* returns within this time period with an application for prolongation, the compulsory care may once again be prolonged, this time for up to six months. This proceeding can be subsequently repeated. If the patient does not consent to the verdict of the LR, this decision can be appealed to the KR. A permit of examination is not necessary in this case. On the other hand, the *chefsöverläkare* lacks the right to appeal against a court's decision about LPT.

*b) Obligation for the personnel to notify the SoS about certain decisions on coercive measures*

Two coercive measures which especially infringe upon personal integrity are *restraint* and *seclusion*. If restraint by means of a belt lasts more than four hours, SoS shall be notified about this. This also applies if seclusion is used for more than eight hours. Thus, SoS is given the possibility to consider whether it shall use its ability to supervise the institution where the coercive measure is taken.

*c) The patient's right to appeal*

Over and above the obligation of the *chefsöverläkare* to let some decisions on compulsory care be taken by a court, *the patient has the right to appeal* against a large number of decisions. Above all, the patient has the possibility to appeal against the admission order established by a psychiatrist. Such an appeal also implies a request to terminate compulsory care. Also, a child has the right to plead his own case on condition that he or she is older than 15 years.

The patient also has the right to request at any time that the compulsory care should be terminated. Such a request shall be considered by the *chefsöverläkare*. If the *chefsöverläkare* rejects the patient's request, the patient can appeal to the LR. The patient also has the right to appeal against the decisions made by the *chefsöverläkare* concerning the destruction or sale of confiscated property. The same is the case if the patient's request for leave of absence was rejected.
The *chefsöverläkare* shall inform the patient about his right to appeal against decisions. The time within which an appeal can be made is *three weeks* beginning with the day when the patient was informed about the decision. Cases of compulsory mental care shall be handled urgently, and a case at LR shall normally be settled within eight days from the day when the appeal came to the court.
In more important cases the patient has the right to a *legal representative* in court. The patient has this right in cases of consent to continued compulsory care, if the patient appeals against an admission order or if his request for termination of the compulsory care was rejected. The costs of the legal representative are paid by the government.
LPT lacks provisions concerning *interpreters*. However, in the local instructions of the care institutions there are, as we have seen, often provisions that foreigners with a main language other than Swedish shall have the right to an interpreter.

*d) Report to the Justitieombudsman, JO*
The *Justitieombudsman*, JO, is a very old Swedish institute created at the beginning of the nineteenth century. According to its instructions, JO has the task of supervising those who exercise public power in Sweden, whether they follow acts of law and other regulations, and fulfil their official duties.[25] Above all, civil servants in governmental and local authorities fall under JO's supervision. The supervision is carried out through the examination of complaints from the public, and through inspections and other investigations that JO finds necessary. If a servant has neglected his duties, JO can report him or her to the public attorney, who can decide on prosecution or report to the proper authority regarding disciplinary actions or withdrawal of authorization.

### 13.6.2 Internal Safeguards

The internal safeguards consist mainly of quality systems. According to regulations of the SoS, all medical care shall be encircled by systems of planning, ac-

---

25 See Lag (1986:765) *med instruktion för riksdagens ombudsmän*. ("Act of instruction for the Ombudsman of the Parliament")

complishing, follow-up and development of the quality of the work.[26] The quality systems shall include routines for cooperation, diagnostic procedures, treatment, nursing care etc. In the field of mental care, it is especially important that the quality systems are defined in a way that the use of compulsory care and coercive measures are limited.

---

[26] *Socialstyrelsens föreskrifter och allmänna råd. Kvalitetssystem i hälso- och sjukvården*, SOSFS 1996:24 (M). ("Regulations and general advice. Quality system in health care").

## Diagram 13.1 Regular Judicial Procedure Concerning Compulsory Admission According to the Swedish Act LPT

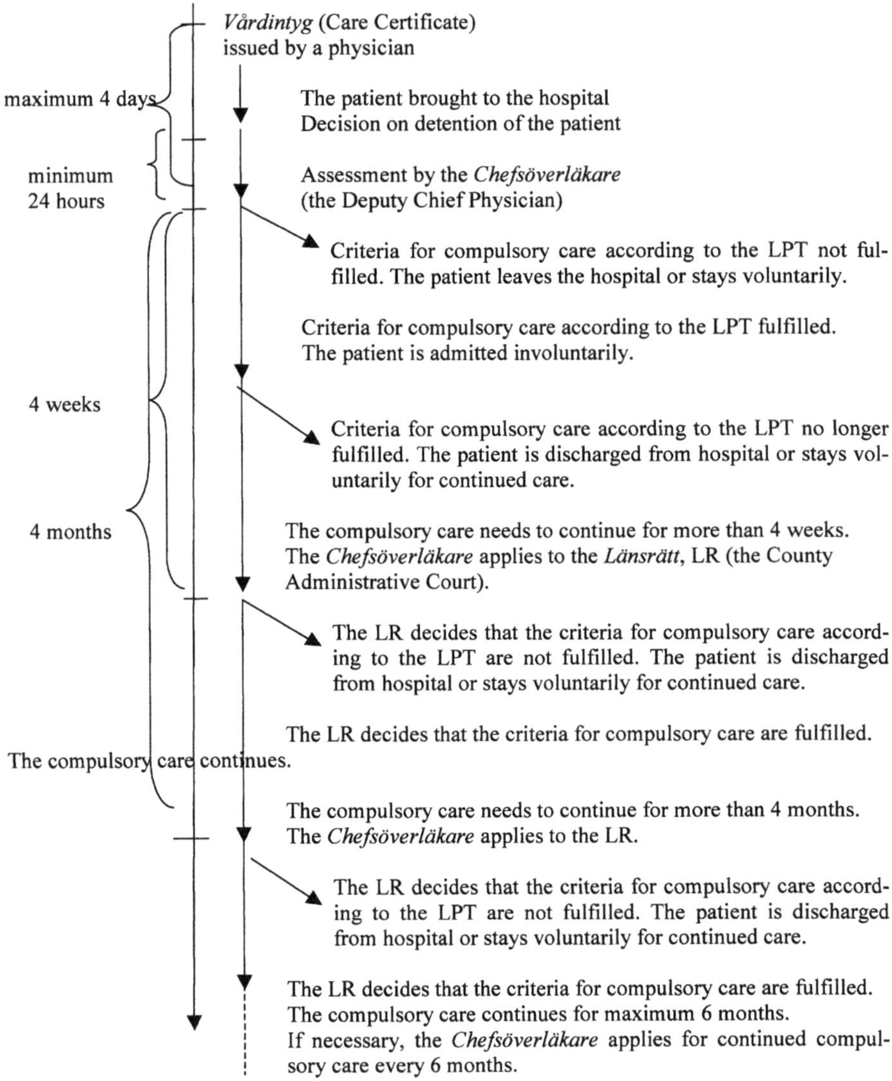

# CHAPTER 14

# The Legal Point of View: Comparing Differences of Legal Regulations Related to Involuntary Admission and Hospital Stay in Twelve European Countries

Jan CONRADY, Tina ROEDER

## 14.1 Introduction

The first part of the article at hand analyses the legal basis for involuntary treatment and involuntary hospitalization in the countries subject to this study, as contained in the preceding country reports. The second part deals with the existing international standards concerning coercion in psychiatry, both at the UN- and at the European level, presenting and defining the relevant provisions and examining observations and recommendations made by UN- and EU-committees.

## 14.2 National Law

Due to a variety of different factors, the requirements concerning the legal basis for involuntary treatment and involuntary hospitalization under national law differ from country to country.
First, some of the countries are federally organized states like Germany, which provides each of the federal states with legislative power. Accordingly, there is no uniform legal situation in Germany because each of the federal states has its own Mental Health Act. Nevertheless, each Mental Health Act has to be consistent with the German Constitution (Grundgesetz). In contrast to federal states like Germany, Bulgaria, for example, is a rather centralized state, where the legal position seems to be *eo ipso* integrative.

Moreover, the diversity of the legal systems is another reason for the different legal positions in the countries analysed in this study. In most countries, whole areas of law are contained in a single code rather than, as in England, being divided between the common law, which is a system of law that is derived from judges' decisions over the centuries, and statute law enacted by Parliament.

The reasons for the very different situations are the differences in the structures of the countries and their non-uniform legal systems.

All countries in this comparison are democracies.

### 14.2.1 Historical Remarks

In order to understand the reasons for the different legal bases in the different countries, it is essential to analyse the historical development of the countries with respect to their constitutional law on the one hand and their general law on the other hand. In every country, history has an impact on the constitution and therefore it is indispensable to bear the history in mind.
The German law, for example – in particular the German Constitution (Grundgesetz) – has to be interpreted in relation to the history of its origins. The constitution came into effect in 1949, four years after World War II, and the deliberations of the Parliamentary Assembly took place under conscious recollection of the Third Reich and the crimes committed therein.

However, not only the historical-political background of the countries matter. The different structures of the states are also important factors for explaining the variety of legal bases. Bulgaria, the Czech Republic, Lithuania, Poland, and the Slovak Republic are young democratic states. Particularly with regard to the collapse of the Soviet Union and, consequently, the independence of the states mentioned, the new states had to face new liabilities including changes concerning the legislative power.
Another state-structural aspect is, on the one hand, the German Reunification, which forced an approximation of laws between the Federal Republic of Germany and the German Democratic Republic, and on the other hand the separation of Czechoslovakia into two sovereign states, the Czech Republic and the Slovak Republic.

Despite the essential changes in world politics that took place during the last two decades, one has to bear in mind that the legal roots of involuntary treatment and involuntary hospitalization can be traced back to the Middle Ages. For example, there have been rules concerning the handling of mentally ill persons in Sweden and Great Britain for centuries. Over the course of time, a paradigm shift has taken place: nowadays the legal system tries to provide not only public safety, but also the safety and adequate treatment that help mentally ill persons.

### 14.2.2 Legal Basis

The comparison of the different legal bases is divided into two parts, the constitutional norms of each country and the general norms of the countries.

#### 14.2.2.1 Constitutional Norms

All countries examined in this analysis are sovereign states. With the exception of England and Israel, all countries taken into account in this study have a written constitution, which serves as the main source of official action.

The constitution of Bulgaria was adopted in 1991 and set a trend towards transferring powers to the local level, although the country has traditionally a rather centralized government. Nevertheless, regulation of medical care has not been transferred to the local level; it has remained centralized.
The constitution of the Republic of Bulgaria does not contain any specific referral to psychiatric treatment. It does guarantee, however, the basic rights relevant for psychiatric treatment, which are the right to life, the prohibition of torture and inhuman and degrading treatment, and the right to liberty. More specifically, the Constitution refers to "medical, scientific and other experiments", which can be performed only with the "voluntary informed consent" of the individual.
However, the Bulgarian Constitution has little practical impact as a guarantee of basic rights in general and no impact at all on the rights of patients and rights of mentally ill persons. This is due to the fact that the Constitutional Court has no power to review complaints of individuals about violations of their basic rights.

Whereas the Constitution of the Republic of Bulgaria – as mentioned before – does not contain any specific referral to psychiatric treatment, the legal situation in the Czech Republic is different. The Charter of Fundamental Rights and Freedoms as adopted after the democratic changes in 1989 is a major part of the constitutional system of the Czech Republic. The Charter was adopted from the constitutional system of former Czechoslovakia by its successor, the Czech Republic, and guarantees personal freedom in Art. 8 (1). However, this is not an absolute right; law may limit it. It shall determine the cases where a person may be admitted to or kept in a medical institution without his or her consent. Such a move shall be reported within 24 hours to a court that shall decide on such placement within seven days.
Anybody who claims that his or her rights have been violated by a decision of a public administration body may turn to a court for a review of the legality of such a decision, unless law stipulates differently. However, a review of the decisions affecting the fundamental rights and freedoms listed in the Charter may not be excluded from the jurisdiction of courts.
As already mentioned, England has no written constitution. Instead, the relationship between the state and its people relies on statute law, common law and conventions.

The German Constitution (Grundgesetz) does not contain any specific rules relating to psychiatric treatment or involuntary hospitalization. However, the general law has to be consistent with the German Constitution (Grundgesetz), which states that human dignity is inviolable, Art. 1 (1). Furthermore, the constitution states that it is the duty of public authority to respect and safeguard human dignity, Art. 1 (3). The term public authority includes the legislative, executive, and judicial powers.

The Constitution guarantees the development of identity, the right to life and physical integrity. However, law may limit personal freedom. Due to the reunification treaty, the German Grundgesetz applies to the new states of Germany, which are Saxony, Saxony-Anhalt, Thuringia, Mecklenburg-Western Pomerania, and Brandenburg.
The fact that the German Constitution only provides very rudimentary rules has to be seen with regard to the state-structural system in Germany. Each of the sixteen states has a wide range of legislative power. The Federal Government has the legislative power only in those cases mentioned in the Constitution.
Anybody who claims that his or her rights have been violated by a decision of a public administration body may turn to a court for a review of the legality of such a decision. If the courts disagree with the complainant, he or she may turn to the Federal Constitutional Court (Bundesverfassungsgericht) claiming his or her constitutional rights have been violated.
This right is not limited to German citizens. Everybody living in Germany is entitled to do so.

A variety of articles of the Constitution of Greece are concerned with involuntary hospitalization, involuntary treatment, and coercive measures. Whereas Germany empowers the states with legislative power, it remains centralized in Greece due to the non-federal structure.
However, the constitution guarantees all persons the right to develop freely their personality and to participate in the social, economic, and political life of the country, insofar as they do not infringe upon the rights of others or violate the constitution or moral values. Torture, any bodily maltreatment, impairment of health or the use of psychological violence as well as any other offence against human dignity are prohibited and subject to punishment, as provided by law. However, the prohibition of coercive measures does not preclude the imposition of measures necessary for the protection of public health or the health of sick persons as specified by law. According to the constitution, restrictions of any kind imposed upon these rights should be provided either directly by the constitution or by law. In case reservations regarding the threat posed or the potential effectiveness of treatment exist, the action taken should respect the principle of proportionality.

Like England, Israel does not have a constitution; it has Basic Laws, which have constitutional status. One of these basic laws – Human Dignity and Freedom – is designed to protect human dignity and liberty. One may not harm the life, body and dignity of a person and every person is entitled to protection of his life, body and dignity.

Therefore, the basic laws of Israel do not contain any specific reference to psychiatric treatment. However, it does guarantee some rights which are relevant for psychiatric treatment.

The Constitution of the Italian Republic came into force in 1948, three years after World War II, and guarantees personal freedom. No type of detention, inspection or personal search or any other kind of personal restriction is permitted unless law provides it. In these exceptional cases, an order must be issued by a judicial authority.
In emergency cases, strictly indicated by the law, the law enforcement authority can carry out temporary measures of which the judicial authority must be informed within 48 hours. If the judicial authority does not validate them, the measures are revoked and rendered null. Any type of physical or moral violence against individuals whose freedom is restricted will be punished.
Furthermore, the Constitution of the Italian Republic guarantees health as a fundamental right of the individual being in the interest of the community and grants free treatments to destitute people. Nobody can be forced to undergo a medical treatment except in cases contemplated by the law.
It is remarkable that the Constitution of the Italian Republic is rather specific on issues dealing with health as a fundamental right compared to other constitutions examined. However, the duty to inform the judicial authority in cases of temporary measures is not limited to the detention, inspection or personal search or any other kind of personal restriction of mentally ill persons.

Following the end of occupation by the Soviet Union, the Lithuanian Republic attained sovereignty, and in 1992, the Constitution of the Lithuanian Republic was passed. Like the other constitutions examined, that of the Lithuanian Republic guarantees personal freedom. No person may be arbitrarily arrested or detained. No person may be deprived of freedom except on the basis, and according to the procedures, which have been established by law. A person detained in flagrante delicto must be brought to court within 48 hours for the purpose of determining the validity of the detention in the presence of the detainee. If the court does not authorize the decision to arrest the person, the detained individual shall be released immediately.
Furthermore, the Constitution prohibits torture, physical injury, and maltreatment. In cases where a person is subjected to scientific or medical testing, his or her knowledge thereof and consent thereto is required.
Besides the guarantee of personal freedom and the safeguarding of human dignity, the Constitution of Poland, like that of the Lithuanian Republic, provides specific constitutional norms with regard to the medical sector.
No one shall be subjected to scientific experimentation, including medical experimentation, without his or her voluntary consent. Personal inviolability and

security shall be ensured to everyone. Any deprivation or limitation of liberty may be imposed only in accordance with the principles and procedures specified by statute.

Due to their history as a single state, the Czech Republic and the Slovak Republic show some parallels to each other in their constitutions.
Like the Constitution of the Czech Republic, that of the Slovak Republic provides some articles concerning involuntary hospitalization in medical facilities. Art. 16 states that the law will stipulate in which cases a person may be admitted or detained in inpatient health care without his or her consent. This measure shall be communicated to the court, which shall make a decision on this placement within seven days.

Whereas the Constitutions of the Czech Republic and the Slovak Republic provide some specific norms relating to mentally ill persons, the Constitution of Spain does not contain any specific referral to psychiatric treatment. However, the constitution guarantees a person's dignity and the free development of his or her personality. Everyone has the right to freedom and security of person. No one may be deprived of his or her freedom except in accordance with the provisions of this section and in the cases and manner envisaged by law.
Furthermore, the Spanish Constitution guarantees the protection of health. The authorities shall implement a policy of prevention, treatment, rehabilitation and integration of the physically and mentally handicapped, providing them with the specialized care they require and affording them enhanced protection.

The Swedish Constitution, in force since 1975, guarantees personal freedom and protects against deprivation of liberty. Deprivation of liberty means that the individual's freedom to move is limited. However, the protection against deprivation of liberty is not absolute. According to the constitution, the freedom to move can be restricted by law, The limitation is never allowed to exceed what is necessary to fulfil its purpose, nor may it be employed due to political, religious, cultural or other such views.
Furthermore, the Constitution of Sweden also refers to the question of compulsory psychiatric care. According to the Swedish Constitution, every citizen in relation to the society is protected against a forced corporal interference. Actually, this term includes not only surgical operations but also milder interference like medication, blood samples and vaccination. Keeping in mind that even an examination of the patient's body carried out by a physician is regarded as a corporal interference, because the aim of the provision is to protect the personal integrity, a psychiatric examination must also be seen as a corporal interference. It is only possible in cases established by law.

Among the constitutions observed, the Swedish Constitution is the only one dealing with the question of involuntary examination.

**Summary**
Under comparison, the constitutions of the twelve European countries covered by this book reveal some remarkable differences with regard to those provisions which are relevant to questions of involuntary treatment and involuntary hospitalization.
Some of the constitutions reviewed guarantee the citizens' protection against involuntary treatment and/or involuntary hospitalization explicitly. However, each constitution provides rules which protect personal freedom in general, but may be restricted in accordance with law.
It is noticeable that the younger constitutions are more likely to contain specific rules concerning involuntary treatment and/or involuntary hospitalization, in contrast to other constitutions, e.g. the German Constitution, that guarantees the protection of personal freedom and the protection of human dignity, but does not refer to the situation of mentally ill persons. Furthermore, their purposes differ. Not all of the constitutions aim to protect the mentally ill against themselves, but restrict their ambition to protecting society.
Another tendency can be revealed: countries having a federal state-structure tend to have less specific rules than countries that are rather centralized. This is due to the fact that, in federally structured states, some of the legislative power is given to local or regional governments.
In addition, the applicability of the constitutions differs. In some countries, it is not possible for the person concerned to turn to the Constitutional Court in order to have his or her case reviewed. In these cases, the constitution has only a small impact on the situation of the people with regard to the enforcement of their rights. Therefore, the general law of the different countries needs to be compared.

**14.2.2.2 General Law**
The synopsis of national general law that follows is based on the twelve country-specific legal expert reports provided in this book.
The basis for comparing the different legal situations is the effective law of the countries observed, as stated in those country-specific reports.

Under Bulgarian law, a person may be placed by the courts against his/her will in a psychiatric establishment for treatment following two different proceedings, an administrative and a criminal procedure. A person, if deprived of his/her legal capacity and placed under guardianship, may also be placed in a psychiatric establishment for treatment by her/his guardian.

Regarding the administrative procedure, only the court, not a prosecutor, can order a detention for assessment, which may not last longer than 14 days with a possibility of a ten-day extension. During the in-patient assessment, no treatment is provided unless informed consent is given or the case is an emergency. The Bulgarian Health Act limits the time for re-examination of the need for placement and treatment, which should take place every three months.
Placement on an emergency basis can be authorized by the head of a psychiatric service for 24 hours, with one-time prolongation of up to 48 hours permitted by a judge. If further treatment is deemed necessary, the head of the psychiatric service should immediately submit an application for obligatory treatment with a detailed explanation to the district court supported by a psychiatrist's statement. The court should, in turn, hold a hearing immediately.
Regarding the criminal procedure, the court may order three alternative measures: first, to surrender the person to the guardianship of his/her next-of-kin, second, to order involuntary treatment at an ordinary psychiatric-neurological facility, or, third, to order treatment at a special psychiatric hospital, or a special ward in an ordinary psychiatric-neurological establishment. A proposal for such treatment may be made by the regional or district prosecutor and should be supported by a psychiatric forensic report. Every six months following the beginning of the treatment, the court should rule ex officio on the need of continued treatment.

Under Czech law, a person may be placed against his/her will in a psychiatric establishment for treatment. The medical care providing institution in which any person is placed without his/her written consent must inform the court in whose district the institution is located within 24 hours of taking charge of that person. The court then shall examine this person, hear the attending doctor, and decide within seven days whether the placement occurred for lawful reasons.
The Criminal Code of the Czech Republic stipulates cases where the court must order compulsory treatment as well as cases where the court may order compulsory treatment. The compulsory treatment shall last until its purpose has been fulfilled, so the court does not specify the length of its duration. The institution in charge of carrying out the compulsory treatment shall inform the court when the treatment has fulfilled its purpose. During the criminal proceedings, the court may decide that the accused person shall be observed in a medical establishment or special prison unit in order to examine his/her mental state. The observation may last up to two months and it can be extended for one additional month.

The English law allows the involuntary admission of a patient for assessment for up to 28 days. This cannot be renewed, as the 28 days are considered sufficient for the assessment of the patient's clinical status. Besides this, the English law allows the involuntary treatment and admission of a patient for up to six months. If it is considered necessary for the patient to stay in hospital longer, this six-month period can be renewed once for another six months. Afterwards it may be extended on a year-to-year-basis. The patient's nearest relative or an approved social worker can submit the application for such a detention. Two medical recommendations or one joint medical recommendation by two doctors demonstrating the criteria for detention are required, but no more than one of them can be employed in the hospital where the patient will be admitted.

In cases of an emergency detention, the application by the nearest relative or social worker is needed along with only one medical recommendation. A patient who is detained under the criteria described can be given medical treatment without his/her consent for the first three months under the direction of a trained psychiatrist. If the responsible Medical Officer believes that the patient should not be detained further, he/she can discharge him/her. If the patient believes that he/she should not be detained anymore, he/she can apply to the Hospital Managers or to a Mental Health Review Tribunal for discharge.

The German law on mental health comprises three different areas of law: civil law, public administrative law, and criminal law. Regarding involuntary measures against patients with mental disorders, a strict distinction has to be made between involuntary treatment and involuntary placement.

The civil law provides the possibility of involuntary placement in case of self-destructive behaviour of a person with mental disorder. If the person is under guardianship, the decision of his/her guardian has to be approved in advance by the Guardianship Court. The public administrative law provides the possibility of involuntary placement in case of self-destructive behaviour of a person with mental disorder and/or if a person represents a significant danger to others. In case of such a placement, the hospital shall immediately inform the court and the administrative authority, at the latest by 10:00 on the day following the day when the confinement of the patient began.

Under Greek law, a person suffering from a mental disorder can be hospitalized without his/her consent if a relative or, in urgent cases, the public prosecutor of the district in which the patient is permanently or temporarily residing makes an application for hospitalization. The application must be accompanied by medical opinions from two psychiatrists. The public prosecutor may, only in the case that the medical opinions differ, order the patient's transfer and then refer the patient's case to the district court. The public prosecutor is entitled to order the patient's transfer to a public psychiatric ward for evaluation and the issue of a medical opinion, but this may not last for more than 48 hours. Patients or, in cases of mentally disabled persons, their representatives are entitled to be informed a priori about the dangers of extraordinary or experimental diagnostic measures or treatment. They have the right to refuse any diagnostic act or treatment. In case of a partial or total mental disability, a person acting for the patient according to the law may exercise this right.

Israel's law gives the power to the district psychiatrist to order forced hospitalization. A person facing commitment in the civil track has no right to legal representation at the initial commitment hearing. On the criminal track, the law grants the patient the right to be legally represented.

Under Italian law, involuntary admission and tests must be supported by initiatives to gain the consent and participation of the individuals forced into the program. The mayor, as the local medical authority, can order involuntary admission and tests with the reservation that this be backed by the well-founded request of a physician. The tutelary judge of the local district has to be informed within 48 hours. Within the next 48 hours, the tutelary judge examines the information, issues a decree validating or rejecting the provision and informs the mayor. If the provision is not validated, the mayor issues another order terminating the involuntary admission. Under criminal law, the judge or the public prosecutor informs the mayor, who is able to order an involuntary admission for mental illness, if the defendant shows symptoms of psychiatric pathology during the criminal proceedings.

Under Lithuanian law, the mental condition of a person may be examined only with his/her consent or the consent of the court. In case of legal incapability, the consent may be given by his/her guardian. A person may be admitted to a mental health facility only with his/her consent or the consent of the court. If a person is suffering from a severe mental illness and if there is a real danger that by his/her actions he/she is likely to commit serious harm to his/her health or to the health, life and property of others, he/she may be hospitalized involuntarily for a time period not longer than 48 hours. Involuntary hospitalization may be prolonged only with the consent of the court. In the case that the person is legally incapable, the consent to involuntary hospitalization may be given by the person's guardian. In case of involuntary treatment, the court has to decide within 48 hours whether the treatment is unlawful or not.
In Poland, the court may decide, based on the expert opinion of two psychiatrists, to commit a person to a health care facility for observation for no longer than six weeks. In exceptional situations, the duration of the observational period may be prolonged for up to three months. A physician may provide medical services only after obtaining a patient's consent. In cases of minors or those incapa-

ble of expressing conscious consent, the consent of their legal representative is required. If a person has no such representative or communication with him/her is impossible, consent is given by the Guardian Court.
A mentally ill person may be admitted to a psychiatric hospital without consent if that person's behaviour to date indicates that, due to the illness, he/she poses an imminent danger to his/her life or to the life or health of others. The decision about the admission of such a person shall be made by the appointed physician following a previous personally conducted examination of that person and, if possible, following consultation with another psychiatrist or psychologist.
The head of the ward shall confirm admission to hospital within 48 hours of admission. The head of the hospital shall notify the Guardianship Court within 72 hours of admission.

In the Slovak Republic, examination and treatment measures including residential health care may be carried out if it is not possible to ask the patient to consent because of his/her health or if it is not possible to contact his/her representative. It is an obligation of the health care institution to inform the district court within 24 hours. The court shall decide on the lawfulness of the hospitalization and treatment. Until the decision of the court is available, only examinations and treatments necessary to save the life and health of the patient may be performed.
Under criminal law, the court is able to impose protective treatment if the person committing an act normally classified as a criminal act is without penal responsibility because of his/her insanity and his/her free movement proves to be dangerous. The court may impose it in addition to another punishment, or independently, as the sole action to reach the aims of the penal law.

Under Spanish law, the confinement due to mental disorders of a person who is in no condition to decide for himself/herself, shall require authorization of the court in the area in which the person resides, even if someone else holds his/her custody or guardianship. Authorization must be obtained prior to confinement, except in a case of emergency when it is necessary to carry out such measures immediately. In such a case, the head of the centre in which the patient is confined shall inform the competent court of this fact as soon as possible and, in all cases, within a period of 24 hours, so that the confinement may be legally ratified. Such ratification must take place within a maximum of 72 hours from the time the court was notified of the confinement. The decision that confinement should take place shall also set out the obligation of the doctors in charge of the person confined to inform the court periodically whether it is necessary to maintain the measure, in addition to providing any other report that the court may require at its discretion. These periodical reports shall be issued every six months, unless the court, taking into account the nature of the disorder that led to confinement, stipulates a shorter period.

In Sweden, the question of admission shall be settled quickly after the patient has been examined, at the latest 24 hours after the patient's arrival to the care institution. Moreover, the "care certificate" must not be older than four days. The physician who has issued the „care certificate", which is to be seen as a guarantee for the patient's legal security, may not issue the admission order. If the Deputy Chief Doctor at the patient's psychiatric care institution finds that compulsory care must be provided for more than four weeks after the day on which the admission order was issued, the physician shall apply to the county administrative court for permission for continued care before the end of the four-weeks-period.
Compulsory psychiatric care shall be provided in a medical institution run by a county council. With "medical institution" is meant a unit at a hospital, which implies that compulsory psychiatric care never can be given in outpatient settings in Sweden. As soon as the patient is admitted to compulsory care, a treatment plan shall be drawn up. The law does not say under which preconditions it is acceptable to treat with medication by coercion; it only says that the care measures – including medication – shall be adjusted to what is needed to fulfil the aim of the compulsory care.

**Summary**

Under comparison, the domestic laws at hand reveal major, remarkable differences with regard to those provisions which are relevant to questions of involuntary treatment and involuntary hospitalization.
One striking example is the difference relating to the competence to order a detention for assessment: In one country, England, the detention for assessment may be ordered by two doctors and may last up to 28 days. In most other countries (e.g.: Bulgaria, Czech Republic, Germany, Lithuania, Poland, Slovak Republic, Spain, and Sweden), only the court has the legal power to do so. In Israel, as has been said before, the district psychiatrist can order the detention, but a court has to rule on this detention within two days.
These differences apparently do not spring from differences rooted in the respective constitutional norms. All examined constitutions, as shown above, contain general clauses protecting the personal freedom of the individual. No specific group of countries can be identified with particular constitutional wording relating to personal freedom from which respective wording in the relevant general norms could be derived. In other words, the form or exact wording of the constitution does not seem to play a major role in relation to the formulation of

rights and reservations concerning involuntary treatment and hospitalization in general domestic law.
Instead, the identified differences seem to be mainly due to the wide scope of discretion left by constitutions in general to the national legislative power for creating the necessary general norms protecting or restricting the constitutional right to personal freedom.

### 14.3 International Standards

Following the synopsis of domestic legal provisions, the international standards for the treatment of individuals involuntarily placed in psychiatric institutions shall be introduced, and the level of their implementation into national legislation and practice briefly examined via reports of UN- und European committees.

#### 14.3.1 Relevant International Conventions

As a first step, it will be necessary to examine briefly the relevant regulations contained in international covenants relating to the treatment of individuals in psychiatry. Not all of the preceding country reports contain sufficient references to relevant international conventions.

##### 14.3.1.1 United Nations

At the UN-level, there are three international conventions with relevance to the treatment of persons with mental disorders in psychiatric establishments: the International Covenant on Civil and Political Rights (CCPR), the International Covenant on Economic, Social and Cultural Rights (CESCR), and the Convention against Torture and Other Cruel, Inhuman or Degrading Treatment or Punishment (CAT). All of the countries subject to this study are party to those conventions; the majority, with the exception of Israel and the United Kingdom, have also signed and ratified the Optional Protocol to the International Covenant on Civil and Political Rights, which provides a certain form of access to the monitoring committee for individuals.
The relevant provisions contained in the two International Covenants and in the Convention against Torture are as follows:

**CCPR**

Art. 7

No one shall be subjected to torture or to cruel, inhuman or degrading treatment or punishment. In particular, no one shall be subjected without his free consent to medical or scientific experimentation.

Art. 9
1. Everyone has the right to liberty and security of person. No one shall be subjected to arbitrary arrest or detention. No one shall be deprived of his liberty except on such grounds and in accordance with such procedure as are established by law. (…)
4. Anyone who is deprived of his liberty by arrest or detention shall be entitled to take proceedings before a court, in order that that court may decide without delay on the lawfulness of his detention and order his release if the detention is not lawful. (…)

Art. 10
1. All persons deprived of their liberty shall be treated with humanity and with respect for the inherent dignity of the human person. (…)

**CESCR**
Art. 12
1. The States Parties to the present Covenant recognize the right of everyone to the enjoyment of the highest attainable standard of physical and mental health. (…)

**CAT**
Art. 2
1. Each State Party shall take effective legislative, administrative, judicial or other measures to prevent acts of torture in any territory under its jurisdiction. (…)

Art. 16
1. Each State Party shall undertake to prevent in any territory under its jurisdiction other acts of cruel, inhuman or degrading treatment or punishment which do not amount to torture (…), when such acts are committed by or at the instigation of or with the consent or acquiescence of a public official or other person acting in an official capacity. (…)

#### 14.3.1.2 European Conventions
Apart from the universal covenants, there are two regional European conventions with relevance to the treatment of the mentally disordered: the European Convention for the Protection of Human Rights and Fundamental Freedoms of 1950, and the so-called 'Oviedo Convention', the European Convention for the Protection of Human Rights and Dignity of the Human Being with Regard to the Application of Biology and Medicine (1997). Those conventions are open for ratification to the member states of the Council of Europe. All of the European states concerned have signed and ratified the European Human Rights Conven-

tion. The Oviedo Convention has been signed by Bulgaria, the Czech Republic, Greece, Italy, Lithuania, Poland, Slovakia, Spain, and Sweden; of these, Italy, Poland, and Sweden have not yet ratified the Convention. Germany and the United Kingdom are not signatories.

The relevant clauses contained in the *European Human Rights Convention* are:
Art. 3
No one shall be subjected to torture or to inhuman or degrading treatment or punishment.

Art. 5
1. Everyone has the right to liberty and security of person.
No one shall be deprived of his liberty save in the following cases and in accordance with a procedure prescribed by law:
(a) the lawful detention of a person after conviction by a competent court;
(b) the lawful arrest or detention of a person for non-compliance with the lawful order of a court or in order to secure the fulfilment of any obligation prescribed by law;
(c) the lawful arrest or detention of a person effected for the purpose of bringing him before the competent legal authority on reasonable suspicion of having committed an offence or when it is reasonably considered necessary to prevent his committing an offence or fleeing after having done so;
(d) the detention of a minor by lawful order for the purpose of educational supervision or his lawful detention for the purpose of bringing him before the competent legal authority;
(e) the lawful detention of persons for the prevention of the spreading of infectious diseases, of persons of unsound mind, alcoholics or drug addicts, or vagrants;
(f) the lawful arrest or detention of a person to prevent his effecting an unauthorized entry into the country or of a person against whom action is being taken with a view to deportation or extradition.
2. Everyone who is arrested shall be informed promptly, in a language which he understands, of the reasons for his arrest and the charge against him.
3. Everyone arrested or detained in accordance with the provisions of paragraph 1(c) of this article shall be brought promptly before a judge or other officer authorized by law to exercise judicial power and shall be entitled to trial within a reasonable time or to release pending trial. Release may be conditioned by guarantees to appear for trial.
4. Everyone who is deprived of his liberty by arrest or detention shall be entitled to take proceedings by which the lawfulness of his detention shall be decided speedily by a court and his release ordered if the detention is not lawful.

5. Everyone who has been the victim of arrest or detention in contravention of the provisions of this article shall have an enforceable right to compensation.

The relevant clauses contained in the *Oviedo Convention* are as follows (special attention should be paid to Art. 7 which relates directly to the treatment of the mentally disordered):
Art. 1
Parties to this Convention shall protect the dignity and identity of all human beings and guarantee everyone, without discrimination, respect for their integrity and other rights and fundamental freedoms with regard to the application of biology and medicine.
Each Party shall take in its internal law the necessary measures to give effect to the provisions of this Convention.

Art. 5
An intervention in the health field may only be carried out after the person concerned has given free and informed consent to it.
This person shall beforehand be given appropriate information as to the purpose and nature of the intervention as well as on its consequences and risks.
The person concerned may freely withdraw consent at any time.

Art. 6
1. Subject to art. 17 and 20 below, an intervention may only be carried out on a person who does not have the capacity to consent, for his or her direct benefit. (...)
3. Where, according to law, an adult does not have the capacity to consent to an intervention because of a mental disability, a disease or for similar reasons, the intervention may only be carried out with the authorization of his or her representative or an authority or a person or body provided for by law. The individual concerned shall as far as possible take part in the authorization procedure. (...)

Art. 7
Subject to protective conditions prescribed by law, including supervisory, control and appeal procedures, a person who has a mental disorder of a serious nature may be subjected, without his or her consent, to an intervention aimed at treating his or her mental disorder only where, without such treatment, serious harm is likely to result to his or her health.

Art. 8
When because of an emergency situation the appropriate consent cannot be obtained, any medically necessary intervention may be carried out immediately for the benefit of the health of the individual concerned.

Art. 9
The previously expressed wishes relating to a medical intervention by a patient who is not, at the time of the intervention, in a state to express his or her wishes shall be taken into account.

### 14.3.1.3 Implementation and Supervision

These international covenants are binding upon the state parties due to the fundamental international principle of '*pacta sunt servanda*', according to which treaties must be abided by. Nevertheless, individual claims can usually not be made in reference to regulations contained in international treaties, since the individual is not normally a subject of public international law. The European Convention on Human Rights constitutes an exception to this rule as it enables individuals to make their demands based on the rights set forth in the Convention before the European Court of Human Rights. Apart from this, individuals are dependent on the implementation of the international rules by their national governments, i.e. the incorporation of international rules in national law. This process of implementation and, more generally, the way state parties abide by the treaties they conclude, are being monitored by certain organs related to the respective treaty. The compliance of state parties with the two UN International Covenants (CCPR, CESCR), for example, is being supervised by the United Nations Human Rights Committee via state reports which have to be submitted to the Committee at regular intervals and which are then assessed and commented by the Committee. The Committee may include certain suggestions in its comments but possesses no means of sanctioning non-compliance with these suggestions. Individual claims can only be made on the basis that the respective individual's state has signed the First Optional Protocol to the International Covenant on Civil and Political Rights, which provides such a possibility. Once more, the Committee will examine the claim and make suggestions. On the other hand, the European Court of Human Rights, which supervises the state parties' compliance with the European Convention on Human Rights, is enabled to render judgements on individuals' claims that are binding upon the state party concerned. These verdicts in relation to countries subject to this study will be explicitly dealt with elsewhere.
To generally assess the level of implementation and incorporation reached by the various countries to date, we would like to point to the synopsis of national regulations given in section 14.2. In the following, a typified evaluation of the presented country-specific situations will be conducted in relation to the above-mentioned international conventions at the UN-level on one hand (CCPR, CESCR, CAT), and data provided by the European Committee on the Prevention of Torture (CPT) on the other.

### 14.3.2 Evaluation at the UN-level: International Covenant on Civil and Political Rights (CCPR), the International Covenant on Economic, Social and Cultural Rights (CESCR), and the Convention Against Torture (CAT)

The scope of the relevant articles contained in the Covenant on Civil and Political Rights (CCPR), the Covenant on Economic, Social and Cultural Rights (CESCR), and the Convention Against Torture (CAT) is often determined by so-called *General Comments*, which the respective Committees responsible for the supervision of the covenant's implementation issues. Based on these definitions and explanations, the Committees issue *Concluding Observations* and *Recommendations* after examining a state report. These express the Committees' concerns about specific domestic shortcomings, and recommend measures to correct these. We will first use the General Comments and the definitions contained therein to show in which respect the norms set forth in the CCPR, the CESCR, and the CAT are applicable to the problem of coercion in psychiatry. In a second step, the relevant Concluding Observations and the recommendations made to countries will be examined.

#### 14.3.2.1 General Comments

The General Comments to the various relevant clauses in the CCPR, the CESCR, and the CAT will be presented under common headings relating to the respective human rights issue.

*Deprivation of Liberty (art. 9 CCPR)*

The first respect in which the international human rights conventions are relevant as concerns coercion in psychiatric treatment is the deprivation of liberty naturally accompanying this kind of treatment. The UN Human Rights Committee, in its General Comment 8 of 1982 (UN Doc. HRI/GEN/1/Rev.1, 1994), states clearly that the respective Article 9 in the CCPR relates not only to persons deprived of their liberty in connection with criminal cases:

> *"Article 9 (...) has often been somewhat narrowly understood in reports by State parties, and they have therefore given incomplete information. The Committee points out that paragraph 1 is applicable to all deprivations of liberty, whether in criminal cases or in other cases such as (...) mental illness (...)."*

Thus, provisions relating to the treatment of persons deprived of their liberty must also be applied to individuals forced into psychiatric treatment against or without their expressed consent, although this is not explicitly mentioned in Article 9 CCPR.

*Human Dignity (art. 10 CCPR)*

Deprivation of liberty is closely related to the second relevant human rights issue, the treatment of detained individuals with respect to their human dignity.

Again, according to the UN Human Rights Committee, this provision is not only applicable to criminal cases:

> *"Article 10, paragraph 1 (...) applies to anyone deprived of liberty under the laws and authority of the State who is held in a prison, hospital – particularly a psychiatric hospitals – (...) or elsewhere. (...) Not only may persons deprived of their liberty not be subjected to treatment that is contrary to article 7 [torture, see below], (...) [they also may not] be subjected to any hardship or constraint other than that resulting from the deprivation of liberty (...)."* (UN Doc. HRI/GEN/1/Rev.1, 1994).

*Torture (art. 7 CCPR;CAT)*

Besides the provisions relating to human dignity of detained individuals in general, Article 7 CCPR and the CAT provide a more specific regulation concerning the use of torture or any other degrading and/or inhuman treatment against such persons, as defined in Article 1 CAT. Once again, these provisions also apply to individuals held in psychiatric institutions, as the Human Rights Committee points out (UN Doc. HRI/GEN/1/Rev.1, 1994):

> *"(...) (A)rticle 7 protects, in particular, (...) patients in (...) medical institutions."*

Besides expressly including individuals held in medical institutions, the Human Rights Committee also clarifies the definition of torture and correspondent treatment:

> *"The aim of the provisions (...) is to protect both the dignity and the physical and mental integrity of the individual. (...) The prohibition in article 7 relates not only to acts that cause physical pain but also to acts that cause mental suffering to the victim. (...) Article 7 expressly prohibits medical or scientific experimentation without the free consent of the person concerned. (...) (S)pecial protection in regard to such experiments is necessary in the case of persons not capable of giving valid consent."*

*Health (art. 12 CESCR)*

The most specific provision relating to coercion in psychiatry is contained in Article 12 CESCR. The General Comment of 2000 (UN Doc. E/2001/22 (2000) 128) notes:

> *"The right to health is not to be understood as a right to be healthy. The right to health includes both freedoms and entitlements. The freedoms include the right to control one's health and body, (...) and the right to be free from interference, such as the right to be free from torture, non-consensual medical treatment and experimentation. (...) Obligations to respect include a State's obligation to refrain from (...) applying coercive medical treatments, unless on an exceptional basis for the treatment of mental illness (...). Such exceptional cases should be subject to specific and restrictive conditions (...)."*

The General Comment also relates to the *Principles for the Protection of Persons with Mental Illness and for the Improvement of Mental Health Care* contained in UN General Assembly resolution 46/119 (annex).

### 14.3.2.2 Concluding Observations

How are the principles and provisions defined in these General Comments inferred by the countries subject to this study? Beforehand, it must be noted that the relevant Concluding Observations on state reports relating to the CCPR, the CESCR, and the CAT contain very little information concerning coercion in psychiatric treatment. These are the findings (the years refer to the publishing date of the respective Concluding Observation, all Concluding Observations mentioned can be obtained online via www.bayefsky.com by searching for the respective country's name):

*Slovakia:* no effective, reliable and independent complaint system relating to allegations of ill-treatment (2000); use of cage beds as a measure of restraint in psychiatric institutions (2003)

*Lithuania:* no comprehensive definition of torture (2002)

*Italy:* torture, as such, is not punishable in domestic law (1994)

*Poland*: national legislation contains no definition of torture (1994, 1997); this shortcoming was rectified by the incorporation of a new constitutional norm prohibiting torture and corresponding treatment, yet no provisions exist for making respective charges (2000)

*Israel:* no implementation of a definition of torture as in Article 1 CAT (1994, 2002)

*Sweden:* CAT provisions not incorporated into domestic law (1997); no definition of torture in domestic legislation in keeping with Article 1 CAT (2002)

*Germany:* precise definition of torture has not been integrated into the legal order (1998)

*Bulgaria:* no implementation of a definition of torture as in art. 1 CAT (1999)

The scarcity of these findings seems mainly related to the already mentioned misinterpretation of states of the relevant human rights clauses, which leads to state reports including information on treatment of prisoners and such, but rarely or not at all on individuals in hospitals and/or psychiatric institutions. Thus, the Concluding Observations generally deal rather with concerns about police or army brutality, prison conditions, the effects of the recent anti-terrorism-strategy employed by many governments or discrimination within health care systems.

#### 14.3.2.3 Jurisprudence

As mentioned above, besides the regular state reports, there exists a possibility of lodging individual complaints relating to rights set forth in the CCPR if the respective state has signed the Optional Protocol I. The CESCR and the CAT system contain similar provisions. In such cases, the respective committee will examine the circumstances at hand and issue a statement concerning its findings and recommendations to the state party. Although the committees cannot issue binding judgements, these statements are generally referred to as "jurisprudence" (the relevant documents can also be found at www.bayefsky.com).

The accessible statements on individual cases concerning *health* issues in general or *health care and health treatment* issues, on *deprivation of liberty* and *torture* issues (in relation to the countries subject to this study) do not contain references to involuntary psychiatric placement, as the complaints lodged mainly concern cases of denied medical treatment in prison or detention. An examination of the jurisprudence related to *human dignity* issues arrives at the same conclusion, with the exception of at least one European state mentioned in relation to involuntary placement, though not included in this study: In the case *Wuyts vs. the Netherlands* (785/1997), the claimant was, in a criminal context, placed by judicial order in a psychiatric institution for two years where actual treatment started only a year after the date of placement. The court then ordered a second two-year-placement, alleging that the claimant's conditions had not approved. The Committee found no violation of art. 10 CCPR.

### 14.3.3 Evaluation at the European Level: Country Reports of the European Committee for the Prevention of Torture (CPT)

While there is not much insight to be gained from the above-presented Concluding Observations on the implementation of the relevant covenants at the UN-level or the UN jurisprudence, we are provided with more detailed and specific data at the European level via the most recent visiting reports of the European Committee for the Prevention of Torture (CPT). Several of these reports contain concerns and/or recommendations relating to involuntary placement in psychiatric institutions.

#### 14.3.3.1 Observations and Recommendations

The essential findings in these reports relating to coercion in psychiatric treatment are listed below (the reports themselves are available on the website of the Committee, www.cpt.coe.int; a number of them are also mentioned in the preceding country reports):

## *Sweden (CPT visit 2004)*

*"The relevant procedures, and the deadlines, for the review of placements and for the discharge of patients appeared to be scrupulously observed in the establishments visited. However, the CPT has proposed the strengthening of certain of the formal safeguards surrounding such procedures; involuntary civil placements should always require the opinion of a psychiatrist independent of the admitting hospital, and greater use should be made of the potentially valuable safeguard of having support persons appointed for patients. The CPT has also suggested that, following the example of Sahlgrenska, information on appeals and complaints procedures be included in the leaflet available at Umeå Forensic and General Psychiatric Unit, and that patients be provided with appropriate appeal and request forms. Further, it has invited the Swedish authorities to consider setting up an independent outside mechanism responsible for the inspection of patients' care."*

## *Czech Republic (CPT visit 2002)*

*"The CPT has also made a number of observations concerning the safeguards surrounding the involuntary placement of persons in psychiatric hospitals and social welfare homes, e.g. regular review of the need for such placements; information on patients'/residents' rights; complaints procedures; external supervision. In particular, the Committee has recommended that all psychiatric establishments in the Czech Republic - including social welfare homes - be visited on a regular basis by an independent outside body."*

## *Bulgaria (CPT visit 2002)*

*"The CPT has also raised a number of issues concerning the safeguards which apply in the context of involuntary hospitalization (observance of the time-limits for court reviews; consent to treatment; information to patients; complaints procedure; external supervision, etc.). In particular, the Committee has recommended that regular visits to psychiatric establishments by independent bodies be encouraged."*

## *Germany (CPT visit 2000)*

*"On account of their vulnerability, the mentally ill and mentally handicapped warrant much attention in order to prevent any form of conduct - or avoid any omission - contrary to their well-being. It follows that the procedure by which involuntary placement is decided should offer guarantees of independence and impartiality, as well as of objective medical expertise. Further, involuntary placement should cease as soon as it is no longer required by the patient's mental state. Consequently, the need for such a placement must be regularly reviewed.*
*The procedure for placements decided on by a judicial authority in accordance with the provisions of the Criminal Code reflects these requirements.*
*However, it appeared that the decision to transfer a patient on secondary referral does not involve any formal procedure whereby the patients concerned receive correct information on their transfer, can make their views known and can appeal against the transfer decision.*
*(S)uch measures should be accompanied by guarantees that the patients are informed in writing of the reasons for their transfer, that they may express their point of view and lodge an appeal against the measure with a clearly defined authority. The CPT recom-*

*mends that the German authorities take the necessary steps to ensure that these guarantees are provided."*

*Poland (CPT visit 2000)*

*"The CPT has also addressed various issues related to safeguards in the context of involuntary hospitalization of psychiatric patients. In particular, the Committee has recommended that an introductory brochure setting forth the hospital routine and patients' rights be devised and issued to each patient on admission, as well as to their families."*

### 14.3.3.2 Conclusions

The Committee's findings reveal shortcomings, to a lesser extent, in the domestic legal systems concerning involuntary psychiatric treatment and/or placement, but more often in relation to the practical aspects. Involuntary psychiatric patients often seem to be left without sufficient information about their rights and their situation in general (Poland, Germany, Czech Republic, Bulgaria, partly also Sweden). More frequent external supervision of psychiatric institutions is encouraged in various cases (Bulgaria, Czech Republic, Sweden). Furthermore, the Committee emphasizes the need to review and reassess the necessity of existing involuntary placements at regular intervals (Germany, Bulgaria).

### 14.3.4 The European Court of Human Rights

Lastly, we shall briefly list some of the relevant individual cases brought before the European Court of Human Rights in relation to involuntary psychiatric treatment and the European Convention on Human Rights (ECHR). Some of these have also been mentioned in the preceding country reports.

*Varbanov vs. Bulgaria,* October 05, 2000
*Kepenerov vs. Bulgaria,* July 31, 2003

*Ashingdane vs. United Kingdom*, May 28, 1985
*Keenan vs. United Kingdom,* April 03, 2001

*Herz vs. Germany,* June 12, 2003
*Storck vs. Germany,* June 16, 2005

### References (i.e. quoted documents and laws)

International Treaties, UN-Resolutions

International Covenant on Civil and Political Rights (CCPR), adopted in UN Doc. A/RES/2200 (XXI), December 16, 1966

International Covenant on Economic, Social and Cultural Rights (CESCR), adopted in UN Doc. A/RES/2200 (XXI), December 16, 1966

Convention against Torture and Other Cruel, Inhuman or Degrading Treatment or Punishment (CAT), adopted in UN Doc. A/RES/39/46, December 10, 1984
European Convention for the Protection of Human Rights and Fundamental Freedoms, European Treaties Series ETS 5, 44, 45, 55, 118
European Convention for the Protection of Human Rights and Dignity of the Human Being with Regard to the Application of Biology and Medicine, European Treaties Series ETS 164
Principles for the Protection of Persons with Mental Illness and for the Improvement of Mental Health Care, UN Doc. A/RES/46/119 (annex), December 17, 1991

UN - General Comments
UN Doc. HRI/GEN/1/Rev.1 (1994)
UN Doc. E/2001/22 (2000)

UN - Concluding Observations
Bulgaria: UN Doc. A/54/44 (1999)
Germany: UN Doc. A/53/44 (1998)
Israel: UN Doc. A/49/44 (1994), A/57/44 (2002)
Italy: UN Doc. A/47/44 (1992)
Lithuania: UN Doc. A/59/44 (2003)
Poland: UN Doc. A/49/44 (1994), A/52/44 (1997), A/55/44 (2000)
Slovakia: UN Doc. A/56/44 (2001), A/58/40 (2003)
Sweden: UN Doc. UN Doc. A/52/44 (1997), A/57/44 (2002)

CPT – Reports
Bulgaria: CPT/Inf (2004) 21
Czech Republic: CPT/Inf (2005) 5
Germany: CPT/Inf (2003) 20
Poland: CPT/Inf (2002) 9
Sweden: CPT/Inf (2004) 32

*Domestic Laws*

| | | |
|---|---|---|
| Bulgaria | - | Constitution of Bulgaria |
| | - | Health Act |
| Czech Republic | - | Constitution of the Czech Republic |
| | - | Charter of Fundamental Rights and Freedoms |
| | - | Act on the Care of the People's Health |
| | - | Civil Procedure Code |
| | - | Criminal Procedure Code |
| | - | Act on Protection against Alcoholism and other Drug Abuse |
| | - | Act on Police |
| England | - | Mental Health Act |
| | - | Human Rights Act |
| | - | Code of Practice |

Germany
- Constitution of Germany
- Civil Code
- Saxon Mental Health Act
- Penal Code

Greece
- Constitution of Greece
- Act for the Modernization and Organization of the Health System
- Civil Law Code
- Civil Procedure Code
- Penal Code

Israel
- Basic Law on Human Dignity and Freedom
- Treatment of Mental Patients Law
- Patient's Right Law
- Youth Care and Supervision Law
- Legal Capacity and Guardianship Law
- Persons in Need Law

Italy
- Constitution of the Italian Republic
- Administrative Law, Law 13, n. 180
- Code of Criminal Procedure
- Penal Code

Lithuania
- Constitution of the Republic of Lithuania
- Criminal Code
- Code of Criminal Procedure
- Law on the Health System
- Law on Ethics of Biomedical Research
- Law on the Rights of Patients and Compensation of the Damage to their Health
- Civil Code
- Law on Mental Health Care

Poland
- Constitution of Poland
- Criminal Code
- Code of Penal Proceedings
- Penal Executive Code
- Civil Code
- Civil Proceedings Code
- Act on Police
- Physician's Profession Act

| | | |
|---|---|---|
| | - Act on Upbringing in Sobriety and Counteracting Alcoholism<br>- Act of Counteracting Drug Addition<br>- Act of Proceedings in Cases of Minors<br>- Mental Health Act |
| Slovak Republic | - Constitution of the Slovak Republic<br>- Health Care Act<br>- Code of Civil Procedure<br>- Penal Law and Code of Penal Procedure<br>- Civil Code<br>- Charter of Patients' Rights<br>- Public Guardian of Rights Act |
| Spain | - Constitution of Spain<br>- Civil Code<br>- Civil Procedure Code<br>- Penal Code<br>- Penal Procedure Code<br>- General Health Care Act<br>- General Prison Act |
| Sweden | - Constitution of Sweden<br>- Act on Compulsory Mental Care<br>- Act on Forensic Mental Care<br>- Act on Health and Medical Care |

**CHAPTER 15**

# The Clinical Point of View: Comparing Differences of Legal Regulations Related to Involuntary Admission and Hospital Stay in Twelve European Countries

Thomas W. KALLERT, Joanna RYMASZEWSKA, Francisco TORRES-GONZÁLEZ

## 15.1 Preliminary Remark

Based on the texts of the twelve individual legal reports published in this book, this chapter aims to compare details relevant to clinical practise that cover involuntary admission and hospital stay as regulated by those countries' civil laws and acts. The limitation to civil commitment results mainly from the clinical research focus of the EUNOMIA-project, and also from the different structure of the participant states' legal systems that do not homogeneously subdivide regulations on civil and forensic commitment.

Issues relevant for clinical practise were identified following the recent international discussion on clinical research, potential misuse, and human rights in this field (Steering Committee on Bioethics of the Council of Europe, 2000). Thus, this chapter will be subdivided in seven main sections:

- Related to involuntary hospital admissions (15.2) we will compare and comment on the basic (15.2.1) conditions (as well as additional criteria (15.2.1.1)) for these admissions, the time period of decision-taking in the different stages of this process (15.2.2), the patients' right to lodge a complaint (15.2.3), the association between involuntary placement and treatment (15.2.4), and the regulations referring to specific involuntary treatment measures during hospitalization (15.2.5).
- The regulations for emergency situations versus the regulations for regular procedures of involuntary admissions (15.3) will be discussed separately as well as
- the different roles of relatives (15.4).
- The professional standard of the physicians involved in these decision processes (15.5) and
- the safeguard procedures of these processes will be critically reviewed (15.6).

  This aim also applies to
- the inclusion and specification of outpatient commitment (15.7).

  And finally,

- the lacking regulations relating to best clinical practise will be outlined (15.8).

## 15.2 Definitions and Regulations Related to Involuntary Hospital Admissions and Hospital Stays

### 15.2.1 Basic Clinical Conditions

These conditions can be subdivided into a general term describing a distinct pathological state of mental health, in addition to some specific conditions that have to be met in order to justify the procedure of involuntary admission to a psychiatric hospital.

The definitions of pathological states of mental health reflect a broad range of general concepts (e.g. Dilling et al. 1993, DSM-IV 1996) and details of descriptions that aim to characterize the nature of these mental health states. These features have to be assessed as positively fulfilled for involuntarily admission to take place. At one end there are general low threshold definitions like "psychological alterations" (Italy) that lack specification of the impairments' nature, disturbances or illnesses which might be included in this definition. Most countries use the term "mental disorder" or "mental illness" (Bulgaria, Czech Republic, England, Germany, Greece, Poland, Slovak Republic, Spain). But, only a few countries outline in detail the diagnostic categories included in these terms. The most detailed description of these categories is given in Bulgaria (in detail: psychosis, severe personality disorder, salient permanent disability due to mental illness, moderate or severe mental retardation, dementia), whereas two other countries (Israel, Poland) use the in itself not further specified term "psychotic"[1] to outline the general pre-conditions for this coercive treatment measure. Two countries using the terms "mental disorder" or "mental illness" explicitly include other terms in describing the medical pre-conditions: "intoxication" in the Czech Republic, and "mental retardation" in Poland (Note: this country has special acts on counteracting alcoholism and drug addiction). At the other end of the spectrum of general concepts are two countries that have introduced a threshold defined by a higher severity degree of pathology. Lithuania uses the in itself not further specified term "severe mental illness", and Sweden[2] introduced the concept of "serious mental disturbance", i.e. psychosis (in detail: a state of mind with a disturbed vision of reality), depression with risk of suicide, severe personality disorder with an impulse breakthrough of psychotic character or severe psychological disturbance with strong obsessive-compulsive behaviour, and

---

1 in detail, Israeli law requires that the psychotic patient's capability to judge reality must be severely defective

2 in preparatory works and general advices of the National Board of Health and Welfare providing guidance for clinicians

(sometimes) also klepto-, pyromania and sexual perversions. The seriousness of a mental disturbance may be judged both by its nature and the extent. The term nature is used to refer to the type of illness, and the extent indicates the psychosocial level of functioning and the severity of the symptoms.
Only three of the assessed countries define conditions that do *not* justify involuntary admission. Greece excludes persons who do not conform to social, moral or political values. The English mental health act states very clearly that people must not be deemed to have a form of mental disorder by reason only of promiscuity or other immoral conduct, sexual deviancy or dependence on alcohol or drugs. And Sweden excludes persons who solely suffer from developmental mental disorders. And, we would like to emphasize that several countries combine the lack of a special capability of the patient with their general concepts of describing the pathological states of mental health. This capability refers to decision making (Davies 1997, Irwin et al. 1985, Vollmann et al. 2003 and 2004) as concerns the consent or the refusal of treatment (England), or to decisions which affect health (Greece), or more precisely decisions relating to the situation of placement (Lithuania, Spain) or urgent medical intervention (Italy).

**Comment**
Independent from legal considerations on and reasons for choosing the discussed formulations of basic clinical conditions, the level of clinical precision in defining the relevant general terms seems to be rather low. In the light of the well-known problem of establishing valid psychiatric diagnoses (Sartorius et al. 1995) particularly in highly acute states and without clear information about the longer-term course of an individual's mental health problems, these low-level definitions might be advantageous for clinicians. However, it must be emphasised that the potential for misuse exists because of the definition's lack of specification – even if the seriousness concept is not considered –, and cross-national harmonization of basic pre-conditions of involuntary admission – one of the main European aims to equalize mental health care opportunities – seems to be far away. Considering the fact that six countries essentially require assessment of the mentally ill person's ability to provide informed consent – this may only refer to placement – criticism has to be raised from a scientific point of view. Clear standards on how to assess this capacity in such acute situations have also not been established (Appelbaum & Grisso 1995, Grisso & Appelbaum 1995, Vollmann 2000), nor do empirical findings exist detailing the numbers and characteristics of patients who are or are not able to make valid decisions.

#### 15.2.1.1 Additional Criteria

Dangerousness criteria are the most frequent criteria that must be met as preconditions for involuntary admissions in addition to or – as in Sweden – included in the positively assessed presence of pathological states of mental health (Dreßing & Salize 2004). In all countries which have established these criteria they do so in terms of these two considerations: a) the existence of a real or present and considerable danger (in the form of self-destructive behaviour) for the individual in question's own life and health (Bulgaria, Czech Republic, England, Germany, Greece, (to some extent) Lithuania, Slovak Republic, Sweden, note: for cases of [involuntary] emergency admissions Poland employed the term "imminent danger"); and/or b) the prevention of a real or present and considerable danger (in the form of dangerous behaviour) for legally protected important interests (normally including health and life, and in Lithuania also property) of other people or of the public (Bulgaria, Czech Republic, England, Germany, Greece, Lithuania, Slovak Republic).

In less concrete formulations Israel and Greece use the same dangerousness criteria, but focus more clearly on the protection of the patient himself (i.e. from inflicting bodily harm on himself or others) or on the society.

As a kind of alternative (Italy, and Poland only for cases of [involuntary] non-emergency admissions), in addition to dangerousness criteria (Greece) or as main pre-requisite on its own (Sweden), the *need* for hospitalization is another important additional criterion. This need has to be absolute in the sense that there are no conditions or circumstances permitting provision of the currently necessary mental health care elsewhere than in a hospital (Israel, Sweden, Lithuania) or there has to be evidence that failure to hospitalize the person in question would cause deterioration in the state of health of the mentally disordered patient.

**Comment**

For clinical practise, two major problems associated with these additional criteria appear. The first is to bridge the gap between the legal and medical view on the attributes attached to the term "danger", and to collect the necessary evidence by including information from external sources within the defined time-limits (see 15.2.2). To further complicate this problem, clinicians at present cannot use broadly accepted national or international guidelines or decision rules that provide some assistance in this difficult task. Secondly, the rarely mentioned criterion of primarily assessing the adequateness of treatment options other than hospitalization clearly depends on the regional availability of a broad range of mental health services (Johnson et al. 2000, Becker et al. 2001) as most recent papers on crisis resolution teams' effects on the frequency and duration of involuntary hospital stays have clearly showed (Johnson et al. 2005). Therefore, it might be assumed that upgrading the structure and availability of mental health services to comparable standards would enhance the clarity and homogeneity of different steps of the decision-making process in order to prevent involuntary admissions.

And, a final comment should address the situation that psychiatry in many of the assessed countries is urged by the legal system's defining elements to execute coercion in order to protect the interests of other people and of the public. This task is not only widely disliked among the professionals, but lacks clarity in the grounding reasons' definition – particularly for those that might be influenced by different cultural and societal contexts.

### 15.2.2 Time-Period of Decision-Taking in the Different Stages of this Process

For the initial period of involuntary hospitalizations which mostly occur on an emergency basis (see section 15.3), all assessed countries have similar regulations (Table 15.1).

The range of these periods varies from 24 (Bulgaria, Czech Republic, Germany, Slovak Republic, Spain, Sweden), and 48 (Italy, Lithuania, Poland) up to 72 (England, Germany) hours. Only in Sweden, it is in the competence of the institution to prolong this initial period for four weeks. Within the given periods, it is the obligation of the institutions – if the patient does not consent to be hospitalized – to inform the authorities, mostly the courts, responsible for deciding on further involuntary stay and treatment of the patient (for more details see section 15.3).

Periods of time until the relevant hearings of the authorities have to be carried out, are defined in seven of the twelve countries. These range from two (Bulgaria, Italy, Poland) to three (Spain), five (Slovak Republic), seven (Czech Republic) and ten days (Greece), following the date on which the information on involuntary hospital admission has been communicated to the relevant authority.

For the next step in this process, the order of further detainment, the variation of the defined periods significantly increases. These periods range from one week (Italy), two weeks (Israel, Poland), one month (Lithuania), six weeks (Germany) and three (Bulgaria, Czech Republic, Slovak Republic, Sweden) months up to six months (England, Greece, Spain[3]).

[3] a first review of the case is held after three months, after this period and the following periods of three months each, the patient or his relatives or his guardian are entitled to request the termination of the involuntary hospitalization by the court via addressing the public prosecutor

**Table 15.1: Most Important Features of Emergency Legal Procedures Referred to Involuntary Hospital Admissions**

| Country | Proposal | Authority to decide | Detention period within the competence of the health institution | Controlling Authority |
|---|---|---|---|---|
| Bulgaria | Relatives<br>Physicians | Head of the Health Service | 24 hours extendable for other 48 hours | Judicial |
| Czech Republic | Parents or relatives<br>Guardian | Physician | 24 hours | Judicial |
| England | *Assessment:*<br>Relatives + Approved Social Worker | Physician + Social worker | 72 hours | Mental Health Act Commission |
| Germany | Administrative Authority | Administrative Authority/Police/ Judicial/Psychiatric hospital | Until 10 a.m., next day* | Judicial, after 10 a.m., next day |
| Greece | Relatives or guardian | Public Attorney** | 48 hours | Judicial |
| Israel | Any psychiatric examination | Hospital director*** | 48 hours | Psychiatric District Committee, Judicial |
| Italy | Physician | 2 physicians | 48 hours | City Mayor.<br>> 48 hours Judicial |
| Lithuania | Psychiatrist | Psychiatrist | 48 hours | Judicial |
| Poland | Physician (preferably psychiatrist (s)) | Psychiatrist (s) | 48 hours | Judicial (followed by Guardianship Court decision) |
| Slovak Republic | Parents or relatives<br>Guardian | Physician | 24 hours | Judicial |
| Spain | Any person | Psychiatrist | 24 hours | Judicial |
| Sweden | Physician | Psychiatrist | 4 weeks | Judicial |

* in 15 of the 16 Federal States (except Baden-Württemberg: 72 h)
** Public Attorney, Public prosecutor, Advocate deputy
*** must refer the case to the district psychiatrist for a hospitalization order (for seven days, can be prolonged for seven more days)

And, if another decision of prolongation is necessary or regular re-assessments are performed by the authorities, the range of permissible time-periods is again considerable. They vary from a one week extension (Italy), to three months from the initial six-weeks-period (Germany), three months (Israel), six months (England, Lithuania, Spain, Sweden) or one year (Czech Republic, Slovak Republic).

Three countries do not state a permissible extension period after the one initially decided by the relevant authority expires (Bulgaria, Greece, Poland). For even more countries it is unclear if there is a maximum duration of detention that might be reached after several decisions on prolongation. Only Germany defines a maximum of twelve (resp. 24) months, whereas some other countries provide further extension periods of six (Israel, Lithuania, Sweden) or twelve months. Although possible limitations of such periods might be reached when patients ask for re-assessment or lodge a complaint (see 15.2.3), it is only Greece that requires a special standard of issuing professional recommendations for deciding on detention periods longer than six months: The necessity of this coercive measure has to be approved by three psychiatrists, one working in the hospital in which the patient is currently treated, and two appointed by the public prosecutor.

Nearly all of the assessed countries (except Bulgaria) clearly assign the competence of terminating involuntary stays before periods defined in the decisions of the authorities expire (Table 15.2) to the hospitals or to (high-ranking) physicians in the hospitals (Czech Republic, Germany, Greece, Israel, Italy, Lithuania, Poland, Slovak Republic, Spain, Sweden). All, except Sweden, are obliged to inform the relevant authorities about these decisions.

It should be mentioned here that four of the twelve countries have special regulations that specifically concern involuntary assessments (and not the process of treatment) in psychiatric hospitals. The periods for these measures range from two days (Greece) to ten days (Poland), and up to 24 (Bulgaria) or 28 (England) days. Poland defined some special periods for this medical undertaking, if addicted persons have to be assessed (two weeks, exceptionally six weeks), and if the legal capacity of patients has to be assessed (normality six weeks, exceptionally maximum of six months).

**Table 15.2: Information on Premature Termination of Involuntary Hospital Stays**

| **Country** | **Authority to decide** | **Criteria for premature termination of involuntary hospital stay** |
|---|---|---|
| Bulgaria | Court | Based on experts' report (psychiatrist) |
| Czech Republic | Health institution | Criteria not explicitly indicated |
| England | The responsible medical officer or a mental health review tribunal | Criteria not explicitly indicated |
| Germany | Physician, municipal public health department | Preconditions for involuntary placement no longer exist |
| Greece | Head doctor<br>Court | Preconditions for involuntary care no longer fulfilled |
| Israel | Hospital director | Criteria not explicitly indicated |
| Italy | Psychiatrist | Preconditions for involuntary care no longer fulfilled |
| Lithuania | The mental health facility administration (following the psychiatrist's recommendations) | Criteria not explicitly indicated |
| Poland | Head of the ward | Preconditions for involuntary care no longer fulfilled |
| Slovak Republic | Health institution | Criteria not explicitly indicated |
| Spain | Psychiatrist | Criteria not explicitly indicated |
| Sweden | Psychiatrist | Preconditions for involuntary care no longer fulfilled |

**Comment**

Because of cross-nationally similar degrees of severity of mental disorders and available treatment options, the clinical rationale for the demonstrated differences in time-periods is hard to explain or understand. Therefore, it could be deemed necessary to suggest a homogeneous solution that tries to consider interests grounded in patients' rights as well as in the needed freedom for clinical decisions. This should include the following components:

A. In order to have enough time to review effects of medication, to improve acute psychopathological symptoms as well as compliance and therapeutic relationship, and to decrease family burden because of early discharge with insufficiently stabilized mental conditions, the initial period of detention should not be shorter than two weeks.

B. The following periods of legal decision making on further detention should not vary across the countries, but should cover clearly defined periods of one or two months.
C. The standard of issuing professional recommendations within the second step should not only involve the psychiatrist in charge, but also one specialist in psychiatry who is independent of the individual care process and the responsible mental health care institution.
D. The obligation to terminate the involuntary hospital stay and to inform the defined legal authority – if the basic conditions have disappeared – should be assigned to the psychiatrist in charge, who should be provided the opportunity to ask for a second specialist's (written) opinion (based on a personal examination of the patient) in cases of doubt.
E. To exceed a defined maximum duration of uninterrupted detention (that should not last longer than six months) should require the decision of a higher court and should take into account professional recommendations issued by two psychiatrists who are independent of the individual care process and the responsible mental health care institution.

In order to evaluate such a proposal it would be necessary from an empirical point of view, to define a two-year time-frame in some model regions in order to carry out the necessary research of effects of these regulations in comparison with the traditional practises. Only in the case of positive results from such a pilot study, should changes of such major importance be introduced at a national or international level.

### 15.2.3 Patients' Rights to Lodge a Complaint

All assessed countries have explicitly included in their legal texts the right to lodge complaints against decisions taken within the official procedures which regulate involuntary admission and hospital stay. However, some details of these regulations show significant variation. This refers to the time-point at which a complaint procedure can be started, time-periods that have to be respected, the number of court instances which can be addressed, the persons/institutions to whom this right is granted, and the provision of legal assistance.

As concerns the starting point, all assessed countries lack clear definitions and leave this issue open – although not explicitly written down – to begun at any time. However, some countries (England, Poland) specifically addressed the option to apply for discharge from a hospital (or the mental health review tribunal in England) at any time (England) or, within 30 days after the court's decision

(Poland), and Germany grants the right to lodge a complaint even before the court's decision is legally valid.
Time-periods for lodging a complaint often start from the day at which the person was informed about the (court's) decision against which the complaint will be filed. Clear periods are named in the legal texts of six countries, and range from ten days (Italy, for the mayor to decide on the complaint) over two (Germany) to three (Sweden) weeks up to 30 (Slovak Republic) and 45 days (Israel) and two months (Greece). Only England's mental health act defines clear periods until which time hearings of the mental health review tribunal have to have been performed (seven days in cases of involuntary hospitalization because of assessment, 21 days in cases of involuntary hospitalization because of treatment), and until which time hospital management (20 days) have to respond to complaints. And Israel's mental health act specifies the period until which time the hearings of the District Psychiatric Committee have to be performed (five days after lodging the initial complaint).
Only in the Slovak Republic it is explicitly stated that complaints can be brought forward to a second higher court's instance. However, it is well-known and common practise that depending on the structure and the tasks of the individual court's systems this is also possible in other countries, even if not written down explicitly in legal texts relating to involuntary hospital admission or stay.
Of course, patients themselves – if legally capable as explicitly defined for the Slovak Republic – can lodge the appeal in all twelve countries. Eight countries grant this right also to other individuals or parties involved in the procedure. Italy and the Czech Republic have chosen the broadest definitions assigning this right to "any other interested individuals" (including e.g. patients' association in Italy) or to "anybody whose rights have been violated by a decision of a public administration body". This clearly includes relatives who are explicitly named in the legal texts of three other countries (England, Israel, Poland[4]), whereas Sweden has excluded this right for relatives. England assigns this right to relatives only in non-emergency cases, and Poland defines that this right can not be executed before 30 days after validation of the decision of the guardianship court (and also defines the brief period of seven days in which an appeal can be lodged to guardianship court if the initial complaint was rejected) in order to decrease the frequency of complaints lodged by relatives. Lithuania and Poland grant the right also to representatives of the patient, and the Slovak Republic grants this right also to the patient's guardian. In three countries (Czech Republic, Italy, Slovak Republic) the right to appeal against court's decisions is also assigned to the mental health institution to which the patient has been admitted or to the health authority which has initially made the decision to detain the pa-

[4] in detail: spouses, children, but also legal representatives

tient (Italy, within 30 days). In Israel[5] and Spain the public prosecutor, and in Spain also the ombudsman can lodge a complaint or initiate a habeas-corpus-procedure (in Spain, lasting twelve to 48 hours).
Only five countries have included clear regulations how legal assistance has to be regularly provided for patients within the judicial procedures of deciding on involuntary hospital admission or stay. German civil and public administrative law defines that a curator (for this procedure) has to be appointed for each patient. Swedish law states that the patient is entitled to a legal representative. The Polish law states that the patient is entitled to a public assistant, curator and/or personal advocate. The law in England entitles the patient to free legal representation, and to the opportunity to choose a solicitor (note: most hospitals offer advocacy services). And in Spain it is the responsibility of the prosecution service to organize the patient's defence before the court.

**Comment**

Empirical findings clearly show the importance of a high standard of procedural quality for decreasing the subjective view of being coerced (Lidz et al. 1995). Therefore, patients' rights to lodge complaints should be enhanced to a cross-nationally comparable standard. In particular, the different steps and the position of those parties to whom roles or activities are assigned within these steps should be defined as transparently as possible. Initially, there should be a clear standard as concerns when, how, to whom, and in which form information on the right to lodge a complaint should be provided. Assignments of legal assistance should be made as a rule. Furthermore, clear time-schedules until which complaints should be lodged and decided on could be helpful for reducing stress and pressure in complicated clinical situations. This also applies to defining homogeneous standards for the form of the personal court hearings in which at least the location, the parties that should participate, and the mode of issuing decisions should be regulated. For patients who may be disturbed in their perceptual and cognitive functions it would be quite helpful if during this process the assignment of several roles to one person (especially to the physician) would be avoided. And, although it might seem easier when making decisions under a certain amount of time-pressure, it would be also helpful for clinicians to concentrate on clinical tasks, and not to mix these with judicial tasks.

### 15.2.4 Association Between Involuntary Placement and Treatment

As concerns this hotly debated issue, the twelve countries can be subdivided into three groups.

---

[5] against the decision of the District Psychiatric Committee (hearing the initial appeal) to the District Court

Only two countries (Bulgaria, Germany) strictly separate legal decisions on involuntary placement and treatment. Two countries have not included special references to involuntary treatment in their legal texts (Greece, Spain). However, indispensable emergency measures including those necessary to protect public health or the health of the patient are not precluded. And, if the patient has no capacity to provide consent to treatment this will provoke special decisions on involuntary treatment or on appointing persons who can provide consent on behalf of the patient.

On the contrary, half of the assessed countries have positively regulated treatment against the will or without consent under the condition of involuntary hospitalization (England, Israel, Lithuania, Poland, Slovak Republic, Sweden). However, a few countries explicitly exclude some measures (Table 15.3) or require special and separate legal consent for these; and the Slovak Republic has defined that until the court's decision on involuntary stay and treatment only emergency measures may be carried out. England requires by law a second opinion as to whether involuntary treatment measures should continue for more than three months. In general, it should be outlined that these six countries bind the decisions on involuntary treatment to the presence of the basic clinical conditions required for involuntary admission.

**Comment**

Although the medical, legal, and patient-centred point of view are clearly different in relation to this hotly debated issue (Steering Committee on Bioethics of the Council of Europe 2000), it seems important to empirically assess if providing consent to placement and to treatment are really distinct mental functions which may be differentially affected by acute states of mental disorders. And, legal practise should be modified following the results in order to avoid unnecessary infringement of patients' rights (in the case of different entities), but also to withhold state-of-the-art treatment options (adequate for rapid decrease of suffering from acute symptoms) from the patient (in the case that different entities cannot be empirically confirmed). Furthermore, to rely on empirical findings relating to this matter would enable decision makers to balance legal safety and other options, helping them decide quickly for the good of both patients and clinicians. To proceed with discussions largely guided by ideological positions in this field, is of no use to clinical practise.

**Table 15.3: Regulations on Specific Treatment Measures**

| Modes of treatment | Explicitly allowed | Allowed by written consent/on defined conditions | Explicitly prohibited |
|---|---|---|---|
| Pharmacological treatment | Israel, Poland (for psychotics), Sweden*, England | | |
| Electro Convulsive Therapy (ECT) | Bulgaria, Israel | Poland, England | |
| Psychotherapy | | Germany | |
| Mechanical restraint | Bulgaria, Israel, Poland, Sweden* | | England (by Code of Practise) |
| Seclusion / Isolation | Bulgaria, Israel, Poland, Sweden* | England (by Code of Practise) | |
| Psychosurgery | | Germany**, Poland, England | Bulgaria, Lithuania |
| Sterilization | | | Bulgaria, Lithuania, Poland |
| Others: lumbal punction | | Poland | |
| Others: comas | | Poland | |
| Forced feeding | Germany | | |
| Treatment of somatic comorbidity | | Germany | |

* The Swedish law stipulates only that a treatment plan should be established and that treatment, decided by the psychiatrist, should be adjusted to what is necessary to achieve the aims of the care (i.e. to get the patient to be able to voluntarily take part in necessary care and to receive the needed support). Fixation and seclusion are explicitly regulated.

** Psychosurgery is not explicitly prohibited in all German States (Laender). E.g., the Saxon Mental Health Act states in section 22 subsection 2 that "medical interventions and methods of treatments pursuant to subsection 1 that are combined with a surgical intervention or a significant danger of serious harm to the life or the health of a patient are permitted only upon the patient's informed and legally relevant consent or, if he or she is not able to assess the significance and implications of such an intervention and of the consent, a legally effective consent of his or her legal representative". And section 22 subsection 4 adds that "all measures may not injure the patient's dignity and may only be carried out by the order of and under direct supervision and responsibility of a physician". Therefore, it depends on the individual case and the interpretation of the judicial body if psychosurgery represents in each case "a measure that injures the patient's dignity". The same is true for sterilisation. In guardianship law some regulations refer to patients unable to provide informed consent.

### 15.2.5 Regulations Referred to Specific Involuntary Treatment Measures During Hospitalization

Although generally mentioned, the legal texts of five countries do not contain standards on the use of restraint and seclusion of psychiatric patients (Bulgaria,

England, Greece, Lithuania, Spain). German civil commitment law regulates the use of preventive measures focussed on dangerous situations (e.g. violent behaviour) or the order of the hospital (e.g. escape attempts) which include isolation and mechanical restraint, but not forced medication. Furthermore, German guardianship law requires consent (of the guardian and the court) if mechanical restraint, forced medication with sedating effect or other measures restricting freedom of movement have to be used.
At the second level of legal norms, four countries (Czech Republic, Israel, Italy, Poland) have defined clear and detailed standards of general use (e.g. preconditions) and clinical application of different coercive treatment measures.
And, two countries (England, Greece) have established nationally binding clinical guidelines outlining how to act clinically in situations which require the use of individual coercive treatment measures (Code of Practise 1983, Special Committee for the Safeguard of the Protection of the Rights of Persons with Mental Disorders 2003).

**Comment**
Independent of a legal level, there should be at least one nationally binding document in each country that is considered as a reference manual for the use of specific involuntary treatment measures (e.g. National Institute for Clinical Excellence 2005). This would provide the opportunity for hospital managers, individual clinicians and patients to check the locally or individually performed standard in order to improve local standards, to lodge complaints or to defend clinical decisions and behaviour against complaints and criticism.

## 15.3 Regulations for Emergency Situations Versus Regular Procedures of Involuntary Admissions

The involuntary placement of a individual in a hospital is not only a relevant clinical decision, it is a breach of one of the most important human rights: the right to freedom. Consequently, this decision, though predominantly taken on clinical grounds, must be externally checked. In countries which have established national constitutions (see chapter 14), this final checking process is carried out exclusively by judicial authorities.
From a clinical point of view, the need for involuntary placement frequently is an urgent one. It is interesting to point out, however, that only five of the twelve countries participating in the EUNOMIA-study (i.e. Czech Republic, Italy, Lithuania, Slovak Republic, Sweden) contemplate only one legal procedure covering emergency placement as well. The majority of national legislative bodies offer two alternatives: regular and emergency procedures. In those cases, undoubtedly, the regular procedure is the one preferred by the legislator and the two approaches are not legally equivalent. The emergency one is considered an

exceptional pathway to manage situations whenever a patient's clinical condition does not allow regular processes to be carried out. Often, according to legislation, the professional in charge has to rely on clinical criteria in order to select which approach is to be taken. The exceptional emergency alternative could be only applied in cases when the mentally ill person's clinical condition does not allow for the time that the regular procedure requires.
In the countries participating in the EUNOMIA-study, the involuntary admission in the case of emergency situations is usually a medical decision (see Table 15.1). This is the case in eleven out of the twelve countries studied. Additionally, within most countries, the authority responsible for looking after the patient's right to freedom is a Judge or a Court, the majority of them being Civil Judges or Courts. In six countries (Bulgaria, England, Greece, Israel, Italy and Sweden), the guarantee of the right to freedom for the mentally ill person is not a direct and immediate judicial responsibility. In Bulgaria and Greece this responsibility is given first to the Public Attorney, in Israel to the District Psychiatrist (appointed by the Minister of Health), and in Italy to the Mayor of the City. In England the responsibility is shared by several public officers, and in Sweden this responsibility is assigned to a medical and judicial authority.

As already mentioned in section 15.2.2, the period of time for which the patient might be placed (in the case of emergencies) in a hospital by the physicians, without the knowledge of a supervisory authority, varies between 24 (four countries) and 72 hours (two countries); Sweden differs here because the patient might be kept in hospital up to four weeks[6] before the case must be presented in front of the County Administrative Court.

In summary, we could say that the involuntary admission within the emergency procedures usually is a two-step procedure: a medical decision followed by a judicial inspection immediately afterwards.

This contrasts the regular legal procedures for involuntary admissions (Table 15.4), the process of which is usually more complex. Most of the relevant laws established specific clinical conditions or behavioural risks which justify involuntary admission (more details have been provided in section 15.2.1 of this chapter) and they frequently mention certain limited purposes of the admission (i.e. assessment, treatment or, simply, placement). Of course, these limitations are implicit also for the emergency procedure. However since it is only a pathway to regular procedure, as we said, the practical schedule is much faster.

---

6 the patient has the right to appeal the decision of the physician at any time during this period

**Table 15.4: Most Important Features of Regular Legal Procedures Referred to Involuntary Hospital Admission and Stay**

| Country | Proposal | Decision Authority | Initial Maximum Period |
|---|---|---|---|
| Bulgaria | Guardian<br>Relatives<br>Physician | Judicial | *For assessment*: 34 days<br>*For involuntary treatment:* 3 months |
| Czech Republic | Physician | Judicial | Up to 3 months |
| England | Relatives + Approved Social Worker | 2 physicians (at least one of these psychiatrist) + social worker | *For assessment*: 28 days<br>*For involuntary treatment:* 6 months |
| Germany | Administrative Authority/ Guardian | Judicial | 6 weeks (or 12 months*) |
| Greece | Application by relatives in front of the Public Attorney | Judicial | 6 months (48 hours for assessment as a preliminary stage of the regular procedure) |
| Israel | District Psychiatrist | District Psychiatrist<br>Psychiatric District Committee | 7 days, extendable for 7 days, and can be prolonged for 3 months |
| Italy** | physician in charge of the psychiatric service | City Mayor | 7 days |
| Lithuania | Psychiatrist | Judicial | 1 month |
| Poland | Relatives or Guardian | Judicial | *For assessment*: 10 days [up to 6 weeks (see text)]<br>*For involuntary treatment:* 6 months |
| Slovak Republic | Psychiatrist | Judicial | 3 months |
| Spain | Parents or relatives<br>Guardian<br>Public Attorney | Judicial | Length not defined. Reporting to judge after each 6-month-period. |
| Sweden*** | Psychiatrist/Deputy Chief Doctor of the care institution | Judicial | 3 months |

* refers to guardianship law
** refers to the situation that the initial admission exceeds 7 days
*** refers to the situation that the initial admission exceeds 4 weeks

In the regular proceeding, the laws also tend to state precisely who is capable of making demands (and on the contrary who is not), as well as from which authority the permission for an involuntary admission of a mentally ill person can be requested. As will be discussed in more detail in this chapter (see section 15.5), the issuance of a professional opinion is needed according to the laws and, in

most cases, sooner or later the judicial authority provides the last word to conclude proceedings.
The clinical problem, reported by several countries, which is associated with the two proceedings is the tendencies that a great proportion of involuntary admissions take place by the application of the fast-track regulations used for emergency situations, instead of the regular proceeding. Some figures indicate that this applies to approx. 80 % of all involuntary admissions (see section 10.2). This means that the fast-track proceeding which was intended to be used as an exception is replacing in practise the regular proceeding. To some extent this could be called a fraud of the law.

The explanation of this phenomenon might be quite simple: the restricted, bureaucratic and lengthy standard procedure is being avoided by using the small door open for emergency situations. Furthermore, the new tendency for community-based care might be an additional factor to be taken into account in most of the countries. The community model of care offers a steady increase in the resources used to keep the person with a mental illness out of the hospital and the mean length of hospital stays has been constantly decreasing across Europe over the last two decades (Becker et al. 2001). All this means that placement into hospital, even that which was already prepared some time in advance, and placement aiming at longer-term inpatient treatment is nowadays less frequent. Admission is mostly opted for when it is unavoidable or cannot be postponed, and is thus usually contemplated for the shortest possible period.

**Comment**
Aiming to face clinical reality adequately we would like to propose that countries should change their legislation according to the frequency of emergency involuntary hospital admissions. This would mean establishing a legally safe time effective method as the standard legal proceeding for placing a mentally ill person in hospital without her or his consent, for both assessment and treatment. This procedure should be based on clinical conditions and be applied through rapid implementation. In every case admission should be followed by an immediate and personal judicial review afterwards, as a necessary guarantee that the patient's right to freedom is not violated.
Contrarily, an exceptional legal procedure should be opened up for involuntary long-stay admissions which are foreseen and prepared in advance. At least in our view, this manner of placement occurs less frequently but remains necessary.

### 15.4 The Different Roles of Relatives
Of special relevance is the struggle that mentally ill person's relatives frequently have to go through when an application has to be put forward in order to achieve

the involuntary placement of that person. In practise and in many cases the mentally ill person's relative has to go from the physician or community psychiatrist to the authority, from the authority to the hospital, from the hospital to the police and back once and again, handling reports and insisting on help.

Nevertheless, the role of relatives within the legal proceedings of involuntary placement is not at all (Germany, Italy, Sweden) or not sufficiently reflected in the studied laws. Whenever the relative is specifically considered a lack of homogeneity among the different national legislations becomes evident, mostly reducing the role of relatives to request primary (England, Lithuania) examinations or earlier discharge (e.g. Poland, Czech Republic, Slovak Republic) as compared to the periods determined by court's decisions. Among the twelve countries assessed, the English law constitutes an exception because the role of the relatives is quite far developed here. The nearest relative has to be identified and consulted by the social worker before involuntary admission takes place. If the nearest relative believes the patient does not need admission, the patient remains in the community. If the social worker believes the nearest relatives objections are unreasonable then the social worker can refer the case to a county court who will decide whether the nearest relative needs to be replaced. The nearest relative can discharge a detained patient and in this case he/she informs the hospital. Then the psychiatrist has 72 hours time to consider the case and stop the discharge but only if there is an acute risk to self or others.

Although a legal representative for the patient is required by several of the countries investigated (see section 15.2.3 of this chapter also covering the relatives' rights to lodge an appeal) very few countries provide the opportunity for a mentally ill person's relative to officially apply for their involuntary admission to the relevant institution. Even when this is the case two extremes could be found: Greece or Poland, for instance, where the type of the link between person with a mental illness and relative is clearly defined and is specifically addressed in the law, while in Spain anybody who happens to know the mentally ill person's need for hospitalization is entitled to declare it before the relevant authority.

**Comment**

The reality seems to be that mentally ill persons' relatives are not sufficiently assisted by the present legal framework of most of the twelve countries considered here. Moreover, when an individual suffering from mental illness lacks insight and suffers a new breakdown and during phases characterised by risk taking behaviour, the relatives suffer the burden of the situation alone and with very little help from legal provisions. Therefore, their role should be clearly stated and protected by the law, and their relationship with the health services, the police or with the judicial procedure itself all need to be addressed in detail. Otherwise, relatives might view themselves as being put aside by the doctor, by the police officer or by the Court authority, with the increasing feeling that the mentally ill member of his or her family is essentially other people's charge. These regulations should include definitions of the relative's rights to be part of a Court hearing or to lodge an appeal on their own initiative against a decision by an authority.

### 15.5 Professional Standard of the Physicians Involved in the Decision Process

In order to systematize the information provided in the legal texts this paragraph will separately deal with the required number and independence or affiliation of physicians, their qualification in the field of psychiatry, their hierarchical position in mental health institutions, and the differentiation of the professional standard between emergency and non-emergency procedures.

Two thirds of the assessed countries rely in the initial phase of involuntarily admitting patients to psychiatric hospitals – before or during an official court procedure in which the court appoints an expert – on the medical recommendation issued by one physician (Bulgaria, Czech Republic, Germany, Israel, Italy, Poland, Slovak Republic, Spain). However, three of these countries (Israel, Italy, Poland) explicitly require that the initial recommendation has to be validated by another independent physician or a board of experts who may be appointed by a court.

On the contrary, one third of the countries (England, Greece, Lithuania, Sweden) require recommendations issued by (at least) two physicians. All of these countries added some further specifications to this mere number of experts. Greece defines the necessary qualification of a specialist in psychiatry as concerns issuing an application for involuntary hospitalization, and – if this professional standard is not available – defines as exception one psychiatrist and one specialist from a related discipline. Sweden requires that the initial recommendation be validated by a specialist in psychiatry, particularly appointed for this task by the head of the mental health facility. Lithuania requires a third recommendation to be issued by a physician who represents the administration of the hospital. And according to the definitions in England – which also provide the option of a joint recommendation – one doctor should be involved who is officially approved to detain patients under the mental health act, another doctor should have previous acquaintance with the patient, and only one of these two should be employed in the hospital where the patient will be admitted.

Except for Italy, the professional standard of the involved physicians issuing recommendations valid for court hearings and decisions in the other eleven countries must be the status of a board-certified specialist in psychiatry. Italian regulations require, however, that the physician validating the initial proposal of another physician should be employed in the local medical unit, e.g. a public medical facility. Three countries explicitly define alternatives to this principle professional standard. Germany also allows the competence of a "medical doctor experienced in psychiatry" without outlining criteria demonstrating the required expertise. Spain defines either a forensic surgeon or an institutional team of various specialists as an alternative. Restricted to the issuing the admission order, Poland accepts the recommendation of any other physician if a specialist in psychiatry is not available.

Concerning the hierarchical positions of psychiatrists in mental health facilities, only two countries have issued some regulations. In Bulgaria, the head physician of the psychiatric facility holds emergency powers for initially detaining patients in the hospital. In Sweden, the head physician appoints a psychiatric specialist to be responsible for validating initial recommendations issued by non-specialists, and for terminating the involuntary hospital stay. Note: countries other than those just mentioned have no explicit regulations as concerns the professional qualifications of physicians responsible for terminating involuntary hospital stay, but implicitly require that their status is a board-certified specialist in psychiatry also for this undertaking.

Only England provides a special regulation for emergency cases in which the number of medical recommendations necessary is reduced to one.

**Comment**

Although it might by unclear if and how (especially complicated and demanding) regulations of required professional qualification will be executed and observed in clinical reality, it would be helpful for the transparency of the legal proceeding if there was at least a common minimum standard which has to be strictly respected. Because of the complexity and difficulty of the clinical task of correctly assessing clinical states that might imply eminent risks for the patient or for others, the initial medical recommendation for involuntary hospitalization should be written by a specialist in psychiatry. Then, following the broadly accepted medical standard to ask for a second opinion, options for having this recommendation reviewed by another psychiatric specialist who was not involved in issuing the initial recommendation and who is not responsible for current decisions relating to involuntary treatment or the patient's hospital stay. These options should be clearly defined in all relevant country-specific legal texts. In general, such regulations should be adapted to the clinical reality of each nation, like the current lack of highly qualified psychiatrists in a range of European countries, and should be embedded in a safeguard system that is dominated by a court's decision in order to subdivide responsibilities as transparently as possible.

## 15.6 Safeguards

As shown in the tables 15.1 and 15.4 the most common authority responsible for checking and monitoring is a qualified Judge or a judicial Court. In fact, it is only in Israel and England that the ordinary judicial authorities do not monitor or review particularly the emergency legal procedures referred to involuntary hospital admission.

In several countries other authorities have a comparatively relevant role, however. A Public Attorney or Public Prosecutor might act as an intermediate agent between the applying family and the Judge, or develop functions of supervision during the hospital stay on behalf of the Judge. Examples of this can be seen in Bulgaria, Czech Republic, Greece or Spain. In a few countries, such as, Bulgaria or Lithuania the health authorities themselves have taken some responsibility for this task. Paradigmatic is the case of Israel, where health professionals appointed as public officers exercise the full safeguarding and monitoring authority, though the Public Attorney might appeal the decision of the Psychiatric District Committee. The ombudsman's institution is mentioned by some legislations (Czech Republic, Greece, Sweden) as a safeguarding or supervising agency, but, according to the details provided in the country-specific legal reports, the practical impact does not seem to be highly significant in relation to mentally ill people admitted into hospital against their will. In Spain, the ombudsman institution's officers were surprised when they were recently asked by the local EUNOMIA-team about eventual complaints by patients or relatives related to coercive measures applied during hospitalization: no complaint was known.
The complex, lengthy and bureaucratic procedural safeguards have been identified several times as a cause for the difficulties faced by the mental ill individual's relatives and as the main reason for explaining that the (legally exceptional) emergency procedure has become the primary method used to achieve involuntary admissions. The Greek legal framework could be taken as an example of this bureaucratic complexity. In that country the Judge, the Public Attorney and the Ombudsman, depending on the stage of the proceeding, share the supervising responsibility. However, the national report emphasizes that the Public Attorney is too often the real protagonist, while the Ombudsman in practise plays a minor role.

Once the person with the mental illness is placed in the hospital, the authorized length of stay varies from country to country (see Table 15.4), but the supervising authority during the hospitalization remains the one which initially authorized involuntary placement.

**Comment**
The general impression from the national legal reports presented in this book is that activities of supervision authorities are largely performed as formal routine. Supervision refers to checking duly filled-in and signed paperwork, but does not stimulate or demand practical changes. Despite of the complexity of the regulations, or perhaps because of that, the face-to-face interview between the person with the mental illness and the supervising authority is exceptional. Changes to the patient's legal status dictated by an authority and not previously suggested by the health professionals are extremely rare. Although appeal proceedings of the patients are foreseen by most of the laws (see section 15.2.3 of this chapter), they rarely occur. We have already discussed how the relatives' role often has not been significantly taken into consideration.

Most of the regulations do not contemplate other coercive measures by which the patient might be affected while staying in hospital. It seems that once the patient is placed in the hospital, the authority delegates the responsibility to the health professionals, assuming that they will always act in the best interests of the patient. And hopefully, this should usually be the case, but nonetheless an external supervision should not be abandoned.
This is not only in the patients' interests. Additionally, care professionals need to be legally protected and considered in the legislation so that they are supported by authorities entitled to supervise the correct application of legal principles.
Supervising authorities should be established not only periodically and routinely. On the contrary, there should be permanent and unbroken activities where the patients and their families have the real opportunity to have face-to face interviews with both the health professionals and the supervising authorities aiming to guarantee the correct application of legal regulations referred to coercive treatment measures.

## 15.7 Inclusion and Specification of Outpatient Commitment
Related to this issue, the twelve countries covered in this book can be subdivided into three parts. Four countries (Czech Republic, Lithuania, Slovak Republic, Spain) have provided the legal framework for ordering outpatient commitment (for up to five years in a medical centre or a specialist social health care institution as in Spain) only in their criminal legislation, but not in their civil laws.
Four countries (Germany, Greece, Poland, Sweden) provide no legal basis whatsoever. However, at least Sweden reports that de facto e.g. depot-injections are carried out in outpatient settings when legally involuntarily admitted patients are on long-term leaves granted by the relevant civil laws.

And, four countries (Bulgaria, England, Israel, Italy) have included options for outpatient commitment in their civil legislation, but three of them have added restrictions indicating special modes of treatment, clinical situations, and procedural aspects. In England, the currently valid mental health act 1995 defines the (clinically rarely used) option of after-care under supervision which refers to residence, and institutions but not relating to medication. In Italy, the local health authority can issue the proposal for involuntary admission not under hospitalization, but this is used only for emergency treatment measures that can be performed at day hospitals or at home. And Israel defines outpatient commitment as an alternative to hospitalization for periods of six months each, and in the case of failure to comply hospitalization will be the automatic consequence.

**Comment**

In contrast to the more widely spread legal regulations on this issue and most recently conducted and controversially discussed empirical research in the United States (Monahan et al. 2003, Steadman et al. 2001, Swanson et al. 2003, Swartz et al. 2001 a-c, Swartz et al. 2002, Swartz & Swanson 2004), European countries seem somewhat hesitant to include outpatient commitment into their civil legislation frameworks. At the moment, the most important reasons for this seem to be: the unclear features of patients who might benefit from such approaches, the not well-defined variables of positive outcomes, and the fear of disproportionately restricting mentally disordered persons' human rights and freedoms. However, it should be mentioned that from a professional point of view this hesitancy remains in opposition to one of the general paradigms of treating mentally ill. This is the requirement of using outpatient and rehabilitative treatment options first (Tansella & Thornicroft 2001), and hospitalization only if these less restrictive measures have failed, are inappropriate or are not available.

## 15.8 Lacking Regulations Related to Best Clinical Practise

In order to avoid repeating individual points of criticism voiced in several subparagraphs of this chapter, the authors would like to briefly summarize and thus emphasize the most important general issues from their point of view that need cross-national harmonization.

- The legal basis for treatment decisions (including the setting of the treatment) must be simplified to the greatest possible extent.
- The powers of decision have to be clearly subdivided and assigned to different professional roles; their standard of professional competency needs to be defined.
- Time periods for the judicial decisions and performance of judicial authorities should be cross-nationally standardized.

- Relevant country-specific laws should be adapted considering the clinical reality of high rates of emergency involuntary hospital admissions.
- At each state of the judicial proceedings assigning involuntary hospitalization and coercive treatment measures the patient should have to the right to a legal representative.
- Regulations to lodge appeals have to be as simple and transparent as possible.
- A similar requirement applies to regulations involving persons from the patient's social environment into the judicial procedures.
- Permanent and active monitoring procedures for supervising authorities should be established in order to increase legal safety for all parties involved in the process of involuntary hospital admission and stay.

## Acknowledgement

The authors gratefully acknowledge the most valuable contributions to this chapter provided by Georgi Onchev, Stepan Peichl, Martin Zinkler, Giorgos Triantaphyllou, Maisam Musallam, Corrado de Rosa, Dalia Zeleckiene, Lars Kjellin, and Gustav Svensson.

## References

Appelbaum PS, Grisso T (1995) The MacArthur Treatment Competence Study. I. Mental illness and competence to consent to treatment. Law and Human Behavior 19:105-126

Becker T, Bauer M, Rutz W, Aktion Psychisch Kranke (eds) (2001) Psychiatric reforms in Europe. Acta Psychiatrica Scandinavica 104 (Suppl. 410)

Code of Practise. Mental Health Act. United Kingdom: 1983

Davies T (1997) Consent to treatment – trust matters as much as information. Psychiatric Bulletin 21:200-201

Diagnostisches und Statistisches Manual Psychischer Störungen DSM-IV (1996). Deutsche Bearbeitung und Einführung von Saß H, Wittchen HU, Zaudig M. Hogrefe-Verlag, Göttingen, Bern, Toronto, Seattle

Dilling H, Mombour W, Schmidt MH (1993) Internationale Klassifikation psychischer Störungen, ICD-10, Kapitel V (F): Klinisch-diagnostische Leitlinien (Tenth revision of the International Classification of Diseases, Chapter V (F): Clinical Descriptions and Diagnostic Guidelines). Huber-Verlag, Bern, Göttingen, Toronto, Seattle

Dreßing H, Salize HJ (2004) Zwangsunterbringung und Zwangsbehandlung psychisch Kranker. Gesetzgebung und Praxis in den Mitgliedsländern der Europäischen Union. Psychiatrie-Verlag, Bonn

Grisso T, Appelbaum PS (1995) The MacArthur Treatment Competence Study. III. Abilities of patients to consent to psychiatric and medical treatments. Law and Human Behavior 19:149-174

Irwin M, Lovitz A, Marder SR, Mintz J, Winslade WJ, van Putten T, Mills MJ (1985) Psychotic patients' understanding of informed consent. American Journal of Psychiatry 142:1351-1354

Johnson S, Kuhlmann R and the EPCAT Group (2000) The European Service Mapping Schedule (ESMS): development of an instrument for the description and classification of mental health services. Acta Psychiatrica Scandinavica 102(Suppl. 405):14-23

Johnson S, Nolan F, Hoult J (2005) The outcomes of crisis before and after introduction of a crisis resolution team: Islington Crisis Studies 1. British Journal of Psychiatry 187:68-75

Lidz CW, Hoge SK, Gardner WP, Bennett NS, Monahan J, Mulvey EP, Roth LH (1995) Perceived coercion in mental hospital admission: Pressures and Process. Archives of General Psychiatry 52: 1034-1039

Monahan J, Swartz M, Bonnie R (2003) Mandated treatment in the community for people with mental disorders. Health Affairs 22:28-38

National Institute for Clinical Excellence (NICE) (2005) Clinical Practise Guidelines for Violence: The short-term management of disturbed/violent behaviour in psychiatric inpatient settings and emergency departments. www.nice.org.uk/page.aspx?o=244477

Sartorius N, Üstün TB, Korten A, Cooper J, Drimmelen J van (1995) Progress toward achieving a common language in psychiatry. II. Results from the international field trials of ICD-10 diagnostic criteria for research for mental and behavioural disorders. American Journal of Psychiatry 152: 1427-1437

Special Committee for the Safeguard of the Protection of the Rights of Persons with Mental Disorders: document number 35, 14 July 2003, Greece

Steadman HJ, Gounis K, Dennis D, Hopper K, Roche B, Swartz M, Robbins PC (2001) Assessing the New York City involuntary outpatient commitment pilot program. Psychiatric Services 52:330-336

Steering Committee on Bioethics of the Council of Europe (2000) White paper on the protection of the human rights and dignity of people suffering from mental disorders, especially those placed as involuntary patients in a psychiatric establishment. www.ijic.org/docs/psychiatry.pdf

Swanson, J., Swartz M, Elbogen E, Wagner H, Burns B (2003) Effects of involuntary outpatient commitment on subjective quality of life in persons with severe mental illness. Behavioral Sciences & the Law 21:473-491

Swartz M, Swanson J, Hiday V, Wagner H, Burns B, Borum R (2001a) A randomized controlled trial of outpatient commitment in North Carolina. Psychiatric Services 52:325-329

Swartz M, Swanson J, Wagner H, Burns B, Hiday V, Borum, W (2001b) Can involuntary outpatient commitment reduce hospital recidivism? Findings from a randomized trial with severely mentally ill individuals. In Talbott J (ed) Year Book of Psychiatry and Applied Mental Health. Elsevier, New York

Swartz M, Wagner H, Swanson J, Hiday V, Burns B (2002) The perceived coerciveness of involuntary outpatient commitment: Findings from an empirical study. Journal of the American Academy of Psychiatry and the Law 30:207-217

Swartz MS, Swanson JW (2004) Involuntary outpatient commitment, community treatment orders, and assisted outpatient treatment: what's in the data? Canadian Journal of Psychiatry 49:585-591

Swartz MS, Swanson JW, Wagner HR, Burns BJ Hiday VA (2001c) Effects of involuntary outpatient commitment and depot antipsychotics on treatment adherence in persons with severe mental illness. Journal of Nervous and Mental Disease 189:583-592

Tansella M, Thornicroft G (2001) The principles underlying community care. In: Thornicroft G, Szmukler G (eds) Textbook of community psychiatry. Oxford University Press, Oxford, p 155-166

Vollmann J (2000) Aufklärung und Einwilligung in der Psychiatrie: Ein Beitrag zur Ethik in der Medizin. Steinkopff, Darmstadt
Vollmann J, Bauer A, Danker-Hopfe H, Helmchen H (2003) Competence of mentally ill patients: a comparative empirical study. Psychological Medicine 33:1463-1471
Vollmann J, Kühl KP, Tilmann A, Hartung HD, Helmchen H (2004) Einwilligungsfähigkeit und neuropsychologische Einschränkungen bei dementen Patienten. Nervenarzt 75:29-35

## GLOSSARY

### Use of terms[1] in the book

| | |
|---|---|
| Act | a law passed formally by a parliament |
| Administration | **1** the organization and running of a business or system. **2** the action of administering. **3** the government in power. |
| Admission | the process or fact of being admitted to a place |
| Agreement | **1** accordance in opinion or feeling. **2** a negotiated and typically legally binding arrangement. **3** consistency or conformity between two things. |
| Ambulatory | movable; mobile |
| Appeal | Law apply to a higher court for a reversal of a lower court's decision. |
| Assess | assess: evaluate or estimate.<br>DERIVATIVES **assessable** adjective **assessment** noun **assessor** noun. |
| Attorney | a person appointed to act for another in legal matters |
| Autonomous | Autonomous: self-governing or independent. |
| Community | ***Community: (pl.*** *communities)* *1* ***a group of people living together in one place.*** *2 (the community)* ***the people of an area or country considered collectively; society.*** |
| Capacity | (pl. **capacities**) **1** the maximum amount that something can contain or produce. **2** the ability or power to do something. **3** a specified role or position |
| Care | **noun 1** the provision of what is necessary for the welfare and protection of someone or something. **2** Brit. protective custody or guardianship provided for children by a local authority. **3** serious attention or consideration applied to avoid damage, risk, or error<br>**verb 1** feel concern or interest. **2** feel affection or liking. **3 (care for/to do)** like to have or be willing to do. **4 (care for)** look after and provide for the needs of. |
| Chart | **noun** a sheet of information in the form of a table, graph, or diagram.<br>**verb** plot or record on a chart. |
| Civil law | **1** law concerned with ordinary citizens, rather than |

[1] selected from the Oxford English Dictionary, revised tenth edition. Oxford University Press 2006

| | |
|---|---|
| | criminal, military, or religious affairs. **2** the system of law predominant on the European continent, influenced by that of ancient Rome. |
| Code | **1** a systematic collection of laws or statutes: the penal code. **2** a set of conventions governing behaviour. |
| Coerce | persuade (an unwilling person) to do something by using force or threats.<br>DERIVATIVES **coercion** noun **coercive** adjective. |
| Commitment | an engagement or obligation that restricts freedom of action. |
| Competence | the quality or extent of being competent |
| Compulsory | required by law or a rule; obligatory |
| Consent | permission or agreement |
| Convention | **1** a way in which something is usually done. **2** an agreement between countries. **3** a body set up by agreement to deal with a particular issue. |
| Council of Ministers | Council: **1** a formally constituted advisory, deliberative, or administrative body. **2** a body elected to manage the affairs of a city, county, or district.<br>Minister: a head of a government department. |
| Court | **1** (also **court of law**) a body of people before whom judicial cases are heard. **2** the place where such a body meets. |
| Criminal | **noun** a person who has committed a crime.<br>**adjective** relating to or constituting a crime. |
| Decision | **1** a conclusion or resolution reached after consideration. **2** the action or process of deciding. |
| Decree | **1** an official order that has the force of law. **2** a judgement or decision of certain law courts. |
| Detain | keep in official custody. |
| Detention | the action of detaining or the state of being detained. |
| Discharge | **noun** the action of discharging<br>**verb** dismiss or allow to leave. |
| District | an area of a town or region, especially one regarded as a unit because of a particular characteristic. |
| Emergency | **1** a serious, unexpected, and potentially dangerous situation requiring immediate action. **2** N. Amer. the casualty department in a hospital. |
| Establishment | **noun 1** the action of establishing or being established. **2** a business organization, public institution, or household. |
| Ethics Committee | Ethics: **1** the moral principles governing or influencing |

| | |
|---|---|
| | conduct. **2** the branch of knowledge concerned with moral principles. |
| | Committee: treated as sing. or pl. a group of people appointed for a specific function by a larger group. |
| Examination | **1** a detailed inspection or investigation. **2** a formal test of knowledge or proficiency in a subject or skill. **3** the action of examining. |
| Expert report | Expert: a person who is very knowledgeable about or skilful in a particular area. |
| | report: **1** an account given of a matter after investigation or consideration. **2** a piece of information about an event or situation. |
| Expertise | great skill or knowledge in a particular field. |
| Facility | a building, service, or piece of equipment provided for a particular purpose. |
| Family | **1** a group consisting of two parents and their children living together as a unit. **2** a group of people related by blood or marriage. **3** the children of a person or couple. |
| Federal | **1** referring to a system of government in which several states form a unity but remain independent in internal affairs. **2** referring to the central government as distinguished from the separate units constituting a federation. |
| Fixation | the action of fixating or the state of being fixated. |
| Force | **noun 1** physical strength or energy as an attribute of action or movement. **2** coercion backed by the use or threat of violence. **3** a person or thing regarded as exerting power or influence. |
| | **verb 1** push into a specified position using force. **2** make (someone) do something against their will. |
| Forcible | done by force. |
| Forensic | **1** relating to or denoting the application of scientific methods to the investigation of crime. **2** of or relating to courts of law. |
| Free will | **noun** the power to act without the constraints of necessity or fate; the ability to act at one's own discretion |
| General Attorney | the principal legal officer of the Crown or a state. |
| Guardian | a person legally responsible for someone unable to manage their own affairs |
| Habeas Corpus | a writ requiring a person to be brought before a judge or into court, especially to investigate the lawfulness of their detention. |

| | |
|---|---|
| Health | **1** the state of being free from illness or injury. **2** a person's mental or physical condition. |
| Hearing | an act of listening to evidence, especially a trial before a judge without a jury. |
| Hospital | an institution providing medical and surgical treatment and nursing care for sick or injured people. |
| Ill | not in full health; unwell. |
| Immobilize | **1** prevent from moving or operating as normal. **2** restrict the movements of (a limb or patient) to allow healing. |
| Instance | **1** an example or single occurrence of something. **2** a particular case. |
| Institution | **1** an important organization or public body. **2** an organization providing residential care for people with special needs. |
| Internal norm | Internal: existing or used within an organization.<br>norm: a required or acceptable standard. |
| Involuntary | done against someone's will. |
| Isolation | the process or fact of isolating or being isolated. |
| Jurisprudence | **1** the theory or philosophy of law. **2** a legal system. |
| Law | **1** a rule or system of rules recognized by a country or community as regulating the actions of its members and enforced by the imposition of penalties. **2** such rules as a subject of study or as the basis of the legal profession. **3** statute law and the common law. |
| Legal representative | an official appointed to investigate individuals' complaints against bad or dishonest administration, especially that of public authorities. |
| Leverage | the exertion of force by means of a lever. |
| Mandate | **noun** an official order or authorization.<br>**verb 1** give (someone) authority to act in a certain way. **2** make compulsory. |
| Mandatory | required by law or mandate; compulsory. |
| Measures | **1** a means of achieving a purpose. **2** a legislative bill. **3** a standard unit used to express size, amount, or degree. |
| Medication | **1** a medicine or drug. **2** treatment with medicines |
| Mental disorder | Mental: **adjective 1** of, done by, or occurring in the mind. **2** relating to disorders or illnesses of the mind.<br>USAGE The use of **mental** (e.g. as in **mental hospital**) is now regarded as old-fashioned, even offensive, and has been largely replaced by **psychiatric** in both general and official use. |

| | |
|---|---|
| | disorder: a disruption of normal physical or mental functions. |
| Nursing home | an institution (for the elderly) providing residential accommodation with health care. |
| Ombudsman | an official appointed to investigate individuals' complaints against bad or dishonest administration, especially that of public authorities. |
| Order | **noun 1** the arrangement of people or things according to a particular sequence or method. **2** a state in which everything is in its correct place. **3** a state in which the laws and rules regulating public behaviour are observed. **4** an authoritative command or direction. **5** a request for something to be made, supplied, or served. **6** the prescribed procedure followed in a meeting, law court, or religious service.<br>**verb 1** request that (something) be made, supplied, or served. **2** arrange methodically. |
| Placement | the action of placing or the fact of being placed. |
| Prevention | a preventive medicine or other treatment. |
| Preventive | designed to prevent something from occurring. |
| Procedure | **1** an established or official way of doing something. **2** a series of actions conducted in a certain manner |
| Prosecutor | **1** a person, especially a public official, who prosecutes someone. **2** a lawyer who conducts the case against a defendant. |
| Protocol | **1** the official procedure or system of rules governing affairs of state or diplomatic occasions. **2** the accepted code of behaviour in a particular situation. |
| Psychiatry | the branch of medicine concerned with the study and treatment of mental illness and emotional disturbance. |
| Public prosecutor | a law officer who conducts criminal proceedings on behalf of the state or in the public interest. |
| Recommend | **1** put forward with approval as being suitable for a purpose or role. **2** advise as a course of action. |
| Record | **1** a piece of evidence or information constituting an account of something that has occurred, been said, etc. **2** the previous conduct or performance of a person or thing. **3** (also **criminal record**) a list of a person's previous criminal convictions. |
| Regional | **1** relating to or characteristic of a region. **2** relating to the regions of a country rather than the capital. |

| | |
|---|---|
| Resolution | **1** a firm decision. **2** an expression of opinion or intention agreed on by a legislative body. |
| Restraint | **1** the action of restraining. **2** a measure or condition that restrains. **3** a device which limits or prevents freedom of movement. |
| Seclusion | the state of being private and away from other people. |
| Sentence | **noun 1** a set of words that is complete in itself, conveying a statement, question, exclamation, or command and typically containing a subject and predicate. **2** the punishment assigned to someone found guilty by a court.<br>**verb** declare the punishment decided for (an offender). |
| State | **noun 1** the condition of someone or something at a particular time. **2** a nation or territory considered as an organized political community under one government. **3** a community or area forming part of a federal republic.<br>**verb** express definitely or clearly in speech or writing.<br>PHRASES **state-of-the-art** incorporating the newest ideas and most up-to-date features. |
| Statement | **1** a definite or clear expression of something in speech or writing. **2** a formal account of facts or events, especially one given to the police or in court. |
| Supreme Court | the highest judicial court in a country or state. |
| Treatment | **1** the process or manner of treating someone or something. **2** medical care for an illness or injury. **3** the use of a substance or process to preserve or give particular properties to something. |
| Trial | **noun 1** a formal examination of evidence in order to decide guilt in a case of criminal or civil proceedings. **2** a test of performance, qualities, or suitability.<br>**verb** test (something) to assess its suitability or performance. |
| Urgent hospitalization | Urgent: requiring immediate action or attention.<br>hospitalize: admit or cause (someone) to be admitted to hospital for treatment. |
| Voluntary | done, given, or acting of one's own free will. |

## LIST OF AUTHORS


| | |
|---|---|
| Bulgaria: | Yonko **Grozev**<br>Bulgarian Helsinki Committee, 7 Varbitsa Street, 1504 Sofia, Bulgaria<br>Georgi **Onchev** MD, PhD<br>Department of Psychiatry, Medical University of Sofia, 1, Sv. Georgy Sofiisky Street, 1431 Sofia, Bulgaria |
| Czech Republic: | MU Dr. Mgr. Štěpán **Peichl**<br>Psychiatric Department, 1st Medical School of Charles University, Ke Karlovu 11, Prague 2, 128 01, Czech Republic |
| England: | Christina **Katsakou**, Dr Martin **Zinkler**<br>Unit for Social and Community Psychiatry, Newham Centre for Mental Health, Glen Road, London E13 8SP, United Kingdom<br>Guy **Davis**<br>East London and City Mental Health Trust, East One, 22 Commercial Street, London E1 6LP, United Kingdom |
| Germany: | Gerhard **Hegendörfer**<br>Bundesministerium für Gesundheit, Grundsatzfragen der europäischen Gesundheitspolitik; Task Force EU-Ratsvorsitz, Wilhelmstrasse 49, 10117 Berlin, Germany<br>Prof. Dr. med. habil. Thomas **Kallert,** Dipl.-Psych. Matthias **Glöckner**<br>Department of Psychiatry and Psychotherapy, University Hospital Carl Gustav Carus, Dresden University of Technology, Dresden, Fetscherstraße 74, 01307 Dresden, Germany<br>Jan **Conrady,** Tina **Roeder**<br>Faculty of Law, Dresden University of Technology, 01062 Dresden, Germany |
| Greece: | Giorgos **Triantaphyllou**<br>Kountourioti 8, 54625, Thessaloniki, Greece |
| Israel: | Maisam **Musallam**<br>Adalah: The Legal Center for Arab Minority Rights in Israel, P.O. Box 510, Shafa'amr, 20200, Israel |

Italy: Prof. Alberto **Manacorda** (†), Dr. Corrado **de Rosa**
University of Naples SUN, Department of Psychiatry
Largo Madonna delle Grazie, 80138 Naples, Italy

Lithuania: Dr. Dalia **Zeleckiene**
J. Basanaviciaus 22/2-11, LT- 03224 Vilnius, Lithuania

Poland: Prof. Stanislaw **Dabrowski**
Institute of Psychiatry and Neurology, Department of Health Care Organization, Al. Sobieskiego 9, 02-957 Warszawa, Poland
Prof. Andrzej **Kiejna,** Dr hab. Joanna **Rymaszewska**
Department of Psychiatry, Medical University, Pasteura 10, 50-367 Wrocław, Poland

Slovak Republic: Mgr. Ján **Farkaš**, JUDr. Jana **Eliášová**, JUDr. Juraj **Biľo**
Psychiatricka nemocnica Michalovce n.o., Stranany, 07101 Michalovce, Slovakia

Spain: Prof. Luis Fernando **Barrios Flores**
Universidad de Alicante, Dpto. Derecho Civil, Apdo. Correos, 99, 3080 Alicante, Spain
Prof. Francisco **Torres-González**
Departamento de Medicina Legal y Psiquiatría, Facultad de Medicina, Universidad de Granada, Avenida de Madrid, 11, 18071 Granada, Spain

Sweden: Ass. Prof. Gustav **Svensson**
Department of Social Work, Göteborg University, P.O.Box 720, SE-405 30 Göteborg, Sweden
Dr. Lars **Kjellin**
Psychiatric Research Centre, P.O. Box 1613, SE-701 16 Örebro, Sweden